ANVIL EDITIONS

Baudelaire
The Complete Verse

CHARLES BAUDELAIRE

The Complete Verse

INTRODUCED AND TRANSLATED BY
FRANCIS SCARFE

SECOND EDITION

Anvil Press Poetry

This edition published in 2012
by Anvil Press Poetry Ltd
Neptune House 70 Royal Hill London SE10 8RF
www.anvilpresspoetry.com
First published in 1986

Copyright © Bruno Scarfe 1986, 2012

This book is published with financial assistance
from Arts Council England

Designed and set in Monotype Bembo by Anvil
Printed and bound in Great Britain
by Hobbs the Printers Ltd

ISBN 978 0 85646 426 3 hardback
ISBN 978 0 85646 427 0 paperback

A catalogue record for this book
is available from the British Library

PUBLISHER'S NOTE

THIS IS the companion volume to Francis Scarfe's edition of Baudelaire's prose poems, originally published as *The Poems in Prose*. Its aim, like that of its forerunner in the Penguin Poets series, is to help readers to negotiate poems without constant recourse to a dictionary and to provide properly prepared texts with expert introductions which are useful to readers at any level of linguistic accomplishment.

Prose translations, aiming primarily to describe the content of poems with a high degree of denotative accuracy, are of course not to be compared with poets' verse translations. Equally, verse translations which aim at independent literary qualities do not compete with the more modest translations offered here. Their purposes are different, as a comparison of Michael Hamburger's separate treatments of Hölderlin (prose translations for *Selected Poems*, verse for *Poems and Fragments*), will show. Editions like this can however provide the stimulus for poets to embark on verse translations, and many versions made in the last fifty years must have been indebted to books like this published in the Penguin Poets series. Such books also offer the more general pleasure, for readers who enjoy the challenge of languages, of approaching the work of great poets with the helping hand of an expert guide, and the safety-net firmly in place below them at the foot of the page.

FRANCIS SCARFE died in March 1986. He had seen this book through proof, and had completed work on the companion volume of Baudelaire's prose poems, our new edition of which is now re-titled *Paris Blues*, the version of the French working title *Le Spleen de Paris* for which he argued in his introduction. He had made some progress with a projected third volume which was to have been called *Baudelaire on Poetry* or *Baudelaire's Poetics*, but only his basic notes remain.

With the permission of Bruno Scarfe, the author's son, we have lightly revised the translations for this second edition. There is always a fine line between translation, even apparently 'plain' and close translation, and freer kinds of interpretation. Our revisions are generally in the direction of increased closeness to the French

phrasing, without, I hope, disturbing the flow or thrust of Francis Scarfe's prose, which makes both his translations and introduction such a pleasure to read. Special thanks are due to E. R. Ashe for his list of suggested corrections, almost all of which we have adopted, and to Stephen Romer for his help in resolving some problematic points. I thank Kit Yee Wong for her careful checking of the text, both French and English, and for her help with the revisions.

We have reinstated and provided a translation for the dozen lines, almost certainly not by Baudelaire but of some interest in context, omitted in the previous edition from one of the doubtful poems, 'Un jour de pluie', pp. 445 ff. These lines ('left' to Ernest Prarond, under whose name the poem was published, by Jules Mouquet, who assigned the rest to Baudelaire) are enclosed in square brackets.

The French text is in the main that of the Pléiade edition of 1976 edited by Claude Pichois. The prose translations are paragraphed according to the French stanzas. On a few occasions translations start on a facing page (e.g. pp. 214, 314) to avoid crowding. The correspondence of the extracts from Longfellow's verse to Baudelaire's treatment of it is of course only approximate. Abbreviations in the notes are: FM, *Les Fleurs du mal*; RDM, *Revue des Deux Mondes*; 'Ed.' signals an editorial addition.

<div align="right">

PETER JAY

</div>

CONTENTS

Publisher's Note 5
Introduction 9
Reading List 49

I Les Fleurs du mal (1861)

Dédicace / Dedication 53
Au lecteur / To the Reader 55
 SPLEEN ET IDÉAL 59
 TABLEAUX PARISIENS 191
 LE VIN 235
 FLEURS DU MAL 247
 RÉVOLTE 265
 LA MORT 275
Projets d'Épilogues / Draft Epilogues 291

II Other Poems

Nouvelles Fleurs du mal (1868) 297
Les Épaves (1866) / Flotsam 313
 PIÈCES CONDAMNÉES 315
 GALANTERIES 335
 ÉPIGRAPHES 347
 PIÈCES DIVERSES 351
 BOUFFONNERIES 359
Bribes / Scraps 365
Poésies de jeunesse / Juvenilia 369
Vers de circonstance / Occasional Verse 389
Amœnitates Belgicœ / The Delights of Belgium 393

III Verse Translations 413

IV Poems Attributed to Baudelaire 429

Appendix

Draft Dedication and Prefaces for Les Fleurs du mal 453

Index of French Titles 467

INTRODUCTION

I

A POET whose work is so complex and diverse, though apparently so simple and unified, as Baudelaire's is not to be summarized in any convenient formula. Yet many attempts of this kind have been made; they are useful and have to be taken seriously. A modern Dante? This suggestion, first made in 1857 by Thierry, has been discussed and modified by T. S. Eliot who would be more satisfied with a comparison with Goethe. In spite of the 'ideal' poems in *Spleen et Idéal*, Baudelaire could at most be described as a Dante without the *Paradiso*. He is also a Dante without a system. There is no consistent metaphysic in Baudelaire, and in spite of the arguments of Pommier and Ferran, the theory of *correspondances* fails to provide one. Then, in spite of the arbitrarily imposed 'architecture' of *Les Fleurs du mal*, expounded by Benedetto and Ruff with a subtlety it does not merit, Baudelaire's work has more of the disorder and fragmentariness of a Leonardo than the powerful structure of a Dante. Yet he does meet Dante at many points: for instance in his 'high-seriousness', to use Matthew Arnold's expression, which leads him so often to take the most important end-problems for his themes. The grave, majestic cadence of his verse at its best, the athletic vigour of his mind, the deep insight he often shows into the nature of mankind, and his intuitive awareness of the mystery of the world – it is these qualities which entitle us to discuss his name with those of the great writers of the past. T. S. Eliot's comparison with Goethe was made in a restrictive sense, in a way that perhaps diminished both: he was thinking of them as being only representative of their own age. Putting aside the romantic apparatus that Baudelaire inherited and which certainly marred some of his work, he was much more than a representative of his own age. What he condemned in society and in the soul of man are evils that are still with us, and the energy with which he defined the human condition enables us to discount the occasional artistic fault because we at once feel ourselves in the presence of problems that are universal, and listening to a universal voice. Baudelaire belongs to that race of poets which includes Blake and Lawrence, fanatics with something to say, and who in order to say it sometimes maltreated

language. The corrections Baudelaire made to his poems are generally directed towards truth and clarity, rather than smoothness.

'The Swift of poetry', Lytton Strachey neatly suggested: but they meet only in their disgust, wit, and gloom, and Baudelaire is the bigger of the two. If he is, as a man, 'the tragic sophist' so ably described by G. T. Clapton, it is debatable whether he is the 'too Christian' or the 'near-Jansenist' portrayed by Bénouville and Ruff. If Aldous Huxley slipped almost as badly as Arthur Symons in calling Baudelaire 'a bored satanist', the admirable phrase of Lionel Johnson, 'Baudelaire sings sermons', while stressing rightly the poet's great claims as a moralist, leaves out that important part of his work which is gratuitous and compels the mind by its supreme aesthetic qualities.

The terms applied to Baudelaire's life are often misleading. It is usually regarded as a tragic failure, whereas it was a triumphant success in the sense of being the kind of life required to produce a certain kind of work, the kind of life which, testing its bearer beyond endurance, led him in the end, as his poems from 1859 onwards show, to a level of heroism and almost saintliness denied to his contemporaries. In Dr René Laforgue's opinion it was psychologically and morally a defeat (*échec*). In Sartre's it was not only a defeat but a 'deliberate failure'. Here we seem to be on the lunatic fringe of moral philosophy: for how can a life be judged as a deliberate failure when it was so inseparable from a precious and beautiful work? According to the philosopher, Baudelaire willed his own misfortune, doomed himself in advance by his worship of the bourgeois values which he flouted, and deliberately failed to live the life for which he was destined by his gifts. Sartre's statements are so framed as to reverberate angrily in the reader's consciousness: 'Baudelaire deliberately isolated himself.' 'Baudelaire is a man who chose to see himself as if he were another man: his life is merely the story of that failure.' 'He is the man who, while most profoundly experiencing his human condition, the most passionately sought to conceal it from himself.' 'He adopted his step-father's moral code without discussion. He was not a revolutionary but a man in revolt.' 'He chose to have a bad conscience.' 'That exceptional soul lived in bad faith.' (For Sartre, bad faith is defined not as cheating others, but as the cheating of oneself.) 'Having chosen Evil, he also chose to feel guilty.' 'Baudelaire submitted to Good in order to violate it.' Sartre does

not even spare the poet in this callous examination: 'All his life, Baudelaire sought sterility.'

Apart from the context of existential philosophy on which Sartre's analysis is based, it is a compliment to Baudelaire to credit him with having 'chosen' so much of his life. But there is no life without Others. Much of Baudelaire's misery came, as we shall see, from the sternness of General Aupick, the unimaginativeness of his mother, the twisted character of Jeanne Duval, the obtuseness of Ancelle, the meanness of Sainte-Beuve who never found a word of praise – in public – for the only poet of the younger generation who really cared for him. His elected master Gautier, in spite of his solid position as a critic on government newspapers, never wrote a line about Baudelaire before the fulsome biography he produced after the poet's death. Baudelaire's suffering did not come from nowhere, and it did not all come from himself. He complained all his life about his bad luck, his *guignon*; but if much of it might have been avoided, it was certainly not his fault if his merits were ignored by the great and fouled by the vulgar, or that the only publisher who really cared for his work was a bankrupt. The whole story of the publication of Baudelaire's works in his lifetime, while containing instances of underhand shifts on Baudelaire's part, was one of disgraceful extortion on the part of his publishers, and to suggest that Baudelaire willed this, that he willingly slaved in poverty to write critical works and translations that were grossly underpaid, is nonsense. Maybe Baudelaire was a *déclassé* and maybe he had an exaggerated grudge against society, but when we read that he told Catulle Mendès, only two years before his death, that he had earned by his pen, in the whole of his life, only *fifteen thousand, eight hundred and ninety-two francs, sixty centimes*, we begin to see the other side of the picture.

The weakness of Sartre's position lies in judging Baudelaire in a vacuum, or as though he were living in a noble state of society, surrounded only by saints. His own arguments are not taken to their proper conclusion. For every case of underhand behaviour on the poet's part it would be possible to quote instances of his generosity to others, but that is not the point, either. We are concerned with a Baudelaire who not only *chose* to suffer, as Sartre suggests, and who not only *chose* to be a misfit, if we can go so far with Sartre, but who also *chose* to write *Les Fleurs du mal* and a dozen books of prose which have stood the tests of time and taste. Perhaps it would be pressing the point too far to say that he

chose, not only to be the poet of evil or of Paris, but to be a European poet (as Valéry described him) and beyond that to be a universal poet. The so-called failure of Baudelaire is, of course, a failure to live a happy and comfortable existence. But his success lies in an unique exchange between a life and a work, the capacity for making a synthesis of sensation and contemplation in an unusual degree the transcendence from the tawdry details of daily life into the life of the spirit, the exchange between ordinary human disgrace and enduring art. It is an insult to a poet to describe him, as one might do on some official form, as an anti-social male suffering from syphilis and an overdraft at the bank. The answer to Sartre is that Baudelaire failed to be a failure.

But it is far from my intention to dismiss all predecessors and then propose a new thesis, equally imperfect. On the contrary, the views quoted above serve to show the complexity of the problem that Baudelaire offers, and the statements quoted need to be borne in mind in any just appreciation of the nature and importance of his life and work. To them we should add P. Mansell-Jones's over-all interpretation of Baudelaire as one who sought justification for his life on the aesthetic plane: he also shows the negative side of Baudelaire in describing in some of the poems 'the intimations they give of a mind in fundamental error'. Dr Enid Starkie, whose final assessment of Baudelaire (1957) is to be read in conjunction with the works of Crépet and Ruff, concludes her book in these terms: 'Many of those in whom Baudelaire today finds an echo, see, in his passionate longing "pour trouver du nouveau", their own aspiration towards something beyond themselves and the pitiable quest for material comfort and happiness, something in which to lose themselves, a return to a spiritual philosophy of life, to a difficult region which will make demands on man for effort and sacrifice, and will not play him false.' Even here the terms are sometimes reversible, for it could also be said that many readers are likely to *find* rather than lose themselves in a proper study of the work of this great poet.

But even 'finding oneself' in Baudelaire will not be as simple as it looks and will be a different experience for every reader. Baudelaire's is a protean and self-contradictory work, the more surprising and baffling the more one studies it. L. J. Austin's *L'Univers poétique de Charles Baudelaire* (1956), despite its rather conventional approach, at least shows the range and complexity of the poet's outlook on the world and on poetic creation. This

complexity and ambiguity are in no way reduced by F. W. Leakey's important *Baudelaire and Nature* (1969) which in analysing Baudelaire's varying attitudes to Nature in its widest sense shows contradictions and fluctuations that point to a cyclic habit of thought. F. W. J. Hemmings in his ostensibly matter-of-fact biography *Baudelaire the Damned* (1982), in which the underlying and old-fashioned thesis about 'damnation' reaches no conclusion, leaves us in the usual dilemma concerning Baudelaire's beliefs and disbeliefs – but surely Baudelaire believed as firmly as Proust in the redemptive value of aesthetic works? It seems that the closer we try to draw to the poet the more remote he becomes. A recent provocative study of *Baudelaire and Freud* by Leo Bersani (1977) comes to the rescue to some extent by comparing the two as creators of 'subjective systems constantly threatened from within'. Most current theories about Baudelaire merely show how foolish it is to try to reduce Baudelaire to some convenient formula. In any case, in over forty years nothing as challenging as Sartre's essay has been produced. The only real advance has been in the scrupulous editing of the texts by Crépet-Blin, Pichois, Bandy, and the chronological investigations of Leakey and others. Some measure of the difficulties facing the reader and critic nowadays is that the Pichois (*Pléiade*) edition of 1975 accompanies 224 pages of Baudelaire's poems with 1,245 pages of notes. Happy is the hypocritical reader who can disregard this academic jungle thus artificially created, and read *Les Fleurs du mal* directly for pleasure or pain and not for its nit-picking potentialities. What is needed now is a critical bomb such as Étiemble's devastating attack on Rimbaud's parasites in *Le Mythe de Rimbaud* (1952) – though if there is a 'mythe de Baudelaire' it was largely of the poet's own creation.

II

CHARLES BAUDELAIRE was born in Paris (rue Hautefeuille) on 9 April 1821 and was thus of that second 'romantic' generation which included Banville, Leconte de Lisle and Flaubert, the Brontës, and Matthew Arnold. His father, François, was born in 1759, taught for a while at the Collège Sainte-Barbe, became a tutor in the house of the duc de Choiseul-Praslin, and after the Revolution was rewarded for his devotion to that family, which he helped to save from the guillotine, with a comfortable post in

the offices of the Senate. It has been recently suggested that François Baudelaire was admitted to holy orders before the Revolution but was released from his vows under the Civil Constitution of the Clergy. His first marriage in 1803 left him with a son, Claude-Alphonse, who later became a lawyer and had only the coolest of relations with his half-brother Charles. At the age of sixty the widowed François remarried, his second wife, the poet's mother, being Caroline Archimbaut-Dufays (or Defayis) who was born in London in 1793. The daughter of a French officer, she was a refined person who communicated to her son something of her knowledge of the English language.

Baudelaire never forgot the elegant manners, artistic tastes, and Jansenist inclinations of his father, whose death in 1827 came as a blow to the sensitive boy. Then followed an idyllic period when the precocious child thrived in the closeness of his mother's undivided love, a happiness nostalgically evoked in such poems as 'Je n'ai pas oublié, voisine de la ville...' and 'La servante au grande cœur...'. A note recalling his childhood background reads: 'Childhood – old Louis XVI furniture, antiques, consulate, pastels, eighteenth-century society' – exactly that old-world atmosphere which is fleetingly suggested in such poems as 'Spleen' ('J'ai plus de souvenirs...'), 'Recueillement', and even 'L'Invitation au voyage'.

Unfortunately for Baudelaire, this interlude was so acutely happy and so short as to become a source of pain in later life, and no doubt the sense of loss and guilt and exclusion, which marks so much of his work, sprang from the experience of being driven from the earthly paradise at an impressionable age. Within eighteen months of his father's death his mother married a Captain Aupick, an energetic officer of Irish descent who later rose to the rank of General and became ambassador to Turkey and Spain. Charles was only about ten years old when he was separated from his mother, becoming a boarder at the Pension Delorme in Lyons, then at the Collège Royal of the same city, to which his stepfather had been posted. When the family regained Paris in 1836 he became a boarder at the Lycée Louis-le-Grand.

Although he was academically a good pupil, excelling in Greek and Latin and later obtaining his *baccalauréat* (or matriculation) with ease, Baudelaire's own comments on his education were unflattering: 'After 1830, the Collège de Lyon – blows, struggles with the teachers and pupils, overwhelming fits of melancholy' –

and, in a letter to his mother towards the end of his life, he referred to the 'lamentable education' that Aupick had given him. He felt himself to be an outsider and wrote of 'the feeling of solitude ever since my childhood. In spite of my family – and especially when I was surrounded by my school-fellows – the feeling of an eternally lonely destiny.' At about the age of fifteen he began devouring the works of the romantics, especially Chateaubriand and Sainte-Beuve (see the Epistle to Sainte-Beuve, p. 381 in the present collection), and showed an aggressive attitude to those in authority. His friend Hignard described him as being 'always a dare-devil . . . sometimes full of the deepest mysticism and sometimes of the grossest immorality – but in conversation only, which often went beyond the bounds of moderation and good sense.'

The beginning of Baudelaire's life as a *déclassé* came with his sudden expulsion from the Lycée Louis-le-Grand in 1839. The reasons given by his headmaster for this humiliation read rather like a pretext, and it seems likely that the masters were glad to be rid of an awkward rather than a bad character. Baudelaire was ordered by the vice-principal to hand over a note which a friend had passed to him in class. In loyalty to his friend, Baudelaire tore up the note and swallowed it. The headmaster accused him of sneering and wrote to Aupick that though the boy was 'certainly endowed with outstanding abilities' he was being dismissed for his bad influence on school discipline.

Meanwhile, though he apparently enjoyed the trip to the Pyrenees with his step-father in 1837, which is commemorated in the poem 'Incompatibilité' (p. 369), Baudelaire was nursing a dislike for the man who, as he thought, had supplanted him in his mother's affections. The boy already wanted to become a writer, but Aupick was determined that he would follow an administrative career. Baudelaire was first sent as a boarder to a Monsieur Lasègue, a tutor at the Pension Bailly, to prepare for his *bachot*, and later, when he was enrolled to study Law at the École de Droit (November 1839) he lived in the famous Pension Bailly, place de l'Estrapade, where he began to enjoy all the diversions of student life. Aupick took his responsibilities with puritanical seriousness and, no doubt in order to save his charge from bad company as well as to change his mind about his career, had him embarked on a ship which left Bordeaux for India in June 1841. For this purpose, 5,000 francs were taken out of Charles's estate. There is no evidence whatever that Baudelaire reached India, and Marcel

Ruff is one of the few biographers who think that he did. All that we know is that he stayed for some time in Mauritius and the Île Bourbon, returned by a different ship from the one in which he set out, and was (according to his mother's evidence) back in Paris by February 1842. The voyage did not have the desired effect. Baudelaire spent most of it in solitude, emerging from his introspection only on one occasion when he showed extraordinary courage in the face of danger and helped the crew to save the ship. The voyage left an indelible mark of exoticism and reverie on the poet's mind and work, as can be seen in poems of such different texture as 'À une dame créole', 'À une Malabaraise', 'Le Voyage', 'Le Cygne', 'L'Albatros', and many of those in which he relies heavily on marine imagery for his effects, such as 'La Chevelure', 'L'Homme et la mer', 'Don Juan aux Enfers'. Perhaps it is not too fanciful to regard this last-named poem as the poet's self-portrait at that time. No doubt this odyssey also gave him his initiation to the 'Black Venus' and explains his profound attachment to the mulatress, Jeanne Duval, whom he met on his return.

Looking back on Baudelaire's youth up to this point, it cannot be said that he was treated by his parents with direct unkindness, though there was a lack of thoughtfulness and insight on their part. Only the combination of a tender sensibility and a streak of intellectual violence can explain the rankling animosity which, in later life, led him to over-dramatize his relationship with his mother, as in 'Bénédiction'. But when we probe under the surface there is more to be said for him than the apologists of the Aupicks would have us believe. The poet's early letters to his mother show nothing but absolute tenderness and respect. When sent to live with M. Lasègue (who later became a mental specialist and was called in to see the poet at the end of his life) he began a letter to his mother in July 1839: 'My dear Mother, my good mother, I hardly know what to say to you, yet I have all kinds of things to tell you. First of all I feel a great need to see you. How different it is, living with strangers – and it isn't exactly your caresses and our laughter that I miss, so much as something which makes our mother always seem the best of women, and her qualities suit us better than those of other women: there's such a harmony between a mother and her son; they live so well in each other's company, so that, God knows, since I came to M. Lasègue's I feel upset.' Such openness and analysis are unusual in a youth of eighteen. At the same time his friend Hignard speaks of him as being 'very

religious', as can be seen in the moving poem beginning 'Hélas, qui n'a gémi sur autrui, sur soi-même?' Until 1842 there is no serious sign of revolt. Even when he was exiled to the East Mme Aupick wrote: 'He would have preferred to stay here, without the slightest doubt, but without showing any repugnance he gave in.' His step-father wrote: 'He yielded to my arguments. When he was leaving Charles wrote us a nice letter which is the first guarantee we have of the good results we expect from this harsh trial.' We can well feel astonished at the hypocrisy of the words 'harsh trial' (*rude épreuve*) since it is obvious that Aupick's policy ever since he married was to keep the boy out of sight as much as possible – five or six boarding establishments followed by a year at sea! The poet was justified in regarding this as selfish, but unfortunately he set a glaze of cynicism, which was to remain, over his wounded feelings.

After his return from Mauritius, Baudelaire was due to come into his inheritance (about 75,000 francs, which was a large sum in those days), but this does not seem to have been handed over to him outright. He lived in rooms in the rue Vaneau, the quai de Béthune, then finally in the Hôtel de Lauzun (Pimodan) on the Île Saint-Louis. He used to send his mother flowers and trinkets and invite her to meals with him. He wrote in one of his letters: 'You speak of making your home pleasant for me, but the simplest way is to invite me when you are alone rather than when you have company.' It was only in 1844, then more seriously in 1847 that his relations with his mother broke down, and till then his revolt was directed only against Aupick. Perhaps he was also in trouble with his half-brother, Claude. Biographers have been slow to note why, while Baudelaire was away on his trip to the Indies, Claude was toadying to the Aupicks and nourishing the fires of resentment. He wrote to Mme Aupick about 'protecting some part of Charles's fortune' and 'other means which you will find as distasteful as I do'. As the two brothers owned adjoining pieces of land at Neuilly, it is not hard to guess why Claude was so anxious to 'protect' his brother's fortune. Be that as it may, the upshot was that Baudelaire's inheritance never came into his own hands: as early as 1843 he agreed that his mother should take care of it and give him remittances from the interest.

By the middle of 1844 all the elements of Baudelaire's future torment were assembled, and the web of circumstance woven round him by himself and his family was only broken with his

death. For the past two years the poet had – openly enough – been leading a kind of double life. While entirely sincere in his devotion to his mother and busily educating himself as well as writing, with his bohemian friends he was smoking hashish and opium, frequenting prostitutes, and squandering money. In the company of members of the so-called 'Norman School', Prarond, Le Vavasseur, and Dozon (who published a book of poems in 1843 which some critics believe to contain unsigned works by Baudelaire) he savoured all the delights of the Latin Quarter. Expecting to come into the inheritance left by his father, he proceeded to spend it in advance: not for him the bourgeois idea that money is to be saved and multiplied. He imagined that a certain social status would enable him to impress editors and publishers. His friends all describe him as incredibly handsome, and so he was. A brilliant conversationalist, he had a grasp of all the arts, was writing impressive poems, and showed every sign of having a brilliant career before him. But he had expensive tastes and indulged them fully after returning from the East. He decorated his room in the Hôtel Pimodan in stripes of red and black, and filled it with rich carpets and hangings, porcelain, fine paintings, and antiques. To quote Dr Starkie, 'Hignard tells us that he sometimes looked like a Titian portrait come to life, in his black velvet tunic, pinched in at the waist by a golden belt, with his dark waving hair and his pointed beard. Sometimes again he wore plain black broadcloth, skin-tight trousers fastened under his patent-leather shoes, with white silk socks, a coat with narrow tails, a fine white shirt with broad turned-back cuffs, and a collar wide-open at the neck, tied loosely with a scarlet tie. Again, according to Nadar, he would wear pale pink gloves.' Dandyism, however, is not always a sign of lack of character: we have to recall Disraeli wearing rings outside his gloves. There is some truth, none the less, in Rimbaud's reproach that Baudelaire 'lived in too artistic a milieu'.

All this was nothing compared with the poet's ostentatious sexual choice (which Nadar dates as early as 1839–40 but which the poet's letters prove to have been in 1842). Though in many respects a chaste man who sought aesthetic rather than sensual satisfaction (Nadar said he died a 'virgin'), he had begun living with a mulatto woman, Jeanne Lemer or Duval, with whom he was to share a short period of happiness followed by many years of misery. Jeanne Duval is the crucible and the cross of his

subsequent life. Though she offered him the poles of ecstasy and disgust which are plainly to be seen in the cycle of poems he wrote for her, though she was unfaithful to him almost from the beginning, cheated and robbed and deliberately hurt him, he never lost his sense of responsibility for her. Baudelaire's nobility of character is seen in his devotion to her needs whenever they separated. If she brought out the worst in him, she also brought out the best. To complete the picture at that time, he had probably contracted the venereal complaint which recurred at intervals for the rest of his life: but it is to be noted that his brother died of the same symptoms.

Such were the conditions when, already in debt to tailors, junk-dealers, and other tradesmen, Baudelaire was suddenly flung from an extravagant and elegant way of life into a poverty from which he was never to recover. The Aupicks suddenly had his fortune sequestrated, it was turned into a trust, and Baudelaire was treated as a minor for the rest of his life, under the guardianship of the lawyer, Ancelle, who made him small monthly payments, often arriving late, on which he was unable to live. His outstanding debts were not all paid at this time, and with accumulating interest they hung round his neck thereafter. He was never able to live in the same lodging for more than a few weeks or months at a time: he explained to his mother some years later how he was obliged to 'flit' on Lady Day to avoid his creditors. In his last years his escape to Belgium in the hope of restoring his fortunes by lecturing and fresh contracts was a flight from their clutches as well as from himself.

The dismay with which Baudelaire faced the prospect of earning his living by his pen and perhaps becoming a hack can be seen in such poems as 'Le Mauvais Moine' and 'La Muse vénale'. Anger and humiliation were for years to override his first feelings of despair. A long letter to his mother in 1844 while the plans were being laid to treat him as a ward, shows much less concern for money, which he did not even discuss, than with the moral aspects of the situation. It came as a hard blow to his pride. 'For my misfortune I am not made as other men – what you regard as a necessity and a painful circumstance is something I cannot bear.' He stressed again and again the humiliation of being put into the hands of strangers: 'Is there not an incredible cruelty in submitting me to the arbitration of a handful of men who find it a nuisance and who do not know me?' Worst of all his mother had in some

way let him down and failed to keep her promises, rushing the affair through without enabling him to prepare any defence (the arrangements were all completed between July and September 1844). The poet was most hurt by the impersonality now imposed on their relationship: 'I would rather have no fortune at all and abandon myself entirely to you, than submit to any other judgement – the first is still a free act: the second is an infringement of my liberty.'

From now on, till Aupick's death in 1857, after which they drew closer together again, relations between mother and son grew cooler: there was a more bitter rupture in 1847, and after that some years in which he hardly saw her or wrote to her at all. In some of his letters we find Baudelaire describing how hungry he was or being unable to go out because he had no clothes, or how he had pawned books and manuscripts and could not carry on with his work. It was not until 1851 when Mme Aupick, returning from Constantinople, found her son living in such abject poverty (she called it *dénuement* or destitution) that her heart melted and she began helping him a little from her own purse – but in every transaction between them it is clear that the poet intended these sums to be set against his credit. Even when her husband was earning 40,000 francs a year as an ambassador, she was never able to give her son more than trifling sums which could only cover his most urgent and immediate needs.

By this time, according to his friends, Baudelaire is supposed to have written a large part of *Les Fleurs du mal*, but in fact only about thirty poems can be attributed with any certainty to the period 1837–45. He was now moving away from the 'Norman School' and numbered among his friends the future Parnassians, Banville and Louis Ménard, also Asselineau (who later wrote a little book about him), Gautier, and the painter Deroy. He had already established contact with Sainte-Beuve and Balzac. With his first published prose work, the *Salon* of 1845, he began laying the basis of his reputation as the greatest art critic of the century. Though this *Salon* is spoiled by a somewhat ambiguous flattery of the 'bourgeois' ('the bourgeois is eminently to be respected, for one has to please those at whose expense one wants to live'), which might have been meant to please the Aupicks or to split the sides of the bohemians, it is notable for its praise of Delacroix, Daumier, and Corot when they were generally misunderstood, and for the coining of the expression 'the heroism of modern

life', which remained one of his constant themes as an art critic and is one of the keys to the understanding of his own poetry. As yet he had published only one poem, 'À une dame créole'.

Only two months after issuing the 1845 *Salon*, which was well received, Baudelaire, no doubt in financial straits and exasperated by his isolation from his mother, wrote a violent letter to the lawyer Ancelle (30 June) announcing that as he was 'useless to others and a danger to himself' he was about to commit suicide and wished to leave all his estate to his mistress Jeanne Duval. 'I am killing myself because I am immortal and because I hope,' he said; characteristically affirming his religious belief at the very moment of an irreligious act. He went on to say that whereas his mother had, in her husband, 'a human being, an affection, a friendship, I have only Jeanne Lemer. I have found peace only in her.' Though some biographers do not take this incident seriously, Baudelaire certainly inflicted a wound on himself. After a reconciliation with his family he stayed for a few months at their home in the aristocratic Place Vendôme. But very soon he wrote 'I have fallen into a terrifying mood of depression and apathy and need a long spell of solitude . . . it's impossible for me to turn myself into what your husband would like me to be, so it would be cheating him to live any longer under his roof.' In the same year (1845) he published an anonymous skit on Balzac (whom he greatly admired) called 'How to pay your debts when you're a genius'.

The following year, 1846, was one of great activity. He first published a short story, *Le Jeune Enchanteur*, which has since been shown to be an unacknowledged translation from an English work. He began contributing to the *avant-garde* magazine *Le Corsaire-Satan* with some 'Consoling Maxims on Love'. In recommending this article to his sister-in-law Mme Claude Baudelaire, with the words 'Be so kind, Madame, as to be my Providence in the career opening to me through the medium of love', he was already showing the tendency, repeated in the case of Marie Daubrun and Mme Sabatier, to seek some idealized person for whom he could write, thus offsetting his unintellectual attachment to Jeanne Duval, whom he was vainly trying to teach to read.

In the same year he published 'Advice to Young Writers', humorous and for the most part useless advice mingled with such anti-romantic wisdom as 'Orgy is not the sister of inspiration – Inspiration is definitely the sister of daily toil', which marks him off from the slovenly bohemians whose life he shared. The *Salon*

of 1846 contains many points which were to become constants in his aesthetic. Much light is thrown on his place in the romantic tradition by such statements as: 'Romanticism, for me, is the most recent, the most up-to-date expression of the beautiful . . . Romanticism will not consist of perfect execution but of a conception analogous to the morality of this century . . . Whoever speaks of romanticism means modern art, that is to say intimacy, spirituality, colour, aspiration towards the infinite.' There is a strong intuition of the theories of Poe (which he did not yet know) in the following almost classical definition of art which anticipates Mallarmé and Valéry: 'There is *no chance* in art, any more than in mechanics . . . A painting is a *machine*, all the systems of which are intelligible to the experienced eye.' The essay also shows the germ of the theory of *correspondances* in the tendency to relate colour to music, and in the statement 'For E. Delacroix, Nature is a vast dictionary'. In Section XVIII ('On the Heroism of Modern Life') he was really defining his own aims as a poet as well as what he was seeking in art: 'Parisian life is fertile in poetic and supernatural subjects. The supernatural (*merveilleux*) envelops us and answers our needs like the atmosphere, but we do not see it.' His postulation of two types of Beauty – however old-fashioned any argument in terms of an abstract beauty may now appear – shows his particular talent for grafting his modernism on to a well-established tradition: 'All forms of beauty contain, like all possible phenomena, something eternal and something transitory – absolute and particular.' This generous and almost impregnable theory of beauty enabled him to graft on to the old rhetoric and aesthetic his own personal symbolism, his vision of the modern world, and indeed his own *anti-aesthetic*, which make him the fore-runner of Symbolism and even Surrealism. Baudelaire was now coming into possession of those few 'general ideas' which Henry James says are necessary to any serious writer. The year closed with the publication of 'L'Impénitent' (later called 'Don Juan aux Enfers') and 'À une Indienne' (otherwise known as 'À une Malabaraise').

Baudelaire referred several times from 1843 onwards, in letters to his mother, to a work over which he was taking great pains. This was the short novel *La Fanfarlo* which was printed in January 1847 in the *Bulletin de la société des gens de lettres*, a society to which Baudelaire was often to turn for financial aid in later years. In this highly artificial work Baudelaire was one of the first to create that

écriture artiste which was to become so widespread towards the end of the century (Wilde, Gide, etc.). The story is told with great detachment and lightness of touch and has the kind of trivial theme of which Musset would have made a sparkling play. The hero, Samuel Cramer, author of a slim volume of poems, *Les Orfraies* (Ospreys), has creole blood in his veins and is very handsome; with a pure and noble forehead, eyes as bright as two drops of coffee, a teasing, mocking proboscis, insolent sensual lips, a square domineering chin, and an ostentatiously Raphaelesque mop of hair.' He suffers from being at once 'an enormous idler, distressingly ambitious, a distinguished misfit', with 'a personality whose dimness was lit by sharp flashes of illumination, so slothful yet so enterprising, so fertile in challenging projects and farcical failures'. Obviously Samuel is at once directly related to Sainte-Beuve's Amaury (hero of the novel *Volupté*, which Baudelaire admired at school), and an ironical portrait of Baudelaire himself. Meeting a Mme de Cosmelly whom he had known in Lyons, who is unhappy because her husband is philandering with the actress La Fanfarlo, Cramer undertakes to lure the actress away from the husband. He achieves this by writing harsh criticism of her in the theatre columns: she yields to him, but much to his disgust Mme de Cosmelly goes away with her husband and La Fanfarlo wreaks her vengeance on the poet. One incident throws a strange light on the reputed sexual inhibition of the poet, for when La Fanfarlo offers herself naked to her lover, Cramer protests that he only wanted *Colombine* and insists that she wear her stage dress.

Baudelaire had little financial benefit from this work, though it was successful enough to be reprinted in 1849. The rest of 1847 was a time of defeat and procrastination, but perhaps it was the moment when he was reading Hoffmann, Swedenborg, Diderot, and others who were to have a decisive influence on his mind. Was he now elaborating his theory of *correspondances*? Swedenborg was already mentioned in *La Fanfarlo*, but though some critics attribute the famous sonnet to the years 1845–6 there is no convincing evidence for this. Now his poverty and sickness overcame him: at one stage he wrote that he had been *locked* in his room by his doctor. He even thought of returning to the Île Bourbon as a tutor. He was also planning a *History of Caricature* and a *History of Sculpture*, but though the first bore fruit in a long essay a few years later, sculpture was an art for which he had

neither sympathy nor understanding – his comments on sculpture in the *Curiosités esthétiques* are mainly deplorable. It was in this year that he first met the actress Marie Daubrun for whom he later wrote the fine cycle of poems between 1850 and 1860 which includes 'L'Invitation au voyage' (and, I am inclined to believe, its pendant, 'Le Jet d'eau'). Apparently he used to stare at her offensively while she was being painted – perhaps by his friend Deroy – but when she rebuffed him he went to the opposite extreme and offered her a purely platonic affection.

1847, that apparently idle year, was thus one which bore fruit later. In the same year, though he was frequenting the ragged bohemian set described by Murger, he was also moving in socialist circles, with Toubin, Proudhon, and the brilliant young painter Courbet. Courbet included a portrait of Baudelaire smoking a pipe in his famous *Atelier de l'artiste*, but in later years they drifted apart as Baudelaire turned against realism. Baudelaire had written mockingly in the last paragraph of *La Fanfarlo*, 'Poor singer of the *Ospreys* – he has fallen very low. I recently heard that he had founded a socialist newspaper and wanted to enter politics – a dishonest intellect, as honest M. Nisard would say.' The poet was now able to revel in the irony of living his fiction – he already believed that nature imitates art.

Baudelaire's activities in the revolutionary period 1848–51 were complicated and often mysterious, but in the main they arose from the emotional commitment, at the outset, which gripped all his generation, even Leconte de Lisle, and which soon faded into disillusionment with the socialist cause, followed by political apathy. Although Baudelaire was active in political journalism, his writings cannot be identified with certainty. He was out with his friends Courbet and Toubin on the violent day of the 'banquets' (22 February 1848) and was shocked by the callous way the military treated unarmed civilians. Two days later he was at the barricades, gun in hand, but the statement that he was demanding the death of Aupick, then director of the École Polytechnique (military academy), was made by a witness who cannot be trusted. He is also known to have attended meetings of Blanqui's Central Republican Society. At the end of February he started a newssheet (*Le Salut public*) which only ran into two numbers because of lack of funds: the poet sold the paper in the streets himself. In April he became editorial secretary of the socialist *La Tribune nationale*. By now he was losing faith in socialist policy. Like Chénier and many

other poets he lacked patience for the day-to-day intrigues and compromises of politics, which he later described as 'a heartless science'. In his hands the paper turned conservative, though his friend Poulet-Malassis was in gaol and Ménard had to flee to Belgium. Towards the end of his life Baudelaire wrote that he understood 'how a man could desert one side to serve the other': this is the ironical fate of thwarted idealists.

With his mother away in Turkey, where Aupick was Ambassador, the poet was left to his own devices. He was in Dijon for a time (with Jeanne) presumably editing another paper, while it is probable that he also worked as an editor in Châteauroux. The influence of the revolutionary period does not show very directly in his poems, which contain few political references, but it helped to cure him of the art for art's sake of his early manner. During this period some of the great 'Spleen' poems were composed, and twenty-six poems in all are known to have been grouped under the title *Les Limbes* (Limbo), a book which the poet announced as being published by Michel-Lévy 'and which is intended to trace the history of the spiritual agitations of modern youth.' Thus the Revolution did, temporarily, give a social significance to poems which might originally have been written without that intention. His outlook as a poet had matured, for whereas in 1846 he was announcing a collection of poems to be called *Les Lesbiennes*, there was no more talk of this. The first of the *Limbes* poems ('Le Vin de l'assassin') appeared in 1848 in *L'Écho des marchands de vin*: two were printed in *Le Magasin des familles* in 1850 and eleven in the following year. The title 'Limbo' is ambiguous, being used in both a religious and a social sense. Fourier had spoken of 'limbic periods' meaning those in which society is making a fresh start accompanied by industrial strife. There is enough stress on both the social and religious aspects for us to take the term in both senses. Such works as 'Châtiment de l'orgueil' and the 'Spleen' poems bear heavily on the idea of excommunication and lack of grace. Together with his rejection of art for art's sake Baudelaire turned against the idea of material progress, but if he abandoned political socialism and artistic realism this did not mean that he welcomed the new régime or ceased hating its materialistic, bourgeois values. Yet he could not become a Liberal because French Liberalism implied atheism or at least agnosticism.

Baudelaire's only other important publication in 1851 was *Du vin et du haschisch*, a short book which appeared in four parts in

Le Messager de l'Assemblée. This prepared the way for the famous *Les Paradis artificiels* published between 1858 and 1860. The section on *Le Vin* contains prose versions of 'L'Âme du vin' and 'Le Vin des chiffonniers.'

In the next five years Baudelaire made enormous progress on all fronts. His interest in Edgar Allan Poe, first stimulated in 1847, now crystallized and became one of his main enthusiasms as well as providing a regular source of income. Beginning with a short study of Poe's life and works – much of it at second-hand – in 1851, by 1856 he had completed the volume of *Histoires extraordinaires* which has remained the standard text in France. Altogether he issued five volumes of Poe's works, but unwisely sold his copyright in them for a sum of only 2,000 francs – a step which reveals his penury and lack of bent for business. In the domain of criticism he produced some good essays which he regarded as 'very Parisian', including those on Caricature and the *Exposition universelle* of 1855. Parallel with these went some articles which were collected later in his book on *L'Art romantique*, including 'L'École païenne' (an attack on the Parnassians and on philosophical poetry, for he was opposed to what he called 'the heresy of teaching'), and the essay on the worker-poet Pierre Dupont.

Perhaps the most important event of all, as Baudelaire had been so slow in publishing his poems, was the appearance of a group of eighteen poems under the title *Les Fleurs du mal* in the highly respectable *Revue des Deux Mondes* in 1855. Baudelaire had abandoned the title *Les Limbes* after another poet used it in 1852, and the new title was suggested to him by Hippolyte Babou. Baudelaire threw away this chance of gaining a new and influential audience by including some of the poems most calculated to shock the review's readers. He wrote to the editor describing an Epilogue he wished to include (but which was rejected) in which occurred the line 'candour and goodness are disgusting', and added, 'that, as you see, makes a nice firework-display of monstrosities.' Only a lack of social maturity could have led Baudelaire to think that such a display would be acceptable in a review of that kind, or to be disappointed when the editors printed nothing more of his.

This is a very important period for two other reasons: it was the time when he was assembling his volume *Les Fleurs du mal*, and when he was living intensely on the emotional plane. He left Jeanne Duval in 1852 after ten years of cohabitation, only to

return to her again in 1855. He wrote a long letter to his mother about this in March 1852, saying 'Jeanne has become an obstacle not only to my happiness but also to the perfecting of my mind.' At the same time he made frantic efforts to provide for her financially.

The emotional picture of these years is extremely involved, because it contained at least three women. It was probably in 1850 or 1851 that Baudelaire wrote to Marie Daubrun: 'Through you, Marie, I shall be strong and great. Like Petrarch I shall immortalize my Laura. By my guardian Angel, my Muse, and my Madonna, and lead me along the paths of the Beautiful.' There was certainly no other satisfaction to be had than this remote adoration, for already Marie was more interested in his friend, Banville. Nor was Baudelaire himself constant. After the separation from Jeanne in the spring of 1852 he began, at the end of the year, a mysterious course of behaviour towards Mme Sabatier, that beautiful and witty but perhaps unprincipled person whose salon, the expenses of which were paid by the banker Mosselmann, was attended by eminent men of letters of the period. Baudelaire had known her for many years, but only in 1851 began frequenting her salon. Having 'lost' both Jeanne and Marie, Baudelaire wrote anonymously to Mme Sabatier in December 1852, enclosing the poem 'À celle qui est trop gaie'. This was followed at intervals by other unsigned letters containing poems. Though Feuillerat points out that his overtures to Mme Sabatier coincide with absences of Marie Daubrun, I cannot believe, as the biographers do, that this series of acts came entirely 'out of the blue' and had nothing to do with feeling. Such a course of action amounted, on both sides, to a tacit understanding, a kind of emotional game, which could only be possible between two persons who knew and respected one another well enough to bear the truth. The poem 'Confession', which has been consistently underestimated, strikes me as one of the most beautiful poems in the love-cycles because of its psychological penetration, the stripping of the mask and laying bare the truth in a manner which still implies the greatest respect and compassion. For once, Baudelaire was entirely disinterested, and there is no sign, in spite of Feuillerat's insinuation, that Baudelaire was trying to exploit Mme Sabatier as soon as Marie was out of sight: he wanted nothing. In the course of 1854 his relationship with Marie became closer: he was even for a time hoping to set up house with her, writing to his mother 'I am

going back to concubinage and if I am not living with Jeanne Lemer by 9 January (1855) I shall be with the *other* one.' His efforts to help Marie's theatre career failed, and she turned again to Banville. From March to September 1856 he again lived with Jeanne, but this time it was she who left him, much to his distress. At the end of the same year he was again writing to Mme Sabatier and in 1857 he threw off his anonymity (which her friend, 'Sisina', had long ago seen through). When in August 1857 Mme Sabatier, in a spontaneous gesture of compassion and admiration, offered herself to him, he rejected her. During 1858–9 Baudelaire again made every effort to help Marie and win her affection, but for the third and last time she went off with Banville, who was ill.

Of all these women Mme Sabatier stands out as the finest and the most profound in spite of her reputation for superficiality. For all her bohemian morals she was beautiful, generous, and sensitive, which the others were not. As for Marie Daubrun, she seems to have been selfish and calculating to a point, as well as pusillanimous. Feuillerat writes 'She bears a great share of responsibility for the crushing sadness that marks the last years of Baudelaire's life.' It can well be asked, however, if Baudelaire ever knew the full exchange of real love. There is no doubt that his relationship with Jeanne was stormy and passionate; that Marie moved him to a protective tenderness, and that between him and Mme Sabatier there was some bond of deep friendship, perhaps based on the idea that they were both in a sense outlaws living beneath the level which their sensibility demanded, and cloaking their wounds with the appearance of cynicism. He knew the enchantments of ecstasy and moments of emotional despair, but perhaps failed to love others because he could not love himself. From all three women he sought a kind of escape and transcendence, but never complete self-recognition or the deep discovery of the other. Love for him was another artificial paradise. Each of the cycles of love-poems is as heavily charged with disillusionment, violence, contempt, and pain as with compassion, tenderness, or delight.

1857 was one of the most active years of Baudelaire's life. During it he published not only the *Nouvelles histoires extraordinaires* by Poe, but his first group of prose-poems (under the title *Poèmes nocturnes*) as well as the famous *Les Fleurs du mal*. At the beginning of the year General Aupick died and after a time the poet drew closer to his mother, despite the interference of busybodies who surrounded her at Honfleur. .

The contract for the *Fleurs* was signed with his friend Poulet-Malassis late in 1856, and in April 1857 the sheets came from the press; but owing to Malassis's delays it was not on sale until the end of June. Already in 1855 the group of *Fleurs du mal* printed in the *Revue des Deux Mondes* had provoked some strong attacks on the poet, and he now feared the worst. He wrote to his mother in July 1857: 'You know that I have never considered literature and the arts except as pursuing an end which is outside morality, and that beauty of conception and style are enough for me. But this book, whose title *Les Fleurs du mal* says everything, is clothed, as you shall see, in a sinister and cold beauty: it was composed in fury and patience. Besides, proof of its positive value can be seen in all the bad that's being said of it. The book enrages people. In any case, appalled myself at the horror I was going to inspire, I cut a third of the book out when it was in proof.' It is enough to read between the lines to see a fundamental contradiction in Baudelaire's outlook. While he might, theoretically, have thought that literature does not pursue a moral end, he clearly realized that his book raised moral problems. It is irrelevant to ask whether poetry pursues a moral end, for at whatever points it touches morality it must face the challenge of moral judgements. When he reacted some years later against Swinburne's remarks on the book's moral import he failed entirely to see that he was writing in the French moral tradition. Why, otherwise, did he print an epigraph from D'Aubigné which so pointedly raised the moral issue: 'But vice has not knowledge for its mother, and virtue is not the daughter of ignorance.' Further, in a prose dedication to Gautier (which Gautier persuaded him not to print) he had written 'I know that in the ethereal regions of true Poetry, there is no longer any evil, any more than good, and that this miserable dictionary of melancholy and crime can justify the reactions of morality, just as the blasphemer confirms religion.' Thus Baudelaire was fully aware of his book's moral significance, and he would have done well to prepare a moral defence instead of claiming that it was beyond good and evil.

Trouble was already brewing. The book was put on sale at the end of June and in July it was attacked by Gustave Bourdin (who had already denounced Baudelaire in 1855) in *Le Figaro*. Bourdin went so far as to doubt the poet's sanity. A further attack followed in a few days, while Baudelaire's faction did little or nothing to defend him. Sainte-Beuve proved to be lily-livered as usual. He

had already failed to say a word in praise of the Poe translations in 1856, and now he asked Thierry to write a review in his place. Thierry had the courage and perception to compare Baudelaire with Dante, though it might well be asked how many would grasp the implications, since at that time Dante was just emerging from the eclipse into which he fell in the seventeenth century. The Ministry of Justice had already prosecuted Flaubert and his publisher for *Madame Bovary* in the same year, and was out for a conviction. All the sheets of *Les Fleurs du mal* were confiscated. Now Baudelaire, throwing off his anonymity, appealed to Mme Sabatier to use her influence, only two days before the trial. On 20 August after a half-hearted defence arguing that other poets such as Béranger had written more shocking things, both poet and publisher were fined and six of the poems were condemned as 'an offence against morality and decency' (*bonnes moeurs*). The fine was reduced after Baudelaire had written a letter of appeal to the Empress.

A final word is necessary at this stage on the additional pain that arose for Baudelaire at this time in his relationship with Mme Sabatier. I have already suggested that this was a valuable relationship: it was certainly so because it encouraged Baudelaire to write poems of exceptional beauty and insight, and because, whereas he wrote about both Jeanne and Marie as though they were animals or children, in this case he was, for the first time, writing for and about a mature person. Critics have asked whether Baudelaire was 'exploiting' Mme Sabatier when he wrote to her in August 1857 asking her to help him in the matter of the trial of *Les Fleurs du mal*. It might be said that there are certain things a man does not ask a woman to do for him. If his action was perhaps not entirely in good taste, it was surely a mark of confidence. What better interpretation can we put on it than that of Mme Sabatier herself? It was too late to help him, but she at once showed her admiration for his poems and her compassion for the poet. Never for a moment did she suggest that she had been asked anything out of the ordinary. Friendship often needs only such a small catalyst to be transformed into love. What happened now was that her spontaneous gesture was to offer herself and her love. In the state of anger and frustration through which he was passing at the time of the trial Baudelaire seems to have misunderstood this gesture, and, reproaching her for immodesty, he wrote 'A few days ago you were a divinity, now you are a woman.' He certainly did not love

her in the proper sense of the term, but the sharpness of his reaction suggests that something valuable was lost. In 'Confession' he had written 'Everything cracks – both love and beauty', and the would-be Petrarch and his idol whom he had used only as a source of poetic inspiration were both knocked off their pedestals together.

The first edition of *Les Fleurs du mal* contained a hundred poems, divided into five sections, as follows: (1) *Spleen et Idéal*, 77 poems; (2) *Fleurs du mal*, 12 poems; (3) *Révolte*, 3 poems; (4) *Le Vin*, 5 poems, and (5) *La Mort*, 3 poems. It can be seen at a glance that although Baudelaire protested that his book was not an 'album' or casual collection as such books usually are, but *un ensemble*, in spite of all that has been written about its 'architecture' the arrangement is loose and unconvincing. There is far too great a disproportion between the first group of seventy-seven poems and the other four with only twenty-three between them. The group of *Tableaux parisiens* was not created until the second edition (1861) when it was made up of eight poems taken from *Spleen et Idéal* and ten new ones. It is also to be noted that the third group (*Révolte*) was miraculously spared by the tribunal, though it consisted of the aggressive trio 'Le Reniement de saint Pierre', 'Abel et Caïn', and 'Les Litanies de Satan'. Baudelaire was at least free from the charge of an offence against religion.

Another point of interest is that in this as in all subsequent editions the three cycles of love-poems were printed in the first section (*Spleen et Idéal*) in the order Jeanne Duval, Mme Sabatier, and Marie Daubrun. In a chronological arrangement the order would be different, if Feuillerat's thesis about the liaison with Marie Daubrun is accepted. The Sabatier cycle begins in 1852 and ends with 'Semper eadem' in 1860. The first poems for Marie were probably written as early as 1850 or 1851, though the dates of publication stretch only from 1855 to 1860, ending with the bitter denunciation of 'L'Amour du mensonge' and 'À une Madone'. (Critics have wondered whether the prose-poem 'Laquelle est la vraie?' refers to Mme Sabatier. This prose-poem, in which the poet buries his beautiful Benedicta and is then faced with a miserable, vulgar replica of her, could just as well refer to Marie Daubrun. The relationship with Mme Sabatier did not end in disgust, but in friendship.) Feuillerat is on sure ground when he claims that Marie Daubrun wrenched the poet free from 'his enslavement to the Black Venus'. If Baudelaire placed Marie last

in the series of cycles, perhaps it was because in 1857 he still had hopes of a permanent liaison with her, whereas he had never contemplated one with Mme Sabatier. It seems logical, then, in a book with a plan that the Daubrun cycle should follow that of Jeanne Duval.

It is hardly surprising if Baudelaire suffered for a long time from the excitement and bitterness of 1857, yet in the next four years he worked very hard and produced a second edition of *Les Fleurs du mal* containing thirty-two 'new' poems – not all of them really new, since he sometimes took years to finish a poem. For instance it has been suggested that 'Le Cygne' (like 'L'Albatros', begun in 1842 and having the final stanza added to it in 1859) might have been started in the 1840s, or consist of several poems or pieces of poems worked into one. 1858 saw the publication of the third Poe volume (*Aventures d'Arthur Gordon Pym*) and the 'Poème du haschisch' which formed the first part of *Les Paradis artificiels* of 1860.

In November 1858 Baudelaire wrote an important letter to Calonne in which he said: 'I have begun the new *Fleurs du mal* . . . perhaps I shall make twenty. Protestant pedants (*professeurs*) will be pained to see that I'm an incorrigible Catholic. I shall take care to make myself thoroughly understood, sometimes very low, and then very high. Thanks to this method I'll be able to descend to the ignoble passions. Nobody but the absolutely dishonest will fail to understand the deliberate impersonality of my poems.'

Several important matters arise from this statement. As for 'incorrigible Catholic', those who are content to approach Baudelaire from a strictly orthodox Catholic position are as likely to be pained as the 'Protestant pedants'. No doubt he meant that his work would shock Protestants through its stress on evil, hell, and Satan, on the notion of excommunication, human vice, and weakness, the reality of sin, the 'poverty of man without God', as Pascal put it. If so, he was underestimating the Protestant mind and perhaps confusing it with that lay puritanism – whether Catholic or Protestant – which refuses to look evil in the face and prefers to console itself with its diet of cups of tea and buns. It is relevant to note that in the period 1842–56 when Baudelaire was composing *Les Fleurs du mal* he was a lapsed Catholic. This amounts to saying that though the poet did not and could not cast off his Catholic formation, the book was not written (i.e. not all the poems were written) with a Catholic intention. Nor can the

structure of the book, ending with death and, noticeably, in some hope for a kind of survival rather than a belief in it (the last three poems were 'La Mort des amants', 'La Mort des pauvres', 'La Mort des artistes'), be regarded as what one would expect from an 'incorrigible Catholic'. Baudelaire's Catholicism will not bear analysis in detail, but became so generalized and laicized as to amount to a prejudice rather than a faith, a disposition rather than a conviction.

As an example of what I mean: in 1860 Flaubert read *Les Paradis artificiels* and commented: 'Here is my only objection. It seems to me that in a subject treated at such a high level, in a study which is the beginning of a natural science, in a work of observation and induction, you have (more than once) insisted too much (?) on the *Spirit of Evil*. One feels a leaven of Catholicism here and there. I would have preferred you not to have condemned hashish, opium, excess. Do you know what will emerge from them later?' Baudelaire's answer was non-committal in the sense that he did not directly quote doctrine in his defence; yet none but a man shaped by Catholicism could have replied quite as he did: 'I have always been obsessed by the impossibility of accounting for some of man's sudden acts and thoughts except by the hypothesis of the intervention of an evil force outside himself.'

On another occasion he wrote to his mother, defending himself against a priest, that his book 'started out from a Catholic idea'. That may be so: but the book did not follow one. It is no condemnation of Baudelaire to point out that an integral Catholic could not have written *Les Fleurs du mal*, and would not have had the need or the courage to write it. The need for such a book arises from the absence of God, not his presence. It is a book which can make Catholics, and which perhaps in the end made Baudelaire into one; but it is not a book made *of* Catholicism, it is a rosary of pain and revolt. Perhaps the truest statement he ever made on the matter was the famous one to Ancelle in February 1866 when he was at the frontier of death: 'Need I tell you, you who haven't guessed it any more than the rest, that in this *atrocious* book I put all my heart, all my tenderness, all my religion (*travestied*), all my hate? It is true that I shall write the opposite, that I'll swear by everything holy that it's a book of pure art, of antics, of entertainment, and I'll be lying like a dentist.'

Nothing can better illustrate the life of a work of art, and its relationship to the author's life, than the way it so often changed

colour in the mind of its author. The reader will not so easily forget the early poems of revolt and nausea, or the projected book *Les Lesbiennes* and the ambiguous aims of *Les Limbes*. The fact that towards the end of his life, when he had learnt to pray and was better disposed towards religion than ever before, he saw *Les Fleurs du mal* as his *travestied* religion does not justify those critics who seek in it his religion in a pure state. The irony of the work depends on our remembering the razor's edge on which its spirituality is poised, and the statement 'incorrigible Catholic' of 1858 is not to be taken at its face value. Baudelaire presents the first case (to be followed by Bloy, Mauriac, Jouhandeau, and Graham Greene) of the modern Catholic adventure towards and beyond the boundary of orthodoxy, the search for God in the nature of evil itself, and for salvation even by our sins.

But if Baudelaire was avowedly seeking beauty in evil, it was perhaps by accident that he found something more? No: what fundamentally kept the work rooted in religion was the author's religious sensibility. He was not a modern, inasmuch as he obstinately believed that the world had an inherent meaning or meanings; that is the sense of 'Correspondances' and it haunts *Les Fleurs du mal*, even in the 'Spleen' poems when he is in despair because the world suddenly closes up and refuses those meanings. Mallarmé, on the other hand, was the very opposite of a mystic because he believed the material world to be meaningless, and it is this which separates Baudelaire from the Symbolists. In spite of all his talk about the gulf, the abyss, the void, nothingness, Baudelaire clung to the end to the meaningfulness of life and things, and the desperate poems of the last period, paralleled in our own language by Hopkins's 'terrible sonnets', represent a virile, muscular protest against the 'dark night of the soul'. Far from being an 'incorrigible Catholic', the saintliness of Baudelaire lies in his struggle for belief against all the odds, though it is likely that he died before the battle was completely won.

I am not certain that the question, whether the poems are 'Catholic' or not, is a legitimate critical question: it is certainly one on which almost any opinion can be offered, and what has been said, in lightly touching on it, may well serve as a warning to the critical mind in its temptation to use the book as a torch to illuminate the life, or vice versa. Oddly enough, the old aesthetic tests are often more satisfactory than those of the biographer, the philosopher, or the theologian, where poetry is concerned. I

would say that 'Le Reniement de saint Pierre' and 'Abel et Caïn' are aesthetic blunders of the first order, and the worst lapses of taste ever committed by Baudelaire, though some people might try to justify them on religious grounds. I see no such aesthetic failure in 'Une charogne' and 'Les Litanies de Satan', and their aesthetic probity is matched instinctively by their religious depth and pureness. A final word on this point: in view of my suggestion (p. 9) that Baudelaire had no consistent metaphysic, how can I assert that he believed the world had a meaning? The answer is, I think, that Baudelaire fails, even in 'Correspondances', to give any idea of what that meaning is, beyond the idea of unity or what he calls elsewhere 'universal harmony'. He does not appear to me to attribute to the world the meaning that an 'incorrigible Catholic' would have given it. His religious sensibility was generalized and only began to focus in the last poems (1859 onwards).

A second point arising from the letter to Calonne is the description he gave of his work ('thanks to this *method*' . . . 'deliberate *impersonality* of my poems'). In the tremendous period of creation on which he was now entering, and which is comparable with the last phase of Beethoven, when in one year, 1859, he produced 'Le Cygne', 'Les Petites Vieilles', 'Le Voyage', and so many other sustained and perfect works, Baudelaire was writing with a confidence of thought and a precision of art that he had never achieved before. It is in this period that without any loss of emotional intensity he became the *deliberate* artist, the *poète volontaire*, described in Poe's *Philosophy of Composition* and, later, in Valéry's critical works. He was writing, as Valéry would put it, 'with the maximum consciousness possible'. He was able to create what he willed and how he willed. The comparison with Beethoven is not accidental: there is nothing in literature comparable with the deliberate *discords* of 'Les Petites Vieilles' where irony and compassion are mercilessly clashed together: nothing comparable with the rising from the simple recitative at the beginning of 'Le Cygne' into the sublime compassion of the aria in the second part, followed by the absolute fall into prose, ending this fine poem on a single note, on a kind of *etcetera*, in 'bien d'autres encore'.

The expression 'deliberate impersonality' also needs comment. It could mean that he was seeing good and evil from above, and that the evil that he described was not only that of his own existence. The great strength and value of all Baudelaire's poetry is

that his theme is always the human being; his most characteristic imagery is always the imagery of the human body and its sensations, as in comparing a street lamp with 'un oeil sanglant qui palpite et qui bouge' or the rustle of dawn 'comme un visage en pleurs que les brises essuient'. In the final period he certainly entered more deeply than ever into the lives of others, but perhaps he misjudged himself in a sense in speaking of his *impersonality* if it was meant to refer to the content of his work. No, it must be taken as referring to his manner of creating, making these superb poems by an act of reason, calculating the extent of his resources and his talent. He was to write in his Journals that he had been accused of all the crimes that he had described. But his poems were now being written according to a set plan, to fit into a framework which already existed but which had little meaning in the first edition. Had Baudelaire died in 1857 his claim on posterity would have remained in doubt. Had the injustice of the trial discouraged him he might have been a distinguished failure, like Musset. But in his remaining years he consolidated his position in every domain and demonstrated the range of his genius as never before.

In November 1858 Baudelaire again set up house with Jeanne Duval, but while he was away at his mother's in April 1859 Jeanne had a paralytic seizure and was taken to hospital. He at once raised money to pay her expenses, but it was characteristic of Jeanne to pretend that she had not received it, so that he had to borrow again. Now he looked after her 'like a father and a guardian'. He set up a home with her at Neuilly, with new furniture. This was a period of tenderness and remorse on his part: he was again insisting with his mother that Jeanne must inherit his estate. Very soon she installed a 'brother' in the apartment, who lived off Baudelaire and tyrannized her and ended by selling the furniture. Now the final parting came: from 1861 onwards Baudelaire was completely alone, fleeing restlessly from one hotel to another, still sending money to Jeanne but never seeing her again, and trying to scrape francs together to go and stay with his mother at Honfleur.

Meanwhile his position as an art critic was finally established by various actions and publications. The idea of the section of *Tableaux parisiens* in the second edition of *Les Fleurs du mal* arose from his efforts to help the eccentric, if not insane artist, Méryon. The poet's idea was to illustrate Méryon's engravings of Paris with poems and prose-poems of his own, but, far from appreciating

this, Méryon thought he was being robbed. The poet had also become a friend of Boudin, then working in obscurity, and was the first to recognize the merits of Manet, who now became a firm friend. He also made Constantin Guys the exemplar of his own theory of the 'heroism of modern life' and celebrated his work in a fine essay which was not issued until 1863. The *Salon* of 1859 is one of his finest and most lucid statements on art, in which he brought Coleridge to his aid in his praise of Imagination which he called 'the queen of the faculties'. Baudelaire rightly saw the work of art as a synthesis and for that reason warned that the pursuit of Truth is not enough. Baudelaire's aesthetic was nearer to that of Croce than to the thinkers of his own time. The same year saw the publication of his fine essays on Wagner (whose work he was the first to evaluate and appreciate in France), and on Hugo, Gautier and other writers. Unfortunately his critical works as well as *Le Spleen de Paris*, that highly original collection of poems in prose, were not collected into volumes until after his death.

Although 1861 was such a remarkable year, including as it did the issue of the famous second edition of *Les Fleurs du mal*, it was one in which Baudelaire was constantly tormented by the urge to commit suicide and by the obscure feeling that he would not live long enough, in any case, to complete all the projects he had undertaken. The frenzy with which he worked was a struggle against time, against solitude and sickness, and against himself. In this period he was writing the notebooks which show the terrible physical and moral struggle in which he was engaged. The point of terror was reached very soon, when he wrote in his journal: 'I am always in a state of vertigo, and today, 23 January 1862, I received a remarkable warning, I felt pass over me the wind from the wing of imbecility.' This mounting mental and physical stress explains the bleak intensity of the poems of this period, the fear of Time in 'L'Horloge', the obsession with the pit and the void in 'Le Gouffre', 'Obsession', and 'Le Goût du néant', the sense of guilt and discouragement in 'La Fin de la journée'. The only two moments of calm occur in 'La Voix' and 'Recueillement', in both of which there are references to the work of Pascal.

The new edition of the *Fleurs* in 1861 failed to receive quite the welcome Baudelaire had expected. He was now in an odd frame of mind, displeased at not being awarded the rosette of the Légion d'Honneur. Perhaps his candidature for the French

Academy in that year was partly intended to draw attention to his work. He made the traditional calls on the Academicians and drew fresh humiliations on his head: Alfred de Vigny was almost the only one to recognize his genius yet did his best to dissuade him. Baudelaire withdrew after Sainte-Beuve, forced at last to mention him in public, described his work as 'Baudelaire's *Folly*', thus dismissing him as an eccentric.

From now on his affairs went from bad to worse. His publisher Poulet-Malassis was imprisoned for debt and declared a bankrupt in 1862. Papers for which he was writing closed down. Charpentier, editor of the *Revue nationale*, had the effrontery to change his text after the proofs were passed. Negotiations with new publishers hung fire. His attacks of nausea and dizziness became more frequent. The few poems he was left to write, though his most powerful, touched the depths of despair: 'Le Coucher du soleil romantique', a condemnation of the literary world as it then was; 'Les Plaintes d'un Icare', a lament for his own destiny; 'Le Couvercle', 'Le Gouffre', and 'L'Examen de minuit', an intense brooding over the cruelty of existence. His last serious poem (for one cannot count the satirical poems about Belgium) was 'L'Imprévu', 1863, a reply to Barbey d'Aurevilly's statement that the author of *Les Fleurs du mal* could only be converted or blow his brains out. This poem, with its usual stress on evil and the power of Satan, gives a glimpse of salvation in the final lines, but the reader must judge for himself whether they refer to Baudelaire. The poet's seriousness can best be judged by looking into his private journal, *Mon Cœur mis à nue* ('My Heart Laid Bare'):

Hygiene. Morality. Conduct. – Too late, perhaps! My mother and Jeanne. – My health, out of charity and duty. – Jeanne's illnesses. My mother's infirmities and solitude.

– Do one's duty every day and trust in God for tomorrow.

– The only way of earning money is to work in a disinterested manner.

– A short formula for wisdom – toilet, prayer, work.

– Prayer: charity, wisdom, and strength.

– Without charity I am but a tinkling cymbal.

– My humiliations have been God's graces.

– Is my period of egotism over?

– The faculty for responding to the needs of each minute, in a word exactness, must inevitably find its reward.

The last page of the journal reads as follows:

Hygiene, Conduct, Method. − I swear to myself to adopt, from now on, the following rules as the permanent rules of my life: Make my prayer every morning to God, the reservoir of all strength and all justice, and to my father, to Mariette, and to Poe as intercessors; pray them to afford me the necessary strength to carry out all my duties, and to grant my mother a long enough life for her to enjoy the change in me; work all day long, or at least as much as my strength allows; trust in God, that is to say in Justice itself, for the success of my undertakings; every evening make a new prayer asking God for life and strength for my mother and me; divide my earnings into four shares, one for daily expenses, one for my creditors, one for my friends, and one for my mother; obey the principles of the strictest sobriety, the first of which is to suppress all stimulants, of whatever kind.

The last chapter of Baudelaire's life was as painful and pointless as can be imagined. To recoup his fortunes he went to Belgium in 1864, and though he made one or two almost furtive visits to France his active life was to end in exile. The lecture-tour was a failure, and with Swiftian scorn and hatred he began writing a fierce attack on *Pauvre Belgique!* which was never completed. His projects for collected editions of his works went awry and he ended by selling his copyright to Michel-Lévy for a pittance. After collapsing (ironically enough, in a church) and losing his powers of speech, Baudelaire had little more before him than the living death of a paralytic before he died in his mother's arms on 31 August 1867. In the meantime, in his absence, the younger generation, Mendès, Mallarmé, Verlaine and others, had been hailing him as the greatest of French poets, but he turned a deaf ear to them. His mother wrote, not long after his death, 'Had Charles let himself be guided by his step-father, his career would have been very different. It is true that he would not have left a name in literature, but all three of us would have been happier.' As a mother, she was right, but she never realized that the dove may be called on to cherish the phoenix. Maybe it could be argued that the romantic fallacy consists in the choice between art and life, which Mme Aupick was lamenting − yet the lives of Molière and Racine are in a sense as lamentable as that of Baudelaire. Yeats put the matter in a nutshell in his lines:

> The intellect of man is forced to choose
> Perfection of the life, or of the work,
> And if it take the second must refuse
> A heavenly mansion, raging in the dark.

But Baudelaire was not entirely the victim of the romantic fallacy: he knew too well that no human life or work can reach perfection.

III

THE TITLE, *Les Fleurs du mal*

In the first place, what about the title itself? It is surprising that in his magisterial *Baudelaire and Nature* F. W. Leakey did not look into the implications of this horticultural image in which there is a built-in confusion between the flower and poem, the natural and the aesthetic, all of them set into an uncertain relationship with evil and therefore with morality.

We know that Baudelaire had considered other titles for his early work, notably the erotic *Les Lesbiennes* in 1846 and the religious/sociological *Les Limbes* in 1848, which are referred to above on p. 25. The first use of *Les Fleurs du mal* was in its application to the eighteen poems published in the *Revue des Deux Mondes* in 1855 (see p. 26 above) where it suited that group of provocative works. As early as 1841 Baudelaire wrote to his mother that he was sending her some 'fleurs' which she would find 'singulières'; using a term which a sentimental woman at that time would understand, while ironically implying that his 'singular' poems might disturb her preconceived female ideas about poetry, or should we say 'poesy'. We all know that the term 'anthology' is based on the Greek for 'flower' and 'choose', meaning 'a collection of the flowers of verse' according to the OED. Throughout the nineteenth century in English fancy words like *treasury*, *thesaurus*, *gems* and even *casket* were used for collections of verse, as well as *bouquet*, *garland* and even *posy*. The term was further extended – it could go no farther – in Stevenson's *A Child's Garden of Verses* in 1885. Meanwhile the French went in for such terms as *album*, *bouquet*, *florilège*. The title *Les Fleurs du mal* is primarily an ironic comment on the romantic notion that verse is something honeyed to charm young ladies, and it reminds us of D. H. Lawrence's equally ironic choice of the title *Pansies* for

his satirical poems. Thus the term 'Flowers of Evil' is primarily an onslaught on the more sentimental aspects of Romantic poetry, at the opposite end to such things as Hégésippe Moreau's *Les Myosotis* (forget-me-nots) of 1838 or even Hugo's *Les Feuilles d'automne* (1831). If the ironic value of Baudelaire's title was not appreciated by the tribunal which in 1857 banned six of the poems, this was the poet's own fault, as instead of insisting on a satirical intention (though his lawyer did in passing) he earnestly stressed the veracity of the pictures he had painted and unwisely, indeed perhaps treacherously, accused other poets of dealing with taboo subjects even more naughtily. The title *Les Fleurs du mal*, then, was a sort of manifesto against the insipid nature-poetry of the lesser Romantics and the sentimentalism perhaps unfairly associated with them.

However the problem does not end there. The title is really a double metaphor meaning (i) the products of evil and (ii) poems about evil or its products. It is interesting to note that Baudelaire himself was led into an extension of the metaphor, as in his Dedications to Gautier he referred to the poems themselves as 'ces fleurs maladives' – as if Evil affected the poems themselves as well as their themes. We thus end with the notion of the book as a collection of sickly or unhealthy flowers (poems) of evil, according to their own creator who spoke elsewhere of 'ce misérable dictionnaire de mélancolie et de crime' and 'ce livre atroce' etc. – thus taking little account himself of the more positive or 'ideal' aspects of his book. But a glance through the first edition of *Les Fleurs du mal* is enough to show that the title was really a misnomer, unless we are to regard love, painting, sculpture, music, poetry, beauty and life itself, as 'evil'. Just as Montaigne said that we experience nothing in its pure state ('nous ne goûtons rien de pur') a large number of poems deal with both good and evil. Also, the delights rather than the evils of existence are the themes of at least thirty-five other poems out of a hundred. The result is that over half of the book has little or nothing to do with its morbid title.

Why all this fuss over a title? What does it matter? It matters because Baudelaire's insistence on Evil as a positive force had an underlying religious significance. This had two odd results: some (Verlaine, Arthur Symons etc.) saw the poet as a Satanist, while others (T. S. Eliot etc.) stole him for Religion. A combination of the two made a whole generation, the Surrealists, reject Baudelaire

almost entirely to their great loss. It is easier to de-christianize
Baudelaire in English than in French by translating *mal* simply as
bad or badness, and in some of the poems that is all that is meant.
For Bertrand Russell, for instance, 'sin' was only a rather preten-
tious word for 'error'. Flowers of badness, flowers of error – such
banalities would take away a significant part of the title's meaning,
which is biblical and related no doubt to 'the wages of sin'. We
must reject such a simplification as Russell suggests, though it
might well please a surrealist; because Baudelaire's label includes
all such interpretations.

To speculate a little further, perhaps something of significance
has been overlooked. The title contains an antithesis between
'flowers' and 'evil'. Baudelaire himself went as far as to describe it
as a punning title – 'un titre-calembour' – in one of his letters.
This is highly unclassical and points to an anti-aesthetic. To quote
Montaigne again, he pointed out a fact which few of us notice
these days, that in Greek there was only one word for beauty and
goodness: 'Un même mot embrasse en Grec le bel et le bon' (*De
la Physionomie*). To 'extract beauty from evil', as Baudelaire
claimed to be doing in one of his prefaces, was to dissociate
beauty from goodness. Éluard and Picasso (in my presence) once
discussed the fact that they had 'created the anti-aesthetic' ('nous
avons créé l'anti-esthétique'). Whether they did so or not, the
roots of that element in Surrealism are to be found in Baudelaire.
And the signpost to the conflict between Spleen and Ideal is to be
found in the title of the collection as a whole. One of the poems
most singularly representing the anti-aesthetic is of course 'Une
charogne', closely followed by the banned poem 'Les Métamor-
phoses du vampire'.

THE BANNED POEMS

While some thirteen poems had to be defended against the public
prosecutor in 1857, only six were actually banned, on the grounds
of 'offence to public morality'. These are given in the *Les Épaves*
section in most editions, an important exception being the
Centenary edition presented by Marcel Ruff. Baudelaire was
acquitted of the accusation of blasphemy or offence against reli-
gion. For him this was a source of great satisfaction; but his
mother's confessor was to burn the book in her presence.

There is nothing in the six banned poems that would offend a
reader today. The two beautiful lesbian poems, 'Lesbos' and 'Femmes

damnées' (pp. 315, 320) are not only written with great delicacy but contain or imply a condemnation of homosexuality. It has not been noted by critics that a recent work by Horace de Viel-Castel had spread rumours about lesbianism at Louis-Napoleon's court; perhaps one undeclared reason why the poems were frowned upon. Three other victims of the tribunal were the frankly erotic poems 'Le Léthé', 'À celle qui est trop gaie' and 'Les Bijoux', all of which have what we would now call sado-masochistic features. 'Les Métamorphoses du vampire' has already been mentioned – the magistrates would have been astonished to know, what they ought to have been told, that this banned work was based on a passage in one of Racine's plays.

<div align="center">EDITIONS</div>

Putting aside the appearance of individual poems in periodicals, collections issued in the poet's lifetime were as follows:

(i) 1857: *Les Fleurs du mal* comprised the introductory 'Au Lecteur', followed by a hundred poems numbered I–C. These were divided into five sections: *Spleen et Idéal*, I–LXXVII; *Fleurs du mal*, LXXVIII–LXXXIX; *Révolte*, XC–XCII; *Le Vin*, XCIII–XCVII; *La Mort*, XCVIII–C. It will be noticed at once that the first group is out of proportion to all the rest. Of the banned poems, three were taken from the first section and three from the second.

(ii) 1861: The second and enlarged edition contained 'Au Lecteur' and 126 poems, now divided into six parts; a new section *Tableaux parisiens* being composed of eight works taken from the former *Spleen et Idéal*, and ten new works. The section *Le Vin* was moved to a less important position as we shall see later.

(iii) 1866: *Les Épaves* (Flotsam) was published by the poet's friend and publisher Poulet-Malassis. It contained twenty-three poems: the six banned poems and seventeen hitherto unpublished. This collection contained one or two early works and half a dozen very good recent ones, including Baudelaire's last 'great' poem 'L'Imprévu' (1863) which could have served as a fitting religious climax to a further edition of *Les Fleurs du mal*. The book unfortunately ends with some trivia or 'Buffooneries' which rather lower the tone of the volume as a whole.

(iv) 1866: sixteen *Nouvelles Fleurs du mal* appeared in *Le Parnasse contemporain* which is sometimes regarded as a manifesto of the (then almost defunct) Parnassian school. It is amusing to note that

Baudelaire had suggested *Sylves* as a possible title for this group – another vegetable label! – but it is just as well that it was not adopted as another poet, Auguste Barbier, had already used it for his collection *Silves, poésies diverses* two years earlier. This group of works is distinguished by its inclusion of the magnificent 'Recueillement', written in 1861.

In 1868 Charles Asselineau and Théodore de Banville issued the first posthumous edition of *Les Fleurs du mal*, imagining that it would remain the definitive text. For copyright reasons it remained the only authorized text until 1917 but since then, for various reasons (notably its questionable arrangement), it has been despised and rejected by subsequent editors. It contained 151 poems. As editors have regarded the second edition of 1861 as the *editio princeps*, unfortunately they have perpetuated a piecemeal arrangement, or lack of it, in dealing with post-1861 works and those written before that date but left unpublished by Baudelaire. In addition a host of 'attributed' pieces have been foisted on Baudelaire by gullible editors.

ARCHITECTURE

The so-called 'architecture' of *Les Fleurs du mal* has already been mentioned (p. 31 above). It was Barbey d'Aurevilly who in 1857, in a statement prepared for the magistrates, first suggested that the collection of poems had 'a secret architecture', without explaining what that might be. This idea was taken up by L. F. Benedetto in a seminal article in 1912 published in the *Zeitschrift für französische Sprache und Literatur*. This was further developed by M. Ruff in 1930 and A. Feuillerat in 1941. The prevailing tendency now is to admit that the sections of the book suggest a certain progression, but that many of the poems seem to be oddly or wrongly situated, and that the term 'architecture' for the 1857 edition is a misnomer, whereas in 1861 Baudelaire made some effort at improving the work's structure.

The weakest part of the argument about 'architecture' is that Baudelaire himself never used the term so happily offered by his friend. His own pronouncements are more modest and only point to his desire for the book to be judged as a whole and not by its parts – a wish which is common to all poets who publish their works. His own term for this was merely 'un ensemble', as in the following from documents prepared for the trial:

– Un livre de poésie doit être apprécié dans son ensemble et par sa conclusion.
– Le livre doit être jugé dans son ensemble, et alors il en ressort une terrible moralité.
– Ce parfait ensemble de mon livre.
– Je répète qu'un livre doit être jugé dans son ensemble.

It will be noted that two of these statements refer to books in general, and two to the poet's own work. In addition, in the four prose pieces which were drafts for a preface, partly written between 1859 and 1861 but not printed by Baudelaire (given as an appendix to the present edition) there was no further mention of this 'ensemble'. At no point anywhere, not even in his letters, did Baudelaire ever use words like plan, architecture, structure, or even arrangement. All the same, Baudelaire's intentions are perhaps sufficiently explained when in connection with the eighteen poems printed in the *Revue des Deux Mondes* in 1855 he wrote that he wished 'les mettre en ordre . . . de manière qu'ils se fassent, pour ainsi dire, suite', that is to say make a logical sequence.

There are signs however that Baudelaire was not indifferent to Barbey's idea, as he made some significant changes in his second edition. Without discussing individual poems this can be shown by simply comparing the distribution of poems in the two editions of *Les Fleurs du mal*:

1857			1861		
Au Lecteur			Au Lecteur		
I.	Spleen et Idéal	77	I.	Spleen et Idéal	5
—			II.	Tableaux parisiens	18
—			III.	Le Vin	5
II.	Fleurs du mal	12	IV.	Fleurs du mal	9
III.	Révolte	3	V.	Révolte	3
IV.	Le Vin	5	—		
V.	La Mort	3	VI.	La Mort	6
		1 + 100			1 + 126

It can be seen at a glance that the second arrangement is more satisfactory than the first. Baudelaire has still not split up the top-heavy first section (perhaps because he wanted to preserve the various 'love' and other cycles within it or to maintain that clash

between ideal and evil in them) but has added substantially to it. He could easily have achieved a better balance, though, if he had created a fresh section, *L'Amour*, by taking the various love-cycles (for Jeanne Duval, Marie Daubrun, Madame Sabatier and various 'amours secondaires'), i.e. 45 poems running from XXII to LXVI. The new *Tableaux parisiens* includes eight poems taken from the first group. The *Le Vin* group has been given a less significant place in 1861 but its composition is unchanged. The *Fleurs du mal* group is reduced by the absence of three banned poems. The final *La Mort* is not greatly increased but the book now ends on the magnificent 'Le Voyage' – the impact of which was to be resumed in T. S. Eliot's 'Fare forward, voyagers' in one of his *Four Quartets*.

In spite of possible objections to the 'hold-all' aspects of the first section, the term 'architecture' may be more satisfactorily applied to the second edition than to the first: there is now a clear progression from the struggle between *Spleen* and *Ideal*, followed by attempted escapes through city life; the temptation to escape through the artificial paradise of intoxication; then a further decline through sin and revolt towards death, the gateway to the unknown. Certainly the new book justifies the title of 'a modern Dante' conferred on Baudelaire by one of his contemporaries. But it is quite certain that if the work does have some claim to a general structure, the individual poems are not all well situated; and it was not one preconceived before 1857 and for which poems could be deliberately written to be slotted in; nor was it much more systematic in 1861. In any case, 'architecture' or not, Baudelaire's poems do not constitute a genuine sequence, nor can they be exempt from individual scrutiny any more than any other poet's. To consider the censorship problem: if we regard the matter from another angle, such as libel, a long poem may contain lines considered libellous, and a collection may contain libellous items, just as a chapter of a novel may do. Thus the defence of an 'ensemble' cannot be maintained, in law, although it may be justified aesthetically.

NOUVELLES FLEURS DU MAL

These poems all appear to have been written after 1857, with the exception of 'La Lune offensée', which is pre-1845. The notion that this poem was about Baudelaire's mother is now discredited.

JUVENILIA

The order given by Pichois (*Pléiade*) is observed here, except that a prose fragment ('Cauchemar') and Baudelaire's school exercises in Latin verse have been omitted.

AMŒNITATES BELGICAE

Only nine of these pieces were published and fourteen known in manuscript before the issue of a complete (?) collection by two publishers in 1925. There followed a lawsuit after which in 1930 the Éditions Excelsior text edited by François Montel was awarded priority. Some of the items might be apocryphal. Written during Baudelaire's unhappy years in Belgium (1864–6), they are of uneven quality; at first reading they are perhaps distasteful, but some have an epigrammatic vitality.

VERSE TRANSLATIONS

Two literal versions of songs by T. F. Walmisley (1783–1866) and Nicholas Breton (1555–1624), which Baudelaire scribbled for Alfred Busquet on a programme of songs from Evans's Music and Supper Rooms, Covent Garden, are omitted. Busquet published them in one of his 'Londres fantastique' articles in 1853.

POEMS ATTRIBUTED TO BAUDELAIRE

The authenticity of most of the poems in this group may be questioned. Only those actually published or mentioned by Baudelaire or for which a manuscript exists should be accepted without question. Those about which I am most sceptical are poems which appeared under other poets' names. Many accounts have been given of a proposed collaboration between Baudelaire and three friends, Prarond, Le Vavasseur and Dozon in a collection of poems, *Vers*, which appeared in 1843 under the names of the three others, Baudelaire having withdrawn. J. Mouquet in *Vers retrouvés* (1929) claimed that a large number of the items in it were in whole or in part by Baudelaire. Since then, J. Pommier, J. Crépet and particularly J. K. Wallace have refuted Mouquet's assertions, but the damage had been done. Subsequently to *Vers* a number of poems published by Prarond and Privat d'Anglemont have been tentatively attributed to Baudelaire. There are also a few others, with such signatures as Antony Bruno and Henry Vernot, which should not be accepted. There is no good reason, in the case of all

the poems in this group, for attributing to Baudelaire anything written by his friends or which mentions corpses, vipers, prostitutes or whatever. All the poems given in the final section of this book are of some interest, but are not certainly Baudelaire's even though they might contain echoes from his work.

Three poems allegedly written in collaboration with other poets have been omitted.

★ ★ ★

This present edition of Baudelaire's poems with prose translations is a complete rehandling of my Penguin *Baudelaire* published in 1961. As the Penguin was a selection only, I then took the liberty of presenting the poems in a more or less chronological order, and the Introduction contained thirteen pages in which the chronology was discussed. Here, in a complete edition, the original order of the poems as prepared for publication in Baudelaire's lifetime is observed.

I offer no apology for translating the poems into prose, as this serves a useful purpose for many overseas readers, some of whom have written to me; while the use of my texts by the BBC, the Arts Council and various scholars both here and abroad shows that there is some need for a version of this kind. Some poets and pedants are bound to grumble; forgetting that Baudelaire chose to translate Poe's verse into prose, and that his text has remained the standard one in the French language.

<div style="text-align: right">

FRANCIS SCARFE

Oxford, 1985

</div>

READING LIST

(WORKS IN ENGLISH ONLY)

ANON. Review of Baudelaire's Collected Works. *Fraser's Magazine*, December 1869
BANDY, W.T. *Baudelaire Judged by his Contemporaries*. Columbia, N.Y., 1933
— 'New Light on Baudelaire and Poe'. *Yale French Studies*, 1953
BENNET, J.D. *Baudelaire, a Criticism*. Oxford, 1944
BERSANI, L. *Baudelaire and Freud*. Berkeley and London, 1977
BOWRA, C.M. *The Romantic Imagination*. Oxford, 1949
CLAPTON, G.T. *Baudelaire, the Tragic Sophist*. London, 1934
ELIOT, T.S. 'Baudelaire'. *Selected Essays*. London, 1934
— 'Baudelaire in Our Time'. *Essays Ancient and Modern*. London, 1936
FAIRLIE, A. *Baudelaire — Les Fleurs du mal*. London, 1960, 1965
GILMAN, M. *Baudelaire the Critic*. New York, 1943
HEMMINGS, F.W.J. *Baudelaire the Damned — a biography*. London, 1982
HUBERT, J.D. 'Baudelaire's Revolutionary Poetics'. *Romanic Review*, 1955
HUXLEY, ALDOUS. 'Baudelaire'. *Do What You Will*. London, 1929
HYSLOP, L.B. and F.E. *Baudelaire, a Self-Portrait*. Oxford, 1957
JAMES, HENRY. 'Baudelaire'. *French Poets and Novelists*. London, 1884
JOHNSON, LIONEL. 'Poets of the 19th Century'. *Daily Chronicle*, 27 December 1900
JONES, P. MANSELL. *Baudelaire*. Cambridge, 1952
LAFORGUE, RENÉ. *The Defeat of Baudelaire*. London, 1932
LEAKEY, F.W. *Baudelaire and Nature*. Manchester, 1969
MOSSOP, D.J. *Baudelaire's Tragic Hero*. London, 1961
MURRY, J.M. 'Baudelaire'. *Countries of the Mind*. London, 1922
NICOLSON, H. *Swinburne and Baudelaire*. Oxford, 1930
PARMEE, D. *Selected Critical Studies of Baudelaire*. Cambridge, 1949
PATTY, J.S. 'Baudelaire's Knowledge of Dante'. *Studies in Philology*, October, 1956
QUENNELL, P. *Baudelaire and the Symbolists*. London, 1955 (revised)
RHODES, S. *The Cult of Beauty in Baudelaire*. New York, 1929

SAINTSBURY, G. 'Baudelaire'. *Miscellaneous Essays*, London, 1892. (Reprinted from *Fortnightly Review*, 1875)

SARTRE, J.-P. *Baudelaire*. (Trans. by M. Turnell.) London, 1940

SCOTT, J.A. 'Petrarch and Baudelaire'. *Revue de littérature comparée*, xxxi, 4, 1957

SIMCOX, H. Review of Baudelaire's Collected Works, in *The Academy*, I, 1869–70

STARKIE, ENID. *Baudelaire*. London, 1957

SWINBURNE, A.C. 'Les Fleurs du mal'. *Spectator*, 6 September 1862. (Reprinted by Edmund Gosse, London, 1913)

SYMONS, A. *Baudelaire, a Study*. London, 1920

TURNELL, M. *Baudelaire: a Study of his Poetry*. London, 1953

—— 'The School of Baudelaire'. *Blackfriars*, 1934

I

Les Fleurs du mal
1861

THE FLOWERS OF EVIL

AU POÈTE IMPECCABLE

AU PARFAIT MAGICIEN ÈS LETTRES FRANÇAISES

À MON TRÈS CHER ET TRÈS VÉNÉRÉ

MAÎTRE ET AMI

THÉOPHILE GAUTIER

AVEC LES SENTIMENTS

DE LA PLUS PROFONDE HUMILITÉ

JE DÉDIE

CES FLEURS MALADIVES

C. B.

To the impeccable Poet and perfect magician of French literature, my most dear and venerable Master and Friend Théophile Gautier, with feelings of the most profound humility, I dedicate these flowers of sickness.

C. B.

AU LECTEUR

La sottise, l'erreur, le péché, la lésine,
Occupent nos esprits et travaillent nos corps,
Et nous alimentons nos aimables remords,
Comme les mendiants nourrissent leur vermine.

Nos péchés sont têtus, nos repentirs sont lâches;
Nous nous faisons payer grassement nos aveux,
Et nous rentrons gaiement dans le chemin bourbeux,
Croyant par de vils pleurs laver toutes nos taches.

Sur l'oreiller du mal c'est Satan Trismégiste
Qui berce longuement notre esprit enchanté,
Et le riche métal de notre volonté
Est tout vaporisé par ce savant chimiste.

C'est le Diable qui tient les fils qui nous remuent!
Aux objets répugnants nous trouvons des appas;
Chaque jour vers l'Enfer nous descendons d'un pas,
Sans horreur, à travers des ténèbres qui puent.

To the Reader

Stupidity, error, sin, and meanness possess our minds and work upon our bodies, and we nourish our fond remorses as beggars suckle their own lice.

Our sins are obstinate, our repentance cowardly. We ensure that our confessions are well rewarded, then gaily we return down the slimy path as if our paltry tears could cleanse our souls of filth.

Satan the thrice-great soothes our spellbound minds on the pillow of evil, this learned alchemist dissolves the precious metal of our will into vapour.

It's the Devil who pulls the strings that make us dance: we take delight in loathsome things; each day we set our feet on a lower step to Hell, yet feel no horror as we descend through the stinking gloom.

Ainsi qu'un débauché pauvre qui baise et mange
Le sein martyrisé d'une antique catin,
Nous volons au passage un plaisir clandestin
Que nous pressons bien fort comme une vieille orange.

Serré, fourmillant, comme un million d'helminthes,
Dans nos cerveaux ribote un peuple de Démons,
Et, quand nous respirons, la Mort dans nos poumons
Descend, fleuve invisible, avec de sourdes plaintes.

Si le viol, le poison, le poignard, l'incendie,
N'ont pas encor brodé de leurs plaisants dessins
Le canevas banal de nos piteux destins,
C'est que notre âme, hélas! n'est pas assez hardie.

Mais parmi les chacals, les panthères, les lices,
Les singes, les scorpions, les vautours, les serpents,
Les monstres glapissants, hurlants, grognants, rampants,
Dans la ménagerie infâme de nos vices,

Like any poverty-stricken lecher who kisses and nibbles an old whore's martyred breasts, we steal more furtive pleasure on the way down and squeeze it to the last drop like a wizened orange.

A compact seething horde of Demons orgies in our brains like a million worms in the bowels; with every breath we take, the invisible stream of Death flows down into our lungs, yet we hear not its dull groans.

If rape and poison, dagger and arson have not yet embroidered the pattern of absurdity on the dreary canvas of our lamentable destinies, that is only, alas, because our souls dare not sin more.

But among the jackals, panthers, bitch-hounds, apes and scorpions, vultures and snakes and monsters which scream and howl and grunt and crawl in the sordid menagerie of our vices,

Il en est un plus laid, plus méchant, plus immonde!
Quoiqu'il ne pousse ni grands gestes ni grands cris,
Il ferait volontiers de la terre un débris
Et dans un bâillement avalerait le monde;

C'est l'Ennui! – l'œil chargé d'un pleur involontaire,
Il rêve d'échafauds en fumant son houka.
Tu le connais, lecteur, ce monstre délicat,
– Hypocrite lecteur, – mon semblable, – mon frère!

there is one even uglier and more wicked and filthier than all the rest. Although it makes no frenzied gestures and utters no deafening cries, yet it would gladly reduce the whole earth to dust, and would gladly swallow the whole world down its yawning maw:

it is Boredom, *taedium vitae*, who with an involuntary tear in his eye dreams of gallows as he smokes his pipe. Dear Reader, you are well acquainted with that fastidious monster – hypocritical Reader – my second self – my brother!

[Published 1855 and in *Les Fleurs du mal*, 1857]

Spleen et Idéal

I
BÉNÉDICTION

Lorsque, par un décret des puissances suprêmes,
Le Poète apparaît en ce monde ennuyé,
Sa mère épouvantée et pleine de blasphèmes
Crispe ses poings vers Dieu, qui la prend en pitié:

– «Ah! que n'ai-je mis bas tout un nœud de vipères,
Plutôt que de nourrir cette dérision!
Maudite soit la nuit aux plaisirs éphémères
Où mon ventre a conçu mon expiation!

«Puisque tu m'as choisie entre toutes les femmes
Pour être le dégoût de mon triste mari,
Et que je ne puis pas rejeter dans les flammes,
Comme un billet d'amour, ce monstre rabougri,

SPLEEN AND IDEAL

Benediction

When, by decree of the supreme Powers the poet enters into this dreary world, his horrified mother, full of blasphemies, clenches her fists against God, who takes pity on her:

'Ah,' she cries, 'I would rather have spawned a clutch of snakes than give suck to this mockery of a creature! Cursed be the night and all its transient pleasures when my womb conceived my own atonement!

Since you have chosen me among all women for my sad husband's loathing, and since I cannot throw this stunted freak like a love-letter into the flames,

«Je ferai rejaillir ta haine qui m'accable
Sur l'instrument maudit de tes méchancetés,
Et je tordrai si bien cet arbre misérable,
Qu'il ne pourra pousser ses boutons empestés!»

Elle ravale ainsi l'écume de sa haine,
Et, ne comprenant pas les desseins éternels,
Elle-même prépare au fond de la Géhenne
Les bûchers consacrés aux crimes maternels.

Pourtant, sous la tutelle invisible d'un Ange,
L'Enfant déshérité s'enivre de soleil,
Et dans tout ce qu'il voit et dans tout ce qu'il mange
Retrouve l'ambroisie et le nectar vermeil.

Il joue avec le vent, cause avec le nuage,
Et s'enivre en chantant du chemin de la croix;
Et l'Esprit qui le suit dans son pèlerinage
Pleure de le voir gai comme un oiseau des bois.

I shall pass the hatred you have heaped upon me, on to this cursed instrument of your spite; so thoroughly will I twist this miserable tree that it will never put forth its evil-smelling buds!'

Thus she swallows her foaming hatred down and, without the least understanding of eternal designs, she herself heaps up those pyres in the depths of Gehenna which are the reward for the crimes of motherhood.

And yet, under the unseen guidance of an Angel, the disinherited child drinks deep of the intoxicating Sun, discovering ambrosia and ruby nectar in all his food and drink.

He plays with the winds and prattles with the clouds; with rapture he sings the way of the Cross, while the Spirit who follows him on his pilgrimage weeps to see him as happy as a woodland bird.

Tous ceux qu'il veut aimer l'observent avec crainte,
Ou bien, s'enhardissant de sa tranquillité,
Cherchent à qui saura lui tirer une plainte,
Et font sur lui l'essai de leur férocité.

Dans le pain et le vin destinés à sa bouche
Ils mêlent de la cendre avec d'impurs crachats;
Avec hypocrisie ils jettent ce qu'il touche,
Et s'accusent d'avoir mis leurs pieds dans ses pas.

Sa femme va criant sur les places publiques:
«Puisqu'il me trouve assez belle pour m'adorer,
Je ferai le métier des idoles antiques,
Et comme elles je veux me faire redorer;

«Et je me soûlerai de nard, d'encens, de myrrhe,
De génuflexions, de viandes et de vins,
Pour savoir si je puis dans un cœur qui m'admire
Usurper en riant les hommages divins!

But all those whom he would gladly love watch him with fear, or else, making bold of his calm bearing, vie with each other to draw a whine from him as they abuse him with their cruelty.

They mingle ash and filthy spit into the bread and wine destined for his lips; hypocritically they cast down what his hands have touched; they falsely blame themselves for following where he led.

His wife goes out and shouts in public places, 'Since he finds me beautiful enough to adore me, I shall follow the trade of those idols of olden days and, as they did, have my body covered with leaf of gold.

'I will make myself drunk with nard, with incense and with myrrh, with the bowing of knees before me, and with flesh and with wines, to find whether I can jeeringly usurp the homage due to God alone, in whatever heart might worship me.

«Et, quand je m'ennuierai de ces farces impies,
Je poserai sur lui ma frêle et forte main;
Et mes ongles, pareils aux ongles des harpies,
Sauront jusqu'à son cœur se frayer un chemin.

«Comme un tout jeune oiseau qui tremble et qui palpite,
J'arracherai ce cœur tout rouge de son sein,
Et, pour rassasier ma bête favorite,
Je le lui jetterai par terre avec dédain!»

Vers le Ciel, où son œil voit un trône splendide,
Le Poète serein lève ses bras pieux,
Et les vastes éclairs de son esprit lucide
Lui dérobent l'aspect des peuples furieux:

– «Soyez béni, mon Dieu, qui donnez la souffrance
Comme un divin remède à nos impuretés
Et comme la meilleure et la plus pure essence
Qui prépare les forts aux saintes voluptés!

'And when I tire of all those impious mockeries I shall lay my delicate but powerful hand on him, and my harpy's nails will surely claw their way into his very heart.

'Yes, like a little bird that trembles and throbs I shall tear the scarlet heart out of his breast, and throw it scornfully into the dust at his feet, to gorge my favourite beast.'

But towards Heaven where his gaze beholds a splendid throne, the serene Poet raises his pious arms, and the great lightning-flashes of his lucid mind shut out the sight of mankind's frenzied hordes.

'Be blessed, O God,' he cries, 'who offer suffering as a divine balm for our impurities – suffering which is the best and purest essence with which the strong may be prepared for those joys that none but saints may know.

«Je sais que vous gardez une place au Poète
Dans les rangs bienheureux des saintes Légions,
Et que vous l'invitez à l'éternelle fête
Des Trônes, des Vertus, des Dominations.

«Je sais que la douleur est la noblesse unique
Où ne mordront jamais la terre et les enfers,
Et qu'il faut pour tresser ma couronne mystique
Imposer tous les temps et tous les univers.

«Mais les bijoux perdus de l'antique Palmyre,
Les métaux inconnus, les perles de la mer,
Par votre main montés, ne pourraient pas suffire
À ce beau diadème éblouissant et clair;

«Car il ne sera fait que de pure lumière,
Puisée au foyer saint des rayons primitifs,
Et dont les yeux mortels, dans leur splendeur entière,
Ne sont que des miroirs obscurcis et plaintifs!»

'I know that you set aside a place for the Poet in the happy ranks of
the holy Legions, and that you will invite him to partake in the eternal
feast of the Thrones and Virtues and Dominations.

'I know that sorrow is the one nobility on which neither earth nor
Hell can lay its fangs, and that all ages and universes must be taxed for
the tressing of my mystic crown.

'But the vanished jewels of antique Palmyra, and metals yet
unknown to man, and all the pearls of the seas, even were they set
together by your hand, would never be enough to complete this beau-
tiful diadem so dazzling and so bright;

'for it will be made of naught but purest Light drawn from the
sacred source of the Sun's first rays, of which all mortal eyes, even in all
their splendour, are no more than dimmed and mortal mirrors.'

[FM 1857]

II

L'ALBATROS

Souvent, pour s'amuser, les hommes d'équipage
Prennent des albatros, vastes oiseaux des mers,
Qui suivent, indolents compagnons de voyage,
Le navire glissant sur les gouffres amers.

À peine les ont-ils déposés sur les planches,
Que ces rois de l'azur, maladroits et honteux,
Laissent piteusement leurs grandes ailes blanches
Comme des avirons traîner à côté d'eux.

Ce voyageur ailé, comme il est gauche et veule!
Lui, naguère si beau, qu'il est comique et laid!
L'un agace son bec avec un brûle-gueule,
L'autre mime, en boitant, l'infirme qui volait!

Le Poète est semblable au prince des nuées
Qui hante la tempête et se rit de l'archer;
Exilé sur le sol au milieu des huées,
Ses ailes de géant l'empêchent de marcher.

The Albatross

Many a time, for their amusement sailors catch albatross, those vast-winged birds of the seas, the indolent companions of their voyages, who follow their ship as it glides upon the bitter depths.

No sooner have the sailors stretched them out upon the deck than those monarchs of the azure, now awkward and ashamed, let their long white wings drag painfully by their side, like oars.

How ungainly and contemptible the winged traveller becomes, how laughable and graceless, he who only a moment ago was so full of beauty. Now a sailor teases his beak with a pipe, and another drags his foot to imitate the cripple who soared through space.

The Poet shares the fate of this prince of the clouds, who rejoices in the tempest and mocks the archer down below: exiled on earth, an object of scorn, his giant wings impede him as he walks.

[1842–59. Published 1859, when the final quatrain was added]

III
ÉLÉVATION

Au-dessus des étangs, au-dessus des vallées,
Des montagnes, des bois, des nuages, des mers,
Par-delà le soleil, par-delà les éthers,
Par-delà les confins des sphères étoilées,

Mon esprit, tu te meus avec agilité,
Et, comme un bon nageur qui se pâme dans l'onde,
Tu sillonnes gaiement l'immensité profonde
Avec une indicible et mâle volupté.

Envole-toi bien loin de ces miasmes morbides;
Va te purifier dans l'air supérieur,
Et bois, comme une pure et divine liqueur,
Le feu clair qui remplit les espaces limpides.

Derrière les ennuis et les vastes chagrins
Qui chargent de leur poids l'existence brumeuse,
Heureux celui qui peut d'une aile vigoureuse
S'élancer vers les champs lumineux et sereins;

Transcendence

Above the pools, above the valleys and mountains, woods, clouds, and seas; beyond the Sun, beyond the expanses of ether, beyond the frontiers of the starry skies –

agile you move, my mind, and as a strong swimmer rejoices in the wavy sea, gaily you cleave the unfathomable vastness with ineffable, virile and voluptuous joy.

Fly far away beyond this deadly slough; go, cleanse yourself in the noblest of the air, drink undiluted the nectar of the gods, that lucid fire which brims the limpid realms of space!

Beyond all cares and vast chagrins that weigh upon our fogged existence, happy is he whose dauntless wing lifts him towards the luminous and serene fields of peace,

Celui dont les pensers, comme des alouettes,
Vers les cieux le matin prennent un libre essor,
– Qui plane sur la vie, et comprend sans effort
Le langage des fleurs et des choses muettes!

he whose thoughts soar free like larks towards the morning skies,
who rides high above life, swift to interpret the speech of flowers and
voiceless things.

[FM 1857]

IV

CORRESPONDANCES

La Nature est un temple où de vivants piliers
Laissent parfois sortir de confuses paroles;
L'homme y passe à travers des forêts de symboles
Qui l'observent avec des regards familiers.

Comme de longs échos qui de loin se confondent
Dans une ténébreuse et profonde unité,
Vaste comme la nuit et comme la clarté,
Les parfums, les couleurs et les sons se répondent.

Il est des parfums frais comme des chairs d'enfants,
Doux comme les hautbois, verts comme les prairies,
– Et d'autres, corrompus, riches et triomphants,

Ayant l'expansion des choses infinies,
Comme l'ambre, le musc, le benjoin et l'encens,
Qui chantent les transports de l'esprit et des sens.

Correlatives

Nature is a temple, in which living pillars sometimes utter a babel of words; mankind traverses it through forests of symbols that watch him with knowing eyes.

Like prolonged echoes which merge far away in an opaque, deep oneness, as vast as darkness and as vast as light, the perfumes, sounds, and colours answer each to each.

There are perfumes fresh and cool as the flesh of children, mellow as oboes, green as fields; and others that are corrupted, rich, triumphant,

that have the infinite expansion of infinite things – such as amber, musk, benjamin, incense, which chant the ecstasies of the mind and senses.

[Variously dated 1845–46, 1855. FM 1857]

V

J'aime le souvenir de ces époques nues,
Dont Phœbus se plaisait à dorer les statues.
Alors l'homme et la femme en leur agilité
Jouissaient sans mensonge et sans anxiété,
Et, le ciel amoureux leur caressant l'échine,
Exerçaient la santé de leur noble machine.
Cybèle alors, fertile en produits généreux,
Ne trouvait point ses fils un poids trop onéreux,
Mais, louve au cœur gonflé de tendresses communes,
Abreuvait l'univers à ses tétines brunes.
L'homme, élégant, robuste et fort, avait le droit
D'être fier des beautés qui le nommaient leur roi;
Fruits purs de tout outrage et vierges de gerçures,
Dont la chair lisse et ferme appelait les morsures!

Le Poète aujourd'hui, quand il veut concevoir
Ces natives grandeurs, aux lieux où se font voir
La nudité de l'homme et celle de la femme,
Sent un froid ténébreux envelopper son âme
Devant ce noir tableau plein d'épouvantement.
Ô monstruosités pleurant leur vêtement!

I love to recall . . .

I love to recall those ancient times when all was naked, those days when Phoebus gladly touched the human frame with gold. Then men and women rejoiced in their lithe bodies without deceit or shame, and with the loving sky caressing their backs, gave free play to their noble organism's health. In those days Cybele, teeming with bountiful harvests, did not regard her sons as too onerous a burden, but like a she-wolf whose heart swelled with tenderness for all things, gave suck to the whole world from her tawny breasts. Elegant, stalwart, strong, Man was rightly proud of those beautiful women who hailed him as their lord – fruits pure of all assault, innocent of all taint, whose smooth, firm flesh was an invitation to be bitten!

But nowadays, when the poet seeks to visualize those natural grandeurs in places where the nudity of men and women may be observed, he feels a dismal chill envelop his soul at such a dismal, dreadful sight.

Ô ridicules troncs! torses dignes des masques!
Ô pauvres corps tordus, maigres, ventrus ou flasques,
Que le dieu de l'Utile, implacable et serein,
Enfants, emmaillota dans ses langes d'airain!
Et vous, femmes, hélas! pâles comme des cierges,
Que ronge et que nourrit la débauche, et vous, vierges,
Du vice maternel traînant l'hérédité
Et toutes les hideurs de la fécondité!

Nous avons, il est vrai, nations corrompues,
Aux peuples anciens des beautés inconnues:
Des visages rongés par les chancres du cœur,
Et comme qui dirait des beautés de langueur;
Mais ces inventions de nos muses tardives
N'empêcheront jamais les races maladives
De rendre à la jeunesse un hommage profond,
– À la sainte jeunesse, à l'air simple, au doux front,
À l'œil limpide et clair ainsi qu'une eau courante,
Et qui va répandant sur tout, insouciante
Comme l'azur du ciel, les oiseaux et les fleurs,
Ses parfums, ses chansons et ses douces chaleurs!

What freaks, bewailing their clothes! What ridiculous trunks, what torsoes worthy of a masquerade, what feeble twisted bodies, so skinny or pot-bellied and flabby, which the pitiless and unmoved god of Utility wrapped in brass swaddling-clothes when they were little babies! – And you women, alas, wax-pale as candles, gnawed away or swollen by debauchery! And you, virgins who drag with you the legacy of your mothers' viciousness and all the hideous stigmata of fertility!

True enough, we decadent nations have beauties unknown to the peoples of old – faces gnawed by the cankers of the heart and, so to speak, the beauties of sickliness; but such inventions of our latter-day muses will never prevent our diseased races from paying a profound tribute to Youth – to saintly Youth with its unaffected mien, its untroubled brow, its eye limpid and clear as running water, and which goes spreading over all things – as carefree as the azure in the sky, the birds and flowers – its perfumes and its songs, its gentle ardours.

[An early poem: influence of A. Chénier. FM 1857]

VI

LES PHARES

Rubens, fleuve d'oubli, jardin de la paresse,
Oreiller de chair fraîche où l'on ne peut aimer,
Mais où la vie afflue et s'agite sans cesse,
Comme l'air dans le ciel et la mer dans la mer;

Léonard de Vinci, miroir profond et sombre,
Où des anges charmants, avec un doux souris
Tout chargé de mystère, apparaissent à l'ombre
Des glaciers et des pins qui ferment leur pays;

Rembrandt, triste hôpital tout rempli de murmures,
Et d'un grand crucifix décoré seulement,
Où la prière en pleurs s'exhale des ordures,
Et d'un rayon d'hiver traversé brusquement;

Michel-Ange, lieu vague où l'on voit des Hercules
Se mêler à des Christs, et se lever tout droits
Des fantômes puissants qui dans les crépuscules
Déchirent leur suaire en étirant leurs doigts;

The Beacons

Rubens, a river of oblivion, a garden of idleness, a pillow of cool
human flesh on which we cannot love, but where life endlessly tides
and heaves like the air into the sky and the sea within the sea:

Leonardo, a fathomless dark glass in which exquisite angels, their
tender smile fraught with mystery, are glimpsed in the shade of the
glaciers and pines that guard the frontiers of their domain:

Rembrandt, drab hospital that echoes whispered woes, furnished
with naught but a vast crucifix, where a weeping prayer sighs from the
filth, and suddenly pierced by a winter sun:

Michelangelo, a no-man's-land where we see Hercules and Christs
together, and, rising stark upright, powerful phantoms who in the
twilights rend their burial shrouds and stretch their fingers long:

Colères de boxeur, impudences de faune,
Toi qui sus ramasser la beauté des goujats,
Grand cœur gonflé d'orgueil, homme débile et jaune,
Puget, mélancolique empereur des forçats;

Watteau, ce carnaval où bien des cœurs illustres,
Comme des papillons, errent en flamboyant,
Décors frais et légers éclairés par des lustres
Qui versent la folie à ce bal tournoyant;

Goya, cauchemar plein de choses inconnues,
De fœtus qu'on fait cuire au milieu des sabbats,
De vieilles au miroir et d'enfants toutes nues,
Pour tenter les démons ajustant bien leurs bas;

Delacroix, lac de sang hanté des mauvais anges,
Ombragé par un bois de sapins toujours vert,
Où, sous un ciel chagrin, des fanfares étranges
Passent, comme un soupir étouffé de Weber;

Puget, with a boxer's fury and a faun's salacity, who could exalt the
beauty of the scum of the earth; that great heart swollen with pride,
that sickly jaundiced man, Puget the sullen emperor of jailbirds:

Watteau, that carnival in which so many illustrious hearts wander
incandescent like butterflies, in cool and frivolous settings where chandeliers pour down the garish light of madness on the swirling dance:

Goya, that nightmare haunted by the unknown, foetuses roasted at
witches' sabbaths, old hags peering into their looking-glasses, un-nubile
girls all naked but for their stockings which they stretch tight to tempt
demons:

Delacroix, that lake of blood haunted by evil angels, with its dark
fringe of fir-trees, evergreen, where under a glowering sky strange
fanfares can be heard, like Weber's muted sigh:

Ces malédictions, ces blasphèmes, ces plaintes,
Ces extases, ces cris, ces pleurs, ces *Te Deum*,
Sont un écho redit par mille labyrinthes;
C'est pour les cœurs mortels un divin opium!

C'est un cri répété par mille sentinelles,
Un ordre renvoyé par mille porte-voix;
C'est un phare allumé sur mille citadelles,
Un appel de chasseurs perdus dans les grands bois!

Car c'est vraiment, Seigneur, le meilleur témoignage
Que nous puissions donner de notre dignité
Que cet ardent sanglot qui roule d'âge en âge
Et vient mourir au bord de votre éternité!

– All these curses and blasphemies, lamentations and ecstasies, cries
and tears and Te Deums echo down a thousand labyrinths, a divine
opium for the hearts of men.

Theirs is a cry repeated by a thousand sentinels, an order passed on
by a thousand messengers, a beacon lit upon a thousand citadels, the call
of the huntsmen lost in the wide woods:

for truly, Lord, this is the best witness we can give of our human
dignity, this impassioned keening which resounds across the ages, and
which shall die only on thine eternal shore!

[Quoted in the 'Exposition universelle de 1855'. FM 1857]

VII
LA MUSE MALADE

Ma pauvre muse, hélas! qu'as-tu donc ce matin?
Tes yeux creux sont peuplés de visions nocturnes,
Et je vois tour à tour réfléchis sur ton teint
La folie et l'horreur, froides et taciturnes.

Le succube verdâtre et le rose lutin
T'ont-ils versé la peur et l'amour de leurs urnes?
Le cauchemar, d'un poing despotique et mutin,
T'a-t-il noyée au fond d'un fabuleux Minturnes?

Je voudrais qu'exhalant l'odeur de la santé
Ton sein de pensers forts fût toujours fréquenté,
Et que ton sang chrétien coulât à flots rythmiques,

Comme les sons nombreux des syllabes antiques,
Où règnent tour à tour le père des chansons,
Phœbus, et le grand Pan, le seigneur des moissons.

The Sick Muse

Alas, my poor Muse, what ails you this morning? Your sunken eyes are
haunted by nocturnal visions, and I see madness and horror, frigid and
speechless, reflected in your complexion each in turn.

Have the green succubus and the pink sprite poured you a draught
of fear and lust from their urns? Has some nightmare's tyrannic and
ungovernable hand drowned you in the depths of some fabulous
Minturnae?

I should be glad if, redolent of health, your breast were always
visited by powerful thoughts, and if your Christian blood would flow in
cadenced waves,

like the harmonious numbers of classical verse, in which Phoebus
the father of songs and mighty Pan the lord of harvests reign turn by
turn.

[The echoes of Sainte-Beuve and A. Chénier suggest
that this was a relatively early poem. FM 1857]

VIII
LA MUSE VÉNALE

Ô muse de mon cœur, amante des palais,
Auras-tu, quand Janvier lâchera ses Borées,
Durant les noirs ennuis des neigeuses soirées,
Un tison pour chauffer tes deux pieds violets?

Ranimeras-tu donc tes épaules marbrées
Aux nocturnes rayons qui percent les volets?
Sentant ta bourse à sec autant que ton palais,
Récolteras-tu l'or des voûtes azurées?

Il te faut, pour gagner ton pain de chaque soir,
Comme un enfant de chœur, jouer de l'encensoir,
Chanter des *Te Deum* auxquels tu ne crois guère,

Ou, saltimbanque à jeun, étaler tes appas
Et ton rire trempé de pleurs qu'on ne voit pas,
Pour faire épanouir la rate du vulgaire.

The Venal Muse

Muse of my heart, lover of palaces, when January unleashes its icy blasts, through the dark tedium of snowy twilights, will you have embers enough to warm your feet when they are purple with cold?

How will you revive your mottled shoulders with nothing but the beams of night that peep through the shutters? When your purse and your mouth are dry, will you harvest the gold of heaven's azure vaults?

To sing for your supper, then you will have to swing the censer like a choirboy, and chant Te Deums in which you scarce believe;

or like a famished acrobat, show off your points, and laugh while you conceal your tears, to make the mob split their sides.

[An early work. FM 1857]

IX

LE MAUVAIS MOINE

Les cloîtres anciens sur leurs grandes murailles
Étalaient en tableaux la sainte Vérité,
Dont l'effet, réchauffant les pieuses entrailles,
Tempérait la froideur de leur austérité.

En ces temps où du Christ florissaient les semailles,
Plus d'un illustre moine, aujourd'hui peu cité,
Prenant pour atelier le champ des funérailles,
Glorifiait la Mort avec simplicité.

– Mon âme est un tombeau que, mauvais cénobite,
Depuis l'éternité je parcours et j'habite;
Rien n'embellit les murs de ce cloître odieux.

Ô moine fainéant! quand saurai-je donc faire
Du spectacle vivant de ma triste misère
Le travail de mes mains et l'amour de mes yeux?

The Bad Monk

The vast walls of ancient cloisters used to display holy Truth, in paint-
ings that warmed the bowels of the faithful, with the effect of temper-
ing the chill of their austerity.

In those olden days when the seed of Christ's word flourished,
many a renowned monk, now rarely spoken of, made the graveyard his
workshop and glorified Death in his simple art.

My soul is a tomb in which for centuries I have moved to and fro
and lived, an unworthy monk, for no work of my hands embellishes the
walls of my hateful close.

Faint-hearted monk, when shall I learn to turn the daily scene of
my sad dejection, into my hands' labour, my eyes' love?

[Ms. 1842–3. FM 1857]

X

L'ENNEMI

Ma jeunesse ne fut qu'un ténébreux orage,
Traversé çà et là par de brillants soleils;
Le tonnerre et la pluie ont fait un tel ravage,
Qu'il reste en mon jardin bien peu de fruits vermeils.

Voilà que j'ai touché l'automne des idées,
Et qu'il faut employer la pelle et les râteaux
Pour rassembler à neuf les terres inondées,
Où l'eau creuse des trous grands comme des tombeaux.

Et qui sait si les fleurs nouvelles que je rêve
Trouveront dans ce sol lavé comme une grève
Le mystique aliment qui ferait leur vigueur?

– Ô douleur! ô douleur! Le Temps mange la vie,
Et l'obscur Ennemi qui nous ronge le cœur
Du sang que nous perdons croît et se fortifie!

The Enemy

My youth was nothing but a glowering storm, pierced here and there
by brilliant shafts of sun; thunder and rain have so ravaged my garden
that very few rosy fruits survive.

Now I have reached the autumn of the mind, and now must toil
with spade and rake to reclaim the flooded land where pits are being
delved as deep as graves.

And who can tell whether the new flowers of which I dream will
ever find, in this soil as thoroughly washed as the seashore, the mystic
manna that will bring them strength?

O sorrow, sorrow – Time eats our life away, and the secret enemy
who gnaws our hearts waxes and thrives upon our wasted blood.

[*Revue des Deux Mondes* 1855, FM 1857]

XI

LE GUIGNON

Pour soulever un poids si lourd,
Sisyphe, il faudrait ton courage!
Bien qu'on ait du cœur à l'ouvrage,
L'Art est long et le Temps est court.

Loin des sépultures célèbres,
Vers un cimetière isolé,
Mon cœur, comme un tambour voilé,
Va battant des marches funèbres.

– Maint joyau dort enseveli
Dans les ténèbres et l'oubli,
Bien loin des pioches et des sondes;

Mainte fleur épanche à regret
Son parfum doux comme un secret
Dans les solitudes profondes.

Unluck

To lift such a burden the courage of Sisyphus would be needed.
However eagerly one labours, Art is long and Time is short.

Far from the graves of the renowned my heart, like a muffled drum,
beats its dead-march towards some desolate graveyard.

Many a gem sleeps buried in darkness and oblivion, far beyond the
reach of pickaxe or sounding-rod;

many a flower squanders its perfume with regret, its scent sweet as
a secret, in the depths of solitude.

[Ms. 1851–2. RDM 1844, FM 1857]

XII
LA VIE ANTÉRIEURE

J'ai longtemps habité sous de vastes portiques
Que les soleils marins teignaient de mille feux,
Et que leurs grands piliers, droits et majestueux,
Rendaient pareils, le soir, aux grottes basaltiques.

Les houles, en roulant les images des cieux,
Mêlaient d'une façon solennelle et mystique
Les tout-puissants accords de leur riche musique
Aux couleurs du couchant reflété par mes yeux.

C'est là que j'ai vécu dans les voluptés calmes,
Au milieu de l'azur, des vagues, des splendeurs
Et des esclaves nus, tout imprégnés d'odeurs,

Qui me rafraîchissaient le front avec des palmes,
Et dont l'unique soin était d'approfondir
Le secret douloureux qui me faisait languir.

A Previous Life

My home was long beneath vast porticoes which the suns of the sea
tinged with a thousand fires, and whose giant columns, straight and
majestic, at evening made them look like basalt caves.

The sea-swells, heaving the patterns of the skies, solemnly and
mystically interwove the overwhelming harmonies of their mellow
music with the hues of sunset mirrored in my eyes.

And there I lived in serene voluptuousness, surrounded by the
azure, waves and splendours, while naked perfume-laden slaves

refreshed my brow with palms, their only care to fathom the secret
grief wherefore I pined.

[RDM 1855, FM 1857]

XIII

BOHÉMIENS EN VOYAGE

La tribu prophétique aux prunelles ardentes
Hier s'est mise en route, emportant ses petits
Sur son dos, ou livrant à leurs fiers appétits
Le trésor toujours prêt des mamelles pendantes.

Les hommes vont à pied sous leurs armes luisantes
Le long des chariots où les leurs sont blottis,
Promenant sur le ciel des yeux appesantis
Par le morne regret des chimères absentes.

Du fond de son réduit sablonneux, le grillon,
Les regardant passer, redouble sa chanson;
Cybèle, qui les aime, augmente ses verdures,

Fait couler le rocher et fleurir le désert
Devant ces voyageurs, pour lesquels est ouvert
L'empire familier des ténèbres futures.

Wandering Gypsies

The tribe of prophets with glowing eyes yesterday took to the road, carrying their little ones on their backs, or offering, for their proud hunger, the inexhaustible treasure of their heavy breasts.

Bearing their glittering weapons aloft, the men stride alongside their caravans, where their folk huddle together, their eyes sweeping the sky, drowsy with mournful nostalgia for departed dreams.

From the shelter of his sandy nook, the cricket watching them go by redoubles his song; while for love of them Cybele puts forth more shoots of green,

makes the rocks gush water and the desert flower before these wanderers' steps, for whom unclose the familiar realms of shades to come.

[Ms. 1852, FM 1857]

XIV
L'HOMME ET LA MER

Homme libre, toujours tu chériras la mer!
La mer est ton miroir; tu contemples ton âme
Dans le déroulement infini de sa lame,
Et ton esprit n'est pas un gouffre moins amer.

Tu te plais à plonger au sein de ton image;
Tu l'embrasses des yeux et des bras, et ton cœur
Se distrait quelquefois de sa propre rumeur
Au bruit de cette plainte indomptable et sauvage.

Vous êtes tous les deux ténébreux et discrets:
Homme, nul n'a sondé le fond de tes abîmes;
Ô mer, nul ne connaît tes richesses intimes,
Tant vous êtes jaloux de garder vos secrets!

Et cependant voilà des siècles innombrables
Que vous vous combattez sans pitié ni remord,
Tellement vous aimez le carnage et la mort,
Ô lutteurs éternels, ô frères implacables!

Man and the Sea

Man, so long as you are free you will always cherish the sea. The sea is
your looking-glass; you contemplate your own soul in the infinite
unfolding of its waves, while your mind is a no less bitter gulf.

You love to plunge into the depths of your own image; you clasp it
into your eyes and arms; sometimes your heart forgets its own throb-
bing, at the sound of that unconquerable and wild lament.

Both of you are dark and secretive: none has ever plumbed your
chasms' depths, O Man, while no man knows what intimate riches you
contain, O Sea, so jealously you guard your enigmas.

And yet you have warred on one another for untold centuries with
neither mercy nor remorse, such is your love of slaughter and death,
you eternal wrestlers, you implacable brothers.

[Published 1852. FM 1857]

XV
DON JUAN AUX ENFERS

Quand Don Juan descendit vers l'onde souterraine
Et lorsqu'il eut donné son obole à Charon,
Un sombre mendiant, l'œil fier comme Antisthène,
D'un bras vengeur et fort saisit chaque aviron.

Montrant leurs seins pendants et leurs robes ouvertes,
Des femmes se tordaient sous le noir firmament,
Et, comme un grand troupeau de victimes offertes,
Derrière lui traînaient un long mugissement.

Sganarelle en riant lui réclamait ses gages,
Tandis que Don Luis avec un doigt tremblant
Montrait à tous les morts errant sur les rivages
Le fils audacieux qui railla son front blanc.

Frissonnant sous son deuil, la chaste et maigre Elvire,
Près de l'époux perfide et qui fut son amant,
Semblait lui réclamer un suprême sourire
Où brillât la douceur de son premier serment.

Don Juan in the Underworld

When Don Juan went down to the underworld stream and paid his ferriage to Charon, a swarthy beggar with an eye as haughty as Antisthenes', laid hold on the oars with avenging powerful arms.

With open gowns, showing their drooping breasts, the womenfolk writhed this way and that under the black firmament, and like a great herd of sacrificial victims broke into endless keening, in his wake.

Chuckling Sganarelle demanded his wages, while with trembling finger Don Luis pointed out to all those dead astray on Lethe's shores, the insolent son who had mocked his hoary head.

The lean and chaste Elvira stood shivering in her mourning weeds, nearby the treacherous spouse who had been her lover, as one awaiting the alms of his final smile in which all the tenderness of his first love would glow.

Tout droit dans son armure, un grand homme de pierre
Se tenait à la barre et coupait le flot noir;
Mais le calme héros, courbé sur sa rapière,
Regardait le sillage et ne daignait rien voir.

Erect in armour, a giant man of stone stood gripping the helm, slicing the black wave: but unmoved, the hero, leaning on his sword, watched only the wake's foam, disdaining other sights.

[Pre-1844. Published 1846 as 'L'Impénitent'. FM 1857]

XVI

CHÂTIMENT DE L'ORGUEIL

En ces temps merveilleux où la Théologie
Fleurit avec le plus de sève et d'énergie,
On raconte qu'un jour un docteur des plus grands,
– Après avoir forcé les cœurs indifférents;
Les avoir remués dans leurs profondeurs noires;
Après avoir franchi vers les célestes gloires
Des chemins singuliers à lui-même inconnus,
Où les purs Esprits seuls peut-être étaient venus, –
Comme un homme monté trop haut, pris de panique,
S'écria, transporté d'un orgueil satanique:
«Jésus, petit Jésus! je t'ai poussé bien haut!
Mais, si j'avais voulu t'attaquer au défaut
De l'armure, ta honte égalerait ta gloire,
Et tu ne serais plus qu'un fœtus dérisoire!»
Immédiatement sa raison s'en alla.
L'éclat de ce soleil d'un crêpe se voila;
Tout le chaos roula dans cette intelligence,
Temple autrefois vivant, plein d'ordre et d'opulence,
Sous les plafonds duquel tant de pompe avait lui.

Pride's Punishment

In those marvellous times when Theology flourished with most sap
and vitality, the story goes that, one day, one of the greatest Doctors of
the Church – after converting lukewarm hearts and stirring them to
their murky depths, after ascending towards heavenly glories along
strange paths unknown even to himself, where the pure Spirits alone
perhaps have been – like someone who has climbed too high, seized
with panic and carried away by some satanic pride, cried out: 'Jesus,
tiny Jesus, I have exalted you to great heights – but had I chosen to
attack you through the chink in your armour, your shame would match
your glory, and you would be no more than a ridiculous foetus!'

At once his reason left him; the light of that sun was veiled with
crape, all chaos swirled into his intelligence that was once a living
temple where all was order and plenty, and under whose vaults so much

Le silence et la nuit s'installèrent en lui,
Comme dans un caveau dont la clef est perdue.
Dès lors il fut semblable aux bêtes de la rue,
Et, quand il s'en allait sans rien voir, à travers
Les champs, sans distinguer les étés des hivers,
Sale, inutile et laid comme une chose usée,
Il faisait des enfants la joie et la risée.

pomp had blazed. Silence and darkness lodged in him as in a burial-vault of which the key is lost. Thereafter he was like to the beasts of the street, and when he wandered through the fields, seeing nothing, unable to tell the summers from winters, as filthy and useless and hideous as some cast-off thing, he was the sport and laughing-stock of children.

[Published 1850. FM 1857]

XVII
LA BEAUTÉ

Je suis belle, ô mortels! comme un rêve de pierre,
Et mon sein, où chacun s'est meurtri tour à tour,
Est fait pour inspirer au poète un amour
Éternel et muet ainsi que la matière.

Je trône dans l'azur comme un sphinx incompris;
J'unis un cœur de neige à la blancheur des cygnes;
Je hais le mouvement qui déplace les lignes,
Et jamais je ne pleure et jamais je ne ris.

Les poètes, devant mes grandes attitudes,
Que j'ai l'air d'emprunter aux plus fiers monuments,
Consumeront leurs jours en d'austères études;

Car j'ai, pour fasciner ces dociles amants,
De purs miroirs qui font toutes choses plus belles:
Mes yeux, mes larges yeux aux clartés éternelles!

Beauty

I am beautiful, O mortals, as a dream in stone, and my breast, on which
every man has bruised himself in his turn, is designed to inspire in poets
a love as eternal and silent as matter itself.

I am enthroned in the azure like a sphinx beyond all understanding;
my heart is of snow that matches my swan-like whiteness; movement I
hate, that disturbs the ideal line; and never do I weep, nor ever smile.

Before the grandeur of my body's poses, as though inspired by the
noblest monuments, poets will consume their days in austere research;

since, to hypnotize the lovers I enslave, I have pure mirrors which
magnify the beauty of all things – my eyes, vast eyes, shining with eter-
nal light.

[FM 1857]

XVIII
L'IDÉAL

Ce ne seront jamais ces beautés de vignettes,
Produits avariés, nés d'un siècle vaurien,
Ces pieds à brodequins, ces doigts à castagnettes,
Qui sauront satisfaire un cœur comme le mien.

Je laisse à Gavarni, poète des chloroses,
Son troupeau gazouillant de beautés d'hôpital,
Car je ne puis trouver parmi ces pâles roses
Une fleur qui ressemble à mon rouge idéal.

Ce qu'il faut à ce cœur profond comme un abîme,
C'est vous, Lady Macbeth, âme puissante au crime,
Rêve d'Eschyle éclos au climat des autans;

Ou bien toi, grande Nuit, fille de Michel-Ange,
Qui tors paisiblement dans une pose étrange
Tes appas façonnés aux bouches des Titans!

The Ideal

Those beauties we see in vignettes, the debased products of our worthless age, shod with their high laced boots, their fingers with castanets, will never appeal to such a heart as mine.

I leave to Gavarni, the poet of anaemias, his simpering bevy of sickly belles fit for the hospital ward; for among those pallid roses I find no flower that recalls my red ideal.

What my chasm-deep heart is seeking is you, Lady Macbeth, a soul prodigious in crime, O dream of Aeschylus reborn in the storm-swept North!

Or you, gigantic Night, daughter of Michelangelo, who calmly twist in your mysterious pose those charms, shaped by the Titans' lips.

[Published 1851. FM 1857]

XIX
LA GÉANTE

Du temps que la Nature en sa verve puissante
Concevait chaque jour des enfants monstrueux,
J'eusse aimé vivre auprès d'une jeune géante,
Comme aux pieds d'une reine un chat voluptueux.

J'eusse aimé voir son corps fleurir avec son âme
Et grandir librement dans ses terribles jeux;
Deviner si son cœur couve une sombre flamme
Aux humides brouillards qui nagent dans ses yeux;

Parcourir à loisir ses magnifiques formes;
Ramper sur le versant de ses genoux énormes,
Et parfois en été, quand les soleils malsains,

Lasse, la font s'étendre à travers la campagne,
Dormir nonchalamment à l'ombre de ses seins,
Comme un hameau paisible au pied d'une montagne.

The Giantess

In olden days when Nature in her lusty exuberance daily conceived monstrous offspring, I would gladly have lived beside some youthful giantess, like a voluptuous cat at the feet of a queen.

I would have loved to watch her body flowering with her soul and developing freely as she played her terrible games, and to speculate whether she was nourishing some tragic passion in her heart, as I saw the liquid mists float in her eyes.

I would have loved to explore her magnificent limbs at my leisure; to climb the slopes of her tremendous knees, and sometimes when the sickly mists of summer
made her stretch out wearily across the fields, to slumber trustfully in the shadow of her breasts, like a quiet hamlet at some mountain's foot.

[FM 1857]

XX
LE MASQUE

STATUE ALLÉGORIQUE DANS LE GOÛT
DE LA RENAISSANCE

À Ernest Christophe, statuaire.

Contemplons ce trésor de grâces florentines;
Dans l'ondulation de ce corps musculeux
L'Élégance et la Force abondent, sœurs divines.
Cette femme, morceau vraiment miraculeux,
Divinement robuste, adorablement mince,
Est faite pour trôner sur des lits somptueux,
Et charmer les loisirs d'un pontife ou d'un prince.

– Aussi, vois ce souris fin et voluptueux
Où la Fatuité promène son extase;
Ce long regard sournois, langoureux et moqueur;
Ce visage mignard, tout encadré de gaze,
Dont chaque trait nous dit avec un air vainqueur:
«La Volupté m'appelle et l'Amour me couronne!»

The Mask

AN ALLEGORICAL STATUE IN RENAISSANCE STYLE

for Ernest Christophe, sculptor

Let us now survey this epitome of the Florentine graces. The rippling contours of this muscular frame abound in Elegance and Strength, those two heavenly sisters. This female form, a truly miraculous piece of work, divinely ample and adorably slim, is designed for majestic poses on palatial couches, to enchant the idle hours of pope or prince.

Observe also that sly voluptuous smile which radiates a mindless ecstasy, that shrewd insistent gaze in which languidness and mockery combine, that enticing face coyly haloed with gauze, whose every feature arrogantly proclaims: 'I am not deaf to the calls of sensuality,

À cet être doué de tant de majesté
Vois quel charme excitant la gentillesse donne!
Approchons, et tournons autour de sa beauté.

Ô blasphème de l'art! ô surprise fatale!
La femme au corps divin, promettant le bonheur,
Par le haut se termine en monstre bicéphale!

– Mais non! ce n'est qu'un masque, un décor suborneur,
Ce visage éclairé d'une exquise grimace,
Et, regarde, voici, crispée atrocement,
La véritable tête, et la sincère face
Renversée à l'abri de la face qui ment.
Pauvre grande beauté! le magnifique fleuve
De tes pleurs aboutit dans mon cœur soucieux;
Ton mensonge m'enivre, et mon âme s'abreuve
Aux flots que la Douleur fait jaillir de tes yeux!

– Mais pourquoi pleure-t-elle? Elle, beauté parfaite
Qui mettrait à ses pieds le genre humain vaincu,
Quel mal mystérieux ronge son flanc d'athlète?

who wear Love's crown.' Observe what titillating charm her readiness to oblige confers on a female so endowed with majesty. Let us draw close, let us hang around her beauty.

But a blasphemy against art awaits us, a sinister surprise: for this woman's divine form, which promised so much joy, proves to be a monster with two heads upon her shoulders.

– No, that is not the case, for that face aglow with the exquisite grimace of a smile is no more than a mask, a disguise meant to seduce us. See how the horribly distorted head, the authentic face of the two, is withdrawn into the shelter of the one that lies. Pitiful great beauty, the awesome fountain of your tears floods into my disconsolate heart, I am stupefied by your deceit, my soul drinks deep of the stream of tears which sorrow brings gushing from your eyes.

Why is she weeping, then, she who is beauty's perfection, she who could bring the vanquished human race to kneel at her feet? What mysterious ill is gnawing her athletic frame?

– Elle pleure, insensé, parce qu'elle a vécu!
Et parce qu'elle vit! Mais ce qu'elle déplore
Surtout, ce qui la fait frémir jusqu'aux genoux,
C'est que demain, hélas! il faudra vivre encore!
Demain, après-demain et toujours! – comme nous!

She is weeping, you fool, because she has already lived and because she goes on living still. But what she mourns for above all, what causes her to tremble from head to heel, is that tomorrow she must go on living, tomorrow and its tomorrow and for always, as each of us must do.

[Published 1859, *Revue contemporaine*. FM 1861]

XXI
HYMNE À LA BEAUTÉ

Viens-tu du ciel profond ou sors-tu de l'abîme,
Ô Beauté? ton regard, infernal et divin,
Verse confusément le bienfait et le crime,
Et l'on peut pour cela te comparer au vin.

Tu contiens dans ton œil le couchant et l'aurore;
Tu répands des parfums comme un soir orageux;
Tes baisers sont un philtre et ta bouche une amphore
Qui font le héros lâche et l'enfant courageux.

Sors-tu du gouffre noir ou descends-tu des astres?
Le Destin charmé suit tes jupons comme un chien;
Tu sèmes au hasard la joie et les désastres,
Et tu gouvernes tout et ne réponds de rien.

Tu marches sur des morts, Beauté, dont tu te moques;
De tes bijoux l'Horreur n'est pas le moins charmant,
Et le Meurtre, parmi tes plus chères breloques,
Sur ton ventre orgueilleux danse amoureusement.

A Hymn to Beauty

O Beauty, do you come from the depths of heaven or do you rise from
the fathomless pit? Your gaze, daemonic and divine, deals out good
deeds and crime together, and in this you are like wine.

Your eye contains the sundown and the dawn, you breathe out
perfumes like a stormy evening; your kisses are a stupefying potion and
your mouth an amphora, filling heroes with cowardice and children
with courage.

Do you rise from the gloom of the underworld, or come down
from the stars? Bewitched Destiny follows your skirts like a dog; you
sow the seeds of joy and disaster impartially; you govern all things and
are responsible for none.

You tread upon the dead, O Beauty, scorning them. Horror is not
the least fascinating of your baubles, and murder, one of your most
cherished trinkets, dances lustfully on your proud navel.

L'éphémère ébloui vole vers toi, chandelle,
Crépite, flambe et dit: Bénissons ce flambeau!
L'amoureux pantelant incliné sur sa belle
A l'air d'un moribond caressant son tombeau.

Que tu viennes du ciel ou de l'enfer, qu'importe,
Ô Beauté! monstre énorme, effrayant, ingénu!
Si ton œil, ton souris, ton pied, m'ouvrent la porte
D'un Infini que j'aime et n'ai jamais connu?

De Satan ou de Dieu, qu'importe? Ange ou Sirène,
Qu'importe, si tu rends, – fée aux yeux de velours,
Rythme, parfum, lueur, ô mon unique reine! –
L'univers moins hideux et les instants moins lourds?

The dazzled ephemerid wings towards you, its candle-light; it sizzles and it flames, yet cries 'Blessed may this torch be!' The breathless lover swooning on his beloved looks like a dying man caressing his tomb.

Whether you come from Heaven or Hell, O Beauty, enormous, terrifying and ingenuous monster, what difference does it make? What does it matter so long as your eye and smile and foot open me the gates of an Infinite which I love and have never known?

What does it matter if you come from Satan or from God? – Angel or Siren, velvet-eyed spirit all rhythm and perfume and light, O my unique queen! – so long as you make the world less hideous and lighten the leaden hours?

[Published 1860. FM 1861]

XXII
PARFUM EXOTIQUE

Quand, les deux yeux fermés, en un soir chaud d'automne,
Je respire l'odeur de ton sein chaleureux,
Je vois se dérouler des rivages heureux
Qu'éblouissent les feux d'un soleil monotone;

Une île paresseuse où la nature donne
Des arbres singuliers et des fruits savoureux;
Des hommes dont le corps est mince et vigoureux,
Et des femmes dont l'œil par sa franchise étonne.

Guidé par ton odeur vers de charmants climats,
Je vois un port rempli de voiles et de mâts
Encor tout fatigués par la vague marine,

Pendant que le parfum des verts tamariniers,
Qui circule dans l'air et m'enfle la narine,
Se mêle dans mon âme au chant des mariniers.

Exotic Perfume

When I lie with both eyes closed on a warm autumn evening, and
breathe the fragrance of your sultry breast, I see a panorama of blissful
shores a-dazzle with the sun's monotonous blaze –
a languid island where Nature lavishes strange trees and luscious
fruits, men who are lean and virile of body, and women's eyes of
astounding candidness.
Led by your odour to enchanting climes, I see a port all filled with
sails and masts that ache still from the briny wave,
while the scent of the green tamarinds that wafts through the air
and fills my nostrils, comes mingling in my soul with the sailors' song.

[An early work (1842–3?). FM 1857]

XXIII
LA CHEVELURE

Ô toison, moutonnant jusque sur l'encolure!
Ô boucles! Ô parfum chargé de nonchaloir!
Extase! Pour peupler ce soir l'alcôve obscure
Des souvenirs dormant dans cette chevelure,
Je la veux agiter dans l'air comme un mouchoir!

La langoureuse Asie et la brûlante Afrique,
Tout un monde lointain, absent, presque défunt,
Vit dans tes profondeurs, forêt aromatique!
Comme d'autres esprits voguent sur la musique,
Le mien, ô mon amour! nage sur ton parfum.

J'irai là-bas où l'arbre et l'homme, pleins de sève,
Se pâment longuement sous l'ardeur des climats;
Fortes tresses, soyez la houle qui m'enlève!
Tu contiens, mer d'ébène, un éblouissant rêve
De voiles, de rameurs, de flammes et de mâts:

Un port retentissant où mon âme peut boire
À grands flots le parfum, le son et la couleur;

Hair

O fleece, billowing down the neck, O ringlets, O fragrance laden with languidness. O ecstasy! This night, to people the dark alcove of our love with all the memories that slumber in this hair, I long to wave it as one waves a handkerchief in farewell.

All languid Asia, blazing Africa, a whole faraway world that is absent, almost dead, survives in the depths of this forest of aromas; and as other minds transcend through music, so mine, O my beloved, shall float afar upon your perfume.

I shall go there where men and trees, full of the sap of life, swoon longly in the ardent torridness; dense tresses, be the swell that carries me afar, for you contain, O sea of ebony, a dazzling dream of sails and oarsmen, pennants and masts;

an echoing port where my soul may drink long waves of perfume,

Où les vaisseaux, glissant dans l'or et dans la moire,
Ouvrent leurs vastes bras pour embrasser la gloire
D'un ciel pur où frémit l'éternelle chaleur.

Je plongerai ma tête amoureuse d'ivresse
Dans ce noir océan où l'autre est enfermé;
Et mon esprit subtil que le roulis caresse
Saura vous retrouver, ô féconde paresse,
Infinis bercements du loisir embaumé!

Cheveux bleus, pavillon de ténèbres tendues,
Vous me rendez l'azur du ciel immense et rond;
Sur les bords duvetés de vos mèches tordues
Je m'enivre ardemment des senteurs confondues
De l'huile de coco, du musc et du goudron.

Longtemps! toujours! ma main dans ta crinière lourde
Sèmera le rubis, la perle et le saphir,
Afin qu'à mon désir tu ne sois jamais sourde!
N'es-tu pas l'oasis où je rêve, et la gourde
Où je hume à longs traits le vin du souvenir?

sound and colour; in which the vessels that glide through gold and through iridescent silk open wide their vast arms to embrace the splendour of a faultless sky that shimmers with eternal heat.

I shall plunge my head, never weary of its rapture, into the jet-black ocean which contains that other sea, and my subtle mind, caressed by the rolling swell, will know how to find you there, O fertile indolence, you infinite lullaby of sweet-scented leisure.

Blue hair, tent draped with shadows, you bring back to me the azure of the vast round sky, and on the downy shores of your plaited locks I grow drunk with the mingling scents of coconut-oil and musk and tar.

O longly, O forever, my hand in your ponderous mane will sow rubies and pearls and sapphires, so that you will never be deaf to my desire: for are you not the oasis where I dream my dreams, the gourd from which I breathe long draughts of the wine of memory?

[Published 1859. FM 1861]

XXIV

Je t'adore à l'égal de la voûte nocturne,
Ô vase de tristesse, ô grande taciturne,
Et t'aime d'autant plus, belle, que tu me fuis,
Et que tu me parais, ornement de mes nuits,
Plus ironiquement accumuler les lieues
Qui séparent mes bras des immensités bleues.

Je m'avance à l'attaque, et je grimpe aux assauts,
Comme après un cadavre un chœur de vermisseaux,
Et je chéris, ô bête implacable et cruelle!
Jusqu'à cette froideur par où tu m'es plus belle!

I adore you . . .

I adore you no less than the vault of Night itself, O urn of sadness, O monument of silence; and I love you the more, my beauty, the more you elude me, and the more, O grace of my nights, you seem ironically to multiply the leagues that deny my arms the blue immensities of heaven.

I press the attack and climb to the assault like a choir of worms upon a corpse, and I cherish, O implacable cruel creature, even the frigidness that makes you ever more beautiful in my eyes.

[1843? FM 1857]

XXV

Tu mettrais l'univers entier dans ta ruelle,
Femme impure! L'ennui rend ton âme cruelle.
Pour exercer tes dents à ce jeu singulier,
Il te faut chaque jour un cœur au râtelier.
Tes yeux, illuminés ainsi que des boutiques
Et des ifs flamboyants dans les fêtes publiques,
Usent insolemment d'un pouvoir emprunté,
Sans connaître jamais la loi de leur beauté.

Machine aveugle et sourde, en cruautés féconde!
Salutaire instrument, buveur du sang du monde,
Comment n'as-tu pas honte et comment n'as-tu pas
Devant tous les miroirs vu pâlir tes appas?
La grandeur de ce mal où tu te crois savante
Ne t'a donc jamais fait reculer d'épouvante,
Quand la nature, grande en ses desseins cachés,
De toi se sert, ô femme, ô reine des péchés,
– De toi, vil animal, – pour pétrir un génie?

Ô fangeuse grandeur! sublime ignominie!

Lewd woman . . .

Lewd woman, you would make the whole world queue at your
bedside. Boredom is making your soul cruel. To sharpen your teeth for
your peculiar game you need a fresh heart every day in your trough.
Dazzling as shop-windows or floodlights blazing on public holidays,
your eyes exert a power not their own, without ever understanding
their beauty's laws.

You blind and deaf machine, fertile in cruelties, you instrument of
health, drinker of human blood, why are you unashamed, why have you
never seen your charms fade in every glass you look into? Has the
enormity of the evil in which you think yourself so expert never made
you shrink with terror, when Nature, so mighty in her obscure designs
makes use of you, O woman, queen of sins, vile animal, to mould a
genius?

What ignoble glory and sublime infamy are yours!

[1842–3 (Prarond), concerning Sara 'La Louchette']

XXVI
SED NON SATIATA

Bizarre déité, brune comme les nuits,
Au parfum mélangé de musc et de havane,
Œuvre de quelque obi, le Faust de la savane,
Sorcière au flanc d'ébène, enfant des noirs minuits,

Je préfère au constance, à l'opium, au nuits,
L'élixir de ta bouche où l'amour se pavane;
Quand vers toi mes désirs partent en caravane,
Tes yeux sont la citerne où boivent mes ennuis.

Par ces deux grands yeux noirs, soupiraux de ton âme,
Ô démon sans pitié! verse-moi moins de flamme;
Je ne suis pas le Styx pour t'embrasser neuf fois,

Hélas! et je ne puis, Mégère libertine,
Pour briser ton courage et te mettre aux abois,
Dans l'enfer de ton lit devenir Proserpine!

Never Satisfied

Outlandish goddess, swarthy as the nights, who smell of a blend of musk and Havana tobacco; creation of some Obi, some Faust of the savannah; ebony-flanked witch, you daughter of all black midnights –

I prefer the elixir of your lustful lips to Africa's Constantia wine, opium, and the burgundy of Nuits-Saint-Georges. When the caravan of my desires sets out towards you on its pilgrimage, your eyes are the reservoir where my cares come to drink.

From those twin vast dark eyes, those skylights of your soul, O pitiless demon, pour me a milder flame: I am no Styx to embrace you ninefold,

alas! – and O lecherous Megaera, in order to break your courage and set you at bay, it is beyond my power to become a Proserpine in the Hades of your bed.

[1842–43. FM 1857]

XXVII

Avec ses vêtements ondoyants et nacrés,
Même quand elle marche on croirait qu'elle danse,
Comme ces longs serpents que les jongleurs sacrés
Au bout de leurs bâtons agitent en cadence.

Comme le sable morne et l'azur des déserts,
Insensibles tous deux à l'humaine souffrance,
Comme les longs réseaux de la houle des mers,
Elle se développe avec indifférence.

Ses yeux polis sont faits de minéraux charmants,
Et dans cette nature étrange et symbolique
Où l'ange inviolé se mêle au sphinx antique,

Où tout n'est qu'or, acier, lumière et diamants,
Resplendit à jamais, comme un astre inutile,
La froide majesté de la femme stérile.

Her Frigid Majesty

With her rippling mother-of-pearl robes, you would think she was dancing even when she walks, like those long snakes which holy fakirs in cadence swing at the end of their long bamboos.

Like the forlorn sands and azures of Saharas, equally insensitive to human suffering, or like the sea-surge's never-ending webs, she glides along in her indifference.

Her burnished eyes are wrought of hypnotic ores, and in her strange symbolic nature in which inviolate angel and ancient sphinx unite,

made all of gold and steel and light and diamonds, forever glitters like a useless star, the frigid majesty of the sterile woman.

[Early poem. FM 1857]

XXVIII
LE SERPENT QUI DANSE

Que j'aime voir, chère indolente,
De ton corps si beau,
Comme une étoffe vacillante,
Miroiter la peau !

Sur ta chevelure profonde
Aux âcres parfums,
Mer odorante et vagabonde
Aux flots bleus et bruns,

Comme un navire qui s'éveille
Au vent du matin,
Mon âme rêveuse appareille
Pour un ciel lointain.

Tes yeux, où rien ne se révèle
De doux ni d'amer,
Sont deux bijoux froids où se mêle
L'or avec le fer.

The Dancing Snake

My indolent darling, how I love watching the skin of your beautiful body glisten like rippling velvet.

On your unfathomable bitter-tanged hair, that pungent restless sea with its waves of blue and brown,

like a ship awakening in the morning wind my dreamy soul sets sail for a distant sky.

Your eyes which show no sign of bitter or sweet are two frigid gems in which gold blends with steel.

À te voir marcher en cadence,
 Belle d'abandon,
On dirait un serpent qui danse
 Au bout d'un bâton.

Sous le fardeau de ta paresse
 Ta tête d'enfant
Se balance avec la mollesse
 D'un jeune éléphant,

Et ton corps se penche et s'allonge
 Comme un fin vaisseau
Qui roule bord sur bord et plonge
 Ses vergues dans l'eau.

Comme un flot grossi par la fonte
 Des glaciers grondants,
Quand l'eau de ta bouche remonte
 Au bord de tes dents,

Je crois boire un vin de Bohême,
 Amer et vainqueur,
Un ciel liquide qui parsème
 D'étoiles mon cœur!

Watching you walk in cadence, lovely in your ease, one would say you were a snake dancing on the tip of a wand.

Lolling with apathy, your girlish head sways to and fro, with the gentle rhythm of a baby elephant's,

 while your body heels and stretches like a trim ship rolling from side to side and dipping its yards into the brine.

Like a stream swollen by the melt of grinding glaciers, when the saliva brims to the tips of your teeth

 I fancy I am sipping a Bohemian wine, tart and triumphant, a liquid sky that flecks my heart with many a star.

[FM 1857]

XXIX
UNE CHAROGNE

Rappelez-vous l'objet que nous vîmes, mon âme,
Ce beau matin d'été si doux:
Au détour d'un sentier une charogne infâme
Sur un lit semé de cailloux,

Les jambes en l'air, comme une femme lubrique,
Brûlante et suant les poisons,
Ouvrait d'une façon nonchalante et cynique
Son ventre plein d'exhalaisons.

Le soleil rayonnait sur cette pourriture,
Comme afin de la cuire à point,
Et de rendre au centuple à la grande Nature
Tout ce qu'ensemble elle avait joint;

Et le ciel regardait la carcasse superbe
Comme une fleur s'épanouir.
La puanteur était si forte, que sur l'herbe
Vous crûtes vous évanouir.

Carrion

Do not forget, O my soul, that thing we saw on that fine summer's morning, that was so mild: there where the path turned, a disgusting corpse on a bed of shingle,

with its legs in the air like a lewd woman's, inflamed and oozing poisons and nonchalantly and cynically laying open its stinking belly.

The sun was blazing down on that rotten meat as if to roast it to a turn, and to render a hundredfold to Nature all that she had brought together;

while the sky looked down on that magnificent carcass as it unfolded its petals like a flower, and the stench was so strong that you all but fainted on the grass.

Les mouches bourdonnaient sur ce ventre putride,
 D'où sortaient de noirs bataillons
De larves, qui coulaient comme un épais liquide
 Le long de ces vivants haillons.

Tout cela descendait, montait comme une vague,
 Ou s'élançait en pétillant;
On eût dit que le corps, enflé d'un souffle vague,
 Vivait en se multipliant.

Et ce monde rendait une étrange musique,
 Comme l'eau courante et le vent,
Ou le grain qu'un vanneur d'un mouvement rythmique
 Agite et tourne dans son van.

Les formes s'effaçaient et n'étaient plus qu'un rêve,
 Une ébauche lente à venir,
Sur la toile oubliée, et que l'artiste achève
 Seulement par le souvenir.

The flies were humming on its putrid belly from which black battalions of maggots crawled, flowing like a turgid fluid along those living rags of flesh.

It was all rising and falling like a wave of the sea, and it seethed and glittered as if the body, swollen with a faint breathing, was alive and being multiplied.

And that horde of life gave out an eerie music like a flow of water or wind, or the sighing of the grain which the winnower's cadenced swing tosses and turns in his basket.

Its forms were blurred as in a dream, nothing but a slowly shaping sketch forgotten on the canvas, which the artist must perfect from memory alone.

Derrière les rochers une chienne inquiète
 Nous regardait d'un œil fâché,
Épiant le moment de reprendre au squelette
 Le morceau qu'elle avait lâché.

— Et pourtant vous serez semblable à cette ordure,
 À cette horrible infection,
Étoile de mes yeux, soleil de ma nature,
 Vous, mon ange et ma passion!

Oui! telle vous serez, ô la reine des grâces,
 Après les derniers sacrements,
Quand vous irez, sous l'herbe et les floraisons grasses,
 Moisir parmi les ossements.

Alors, ô ma beauté! dites à la vermine
 Qui vous mangera de baisers,
Que j'ai gardé la forme et l'essence divine
 De mes amours décomposés!

 From behind the rocks a fretful bitch glared at us with anger in its eyes, judging the moment when it could snatch from the skeleton the morsel of flesh it had left behind.
 — Yet you will come to resemble that offal, that loathsome corruption, O star of my eyes, O Sun of my nature, my angel and my passion!
 Yes, such will you be, O queen of graces, after the last sacraments, when you will go down beneath the grass and unctuous flowers to grow green among the bones.
 Then, O my beauty, tell the vermin which will devour you with their kisses, how I have immortalized the image and divine essence of my putrefied loves.

[1843? FM 1857]

XXX
DE PROFUNDIS CLAMAVI

J'implore ta pitié, Toi, l'unique que j'aime,
Du fond du gouffre obscur où mon cœur est tombé.
C'est un univers morne à l'horizon plombé,
Où nagent dans la nuit l'horreur et le blasphème;

Un soleil sans chaleur plane au-dessus six mois,
Et les six autres mois la nuit couvre la terre;
C'est un pays plus nu que la terre polaire;
– Ni bêtes, ni ruisseaux, ni verdure, ni bois!

Or il n'est pas d'horreur au monde qui surpasse
La froide cruauté de ce soleil de glace
Et cette immense nuit semblable au vieux Chaos;

Je jalouse le sort des plus vils animaux
Qui peuvent se plonger dans un sommeil stupide,
Tant l'écheveau du temps lentement se dévide!

I Cried from the Depths

I implore your pity, you whom alone I love, from the depths of the dark pit into which my soul has sunk, this forlorn world with leaden-grey horizons in which horror and blasphemy come swimming through the gloom,

where a heatless sun hangs over it half the year, then for six months a midnight shrouds the earth. This land is barer than the Arctic desert, with never an animal or stream, no wood or anything that is green.

No horror in the world can outdo the chill cruelty of this Sun of Ice, or this vast nightness like the Chaos of olden days;

and so slowly does the skein of Time unwind, that I envy the lot of the lowliest of creatures, which can take refuge in their stupid winter sleep.

[Original titles: 'La Béatrix' and 'Spleen'.
Listed for *Les Limbes*, 1855. FM 1857]

XXXI
LE VAMPIRE

Toi qui, comme un coup de couteau,
Dans mon cœur plaintif es entrée;
Toi qui, forte comme un troupeau
De démons, vins, folle et parée,

De mon esprit humilié
Faire ton lit et ton domaine;
— Infâme à qui je suis lié
Comme le forçat à la chaîne,

Comme au jeu le joueur têtu,
Comme à la bouteille l'ivrogne,
Comme aux vermines la charogne,
— Maudite, maudite sois-tu!

J'ai prié le glaive rapide
De conquérir ma liberté,
Et j'ai dit au poison perfide
De secourir ma lâcheté.

The Vampire

You who plunged into my despondent heart like the stab of a knife,
who with all the power of a pack of devils came with your wantonness
and glamour
 to make my humiliated mind your bed, your empire; foul creature
to whom I am shackled like a galley-slave to his chains,
 a dogged gambler to his game, a boozer to his bottle, a corpse to its
own maggots: may you be doubly damned.
 I begged the swift dagger to retrieve my liberty, I implored the
treacherous poison to stiffen my cowardice;

Hélas! le poison et le glaive
M'ont pris en dédain et m'ont dit:
«Tu n'es pas digne qu'on t'enlève
À ton esclavage maudit,

«Imbécile! – de son empire
Si nos efforts te délivraient,
Tes baisers ressusciteraient
Le cadavre de ton vampire!»

but the poison and the blade turned away from me in scorn and said, 'Fool, you don't deserve to be saved from your hellish abjection; for even if our efforts could set you free, you would soon give your vampire the kiss of life.'

[Published 1855 as 'La Beatrice']

XXXII

Une nuit que j'étais près d'une affreuse Juive,
Comme au long d'un cadavre un cadavre étendu,
Je me pris à songer près de ce corps vendu
À la triste beauté dont mon désir se prive.

Je me représentai sa majesté native,
Son regard de vigueur et de grâces armé,
Ses cheveux qui lui font un casque parfumé,
Et dont le souvenir pour l'amour me ravive.

Car j'eusse avec ferveur baisé ton noble corps,
Et depuis tes pieds frais jusqu'à tes noires tresses
Déroulé le trésor des profondes caresses,

Si, quelque soir, d'un pleur obtenu sans effort
Tu pouvais seulement, ô reine des cruelles!
Obscurcir la splendeur de tes froides prunelles.

One night as I lay . . .

One night as I lay beside an abominable jewess, stretched like a corpse against another corpse, my thoughts turned, beside this bartered body, to the sad beauty whom my desire makes me renounce.

In my mind's eye I pictured her inborn majesty, the vitality and the graces that give her eyes such power, the sweet-smelling helmet of her hair, – the one whose memory makes me live again to love.

For most fervently I would have kissed your noble form, from your cool feet to your black locks; I would have poured out for you a wealth of profound caresses –

if only some evening, O queen of all heartless women, a spontaneous tear would dim the splendour of your frigid eyes.

[1842–3. See XXXIII, 'Remords posthume']

XXXIII
REMORDS POSTHUME

Lorsque tu dormiras, ma belle ténébreuse,
Au fond d'un monument construit en marbre noir,
Et lorsque tu n'auras pour alcôve et manoir
Qu'un caveau pluvieux et qu'une fosse creuse;

Quand la pierre, opprimant ta poitrine peureuse
Et tes flancs qu'assouplit un charmant nonchaloir,
Empêchera ton cœur de battre et de vouloir,
Et tes pieds de courir leur course aventureuse,

Le tombeau, confident de mon rêve infini
(Car le tombeau toujours comprendra le poète),
Durant ces grandes nuits d'où le somme est banni,

Te dira: «Que vous sert, courtisane imparfaite,
De n'avoir pas connu ce que pleurent les morts?»
— Et le ver rongera ta peau comme un remords.

Posthumous Remorse

My darkling beauty, when you sleep in your black marble tomb and
have only a dripping vault and shallow grave for bed and mansion;
 when the tombstone crushes your cringing breast and those flanks
which are now so lithe and full of endearing nonchalance; when it
slows the beat and longings of your heart and curbs the roving of your
adventurous feet:
 then the grave, that shares my infinite dreams and never fails to
understand a poet, the grave will whisper to you, in those enormous
nights that banish sleep,
 'You defective harlot, what have you gained by ignoring all that the
dead mourn for?' Then the worm will gnaw your hide, like a remorse.

[1842–3. Published 1855]

XXXIV
LE CHAT

Viens, mon beau chat, sur mon cœur amoureux;
 Retiens les griffes de ta patte,
Et laisse-moi plonger dans tes beaux yeux,
 Mêlés de métal et d'agate.

Lorsque mes doigts caressent à loisir
 Ta tête et ton dos élastique,
Et que ma main s'enivre du plaisir
 De palper ton corps électrique,

Je vois ma femme en esprit. Son regard,
 Comme le tien, aimable bête,
Profond et froid, coupe et fend comme un dard,

 Et, des pieds jusques à la tête,
Un air subtil, un dangereux parfum
 Nagent autour de son corps brun.

The Cat

Come now, my handsome cat, stretch on my loving heart, draw your claws in and let me lose myself in the metal and agate of your lovely eyes.

When leisurely my fingers stroke your head and your elastic back, and my hand thrills from the feel of your electric body,

then the image of the woman I love rises before me: her gaze, like yours, dear creature, is fathomless and cold, and as sharp and penetrating as a sting,

and from head to foot an elusive atmosphere, a threatening perfume, swirls round her dusky limbs.

[Pre-1844. Published 1854, FM 1857]

XXXV
DUELLUM

Deux guerriers ont couru l'un sur l'autre; leurs armes
Ont éclaboussé l'air de lueurs et de sang.
Ces jeux, ces cliquetis du fer sont les vacarmes
D'une jeunesse en proie à l'amour vagissant.

Les glaives sont brisés! comme notre jeunesse,
Ma chère! Mais les dents, les ongles acérés,
Vengent bientôt l'épée et la dague traîtresse.
Ô fureur des cœurs mûrs par l'amour ulcérés!

Dans le ravin hanté des chats-pards et des onces
Nos héros, s'étreignant méchamment, ont roulé,
Et leur peau fleurira l'aridité des ronces.

– Ce gouffre, c'est l'enfer, de nos amis peuplé!
Roulons-y sans remords, amazone inhumaine,
Afin d'éterniser l'ardeur de notre haine!

The Duel

Two fighters fell upon each other; their weapons splashed the air with glints and blood. Those contests and clashes of steel are the tumults of youth in the throes of adolescent love.

The blades are snapped like our youth, my darling! But teeth and sharpened fingernails are quick to avenge the sword and treacherous dirk – O frenzy of hearts matured, by love embittered!

In the ravine haunted by lynxes and leopards our heroes, wickedly grappling, have rolled, and their hides will flower the brambles' barrenness.

That pit is hell itself, and peopled by our friends. Let us wallow there without remorse, inhuman Amazon, to make the ardour of our hate eternal.

[Published 1858, FM 1861]

XXXVI

LE BALCON

Mère des souvenirs, maîtresse des maîtresses,
Ô toi, tous mes plaisirs! ô toi, tous mes devoirs!
Tu te rappelleras la beauté des caresses,
La douceur du foyer et le charme des soirs,
Mère des souvenirs, maîtresse des maîtresses!

Les soirs illuminés par l'ardeur du charbon,
Et les soirs au balcon, voilés de vapeurs roses.
Que ton sein m'était doux! que ton cœur m'était bon!
Nous avons dit souvent d'impérissables choses
Les soirs illuminés par l'ardeur du charbon.

Que les soleils sont beaux dans les chaudes soirées!
Que l'espace est profond! que le cœur est puissant!
En me penchant vers toi, reine des adorées,
Je croyais respirer le parfum de ton sang.
Que les soleils sont beaux dans les chaudes soirées!

The Balcony

Mother of memories, mistress of mistresses, you who are my every pleasure, you who are my every obligation – you will remember the beauty of caresses, the bliss of home and fireside and the charm of evenings, mother of memories, mistress of mistresses.

In those evenings lit by the glowing coal, evenings on the balcony, veiled with rosy mists, how gentle I found your breast, how kind your heart was to me: we often said things that will never perish, on those evenings lit by the glowing coals.

How lovely are the suns of sultry evenings; how space grows deep; how the heart compels! As I leaned towards you, my beloved queen, I seemed to breathe the bouquet of your blood. How lovely are the suns of sultry evenings!

La nuit s'épaississait ainsi qu'une cloison,
Et mes yeux dans le noir devinaient tes prunelles,
Et je buvais ton souffle, ô douceur! ô poison!
Et tes pieds s'endormaient dans mes mains fraternelles.
La nuit s'épaississait ainsi qu'une cloison.

Je sais l'art d'évoquer les minutes heureuses,
Et revis mon passé blotti dans tes genoux.
Car à quoi bon chercher tes beautés langoureuses
Ailleurs qu'en ton cher corps et qu'en ton cœur si doux?
Je sais l'art d'évoquer les minutes heureuses!

Ces serments, ces parfums, ces baisers infinis,
Renaîtront-ils d'un gouffre interdit à nos sondes,
Comme montent au ciel les soleils rajeunis
Après s'être lavés au fond des mers profondes?
– Ô serments! ô parfums! ô baisers infinis!

The night came thickening round us like a wall, my eyes sought and found your pupils in the dark, and I drank deep of the sweetness and poison of your breath, and your feet went to sleep in my fraternal hands, as the night came thickening round us like a wall.

I know the art of evoking happy moments, and live my past again nestled at your knees; for what would it avail to seek your drowsy beauties save in your most dear body and so tender heart? I know the art of evoking happy moments.

Those vows, those perfumes, infinity of kisses – will they ever live once more in a fathomless underworld, like suns reborn returning to the sky after their cleansing in the deepnesses of seas? O vows, O perfumes, O infinite kisses!

[Published 1857, and FM 1857. Set to music by Debussy]

XXXVII
LE POSSÉDÉ

Le soleil s'est couvert d'un crêpe. Comme lui,
Ô Lune de ma vie! emmitoufle-toi d'ombre;
Dors ou fume à ton gré; sois muette, sois sombre,
Et plonge tout entière au gouffre de l'Ennui;

Je t'aime ainsi! Pourtant, si tu veux aujourd'hui,
Comme un astre éclipsé qui sort de la pénombre,
Te pavaner aux lieux que la Folie encombre,
C'est bien! Charmant poignard, jaillis de ton étui!

Allume ta prunelle à la flamme des lustres!
Allume le désir dans les regards des rustres!
Tout de toi m'est plaisir, morbide ou pétulant;

Sois ce que tu voudras, nuit noire, rouge aurore;
Il n'est pas une fibre en tout mon corps tremblant
Qui ne crie: *Ô mon cher Belzébuth, je t'adore!*

The Possessed

The Sun has shrouded himself in crape. Like him, O Moon of my existence, wrap yourself in gloom, sleep or smoke as much as you desire, be taciturn, morose, and fling yourself entire into the pit of tedium.

I love you when you are that way – but if, like an eclipsed star emerging from its penumbra, you want to parade yourself today in places where madness stalks, all right then, let the charming dagger shoot from your sheath.

Kindle your pupils from the lustres flame, set lust alight in the eyes of oafs! Morbid or petulant, all that is you is my delight.

Be whatever you wish, dun midnight or red dawn: there is no fibre in my body that does not cry 'O my beloved Beelzebub, I worship you!'

[1858. FM 1861]

XXXVIII
UN FANTÔME

I
LES TÉNÈBRES

Dans les caveaux d'insondable tristesse
Où le Destin m'a déjà relégué;
Où jamais n'entre un rayon rose et gai;
Où, seul avec la Nuit, maussade hôtesse,

Je suis comme un peintre qu'un Dieu moqueur
Condamne à peindre, hélas! sur les ténèbres;
Où, cuisinier aux appétits funèbres,
Je fais bouillir et je mange mon cœur,

Par instants brille, et s'allonge, et s'étale
Un spectre fait de grâce et de splendeur.
À sa rêveuse allure orientale,

Quand il atteint sa totale grandeur,
Je reconnais ma belle visiteuse:
C'est Elle! noire et pourtant lumineuse.

An Apparition

I THE SHADOWS

Deep in the burial-vaults of unfathomable sadness to which Fate has already consigned me, into which no rosy cheerful beam ever enters and in which, alone with that surly landlady, the Night,

I am as a painter doomed by a jeering God to paint, alas, upon the shadows. There, like some cook with morbid tastes I boil and eat my own heart,

and sometimes there shines and lengthens out and spreads a phantom of grace and splendour. From its dreamy oriental form,

when it reaches its full height I recognize my beautiful visitor: it is She herself, so black yet luminous.

II

LE PARFUM

Lecteur, as-tu quelquefois respiré
Avec ivresse et lente gourmandise
Ce grain d'encens qui remplit une église,
Ou d'un sachet le musc invétéré?

Charme profond, magique, dont nous grise
Dans le présent le passé restauré!
Ainsi l'amant sur un corps adoré
Du souvenir cueille la fleur exquise.

De ses cheveux élastiques et lourds,
Vivant sachet, encensoir de l'alcôve,
Une senteur montait, sauvage et fauve,

Et des habits, mousseline ou velours,
Tout imprégnés de sa jeunesse pure,
Se dégageait un parfum de fourrure.

II THE PERFUME

Reader, have you ever inhaled with rapture and mounting relish
the grain of incense which saturates a church, or a sachet of enduring
musk –

a profound magic spell, with which the past, reliving in the present,
intoxicates our being? Likewise a lover plucks the exquisite flower of
memory on the body he adores.

From her elastic ponderous hair, a living sachet, the censer of the
alcove, a perfume rose up, savage, wild,

and her muslin or velvet garments, imbued with her immaculate
youthfulness, breathed out a smell of fur.

III

LE CADRE

Comme un beau cadre ajoute à la peinture,
Bien qu'elle soit d'un pinceau très vanté,
Je ne sais quoi d'étrange et d'enchanté
En l'isolant de l'immense nature,

Ainsi bijoux, meubles, métaux, dorure,
S'adaptaient juste à sa rare beauté;
Rien n'offusquait sa parfaite clarté,
Et tout semblait lui servir de bordure.

Même on eût dit parfois qu'elle croyait
Que tout voulait l'aimer; elle noyait
Sa nudité voluptueusement

Dans les baisers du satin et du linge,
Et, lente ou brusque, à chaque mouvement
Montrait la grâce enfantine du singe.

III THE FRAME

As a beautiful frame adds something to a painting, though it be the
work of a master's brush, something strange and bewitched that
isolated her from immense Nature –
 jewels, furniture, metals, gilding – adapted themselves exactly to the
rareness of her beauty; nothing diminished her perfect radiance, and all
things seemed to serve her as a frame.
 Sometimes, one might even have said that she thought all things
ought to love her – sensually she drowned her nakedness
 in the kisses of satin and lingerie, and slow or abrupt, in her every
movement she showed a monkey's childlike grace.

IV

LE PORTRAIT

La Maladie et la Mort font des cendres
De tout le feu qui pour nous flamboya.
De ces grands yeux si fervents et si tendres,
De cette bouche où mon cœur se noya,

De ces baisers puissants comme un dictame,
De ces transports plus vifs que des rayons,
Que reste-t-il? C'est affreux, ô mon âme!
Rien qu'un dessin fort pâle, aux trois crayons,

Qui, comme moi, meurt dans la solitude,
Et que le Temps, injurieux vieillard,
Chaque jour frotte avec son aile rude . . .

Noir assassin de la Vie et de l'Art,
Tu ne tueras jamais dans ma mémoire
Celle qui fut mon plaisir et ma gloire!

IV THE PORTRAIT

Sickness and death reduce to ashes all the fire that once flamed for us.
Of those great eyes so fervent and so tender, of that mouth where my
heart drowned,

of those kisses powerful as balm, of those ecstasies more swift than
sunbeams – what remains? It is lamentable, O my soul – there is noth-
ing but a faded drawing in three colours,

which like myself is dying in loneliness, and which that insolent
greybeard, Time, rubs every day with his rough wing.

Black murderer of life and art, you will never kill in my memory the
one who was all my pleasure and my glory!

[1858–60]

XXXIX

Je te donne ces vers afin que si mon nom
Aborde heureusement aux époques lointaines,
Et fait rêver un soir les cervelles humaines,
Vaisseau favorisé par un grand aquilon,

Ta mémoire, pareille aux fables incertaines,
Fatigue le lecteur ainsi qu'un tympanon,
Et par un fraternel et mystique chaînon
Reste comme pendue à mes rimes hautaines;

Être maudit à qui, de l'abîme profond
Jusqu'au plus haut du ciel, rien, hors moi, ne répond!
– Ô toi qui, comme une ombre à la trace éphémère,

Foules d'un pied léger et d'un regard serein
Les stupides mortels qui t'ont jugée amère,
Statue aux yeux de jais, grand ange au front d'airain!

To you I give these lines . . .

To you I give these lines, so that if ever my name comes safely to the
shores of future times like a ship favoured by a good north wind, and
of an evening makes men's minds to muse,

your memory, like those enigmatic legends handed down, will tease
the reader like a dulcimer, and by some mystical fraternal bond, survive
suspended from my arrogant rhymes –

O cursed being, to whom from the lowest depths to the world's
highest heavens, nothing but I responds; you who, like a shade that
leaves no more than a fleeting trace,

tread under your frivolous foot, with indifferent gaze, those foolish
mortals who take you for a shrew, my statue with jet eyes, great angel
of the brazen brow!

[FM 1857]

XL

SEMPER EADEM

«D'où vous vient, disiez-vous, cette tristesse étrange,
Montant comme la mer sur le roc noir et nu?»
– Quand notre cœur a fait une fois sa vendange,
Vivre est un mal. C'est un secret de tous connu,

Une douleur très simple et non mystérieuse,
Et, comme votre joie, éclatante pour tous.
Cessez donc de chercher, ô belle curieuse!
Et, bien que votre voix soit douce, taisez-vous!

Taisez-vous, ignorante! âme toujours ravie!
Bouche au rire enfantin! Plus encor que la Vie,
La Mort nous tient souvent par des liens subtils.

Laissez, laissez mon cœur s'enivrer d'un *mensonge*,
Plonger dans vos beaux yeux comme dans un beau songe,
Et sommeiller longtemps à l'ombre de vos cils!

Always the Same

'Whence comes', you ask, 'this strange sadness of yours, that wells like
the sea over a bare black rock?' – When once our heart has reaped its
harvest and all the grapes are plucked, then living is an evil. This is a
secret known to all,
 the simplest of sorrows and in no way mysterious, and like your joy,
impossible to conceal. Ask no more questions then, inquisitive beauty,
and though your voice be gentle, hold your tongue!
 Be quiet, ignorant woman, forever delighted soul with childish
laughter bubbling on your lips; for even more than Life itself, Death
grapples us with many a subtle bond.
 Leave, then, my heart to drink deep of a falsehood, to lose itself in
your lovely eyes as in a perfect dream, to sleep long hours in your
eyelashes' shade.

[1860, FM 1861]

XLI
TOUT ENTIÈRE

Le Démon, dans ma chambre haute,
Ce matin est venu me voir,
Et, tâchant à me prendre en faute,
Me dit: «Je voudrais bien savoir,

«Parmi toutes les belles choses
Dont est fait son enchantement,
Parmi les objets noirs ou roses
Qui composent son corps charmant,

«Quel est le plus doux.» – Ô mon âme!
Tu répondis à l'Abhorré:
«Puisqu'en Elle tout est dictame,
Rien ne peut être préféré.

«Lorsque tout me ravit, j'ignore
Si quelque chose me séduit.
Elle éblouit comme l'Aurore
Et console comme la Nuit;

Entire

Satan visited me this morning in my high attic, and said, in an attempt
to trick me, 'It would please me to know
 which is the loveliest of all the beautiful things of which her magic
is composed; which is the loveliest of all those black or rosy features
that combine to make her charming person?'
 And you, my soul, answered the hateful Demon, 'Since all her being
is my solace, there is nothing in her to be preferred.
 'When all delights me, I am not even aware whether one thing
entrances me more than any other. She dazzles me like Dawn, and
comforts me like Night.

« Et l'harmonie est trop exquise,
Qui gouverne tout son beau corps,
Pour que l'impuissante analyse
En note les nombreux accords.

« Ô métamorphose mystique
De tous mes sens fondus en un !
Son haleine fait la musique,
Comme sa voix fait le parfum ! »

'The unison that governs all her beautiful form is too exquisite for sterile analysis to detail its countless harmonies.'

– O mystic transformation, whereby all my senses are fused into one: her breath becomes music, and her voice, perfume.

[For Mme Sabatier, 1857; FM 1857]

XLII

Que diras-tu ce soir, pauvre âme solitaire,
Que diras-tu, mon cœur, cœur autrefois flétri,
À la très belle, à la très bonne, à la très chère,
Dont le regard divin t'a soudain refleuri?

– Nous mettrons notre orgueil à chanter ses louanges:
Rien ne vaut la douceur de son autorité;
Sa chair spirituelle a le parfum des Anges,
Et son œil nous revêt d'un habit de clarté.

Que ce soit dans la nuit et dans la solitude,
Que ce soit dans la rue et dans la multitude,
Son fantôme dans l'air danse comme un flambeau.

Parfois il parle et dit: «Je suis belle, et j'ordonne
Que pour l'amour de moi vous n'aimiez que le Beau;
Je suis l'Ange gardien, la Muse et la Madone.»

What will you say tonight . . .

What will you say tonight, poor lonely soul: what will you say, my heart
that once was blighted, to her who is most beautiful, most good, most
dear, and whose divine gaze has suddenly made you flower again?

We shall set all our pride in singing her praises; there is nothing to
rival her gentle authority; her spiritual flesh has the fragrance of angels';
her eye clothes us in garments of light.

Whether I am in darkness, in solitude, or in the crowded street, her
image hovers like a torch in the air.

Sometimes it speaks and says, 'I am beautiful, and bid you, for love
of me, to love the Beautiful alone – for I am your guardian Angel, I am
your Muse and your Madonna.'

[Sent to Mme Sabatier 1854. Published 1855]

XLIII
LE FLAMBEAU VIVANT

Ils marchent devant moi, ces Yeux pleins de lumières,
Qu'un Ange très savant a sans doute aimantés;
Ils marchent, ces divins frères qui sont mes frères,
Secouant dans mes yeux leurs feux diamantés.

Me sauvant de tout piège et de tout péché grave,
Ils conduisent mes pas dans la route du Beau;
Ils sont mes serviteurs et je suis leur esclave;
Tout mon être obéit à ce vivant flambeau.

Charmants Yeux, vous brillez de la clarté mystique
Qu'ont les cierges brûlant en plein jour; le soleil
Rougit, mais n'éteint pas leur flamme fantastique;

Ils célèbrent la Mort, vous chantez le Réveil;
Vous marchez en chantant le réveil de mon âme,
Astres dont nul soleil ne peut flétrir la flamme!

The Living Torch

They go before me, those eyes full of many lights, which some angel's craft must have made magnetic; they advance, those divine brothers, my own brothers, flashing into my eyes their diamond-lustred flames.

Preserving me from every snare and every grievous sin, they guide my steps along the paths of Beauty: although they serve me I am their bondsman; my entire being obeys this living torch.

Entrancing eyes, you glitter with the mysterious radiance of candles lit in the broad light of day; the sun glows red but cannot douse their eerie flame.

The candles honour Death, but you hymn the Resurrection: as you advance you sing the awakening of my soul, O stars whose fire no Sun has power to dim.

[Sent to Mme Sabatier 1854. FM 1857]

XLIV
RÉVERSIBILITÉ

Ange plein de gaieté, connaissez-vous l'angoisse,
La honte, les remords, les sanglots, les ennuis,
Et les vagues terreurs de ces affreuses nuits
Qui compriment le cœur comme un papier qu'on froisse?
Ange plein de gaieté, connaissez-vous l'angoisse?

Ange plein de bonté, connaissez-vous la haine,
Les poings crispés dans l'ombre et les larmes de fiel,
Quand la Vengeance bat son infernal rappel,
Et de nos facultés se fait le capitaine?
Ange plein de bonté, connaissez-vous la haine?

Ange plein de santé, connaissez-vous les Fièvres,
Qui, le long des grands murs de l'hospice blafard,
Comme des exilés, s'en vont d'un pied traînard,
Cherchant le soleil rare et remuant les lèvres?
Ange plein de santé, connaissez-vous les Fièvres?

Reversibility

Angel of gaiety, do you know anguish, the shame and remorses, sobs
and cares, the nameless terror of those awful nights which tighten the
heart like crushed paper? Angel of gaiety, do you know that anguish?

Angel of goodness, do you know hatred, the fists clenched in the
dark, the tears of gall, when revenge drums its devilish tattoo and takes
command of all our faculties? Angel of goodness, do you know that
hatred?

Angel of health, do you know the fevers that stalk between high
walls of drab hospitals, like exiles dragging their feet in quest of the rare
sun, chattering with speechless lips? Angel of health, do you know
those fevers?

Ange plein de beauté, connaissez-vous les rides,
Et la peur de vieillir, et ce hideux tourment
De lire la secrète horreur du dévouement
Dans des yeux où longtemps burent nos yeux avides?
Ange plein de beauté, connaissez-vous les rides?

Ange plein de bonheur, de joie et de lumières,
David mourant aurait demandé la santé
Aux émanations de ton corps enchanté;
Mais de toi je n'implore, ange, que tes prières,
Ange plein de bonheur, de joie et de lumières!

Angel of beauty, do you know of wrinkles, the terror of growing old, the hideous torture of reading the secret horror of their devotion, in eyes that our own thirsting eyes drank from for years? Angel of beauty, do you know those wrinkles?

Angel of happiness and joy and radiance, David at the hour of death would have sought health in the fragrance of your enchanted body: but all I beg of you, my angel, is your prayers, Angel of happiness and joy and radiance!

[For Mme Sabatier 1853. Published 1855]

XLV
CONFESSION

Une fois, une seule, aimable et douce femme,
 À mon bras votre bras poli
S'appuya (sur le fond ténébreux de mon âme
 Ce souvenir n'est point pâli);

Il était tard; ainsi qu'une médaille neuve
 La pleine lune s'étalait,
Et la solennité de la nuit, comme un fleuve,
 Sur Paris dormant ruisselait.

Et le long des maisons, sous les portes cochères,
 Des chats passaient furtivement,
L'oreille au guet, ou bien, comme des ombres chères,
 Nous accompagnaient lentement.

Tout à coup, au milieu de l'intimité libre
 Éclose à la pâle clarté,
De vous, riche et sonore instrument où ne vibre
 Que la radieuse gaieté,

Confession

Once and once only, lovable and gentle woman, you leaned your smooth arm on mine: the memory of it has never faded from the dark background of my soul.

The hour was late, when like a freshly-minted medallion the full moon was spread out, and the solemnness of night streamed down like a river on sleeping Paris;

and along by the houses and under the carriage-gates, the cats went creeping furtively with pricking ears, or walked beside us slowly like familiar shades.

Then suddenly in the midst of our easy intimacy, grown frank and open in the milky light, there escaped from you – from you who are such a rich sonorous instrument, vibrating always with radiant cheer –

De vous, claire et joyeuse ainsi qu'une fanfare
 Dans le matin étincelant,
Une note plaintive, une note bizarre
 S'échappa, tout en chancelant

Comme une enfant chétive, horrible, sombre, immonde,
 Dont sa famille rougirait,
Et qu'elle aurait longtemps, pour la cacher au monde,
 Dans un caveau mise au secret.

Pauvre ange, elle chantait, votre note criarde:
 «Que rien ici-bas n'est certain,
Et que toujours, avec quelque soin qu'il se farde,
 Se trahit l'égoïsme humain;

«Que c'est un dur métier que d'être belle femme,
 Et que c'est le travail banal
De la danseuse folle et froide qui se pâme
 Dans un sourire machinal;

from you who are bright and lively as a trumpet sounding through the glittering dawn – there escaped from you a strange lamenting cry, a faltering note

like some sickly repulsive child, sullen and foul, whose ashamed parents would hide away for years in a secret cellar, far from the eyes of the world.

My poor angel, it sang, your piercing note: 'That nothing on earth is certain; that in spite of every disguise human selfishness is forever breaking through;

'that it's a thankless occupation, being a beautiful woman, like the inane toil of a crazy numbed dancing-girl, who goes on dancing till she drops, with the same mechanical smile:

«Que bâtir sur les cœurs est une chose sotte;
 Que tout craque, amour et beauté,
Jusqu'à ce que l'Oubli les jette dans sa hotte
 Pour les rendre à l'Éternité!»

J'ai souvent évoqué cette lune enchantée,
 Ce silence et cette langueur,
Et cette confidence horrible chuchotée
 Au confessionnal du cœur.

'that it's foolish to build anything on human hearts – for everything cracks, yes, even love and beauty, till oblivion flings them into its hod and gives them over to eternity . . .'

I have often recalled that entrancing moonlight, that silence, that languor, that fearful secret whispered in the heart's confessional.

[Sent to Mme Sabatier 1853. Published 1855]

XLVI
L'AUBE SPIRITUELLE

Quand chez les débauchés l'aube blanche et vermeille
Entre en société de l'Idéal rongeur,
Par l'opération d'un mystère vengeur
Dans la brute assoupie un ange se réveille.

Des Cieux Spirituels l'inaccessible azur,
Pour l'homme terrassé qui rêve encore et souffre,
S'ouvre et s'enfonce avec l'attirance du gouffre.
Ainsi, chère Déesse, Être lucide et pur,

Sur les débris fumeux des stupides orgies
Ton souvenir plus clair, plus rose, plus charmant,
À mes yeux agrandis voltige incessamment.

Le soleil a noirci la flamme des bougies;
Ainsi, toujours vainqueur, ton fantôme est pareil,
Âme resplendissante, à l'immortel soleil!

The Spiritual Dawn

When the white and ruby dawn enters rakes' rooms, and with it the Ideal that frets the mind, then some avenging power of mystery sets to work, and in the slothful beast an angel wakes.

The unattainable azure of the Spiritual Heavens opens for the still dreaming, felled man, and floods into his being as though drawn by a precipice. Thus, my beloved goddess, O translucent and pure being,

above the fuddled ruins of stupefying debauch, your memory, ever brighter and rosier and more enchanting, ceaselessly hovers before my dilated eyes.

The sun has blackened the candle-flames: likewise, O radiant spirit, your invincible image is sister to the immortal Sun.

[1854. Published 1855]

XLVII
HARMONIE DU SOIR

Voici venir les temps où vibrant sur sa tige
Chaque fleur s'évapore ainsi qu'un encensoir;
Les sons et les parfums tournent dans l'air du soir;
Valse mélancolique et langoureux vertige!

Chaque fleur s'évapore ainsi qu'un encensoir;
Le violon frémit comme un cœur qu'on afflige;
Valse mélancolique et langoureux vertige!
Le ciel est triste et beau comme un grand reposoir.

Le violon frémit comme un cœur qu'on afflige,
Un cœur tendre, qui hait le néant vaste et noir!
Le ciel est triste et beau comme un grand reposoir;
Le soleil s'est noyé dans son sang qui se fige.

Un cœur tendre, qui hait le néant vaste et noir,
Du passé lumineux recueille tout vestige!
Le soleil s'est noyé dans son sang qui se fige . . .
Ton souvenir en moi luit comme un ostensoir!

Evening Harmony

Now the days are coming when, throbbing on its stalk, each flower
sheds its perfume like a censer; the sounds and perfumes spiral in the
evening air, in a melancholy waltz, a slow sensual gyre.

Each flower sheds its perfume like a censer; the violin trembles like
a wounded heart, in a melancholy waltz, a slow sensual gyre; the sky is
sad and beautiful like a vast altar.

The violin trembles like a wounded heart, a tender heart that hates
the huge black void; the sky is sad and beautiful like a vast altar; the sun
has drowned in its congealing blood.

A tender heart that hates the huge black void is gathering to itself all
traces of the luminous past; the sun has drowned in its congealing
blood – and like a monstrance your memory shines within me.

[F. W. Leakey dates this 1845–6 but it was
offered to Mme Sabatier in 1857]

XLVIII
LE FLACON

Il est de forts parfums pour qui toute matière
Est poreuse. On dirait qu'ils pénètrent le verre.
En ouvrant un coffret venu de l'Orient
Dont la serrure grince et rechigne en criant,

Ou dans une maison déserte quelque armoire
Pleine de l'âcre odeur des temps, poudreuse et noire,
Parfois on trouve un vieux flacon qui se souvient,
D'où jaillit toute vive une âme qui revient.

Mille pensers dormaient, chrysalides funèbres,
Frémissant doucement dans les lourdes ténèbres,
Qui dégagent leur aile et prennent leur essor,
Teintés d'azur, glacés de rose, lamés d'or.

Voilà le souvenir enivrant qui voltige
Dans l'air troublé; les yeux se ferment; le Vertige
Saisit l'âme vaincue et la pousse à deux mains
Vers un gouffre obscurci de miasmes humains;

The Scent-Bottle

There are pungent perfumes for which all matter is porous. They seem
able to penetrate through glass. Opening a casket from the East, with its
lock grating and protesting, crying out;

or in some empty house, when you open a wardrobe that is redo-
lent of the acrid smell of the years, all dusty and dark, perhaps you will
find an old scent-bottle which remembers all the past, and from which
a returning spirit springs fully alive.

A thousand thoughts lay slumbering there, chrysalids of death
gently rustling in the thick shadows, but which now unfold their wings
and take flight once more, tinged with azure and glazed with rosy hues
and threaded with gold.

Now memory spirals entrancing on the troubled air; your eyes close
and the gyre grips the vanquished soul, thrusting it with both hands
down to the Pit all darkened with the foul vapours of mortal decay,

Il la terrasse au bord d'un gouffre séculaire,
Où, Lazare odorant déchirant son suaire,
Se meut dans son réveil le cadavre spectral
D'un vieil amour ranci, charmant et sépulcral.

Ainsi, quand je serai perdu dans la mémoire
Des hommes, dans le coin d'une sinistre armoire
Quand on m'aura jeté, vieux flacon désolé,
Décrépit, poudreux, sale, abject, visqueux, fêlé,

Je serai ton cercueil, aimable pestilence!
Le témoin de ta force et de ta virulence,
Cher poison préparé par les anges! liqueur
Qui me ronge, ô la vie et la mort de mon cœur!

striking the soul down to the brim of the ageless pit, where like a
stinking Lazarus rending his shroud, the spectral corpse of an old rancid
love, full of charm and death, writhes into wakefulness.

Thus, when I no longer live in the memories of men, when I am
cast aside in the corner of some sinister cupboard like an old useless
scent-bottle, decrepit and covered with dust, foul and abject, slimy and
cracked –

then I shall be your funeral casket, O seductive plague, proof of your
strength and virulence, O poison brewed by angels' hands, corroding
ichor, O life and death of my heart.

[Published 1857, FM 1857]

XLIX
LE POISON

Le vin sait revêtir le plus sordide bouge
 D'un luxe miraculeux,
Et fait surgir plus d'un portique fabuleux
 Dans l'or de sa vapeur rouge,
Comme un soleil couchant dans un ciel nébuleux.

L'opium agrandit ce qui n'a pas de bornes,
 Allonge l'illimité,
Approfondit le temps, creuse la volupté,
 Et de plaisirs noirs et mornes
Remplit l'âme au-delà de sa capacité.

Tout cela ne vaut pas le poison qui découle
 De tes yeux, de tes yeux verts,
Lacs où mon âme tremble et se voit à l'envers . . .
 Mes songes viennent en foule
Pour se désaltérer à ces gouffres amers.

Her Poison

Wine can clothe the most sordid hovel in miraculous luxury, and
conjure up many a fabulous portico in its red vapour's gold, like a
setting sun's fire in a clouded sky.

Opium magnifies things that have no limits, it prolongs the bound-
less, makes Time more profound, deepens voluptuousness, and fills the
soul to overbrimming with dark and melancholy pleasures.

None of these things can rival the poison that flows from your eyes,
from your green eyes, which are lakes wherein my soul trembles and
sees its own image reversed. My dreams come flocking to quench their
thirst in those bitter depths.

Tout cela ne vaut pas le terrible prodige
 De ta salive qui mord,
Qui plonge dans l'oubli mon âme sans remords,
 Et, charriant le vertige,
La roule défaillante aux rives de la mort!

None of those things can equal the fearsome marvel of your piquant saliva, which plunges my remorseless soul into oblivion, that sets it spinning and swirls it swooning towards the shores of death.

[FM 1857]

L

CIEL BROUILLÉ

On dirait ton regard d'une vapeur couvert;
Ton œil mystérieux (est-il bleu, gris ou vert?)
Alternativement tendre, rêveur, cruel,
Réfléchit l'indolence et la pâleur du ciel.

Tu rappelles ces jours blancs, tièdes et voilés,
Qui font se fondre en pleurs les cœurs ensorcelés,
Quand, agités d'un mal inconnu qui les tord,
Les nerfs trop éveillés raillent l'esprit qui dort.

Tu ressembles parfois à ces beaux horizons
Qu'allument les soleils des brumeuses saisons . . .
Comme tu resplendis, paysage mouillé
Qu'enflamment les rayons tombant d'un ciel brouillé!

Ô femme dangereuse, ô séduisants climats!
Adorerai-je aussi ta neige et vos frimas,
Et saurai-je tirer de l'implacable hiver
Des plaisirs plus aigus que la glace et le fer?

An Uncertain Sky

Your gaze seems veiled with vapour; your mysterious eyes – blue, grey,
or green? – fitfully tender, dreamy, cruel, echo the indolence and pale-
ness of the sky.

Sometimes you make me think of those blank days, listless and hazy,
which melt enamoured hearts to tears, when they fret with some inex-
plicable twisting unease, when the taut nerves mock the numbness of
the mind.

At other times you recall delightful vistas lit by the misty seasons'
suns, then how splendid you are, a landscape all bedewed yet aglow
with the rays of a cloud-dappled sky.

O dangerous woman, with your seductive moods: perhaps some day
I shall worship your snows and frosts, and learn to draw from your
pitiless winter, pleasures more sharply-edged than ice or steel?

[FM 1857]

LI

LE CHAT

I

Dans ma cervelle se promène,
Ainsi qu'en son appartement,
Un beau chat, fort, doux et charmant.
Quand il miaule, on l'entend à peine,

Tant son timbre est tendre et discret;
Mais que sa voix s'apaise ou gronde,
Elle est toujours riche et profonde.
C'est là son charme et son secret.

Cette voix, qui perle et qui filtre
Dans mon fonds le plus ténébreux,
Me remplit comme un vers nombreux
Et me réjouit comme un philtre.

Elle endort les plus cruels maux
Et contient toutes les extases;
Pour dire les plus longues phrases,
Elle n'a pas besoin de mots.

The Cat

I

A handsome cat, strong and gentle and full of charm, prowls in my brain as if in its own home. When he mews you can hardly hear him at all,

so tender and discreet are his tones. But whether his voice be meek or vexed it is always rich and deep. That is his special charm, his special secret.

This voice which purls and filters down to the most opaque depths of my being, expands within me like a long harmonious line of verse and delights me like some magic potion.

It soothes the cruellest pangs of suffering and brings me every possible ecstasy. To utter the longest sentences it has no need of words.

Non, il n'est pas d'archet qui morde
Sur mon cœur, parfait instrument,
Et fasse plus royalement
Chanter sa plus vibrante corde,

Que ta voix, chat mystérieux,
Chat séraphique, chat étrange,
En qui tout est, comme en un ange,
Aussi subtil qu'harmonieux!

II

De sa fourrure blonde et brune
Sort un parfum si doux, qu'un soir
J'en fus embaumé, pour l'avoir
Caressée une fois, rien qu'une.

C'est l'esprit familier du lieu;
Il juge, il préside, il inspire
Toutes choses dans son empire;
Peut-être est-il fée, est-il dieu?

No, there is no violin-bow in the world that, biting on my heart,
that most perfect of instruments, more richly draws a melody from its
most vibrant string,

than does your voice, O most mysterious, seraphic, extraordinary
cat, in whom everything, as in an angel, is as subtle as it is harmonious.

II

From its blond and brown fur there rises such a sweet aroma that, one
evening, I was steeped in its fragrance after caressing it but once, yes,
only once.

It is the house's familiar spirit, judging, presiding, inspiring all things
within its empire: can it be a fairy, or a god?

Quand mes yeux, vers ce chat que j'aime
Tirés comme par un aimant,
Se retournent docilement
Et que je regarde en moi-même,

Je vois avec étonnement
Le feu de ses prunelles pâles,
Clairs fanaux, vivantes opales,
Qui me contemplent fixement.

When my eyes are drawn as by a magnet towards my beloved cat, and obediently I turn them upon him and find I am looking into myself,

I am amazed to see the fire of his pale pupils, bright lamps, living opals, hypnotically fixed on me.

[Marie Daubrun cycle. FM 1857]

LII
LE BEAU NAVIRE

Je veux te raconter, ô molle enchanteresse!
Les diverses beautés qui parent ta jeunesse;
 Je veux te peindre ta beauté,
Où l'enfance s'allie à la maturité.

Quand tu vas balayant l'air de ta jupe large,
Tu fais l'effet d'un beau vaisseau qui prend le large,
 Chargé de toile, et va roulant
Suivant un rythme doux, et paresseux, et lent.

Sur ton cou large et rond, sur tes épaules grasses,
Ta tête se pavane avec d'étranges grâces;
 D'un air placide et triomphant
Tu passes ton chemin, majestueuse enfant.

Je veux te raconter, ô molle enchanteresse!
Les diverses beautés qui parent ta jeunesse;
 Je veux te peindre ta beauté,
Où l'enfance s'allie à la maturité.

The Beautiful Ship

I want to describe to you, my gentle enchantress, the various beauties which adorn your youth: I want to depict your loveliness in which childhood and maturity combine.

When you walk, sweeping the air with your ample skirts, you give the impression of a handsome ship setting out to sea with all its canvas spread, and swinging away, sailing on with a gentle, languid, easy rhythm.

On your broad rounded throat, on your plump shoulders, your head sways to and fro with many a strange grace; with a placid, conquering air you go your way, majestic child.

I want to describe to you, my gentle enchantress, the various beauties which adorn your youth; I want to depict your loveliness in which childhood and maturity combine.

Ta gorge qui s'avance et qui pousse la moire,
Ta gorge triomphante est une belle armoire
 Dont les panneaux bombés et clairs
Comme les boucliers accrochent des éclairs;

Boucliers provocants, armés de pointes roses!
Armoire à doux secrets, pleine de bonnes choses,
 De vins, de parfums, de liqueurs
Qui feraient délirer les cerveaux et les cœurs!

Quand tu vas balayant l'air de ta jupe large,
Tu fais l'effet d'un beau vaisseau qui prend le large,
 Chargé de toile, et va roulant
Suivant un rythme doux, et paresseux, et lent.

Tes nobles jambes, sous les volants qu'elles chassent,
Tourmentent les désirs obscurs et les agacent,
 Comme deux sorcières qui font
Tourner un philtre noir dans un vase profond.

 Your jutting breast which curves the watered silk, your triumphant bosom is like some beautiful press, whose curved bright panels catch the light like shields –
 provoking shields that are armed with rosy tips – a press full of delicious secrets, full of good things, with wines and perfumes and liqueurs to exhilarate men's minds and hearts.
 When you go sweeping the air with your ample skirts, you give the impression of a handsome ship setting out to sea, with all its canvas spread, and swinging away, sailing on with a gentle, languid, easy rhythm.
 Your noble legs, under the flounces which they thrust before them, torment and tease obscure desires, like twin witches stirring a black potion in a deep vase.

Tes bras, qui se joueraient des précoces hercules,
Sont des boas luisants les solides émules,
 Faits pour serrer obstinément,
Comme pour l'imprimer dans ton cœur, ton amant.

Sur ton cou large et rond, sur tes épaules grasses,
Ta tête se pavane avec d'étranges grâces;
 D'un air placide et triomphant
Tu passes ton chemin, majestueuse enfant.

Your arms, which could outmatch any youthful Hercules, are worthy rivals of glistening boas, fashioned for relentless embraces, as though to imprint your lover on your heart.

On your broad rounded throat, on your plump shoulders, your head sways to and fro with many a strange grace; with a placid, conquering air you go your way, majestic child.

[Marie Daubrun cycle. FM 1857]

LIII
L'INVITATION AU VOYAGE

Mon enfant, ma sœur,
Songe à la douceur
D'aller là-bas vivre ensemble!
Aimer à loisir,
Aimer et mourir
Au pays qui te ressemble!
Les soleils mouillés
De ces ciels brouillés
Pour mon esprit ont les charmes
Si mystérieux
De tes traîtres yeux,
Brillant à travers leurs larmes.

Là, tout n'est qu'ordre et beauté,
Luxe, calme et volupté.

Des meubles luisants,
Polis par les ans,
Décoreraient notre chambre;
Les plus rares fleurs
Mêlant leurs odeurs
Aux vagues senteurs de l'ambre,
Les riches plafonds,
Les miroirs profonds,

The Invitation to the Voyage

My child, my sister, just imagine the happiness of voyaging there to spend our lives together, to love to our hearts' content, to love and die in the land which is the image of yourself. The misty suns of those unsettled skies have the same mysterious hold on my mind as your fickle eyes, shining through their tears.

Everything there is order and beauty, luxury, calm, voluptuousness.

Furniture gleaming with the patina of the years would grace our bedroom; the rarest of flowers, mingling their scents with the vague fragrances of amber; the richly decorated ceilings, the fathomless mirrors,

La splendeur orientale,
Tout y parlerait
À l'âme en secret
Sa douce langue natale.

Là, tout n'est qu'ordre et beauté,
Luxe, calme et volupté.

Vois sur ces canaux
Dormir ces vaisseaux
Dont l'humeur est vagabonde;
C'est pour assouvir
Ton moindre désir
Qu'ils viennent du bout du monde.
– Les soleils couchants
Revêtent les champs,
Les canaux, la ville entière,
D'hyacinthe et d'or;
Le monde s'endort
Dans une chaude lumière.

Là, tout n'est qu'ordre et beauté,
Luxe, calme et volupté.

the splendour of the East – all would whisper in secret to our souls in their own gentle mother-tongue.

Everything there is order and beauty, luxury, calm, voluptuousness.

See how the ships that love to roam are slumbering in the canals: it's to gratify your slightest whim that they sail in from the ends of the world. The westering sun enwraps the fields and the canals and the entire city in hyacinth and gold, and the world falls asleep in the warm gloaming.

Everything there is order and beauty, luxury, calm, voluptuousness.

[Marie Daubrun cycle, 1854. Published 1855, FM 1857]

LIV

L'IRRÉPARABLE

Pouvons-nous étouffer le vieux, le long Remords,
Qui vit, s'agite et se tortille,
Et se nourrit de nous comme le ver des morts,
Comme du chêne la chenille?
Pouvons-nous étouffer l'implacable Remords?

Dans quel philtre, dans quel vin, dans quelle tisane,
Noierons-nous ce vieil ennemi,
Destructeur et gourmand comme la courtisane,
Patient comme la fourmi?
Dans quel philtre? – dans quel vin? – dans quelle tisane?

Dis-le, belle sorcière, oh! dis, si tu le sais,
À cet esprit comblé d'angoisse
Et pareil au mourant qu'écrasent les blessés,
Que le sabot du cheval froisse,
Dis-le, belle sorcière, oh! dis, si tu le sais,

The Irreparable

Can we ever stifle the old and long Remorse which lives, writhes, coils
and feeds on us as the worm feeds on the dead, as the caterpillar battens
on the oak? Can we ever stifle implacable Remorse?

In what potion, in what wine, in what brew shall we drown this
ancient enemy, as destructive and greedy as a harlot, as patient as an
ant? In what potion, in what wine, in what brew?

Tell us, lovely witch, oh tell us if you know what that potion is, to
the anguish-laden mind which is like some dying man crushed under
piles of wounded, bruised by the horse's hoof – tell it, you lovely witch,
if you know what it is,

À cet agonisant que le loup déjà flaire
 Et que surveille le corbeau,
À ce soldat brisé! s'il faut qu'il désespère
 D'avoir sa croix et son tombeau;
Ce pauvre agonisant que déjà le loup flaire!

Peut-on illuminer un ciel bourbeux et noir?
 Peut-on déchirer des ténèbres
Plus denses que la poix, sans matin et sans soir,
 Sans astres, sans éclairs funèbres?
Peut-on illuminer un ciel bourbeux et noir?

L'Espérance qui brille aux carreaux de l'Auberge
 Est soufflée, est morte à jamais!
Sans lune et sans rayons, trouver où l'on héberge
 Les martyrs d'un chemin mauvais!
Le Diable a tout éteint aux carreaux de l'Auberge!

Adorable sorcière, aimes-tu les damnés?
 Dis, connais-tu l'irrémissible?
Connais-tu le Remords, aux traits empoisonnés,
 À qui notre cœur sert de cible?
Adorable sorcière, aimes-tu les damnés?

to the man in the throes of death whom the wolf has already scented and over whom the raven is watching – tell the broken soldier whether he must despair of his medal and his tomb – the poor man in the throes of death, whom the wolf has already scented.

Can we illumine a mud-sodden black sky? Can we pierce shadows denser than pitch, with no morning and no evening, with no stars, with not even a deadly flash of lightning? Can we illuminate the grime of a black sky?

The Hope that shines in the windows of the Inn is doused, is dead for ever. Without moonlight, without beams, where find a place to shelter the martyrs of a cruel journey? The Devil has snuffed the light at the windows of the Inn.

Adorable witch, do you love the damned? Say, do you know the unforgivable sin? Do you know Remorse with its poisoned barbs, for which our heart serves as target? Adorable witch, do you love the damned?

L'Irréparable ronge avec sa dent maudite
Notre âme, piteux monument,
Et souvent il attaque, ainsi que le termite,
Par la base le bâtiment.
L'Irréparable ronge avec sa dent maudite!

– J'ai vu parfois, au fond d'un théâtre banal
Qu'enflammait l'orchestre sonore,
Une fée allumer dans un ciel infernal
Une miraculeuse aurore;
J'ai vu parfois au fond d'un théâtre banal

Un être, qui n'était que lumière, or et gaze,
Terrasser l'énorme Satan;
Mais mon cœur, que jamais ne visite l'extase,
Est un théâtre où l'on attend
Toujours, toujours en vain, l'Être aux ailes de gaze!

The Irreparable gnaws with its accursed tooth that pitiful monument, our soul, and like the white ant it often attacks a building at its foundations. The Irreparable gnaws with its accursed tooth.
Sometimes I have seen, in a third-rate theatre, lit up by the sonorous orchestra, a fairy kindle a miraculous dawn in an infernal sky: sometimes I have seen, on a third-rate stage,
a being who was naught but light and gold and gauze, overthrow the gigantic Satan: but my heart, never visited by any ecstasy, is a theatre in which the gauze-winged being is for ever awaited in vain.

[Marie Daubrun cycle: in 1855 dedicated to
'the golden-haired beauty', a part she played in 1847–8]

LV

CAUSERIE

Vous êtes un beau ciel d'automne, clair et rose!
Mais la tristesse en moi monte comme la mer,
Et laisse, en refluant, sur ma lèvre morose
Le souvenir cuisant de son limon amer.

— Ta main se glisse en vain sur mon sein qui se pâme;
Ce qu'elle cherche, amie, est un lieu saccagé
Par la griffe et la dent féroce de la femme.
Ne cherchez plus mon cœur; les bêtes l'ont mangé.

Mon cœur est un palais flétri par la cohue;
On s'y soûle, on s'y tue, on s'y prend aux cheveux!
— Un parfum nage autour de votre gorge nue!...

Ô Beauté, dur fléau des âmes, tu le veux!
Avec tes yeux de feu, brillants comme des fêtes,
Calcine ces lambeaux qu'ont épargnés les bêtes!

Monologue

You are a fine autumn sky, clear and rosy — but sadness is rising within
me like the sea, and leaves, as it ebbs, the sharp after-taste of bitter lime
on my sullen lips.

In vain your hand glides over my numb breast: what it seeks, my
dear, is now a place laid waste by women's claws and fangs — so seek no
more my heart; wild beasts have fed on it.

The rabble have deified the palace of my heart, they swill and
murder in it, clutching each other's hair — but such a perfume hovers
round your naked throat —

O Beauty, the stern scourge of human souls — if it is your will, may
your eyes of fire, as dazzling as festivals, consume these mortal shreds
the beasts have spared.

[Marie Daubrun cycle. FM 1857]

LVI

CHANT D'AUTOMNE

I

Bientôt nous plongerons dans les froides ténèbres;
Adieu, vive clarté de nos étés trop courts!
J'entends déjà tomber avec des chocs funèbres
Le bois retentissant sur le pavé des cours.

Tout l'hiver va rentrer dans mon être: colère,
Haine, frissons, horreur, labeur dur et forcé,
Et, comme le soleil dans son enfer polaire,
Mon cœur ne sera plus qu'un bloc rouge et glacé.

J'écoute en frémissant chaque bûche qui tombe;
L'échafaud qu'on bâtit n'a pas d'écho plus sourd.
Mon esprit est pareil à la tour qui succombe
Sous les coups du bélier infatigable et lourd.

Autumn Song

I

Soon we shall plunge into the chill shadows. Farewell to the vivid sunlight of our summers, all too short! Already I hear the falling of the logs of winter fuel, their forlorn thuds resounding in the courtyards.

The whole winter will lodge itself once more within my being: anger and hatred, ague and horror and hard forced labour, and like the sun in its arctic hell my heart will be no more than a block of scarlet ice.

I tremble as I hear the logs drop one by one; the hammering of the scaffold makes no duller echo than this; my mind is like a tower, crashing beneath the blows of the ponderous tireless ram.

Il me semble, bercé par ce choc monotone,
Qu'on cloue en grande hâte un cercueil quelque part.
Pour qui? – C'était hier l'été; voici l'automne!
Ce bruit mystérieux sonne comme un départ.

II

J'aime de vos longs yeux la lumière verdâtre,
Douce beauté, mais tout aujourd'hui m'est amer,
Et rien, ni votre amour, ni le boudoir, ni l'âtre,
Ne me vaut le soleil rayonnant sur la mer.

Et pourtant aimez-moi, tendre cœur! soyez mère,
Même pour un ingrat, même pour un méchant;
Amante ou sœur, soyez la douceur éphémère
D'un glorieux automne ou d'un soleil couchant.

Courte tâche! La tombe attend; elle est avide!
Ah! laissez-moi, mon front posé sur vos genoux,
Goûter, en regrettant l'été blanc et torride,
De l'arrière-saison le rayon jaune et doux!

As I am rocked this way and that by the monotonous thuds, I fancy that somewhere a coffin is being hastily nailed together – and for whom? Yesterday it was summer, but now autumn is with us. The mysterious noise resounds like a farewell.

II

I love the emerald light of your long eyes, my gentle beauty; but today I find all things full of bitterness, and nothing, not even your love nor the boudoir nor the hearth, means as much to me as the sunlight glittering on the sea.

Yet love me still, O tender heart, and be as a mother, however ungrateful I may be and however unworthy; whether as mistress or sister, be as the transient bliss of a splendid autumn or a setting sun.

Your task will not be long, for the famished grave is waiting. Ah, let me rest my brow upon your knees, regretting the white and torrid summertime, and enjoying the yellow, gentle rays of autumntide.

[Dedicated to Marie Daubrun, 1859]

LVII
À UNE MADONE

EX-VOTO DANS LE GOÛT ESPAGNOL

Je veux bâtir pour toi, Madone, ma maîtresse,
Un autel souterrain au fond de ma détresse,
Et creuser dans le coin le plus noir de mon cœur,
Loin du désir mondain et du regard moqueur,
Une niche, d'azur et d'or tout émaillée,
Où tu te dresseras, Statue émerveillée.
Avec mes Vers polis, treillis d'un pur métal
Savamment constellé de rimes de cristal,
Je ferai pour ta tête une énorme Couronne;
Et dans ma Jalousie, ô mortelle Madone,
Je saurai te tailler un Manteau, de façon
Barbare, roide et lourd, et doublé de soupçon,
Qui, comme une guérite, enfermera tes charmes;
Non de Perles brodé, mais de toutes mes Larmes!
Ta Robe, ce sera mon Désir, frémissant,
Onduleux, mon Désir qui monte et qui descend,

To a Madonna

AN EX-VOTO IN THE SPANISH STYLE

My Madonna and mistress, let me build you an underground shrine in
the depths of my distress; and in the darkest corner of my heart, far
from all worldly desires and mocking eyes, hew a niche for you enam-
elled in blue and gold in which, a spellbound statue, you will stand.
 With my smooth verses' network of unalloyed metal cunningly
starred with crystal rhymes, I will fashion a vast Crown upon your
head; and out of my Jealousy, O mortal Madonna, carve you a mantle
of primitive design, stiff, massy, lined with Suspicion, to imprison your
charms as in a sentry-box, embroidered not with pearls but with my
tears. Your gown will be the rippling tide of my Desire, billowing at the

Aux pointes se balance, aux vallons se repose,
Et revêt d'un baiser tout ton corps blanc et rose.
Je te ferai de mon Respect de beaux Souliers
De satin, par tes pieds divins humiliés,
Qui, les emprisonnant dans une molle étreinte,
Comme un moule fidèle en garderont l'empreinte.
Si je ne puis, malgré tout mon art diligent,
Pour Marchepied tailler une Lune d'argent,
Je mettrai le Serpent qui me mord les entrailles
Sous tes talons, afin que tu foules et railles,
Reine victorieuse et féconde en rachats,
Ce monstre tout gonflé de haine et de crachats.
Tu verras mes Pensers, rangés comme les Cierges
Devant l'autel fleuri de la Reine des Vierges,
Étoilant de reflets le plafond peint en bleu,
Te regarder toujours avec des yeux de feu;
Et comme tout en moi te chérit et t'admire,
Tout se fera Benjoin, Encens, Oliban, Myrrhe,
Et sans cesse vers toi, sommet blanc et neigeux,
En Vapeurs montera mon Esprit orageux.

fringes, settling in the folds, clothing your body's white and rosiness as with a single kiss.

From my Respect I'll fashion you dainty satin shoes to be the slaves of your celestial feet, to grip them in a gentle clasp and keep their imprint like a loyal mould.

If with all my earnest craft I fail to carve a silver Moon to be your footstool, then at your heels I'll set the serpent which devours my bowels, to make you crush and scold that monster bloated with hate and spitting venom, O my victorious Queen grown rich on ransoming.

There you will see my thoughts displayed like candles before the flowered altar of the queen of vestals, starring the blue-painted vault with their reflected flames and watching you with eyes of fire; and as all my being admires and cherishes you, all will be transmuted into benjamin and incense, frankincense and myrrh, and my tempestuous spirit will ever rise in clouds to your white snowy peak.

Enfin, pour compléter ton rôle de Marie,
Et pour mêler l'amour avec la barbarie,
Volupté noire! des sept Péchés capitaux,
Bourreau plein de remords, je ferai sept Couteaux
Bien affilés, et, comme un jongleur insensible,
Prenant le plus profond de ton amour pour cible,
Je les planterai tous dans ton Cœur pantelant,
Dans ton Cœur sanglotant, dans ton Cœur ruisselant!

And finally, to complete your role as Mary, and to mingle love with barbarity, O blackest pleasure! from the seven deadly sins, your pitiless executioner, I'll fashion seven keen blades for you and, like some dispassionate juggler, I shall aim at the deep centre of your love and plunge them one by one into your throbbing heart, your sobbing, gushing heart.

[The poem refers to Marie Daubrun. Published 1860]

LVIII
CHANSON D'APRÈS-MIDI

Quoique tes sourcils méchants
Te donnent un air étrange
Qui n'est pas celui d'un ange,
Sorcière aux yeux alléchants,

Je t'adore, ô ma frivole,
Ma terrible passion!
Avec la dévotion
Du prêtre pour son idole.

Le désert et la forêt
Embaument tes tresses rudes,
Ta tête a les attitudes
De l'énigme et du secret.

Sur ta chair le parfum rôde
Comme autour d'un encensoir;
Tu charmes comme le soir,
Nymphe ténébreuse et chaude.

Ah! les philtres les plus forts
Ne valent pas ta paresse,
Et tu connais la caresse
Qui fait revivre les morts!

Afternoon Song

Although your scowling eyebrows give you an unusual appearance,
which is no angel's, you witch with alluring eyes,

I adore you, my frivolous one, my terrible passion, with a priest's
devotion to his idol.

Both desert and forest perfume your primitive tresses; your head
affects the poises of enigmas and secrecy.

The perfume hovers round your flesh as round a censer; you
bewitch like eventide, O darkling sultry nymph.

Ah, the strongest potions are no match for your indolence, and you
know caresses that could raise the dead.

Tes hanches sont amoureuses
De ton dos et de tes seins,
Et tu ravis les coussins
Par tes poses langoureuses.

Quelquefois, pour apaiser
Ta rage mystérieuse,
Tu prodigues, sérieuse,
La morsure et le baiser;

Tu me déchires, ma brune,
Avec un rire moqueur,
Et puis tu mets sur mon cœur
Ton œil doux comme la lune.

Sous tes souliers de satin,
Sous tes charmants pieds de soie,
Moi, je mets ma grande joie,
Mon génie et mon destin,

Mon âme par toi guérie,
Par toi, lumière et couleur!
Explosion de chaleur
Dans ma noire Sibérie!

Your hips are enamoured of your back and breasts, and you delight the cushions with your languid poses.

Sometimes, to appease your mysterious rage, gravely you lavish bites and kisses.

O dark-haired one, you rend me with mocking laughter, then on my heart you lay your eye as gentle as the Moon.

Under your satin slippers, under your charming silky feet, I lay down my great joy, my genius and my destiny,

my soul restored to health by you, who are all light, all colour, an explosion of warmth in my sunless Siberia.

[Beginning of the 'secondary loves' group. Published 1860]

LIX
SISINA

Imaginez Diane en galant équipage,
Parcourant les forêts ou battant les halliers,
Cheveux et gorge au vent, s'enivrant de tapage,
Superbe et défiant les meilleurs cavaliers!

Avez-vous vu Théroigne, amante du carnage,
Excitant à l'assaut un peuple sans souliers,
La joue et l'œil en feu, jouant son personnage,
Et montant, sabre au poing, les royaux escaliers?

Telle la Sisina! Mais la douce guerrière
A l'âme charitable autant que meurtrière;
Son courage, affolé de poudre et de tambours,

Devant les suppliants sait mettre bas les armes,
Et son cœur, ravagé par la flamme, a toujours,
Pour qui s'en montre digne, un réservoir de larmes.

Sisina

Imagine Sisina clad for the chase, galloping through the forests or beating through the brakes, her hair and bosom loose to the wind as she revels in the uproar of the hunt, sublime as she challenges the finest horsemen there.

Did you ever see Théroigne, the virago who rejoiced in the blood of the guillotine, as she stirred the barefoot rabble to riot, her cheeks and eyes afire when she played the Jacobin, leaping the royal stairs with a sabre in her hand?

Such is Sisina; but her gentle amazon's soul is as kind as cruel. When her courage is stirred by gunshot or drumbeat

she knows when to down arms before her suppliants, and her heart, scorched by love's fires, has always a fund of tears for those who are not unworthy of them.

[Published 1859]

LX
FRANCISCÆ MEÆ LAUDES

VERS COMPOSÉS POUR UNE MODISTE
ÉRUDITE ET DÉVOTE

Novis te cantabo chordis,
O novelletum quod ludis
In solitudine cordis.

Esto sertis implicata,
O femina delicata
Per quam solvuntur peccata!

Sicut beneficum Lethe,
Hauriam oscula de te,
Quæ imbuta es magnete.

Quum vitiorum tempestas
Turbabat omnes semitas,
Apparuisti, Deitas,

Velut stella salutaris
In naufragiis amaris . . .
Suspendam cor tuis aris!

In Praise of my Francisca

FOR A LEARNED AND DEVOUT MILLINER

I shall sing your praises on fresh strings, O stripling who play in the solitude of my heart.

May you be wreathed in garlands, delicious girl through whom sins are absolved.

As from some health-giving Lethe I shall draw kisses from you, who are alive with magnetism.

When the storm of vices wrought havoc in all my paths, then you appeared, a divinity,

a star of salvation above the bitter doom of ships; wherefore I shall hang my heart over your altars.

Piscina plena virtutis,
Fons æternæ juventutis,
Labris vocem redde mutis!

Quod erat spurcum, cremasti;
Quod rudius, exæquasti;
Quod debile, confirmasti.

In fame mea taberna,
In nocte mea lucerna,
Recte me semper guberna.

Adde nunc vires viribus,
Dulce balneum suavibus
Unguentatum odoribus!

Meos circa lumbos mica,
O castitatis lorica,
Aqua tincta seraphica;

Patera gemmis corusca,
Panis salsus, mollis esca,
Divinum vinum, Francisca!

Vessel of virtue, fountain of everlasting youth, I beg you to restore the voice to my speechless lips.

You have burnt my baseness all away, you have made smooth all that was rough and all that was weak you have made strong.

My tavern in hunger, my lantern in the night, guide me always in the paths of righteousness.

Fortify my strength, sweet bath of sublime aromas.

Circle my reins with your illumination, O girdle of chastity purged in the holy waters,

O chalice glittering with gems, O bread well salted, ambrosial manna, elixir of the gods, Francisca.

[Written (?) and published in 1857. *Fresh strings*: i.e. the Latin tongue. The Francisca in question has not been traced.]

LXI
À UNE DAME CRÉOLE

Au pays parfumé que le soleil caresse,
J'ai connu, sous un dais d'arbres tout empourprés
Et de palmiers d'où pleut sur les yeux la paresse,
Une dame créole aux charmes ignorés.

Son teint est pâle et chaud; la brune enchanteresse
A dans le cou des airs noblement maniérés;
Grande et svelte en marchant comme une chasseresse,
Son sourire est tranquille et ses yeux assurés.

Si vous alliez, Madame, au vrai pays de gloire,
Sur les bords de la Seine ou de la verte Loire,
Belle digne d'orner les antiques manoirs,

Vous feriez, à l'abri des ombreuses retraites,
Germer mille sonnets dans le cœur des poètes,
Que vos grands yeux rendraient plus soumis que vos noirs.

To a Creole Lady

In that perfumed land, by the sun caressed, I knew – beneath a canopy
of trees aglow with crimson, and palms which pour languor in your
eyes – a Creole lady whose charms are unknown to the world.

 She is of a pale and warm complexion; that dark-haired enchantress
has poses of aristocratic grace in the poise of her neck; tall and slender,
as she strides like a huntress, her smile is peaceful and her eyes assured.

 Should you go, Lady, to the true home of women's fame, to the
banks of the Seine or of the verdant Loire, your beauty might well
grace some ancient manor-house,

 and in many a shady arbour you would inspire a thousand sonnets
in the hearts of poets, whom your wide eyes would make more submis-
sive than your black slaves.

[1841. Baudelaire's first poem to be published, 1845,
under the name Baudelaire Dufays. FM 1857]

LXII

MŒSTA ET ERRABUNDA

Dis-moi, ton cœur parfois s'envole-t-il, Agathe,
Loin du noir océan de l'immonde cité,
Vers un autre océan où la splendeur éclate,
Bleu, clair, profond, ainsi que la virginité?
Dis-moi, ton cœur parfois s'envole-t-il, Agathe?

La mer, la vaste mer, console nos labeurs!
Quel démon a doté la mer, rauque chanteuse
Qu'accompagne l'immense orgue des vents grondeurs,
De cette fonction sublime de berceuse?
La mer, la vaste mer, console nos labeurs!

Emporte-moi, wagon! enlève-moi, frégate!
Loin! loin! ici la boue est faite de nos pleurs!
– Est-il vrai que parfois le triste cœur d'Agathe
Dise: Loin des remords, des crimes, des douleurs,
Emporte-moi, wagon, enlève-moi, frégate?

Sad and Restless

Tell me, Agatha, does your heart sometimes soar far away from the black ocean of the foul city, towards another ocean where splendour blazes blue and bright and deep, like virginity itself? Tell me, Agatha, does your heart sometimes soar away?

The sea, the enormous sea consoles us for our labours. What demon endowed the sea – that hoarse contralto accompanied by the mighty organ of the growling winds – with the supreme task of singing lullabies? The sea, the enormous sea consoles us for our labours.

Let some railway car take me away, some frigate kidnap me, far, far away! Here the city slime is made of our human tears. Is it true that sometimes Agatha's sad heart cries out: 'Far from remorses, crimes and sufferings, O railway car take me away, O frigate kidnap me?'

Comme vous êtes loin, paradis parfumé,
Où sous un clair azur tout n'est qu'amour et joie,
Où tout ce que l'on aime est digne d'être aimé,
Où dans la volupté pure le cœur se noie!
Comme vous êtes loin, paradis parfumé!

Mais le vert paradis des amours enfantines,
Les courses, les chansons, les baisers, les bouquets,
Les violons vibrant derrière les collines,
Avec les brocs de vin, le soir, dans les bosquets,
– Mais le vert paradis des amours enfantines,

L'innocent paradis, plein de plaisirs furtifs,
Est-il déjà plus loin que l'Inde et que la Chine?
Peut-on le rappeler avec des cris plaintifs,
Et l'animer encor d'une voix argentine,
L'innocent paradis plein de plaisirs furtifs?

How distant you are now, O perfumed paradise, where under the lucid azure all is love and joy; where all one loves is worthy to be loved; where the heart drowns in pure voluptuousness – how distant you are now, O perfumed paradise!

But the green paradise of childhood loves, with its romps and songs, its kisses and bouquets, the violins vibrating beyond the braes, the jugs of wine at twilight in the groves – O the green paradise of childhood loves,

the innocent paradise of secret pleasures – is it really farther away than India or China? Can we ever call it back with plaintive cries, make it alive again with silvery voices, that innocent paradise, full of furtive pleasures?

[RDM 1855. Identity of Agatha not known. FM 1857]

LXIII
LE REVENANT

Comme les anges à l'œil fauve,
Je reviendrai dans ton alcôve
Et vers toi glisserai sans bruit
Avec les ombres de la nuit;

Et je te donnerai, ma brune,
Des baisers froids comme la lune
Et des caresses de serpent
Autour d'une fosse rampant.

Quand viendra le matin livide,
Tu trouveras ma place vide,
Où jusqu'au soir il fera froid.

Comme d'autres par la tendresse,
Sur ta vie et sur ta jeunesse,
Moi, je veux régner par l'effroi.

The Ghost

Like angels with wild eyes I shall return to your bedside, slinking towards you noiselessly with the shadows of the night.

And then, my brown beauty, I'll give you kisses cold as moonlight, the caresses of serpents writhing round a grave.

When livid morning dawns you will find my place beside you empty, and there till evening falls the cold will stay.

As others rule by means of tenderness, I shall govern your youthful days and all your life, through terror.

[Attributed by Crépet-Blin to the Jeanne Duval cycle. FM 1857]

LXIV
SONNET D'AUTOMNE

Ils me disent, tes yeux, clairs comme le cristal:
«Pour toi, bizarre amant, quel est donc mon mérite?»
– Sois charmante et tais-toi! Mon cœur, que tout irrite,
Excepté la candeur de l'antique animal,

Ne veut pas te montrer son secret infernal,
Berceuse dont la main aux longs sommeils m'invite,
Ni sa noire légende avec la flamme écrite.
Je hais la passion et l'esprit me fait mal!

Aimons-nous doucement. L'Amour dans sa guérite,
Ténébreux, embusqué, bande son arc fatal.
Je connais les engins de son vieil arsenal:

Crime, horreur et folie! – Ô pâle marguerite!
Comme moi n'es-tu pas un soleil automnal,
Ô ma si blanche, ô ma si froide Marguerite?

Autumn Sonnet

They say to me, your eyes lucid as crystal, 'Strange lover, what merit do
you find in me?' – Be charming, and hold your tongue! My heart, on
which everything jars except the candour of the primitive animal,
 is unwilling to disclose its hellish secret or its black legend written
in flame, O sleep-giver whose hand invites me to long slumbers. I hate
all passion, and wit grates on me.
 Let us love each other gently. Love in his watch-tower, darkling in
ambush, is stretching his deadly bow. I know the weapons of his age-
old arsenal,
 which are crime and horror and madness. O my pale marguerite, are
you not, like me, an autumn sun, O my so white, my frigid Marguerite?

[Published 1859: the addressee unknown]

LXV
TRISTESSES DE LA LUNE

Ce soir, la lune rêve avec plus de paresse;
Ainsi qu'une beauté, sur de nombreux coussins,
Qui d'une main distraite et légère caresse
Avant de s'endormir le contour de ses seins,

Sur le dos satiné des molles avalanches,
Mourante, elle se livre aux longues pâmoisons,
Et promène ses yeux sur les visions blanches
Qui montent dans l'azur comme des floraisons.

Quand parfois sur ce globe, en sa langueur oisive,
Elle laisse filer une larme furtive,
Un poète pieux, ennemi du sommeil,

Dans le creux de sa main prend cette larme pâle,
Aux reflets irisés comme un fragment d'opale,
Et la met dans son cœur loin des yeux du soleil.

Sorrows of the Moon

Tonight, the Moon is more languidly than usual dreaming. Like some lovely woman reclining on her pile of cushions, who caresses the curve of her breasts with her light, discreet hand before she sleeps,

on the satined pillow of soft drifts of cloud, she dies away into deep swoons, and her eyes sweep the white visions which rise like opening flowers into the azure sky.

When sometimes in her idle languor she lets fall a secret tear upon our globe, a pious poet, the enemy of sleep,

takes in the hollow of his hand that pale tear, veined with glinting hues like a chip of opal, and stores it in his heart, far from the sun's eyes.

[Mentioned in a letter to Ancelle, 1850. FM 1857]

LXVI

LES CHATS

Les amoureux fervents et les savants austères
Aiment également, dans leur mûre saison,
Les chats puissants et doux, orgueil de la maison,
Qui comme eux sont frileux et comme eux sédentaires.

Amis de la science et de la volupté,
Ils cherchent le silence et l'horreur des ténèbres;
L'Érèbe les eût pris pour ses coursiers funèbres,
S'ils pouvaient au servage incliner leur fierté.

Ils prennent en songeant les nobles attitudes
Des grands sphinx allongés au fond des solitudes,
Qui semblent s'endormir dans un rêve sans fin;

Leurs reins féconds sont pleins d'étincelles magiques,
Et des parcelles d'or, ainsi qu'un sable fin,
Étoilent vaguement leurs prunelles mystiques.

Cats

Fervent lovers and austere scholars share the same love, in their riper years, for powerful but gentle cats, the pride of the household, who like them are sedentary and sensitive to draughts.

The friends of learning and sensuality, cats ever seek silence and dreadful night; Erebus would have employed them as messengers of gloom, could they lower their pride to slavery.

They assume, when their minds wander, the majestic poses of those colossal sphinxes who stretch their limbs in the realms of solitude, and who appear to be sleeping in an eternal dream.

Magical sparks teem in their fertile loins, and particles of gold, like delicate grains of sand, vaguely fleck their mystic pupils with stars.

[An early poem, published 1847, 1851, 1853. FM 1857]

LXVII
LES HIBOUX

Sous les ifs noirs qui les abritent,
Les hiboux se tiennent rangés,
Ainsi que des dieux étrangers,
Dardant leur œil rouge. Ils méditent.

Sans remuer ils se tiendront
Jusqu'à l'heure mélancolique
Où, poussant le soleil oblique,
Les ténèbres s'établiront.

Leur attitude au sage enseigne
Qu'il faut en ce monde qu'il craigne
Le tumulte et le mouvement;

L'homme ivre d'une ombre qui passe
Porte toujours le châtiment
D'avoir voulu changer de place.

Owls

In the shelter of the black yews, the owls perch in a row like alien gods, darting their red eyes. They are meditating.

They will stand there motionless until the melancholy hour when, thrusting down the slanting sun, the shadows settle into place.

Their attitude teaches the wise man that in this world all tumult and movement are to be feared;

for man, intoxicated by every fleeting shadow, is always punished for his desire to roam.

[1851. FM 1857]

LXVIII
LA PIPE

Je suis la pipe d'un auteur;
On voit, à contempler ma mine
D'Abyssinienne ou de Cafrine,
Que mon maître est un grand fumeur.

Quand il est comblé de douleur,
Je fume comme la chaumine
Où se prépare la cuisine
Pour le retour du laboureur.

J'enlace et je berce son âme
Dans le réseau mobile et bleu
Qui monte de ma bouche en feu,

Et je roule un puissant dictame
Qui charme son cœur et guérit
De ses fatigues son esprit.

The Pipe

I am an author's pipe. You can see, by a glance at my complexion, as jet as any Abyssinian or Kaffir woman's, that my master is a heavy smoker.

When he is overcome with grief, then I puff smoke, like a cottage in which supper is being cooked for the ploughman when he comes home from his toil.

I embrace and lull his soul in the hovering net of blueness that floats up from my fiery mouth,

and make rings of pungent balm that gladdens his heart and cures his mind of every strain.

[FM 1857]

LXIX
LA MUSIQUE

La musique souvent me prend comme une mer !
 Vers ma pâle étoile,
Sous un plafond de brume ou dans un vaste éther,
 Je mets à la voile ;

La poitrine en avant et les poumons gonflés
 Comme de la toile,
J'escalade le dos des flots amoncelés
 Que la nuit me voile ;

Je sens vibrer en moi toutes les passions
 D'un vaisseau qui souffre ;
Le bon vent, la tempête et ses convulsions

 Sur l'immense gouffre
Me bercent. D'autres fois, calme plat, grand miroir
 De mon désespoir !

Music

Music often sweeps me away like a sea, and under a canopy of mist or through a vast ether, I set sail towards my faint star.

 Breasting the swell, with my lungs dilated like a ship's canvas, I ride up the backs of the piling waves veiled from me by the dark;

 I feel all the passions of a groaning ship vibrate within me; the fair wind and the tempest's rage

cradle me on the fathomless deep – at other times it brings flat calm, the gigantic mirror of my own despair.

[Sent to Gautier 1852. FM 1857. Dubiously related
by some critics to Wagner, Beethoven etc.]

LXX

SÉPULTURE

Si par une nuit lourde et sombre
Un bon chrétien, par charité,
Derrière quelque vieux décombre
Enterre votre corps vanté,

À l'heure où les chastes étoiles
Ferment leurs yeux appesantis,
L'araignée y fera ses toiles,
Et la vipère ses petits;

Vous entendrez toute l'année
Sur votre tête condamnée
Les cris lamentables des loups

Et des sorcières faméliques,
Les ébats des vieillards lubriques
Et les complots des noirs filous.

A Grave

If on some sullen darksome night a good christian is charitable enough
to bury your precious carcass at the back of some old ruin,
 at the hour when the chaste stars close their heavy eyes, the spider
will spin its webs there, and the viper hatch its brood.
 Then all year long, over your condemned head you will hear the
mournful howling of the wolves
 and starving witches, the obscenities of lewd old men, and shady
gangsters plotting crimes.

[FM 1857. Entitled 'Sépulture d'un poète maudit' –
a damned poet's grave – 1868. Without evidence,
some critics say it refers to an actress.]

LXXI
UNE GRAVURE FANTASTIQUE

Ce spectre singulier n'a pour toute toilette,
Grotesquement campé sur son front de squelette,
Qu'un diadème affreux sentant le carnaval.
Sans éperons, sans fouet, il essouffle un cheval,
Fantôme comme lui, rosse apocalyptique,
Qui bave des naseaux comme un épileptique.
Au travers de l'espace ils s'enfoncent tous deux,
Et foulent l'infini d'un sabot hasardeux.
Le cavalier promène un sabre qui flamboie
Sur les foules sans nom que sa monture broie,
Et parcourt, comme un prince inspectant sa maison,
Le cimetière immense et froid, sans horizon,
Où gisent, aux lueurs d'un soleil blanc et terne,
Les peuples de l'histoire ancienne et moderne.

A Fantastic Engraving

This spectacular wraith is wearing nothing but a garish crown of the carnival sort, set grotesquely awry on his skull. With neither spur nor whip, he goads his panting horse along, a ghost like himself, a hack of the Apocalypse which foams at the nostrils like an epileptic. They go galloping through Space together, trampling the infinite void with merciless hooves. The horseman is waving a sabre of fire over the nameless hordes which his mount is grinding underfoot. Like some prince surveying his domain, he is charging now across a vast cold graveyard which stretches beyond the horizon, where under the sickly rays of a leaden sun, the nations of ancient and modern history lie buried.

[A note in 1857 gives 'an engraving by Mortimer' (1741–99).
Traced by F. W. Leakey to a work by Joseph Haynes.
Manuscript evidence dates the poem 1843–7.]

LXXII
LE MORT JOYEUX

Dans une terre grasse et pleine d'escargots
Je veux creuser moi-même une fosse profonde,
Où je puisse à loisir étaler mes vieux os
Et dormir dans l'oubli comme un requin dans l'onde.

Je hais les testaments et je hais les tombeaux;
Plutôt que d'implorer une larme du monde,
Vivant, j'aimerais mieux inviter les corbeaux
À saigner tous les bouts de ma carcasse immonde.

Ô vers! noirs compagnons sans oreille et sans yeux,
Voyez venir à vous un mort libre et joyeux;
Philosophes viveurs, fils de la pourriture,

À travers ma ruine allez donc sans remords,
Et dites-moi s'il est encor quelque torture
Pour ce vieux corps sans âme et mort parmi les morts!

Dead But Happy

In a rich soil full of snails I want to dig a deep grave for myself, where
I can stretch my old bones at leisure and sleep in oblivion like a shark
in the sea.

I hate last wills and testaments, and I hate tombs. Rather than beg a
tear from the world, I'd prefer, still alive, to invite the crows to drink
blood from every tatter of my loathsome carcass.

O worms, black cronies without eyes or ears, behold: a free and
happy dead man is on his way to you, you gourmet-philosophers,
putrefaction's sons:

wind through my ruins, then, without remorse, and tell me if there
is still some other torture left for this old body, soulless and dead among
the dead.

[Published 1851 under the title 'Le Spleen'. FM 1857]

LXXIII
LE TONNEAU DE LA HAINE

La Haine est le tonneau des pâles Danaïdes;
La Vengeance éperdue aux bras rouges et forts
A beau précipiter dans ses ténèbres vides
De grands seaux pleins du sang et des larmes des morts,

Le Démon fait des trous secrets à ces abîmes,
Par où fuiraient mille ans de sueurs et d'efforts,
Quand même elle saurait ranimer ses victimes,
Et pour les pressurer ressusciter leurs corps.

La Haine est un ivrogne au fond d'une taverne,
Qui sent toujours la soif naître de la liqueur
Et se multiplier comme l'hydre de Lerne.

— Mais les buveurs heureux connaissent leur vainqueur,
Et la Haine est vouée à ce sort lamentable
De ne pouvoir jamais s'endormir sous la table.

The Cask of Hatred

Hate is a Sisyphean task [*lit.* the cask of the pale Danaïds]. Furious Revenge with her strong red arms in vain pours huge pails of blood and the tears of the dead into her empty blackness,

for the Demon drills hidden holes in it below, through which the sweats and tears of a thousand years could easily escape, even if Hate could revive her victims and resurrect their bodies only to crush them dry again.

Hate is a drunkard in the pit of a pothouse, who feels his thirst endlessly renewed by his liquor, multiplying like the Lernaean hydra's hundred heads.

But the fortunate tipplers know when they are beaten; whereas Hate is doomed to the miserable fate of never being able to nap under the table.

- [Published 1851, part of the *Limbo* series]

LXXIV
LA CLOCHE FÊLÉE

Il est amer et doux, pendant les nuits d'hiver,
D'écouter, près du feu qui palpite et qui fume,
Les souvenirs lointains lentement s'élever
Au bruit des carillons qui chantent dans la brume.

Bienheureuse la cloche au gosier vigoureux
Qui, malgré sa vieillesse, alerte et bien portante,
Jette fidèlement son cri religieux,
Ainsi qu'un vieux soldat qui veille sous la tente!

Moi, mon âme est fêlée, et lorsqu'en ses ennuis
Elle veut de ses chants peupler l'air froid des nuits,
Il arrive souvent que sa voix affaiblie

Semble le râle épais d'un blessé qu'on oublie
Au bord d'un lac de sang, sous un grand tas de morts,
Et qui meurt, sans bouger, dans d'immenses efforts.

The Cracked Bell

It is bitter-sweet, of a winter's night, sitting by the crackling smoking fire, to listen to distant memories which slowly rise to the sound of the chiming angelus singing through the fog.

Happy is the strong-throated bell which despite its great age is still alert and hale, and faithfully voices its pious call, like some old veteran on watch in his tent.

But as for me, my soul is cracked and when, with all its cares, it would fain fill the night's chill air with its hymns, most often its faded voice

sounds like the thick death-rattle of a wounded soldier, who lies forgotten near a pool of blood, beneath a great pile of dead, and who dies, unable to stir despite his tremendous efforts.

[Published 1851 under the title 'Le Spleen',
also in RDM 1855 and FM 1857]

LXXV

SPLEEN

Pluviôse, irrité contre la ville entière,
De son urne à grands flots verse un froid ténébreux
Aux pâles habitants du voisin cimetière
Et la mortalité sur les faubourgs brumeux.

Mon chat sur le carreau cherchant une litière
Agite sans repos son corps maigre et galeux;
L'âme d'un vieux poète erre dans la gouttière
Avec la triste voix d'un fantôme frileux.

Le bourdon se lamente, et la bûche enfumée
Accompagne en fausset la pendule enrhumée,
Cependant qu'en un jeu plein de sales parfums,

Héritage fatal d'une vieille hydropique,
Le beau valet de cœur et la dame de pique
Causent sinistrement de leurs amours défunts.

Spleen

Pluviôse [the rain-month], vexed with the entire city, is pouring great
waves of Stygian cold on the pale inmates of the nearby graveyard, and
pouring the essence of death on the fogbound suburbs.

My cat, trying to bed down on the floor, is feverishly jerking its
skinny, mangy body. An old poet's soul is walking the tiles, lifting a
voice as miserable as a shivering ghost's.

The master-bell is groaning and the smoking log's falsetto whistles
in time with the rheumy wheezing clock, while in a smelly pack of
cards –

the deadly legacy of a dropsical old hag – the dapper Knave of Hearts
and the Queen of Spades chat sinisterly about their perished loves.

[One of the *Limbo* poems, 1851. FM 1857]

[Pluviôse was a month (mid-January to mid-February) in the
Republican Calendar of 1793. The name is from the Latin
pluviosus, rainy, and the god of rain, Jupiter Pluvius. – Ed.]

LXXVI
SPLEEN

J'ai plus de souvenirs que si j'avais mille ans.

Un gros meuble à tiroirs encombré de bilans,
De vers, de billets doux, de procès, de romances,
Avec de lourds cheveux roulés dans des quittances,
Cache moins de secrets que mon triste cerveau.
C'est une pyramide, un immense caveau,
Qui contient plus de morts que la fosse commune.
– Je suis un cimetière abhorré de la lune,
Où comme des remords se traînent de longs vers
Qui s'acharnent toujours sur mes morts les plus chers.
Je suis un vieux boudoir plein de roses fanées,
Où gît tout un fouillis de modes surannées,
Où les pastels plaintifs et les pâles Boucher,
Seuls, respirent l'odeur d'un flacon débouché.

Rien n'égale en longueur les boiteuses journées,
Quand sous les lourds flocons des neigeuses années

Spleen

I am fuller of memories than if I had lived a thousand years.

Not even an enormous chest of drawers stuffed with accounts and verses, love-letters and law-suits, drawing-room ballads, and heavy plaits of hair rolled in receipts, has fewer secrets to hide than has my unhappy brain. It is a pyramid, a vast burial-vault, more packed with dead than any charnel-house.

I am a graveyard that the Moon abhors, in which long worms crawl like remorses, always battening on those dead I hold most dear. I am a bygone boudoir full of faded roses, in which a medley of old-fashioned dresses lie scattered everywhere, with only the plaintive pastels and pale Boucher canvases to breathe the fragrance of a scent-bottle left uncorked.

Nothing could be as long-drawn-out as the limping days, when under the heavy flakes of the snowy years, boredom, the fruit of sullen

L'ennui, fruit de la morne incuriosité,
Prend les proportions de l'immortalité.
– Désormais tu n'es plus, ô matière vivante!
Qu'un granit entouré d'une vague épouvante,
Assoupi dans le fond d'un Sahara brumeux;
Un vieux sphinx ignoré du monde insoucieux,
Oublié sur la carte, et dont l'humeur farouche
Ne chante qu'aux rayons du soleil qui se couche.

indifference, takes on the proportions of immortality. Henceforth, O
living matter, you are but a granite form shrouded in vague horror, list-
lessly sunken in the depths of a mist-bound Sahara, an old Sphinx
unknown to the uncaring world, forgotten on the map, and whose
grim humour is to sing only in the rays of the setting sun.

[A *Limbo* poem, 1851. FM 1857]

LXXVII
SPLEEN

Je suis comme le roi d'un pays pluvieux,
Riche, mais impuissant, jeune et pourtant très vieux,
Qui, de ses précepteurs méprisant les courbettes,
S'ennuie avec ses chiens comme avec d'autres bêtes.
Rien ne peut l'égayer, ni gibier, ni faucon,
Ni son peuple mourant en face du balcon.
Du bouffon favori la grotesque ballade
Ne distrait plus le front de ce cruel malade;
Son lit fleurdelisé se transforme en tombeau,
Et les dames d'atour, pour qui tout prince est beau,
Ne savent plus trouver d'impudique toilette
Pour tirer un souris de ce jeune squelette.
Le savant qui lui fait de l'or n'a jamais pu
De son être extirper l'élément corrompu,
Et dans ces bains de sang qui des Romains nous viennent,
Et dont sur leurs vieux jours les puissants se souviennent,
Il n'a su réchauffer ce cadavre hébété
Où coule au lieu de sang l'eau verte du Léthé.

Spleen

I am like the monarch of some rainy kingdom, rich but impotent, young but senile, and who, despising the bowing and scraping of his tutors, is bored with his hounds, as with all other creatures.

Nothing can cheer him, neither game nor falcon, nor his subjects who come to die beneath his balcony. His favourite jester's drollest ballad can no longer smooth the cruelly sick man's brow; his couch, adorned with fleurs-de-lys, becomes his tomb, and the ladies-in-waiting, who find all princes handsome, can invent no new wanton costume to draw a smile from this youthful skeleton.

The alchemist who fabricates his gold has never managed to eliminate the corrupt element from his being, and in those blood-baths which we inherit from the Romans, and which men of power recall in their declining days, he has failed to rewarm that stupefied living corpse, in which not blood but Lethe's green tide flows.

[1857]

LXXVIII
SPLEEN

Quand le ciel bas et lourd pèse comme un couvercle
Sur l'esprit gémissant en proie aux longs ennuis,
Et que de l'horizon embrassant tout le cercle
Il nous verse un jour noir plus triste que les nuits;

Quand la terre est changée en un cachot humide,
Où l'Espérance, comme une chauve-souris,
S'en va battant les murs de son aile timide
Et se cognant la tête à des plafonds pourris;

Quand la pluie étalant ses immenses traînées
D'une vaste prison imite les barreaux,
Et qu'un peuple muet d'infâmes araignées
Vient tendre ses filets au fond de nos cerveaux,

Spleen

When the low, leaden sky weighs like a lid on the groaning mind
tortured by endless cares, and when, embracing the whole ring of the
horizon it pours on us dark day more sad than any night;

when the earth is transformed into a dripping prison-cell in which
Hope reels like a bat bruising its timid wings against the walls and
knocking its head against the rotted ceilings;

when the rain, fanning out its long streaks of water, shapes itself into
the bars of an enormous gaol, and a silent horde of loathsome spiders
come and weave their webs inside our brains;

Des cloches tout à coup sautent avec furie
Et lancent vers le ciel un affreux hurlement,
Ainsi que des esprits errants et sans patrie
Qui se mettent à geindre opiniâtrement.

— Et de longs corbillards, sans tambours ni musique,
Défilent lentement dans mon âme; l'Espoir,
Vaincu, pleure, et l'Angoisse atroce, despotique,
Sur mon crâne incliné plante son drapeau noir.

then suddenly the bells swing angrily and hurl their horrible howl
into the sky, like wandering homeless spirits beginning their endless
wailing,
— and long trails of mourners and hearses, with neither drums nor
music, move slowly in procession through my soul, and Hope in its
defeat bursts into tears, and the cruel tyrant, Anguish, plants her black
flag on my bowed head.

[FM 1857]

LXXIX
OBSESSION

Grands bois, vous m'effrayez comme des cathédrales;
Vous hurlez comme l'orgue; et dans nos cœurs maudits,
Chambres d'éternel deuil où vibrent de vieux râles,
Répondent les échos de vos *De profundis*.

Je te hais, Océan! tes bonds et tes tumultes,
Mon esprit les retrouve en lui; ce rire amer
De l'homme vaincu, plein de sanglots et d'insultes,
Je l'entends dans le rire énorme de la mer.

Comme tu me plairais, ô nuit! sans ces étoiles
Dont la lumière parle un langage connu!
Car je cherche le vide, et le noir, et le nu!

Mais les ténèbres sont elles-mêmes des toiles
Où vivent, jaillissant de mon œil par milliers,
Des êtres disparus aux regards familiers.

Obsession

Vast woods, you terrify me like cathedrals. You roar like an organ, and in our condemned hearts – those chambers of eternal mourning in which death-rattles vibrate from gone times – the echoes of your *De profundis* reverberate responses.

Ocean, I hate you, whose leaping waves and pandemonium battle in my own mind. In the enormous laughter of the sea I hear the bitter laughter of man in his defeat, his sobs and blasphemies.

How you would please me, O Night, without those stars whose brilliance speaks a language I understand! For my quest is for the bleak, the black, the bare.

But the shadows themselves are canvases in which, leaping in their thousands from my eye, live vanished beings with their familiar gaze.

[Published 1860. FM 1861]

LXXX
LE GOÛT DU NÉANT

Morne esprit, autrefois amoureux de la lutte,
L'Espoir, dont l'éperon attisait ton ardeur,
Ne veut plus t'enfourcher! Couche-toi sans pudeur,
Vieux cheval dont le pied à chaque obstacle bute.

Résigne-toi, mon cœur; dors ton sommeil de brute.

Esprit vaincu, fourbu! Pour toi, vieux maraudeur,
L'amour n'a plus de goût, non plus que la dispute;
Adieu donc, chants du cuivre et soupirs de la flûte!
Plaisirs, ne tentez plus un cœur sombre et boudeur!

Le Printemps adorable a perdu son odeur!

Et le Temps m'engloutit minute par minute,
Comme la neige immense un corps pris de roideur;
Je contemple d'en haut le globe en sa rondeur
Et je n'y cherche plus l'abri d'une cahute.

Avalanche, veux-tu m'emporter dans ta chute?

The Longing for Nothingness

Disconsolate mind, once amorous of the struggle, now Hope whose
spur used to add fuel to your ardour no longer desires to mount you. Lay
you down without shame, old nag whose foot now stumbles at every
obstacle.

Resign yourself, my heart, and sleep the sleep of the brute.

O vanquished worn-out mind, for you, old prowler, there's no more
pleasure in loving than in dispute. Farewell, then, brassy melodies and the
sighings of the flute! Pleasures, entice no more this sombre, sullen heart!

Adorable Spring has lost its perfume now.

Time is engulfing me, minute by minute, as the interminable snow
swallows a stiffening body. I gaze down from on high on the roundness
of the globe, and seek no hut for shelter any more.

O avalanche, will you take me with you when you fall?

[Published 1859. FM 1861]

LXXXI
ALCHIMIE DE LA DOULEUR

L'un t'éclaire avec son ardeur,
L'autre en toi met son deuil, Nature!
Ce qui dit à l'un: Sépulture!
Dit à l'autre: Vie et splendeur!

Hermès inconnu qui m'assistes
Et qui toujours m'intimidas,
Tu me rends l'égal de Midas,
Le plus triste des alchimistes;

Par toi je change l'or en fer
Et le paradis en enfer;
Dans le suaire des nuages

Je découvre un cadavre cher,
Et sur les célestes rivages
Je bâtis de grands sarcophages.

The Alchemy of Grief

One man illuminates you with his ardour's light; another sets his grief
in you, O Nature. What spells the Grave to one, means Life and splen-
dour to the other.

Unknown Hermes, who are my helpmate, but of whom I ever went
in fear, you make me equal in skill to Midas, yet the unhappiest of all
alchemists.

For through you I transmute gold to iron, and Paradise into an
Inferno; in the winding-sheet of the clouds

I find the corpse of what I loved, and build colossal sarcophagi on
the shores of heaven.

[Published 1860. FM 1861]

LXXXII
HORREUR SYMPATHIQUE

De ce ciel bizarre et livide,
Tourmenté comme ton destin,
Quels pensers dans ton âme vide
Descendent? réponds, libertin.

– Insatiablement avide
De l'obscur et de l'incertain,
Je ne geindrai pas comme Ovide
Chassé du paradis latin.

Cieux déchirés comme des grèves,
En vous se mire mon orgueil;
Vos vastes nuages en deuil

Sont les corbillards de mes rêves,
Et vos lueurs sont le reflet
De l'Enfer où mon cœur se plaît.

Sympathetic Horror

From that grotesque and livid sky, as tortured as your destiny, what thoughts descend into your empty soul? Freethinker, reply.

– Insatiably hungering for whatever is obscure and uncertain, I shall not whimper like Ovid when he was cast out from the Latin paradise.

Skies split asunder like sea-shores, my pride reflects itself in you; your vast mourning clouds

are the hearses of my dreams, your glimmering rays reflect the Inferno in which my heart delights.

[Published 1860. FM 1861]

LXXXIII
L'HÉAUTONTIMOROUMÉNOS

À J. G. F.

Je te frapperai sans colère
Et sans haine, comme un boucher,
Comme Moïse le rocher!
Et je ferai de ta paupière,

Pour abreuver mon Sahara,
Jaillir les eaux de la souffrance.
Mon désir gonflé d'espérance
Sur tes pleurs salés nagera

Comme un vaisseau qui prend le large,
Et dans mon cœur qu'ils soûleront
Tes chers sanglots retentiront
Comme un tambour qui bat la charge!

Ne suis-je pas un faux accord
Dans la divine symphonie,
Grâce à la vorace Ironie
Qui me secoue et qui me mord?

Heautontimoroumenos

THE SELF-PUNISHER

for J. G. F.

I shall strike you without anger or hatred, like a butcher, as Moses struck the rock, and from your eyelids,
 to slake my Sahara's thirst, I shall make the springs of suffering gush forth. My desire, swollen with hope, will swim in your salt tears
 like a ship faring out to sea; while in my heart, elated by your weeping, your sobs which I love will resound like a drum beating to the attack.
 – Am I not a dissonant chord in the divine symphony, thanks to the insatiable Irony that shakes and bites me?

Elle est dans ma voix, la criarde!
C'est tout mon sang, ce poison noir!
Je suis le sinistre miroir
Où la mégère se regarde.

Je suis la plaie et le couteau!
Je suis le soufflet et la joue!
Je suis les membres et la roue,
Et la victime et le bourreau!

Je suis de mon cœur le vampire,
– Un de ces grands abandonnés
Au rire éternel condamnés,
Et qui ne peuvent plus sourire!

That spitfire irony is in my voice and all my blood is her black poison: I am the sinister glass in which the shrew looks on herself.

I am the wound and the knife, I am the blow and the cheek, the limbs and the rack, the victim and the executioner.

I am the vampire of my own heart, one of the totally abandoned, condemned to eternal laughter but who can never smile again.

[The title is from the Latin playwright Terence.
The dedicatee is unidentified. 1855, FM 1857]

LXXXIV
L'IRRÉMÉDIABLE

I

Une Idée, une Forme, un Être
Parti de l'azur et tombé
Dans un Styx bourbeux et plombé
Où nul œil du Ciel ne pénètre;

Un Ange, imprudent voyageur
Qu'a tenté l'amour du difforme,
Au fond d'un cauchemar énorme
Se débattant comme un nageur,

Et luttant, angoisses funèbres!
Contre un gigantesque remous
Qui va chantant comme les fous
Et pirouettant dans les ténèbres;

Un malheureux ensorcelé
Dans ses tâtonnements futiles,
Pour fuir d'un lieu plein de reptiles,
Cherchant la lumière et la clé;

The Irremediable

I

An Idea, a Form, a Being – lapsed from the azure and fallen into the slough of a leaden Styx no Heavenly eye can ever penetrate:

an Angel, an unwary traveller tempted by a lust for the deformed, lashing out like a swimmer in the depths of an enormous nightmare,

struggling in funereal anguish against a gigantic undertow which goes singing like a horde of madmen and pirouetting through the gloom:

an unfortunate man under a spell, futilely groping to escape from a place full of reptiles, searching for the light, the key:

Un damné descendant sans lampe,
Au bord d'un gouffre dont l'odeur
Trahit l'humide profondeur,
D'éternels escaliers sans rampe,

Où veillent des monstres visqueux
Dont les larges yeux de phosphore
Font une nuit plus noire encore
Et ne rendent visibles qu'eux;

Un navire pris dans le pôle,
Comme en un piège de cristal,
Cherchant par quel détroit fatal
Il est tombé dans cette geôle;

— Emblèmes nets, tableau parfait
D'une fortune irrémédiable,
Qui donne à penser que le Diable
Fait toujours bien tout ce qu'il fait!

a damned man, descending lampless down the edge of a pit whose
stench hints at its watery depths, descending endless banisterless stairs
where slimy monsters glare with great phosphorescent eyes that
deepen the night's dark and make naught but themselves visible:
a ship caught at the arctic pole as if in a crystal trap, seeking the fatal
passage through which it foell into this prison:
— all these are plain emblems, a perfect picture of an irremediable
fate, which makes one reflect that Satan makes a perfect job of all he
does.

II

Tête-à-tête sombre et limpide
Qu'un cœur devenu son miroir!
Puits de Vérité, clair et noir,
Où tremble une étoile livide,

Un phare ironique, infernal,
Flambeau des grâces sataniques,
Soulagement et gloire uniques,
— La conscience dans le Mal!

II

What a sombre but lucid exchange there is, in a heart that has become its own mirror — a well of truth, clear though black, in which there trembles a livid star,

an ironic, infernal beacon, a torch of satanic graces, unique relief and glory — our consciousness in Evil!

[FM 1857]

LXXXV
L'HORLOGE

Horloge! dieu sinistre, effrayant, impassible,
Dont le doigt nous menace et nous dit: «*Souviens-toi!*
Les vibrantes Douleurs dans ton cœur plein d'effroi
Se planteront bientôt comme dans une cible;

«Le Plaisir vaporeux fuira vers l'horizon
Ainsi qu'une sylphide au fond de la coulisse;
Chaque instant te dévore un morceau du délice
À chaque homme accordé pour toute sa saison.

«Trois mille six cents fois par heure, la Seconde
Chuchote: *Souviens-toi!* – Rapide, avec sa voix
D'insecte, Maintenant dit: Je suis Autrefois,
Et j'ai pompé ta vie avec ma trompe immonde!

«*Remember! Souviens-toi*, prodigue! *Esto memor!*
(Mon gosier de métal parle toutes les langues.)
Les minutes, mortel folâtre, sont des gangues
Qu'il ne faut pas lâcher sans en extraire l'or!

The Clock

The Clock is a sinister, terrifying, inscrutable god, whose finger threatens us and says '*Remember!* – throbbing pains will soon be stabbing your cringing heart as if it were a target.

'Pleasure will vanish away like a cloud over the horizon as a sylph flits into the stage's wings. Every instant devours a grain of that delight which every man is granted for the season of his life.

'Three thousand and six hundred times an hour the Second whispers, *Remember!* Swift, with its insect's voice, Now says, "Already I am Then, I have drained your life with my loathsome suckers!"

'*Remember! Souviens-toi!* O spendthrift, *Esto memor!* – My metal throat can speak all languages. – The Minutes, playful mortal, are seams that should not be abandoned before you have extracted all their gold.

«*Souviens-toi* que le Temps est un joueur avide
Qui gagne sans tricher, à tout coup! c'est la loi.
Le jour décroît; la nuit augmente; *souviens-toi!*
Le gouffre a toujours soif; la clepsydre se vide.

«Tantôt sonnera l'heure où le divin Hasard,
Où l'auguste Vertu, ton épouse encor vierge,
Où le Repentir même (oh! la dernière auberge!),
Où tout te dira: Meurs, vieux lâche! il est trop tard!»

'Time is a greedy gambler who at every turn of the wheel wins
without cheating. Such is the Law! The Day is declining and Night
waxes fat; *do not forget!* The thirst of the pit is endless, the water-clock
runs dry.

'The hour will shortly strike when divine Chance or august Virtue
– your still-virgin spouse! – or even Repentance, the last tavern of all,
in fact everything will say to you – "Die, old faint-hearted coward – for
now it is too late!"'

[1860, FM 1861. See the prose-poem 'La Chambre double']

Tableaux parisiens

LXXXVI
PAYSAGE

Je veux, pour composer chastement mes églogues,
Coucher auprès du ciel, comme les astrologues,
Et, voisin des clochers, écouter en rêvant
Leurs hymnes solennels emportés par le vent.
Les deux mains au menton, du haut de ma mansarde,
Je verrai l'atelier qui chante et qui bavarde;
Les tuyaux, les clochers, ces mâts de la cité,
Et les grands ciels qui font rêver d'éternité.

Il est doux, à travers les brumes, de voir naître
L'étoile dans l'azur, la lampe à la fenêtre,
Les fleuves de charbon monter au firmament
Et la lune verser son pâle enchantement.
Je verrai les printemps, les étés, les automnes;
Et quand viendra l'hiver aux neiges monotones,

PARISIAN SCENES

Townscape

PARISIAN SCENES

Townscape

Chastely to compose my eclogues, I want to have my bed beside the
sky, as astrologers do; I want to lodge beside the belfries and dreamily
listen to their solemn songs being borne away on the wind. With my
chin cupped in my hands, from my lofty attic I shall watch the work-
shop full of singing and gossip, and the chimney-pots and steeples, the
city's masts, and the wide skies that make one dream of eternity.

It is pleasant, through the mists, to watch the star being born in the
blueness of the sky, or the lamp appearing at a window, or the streams
of coal-smoke floating heavenwards, and the Moon pouring out her
pale enchantment. There I shall see the springs and summers and
autumns through, and when winter comes with its monotonous snows,

Je fermerai partout portières et volets
Pour bâtir dans la nuit mes féeriques palais.
Alors je rêverai des horizons bleuâtres,
Des jardins, des jets d'eau pleurant dans les albâtres,
Des baisers, des oiseaux chantant soir et matin,
Et tout ce que l'Idylle a de plus enfantin.
L'Émeute, tempêtant vainement à ma vitre,
Ne fera pas lever mon front de mon pupitre;
Car je serai plongé dans cette volupté
D'évoquer le Printemps avec ma volonté,
De tirer un soleil de mon cœur, et de faire
De mes pensers brûlants une tiède atmosphère.

I shall close all my doors and shutters to build my faery palaces in the night.

Then I shall dream of blue-tinted horizons, and gardens, and fountains shedding their tears on alabaster forms. I'll dream of kisses, of birds at song at twilight and dawn, and of all that is most unsophisticated in the Idyll. The riots of the mob, vainly beating on my windowpane, will not make me lift my head from my desk; for I shall be deep in the sensuous pleasure of evoking the Springtime at will, drawing a sun out of my own heart, making a genial atmosphere with my burning thoughts.

[This poem shows the influence of Chénier ('mon Louvre est sous le toit') and is no doubt an early work. Crépet-Blin suggests 1848, taking *émeute* to refer to the revolution. FM 1857]

LXXXVII

LE SOLEIL

Le long du vieux faubourg, où pendent aux masures
Les persiennes, abri des secrètes luxures,
Quand le soleil cruel frappe à traits redoublés
Sur la ville et les champs, sur les toits et les blés,
Je vais m'exercer seul à ma fantasque escrime,
Flairant dans tous les coins les hasards de la rime,
Trébuchant sur les mots comme sur les pavés,
Heurtant parfois des vers depuis longtemps rêvés.

Ce père nourricier, ennemi des chloroses,
Éveille dans les champs les vers comme les roses;
Il fait s'évaporer les soucis vers le ciel,
Et remplit les cerveaux et les ruches de miel.
C'est lui qui rajeunit les porteurs de béquilles
Et les rend gais et doux comme des jeunes filles,
Et commande aux moissons de croître et de mûrir
Dans le cœur immortel qui toujours veut fleurir!

The Sun

Through the old suburb, where the venetian blinds hang at the windows of tumbledown houses, concealing furtive lecheries, when the cruel sun strikes blow after blow on the city and the meadows, roofs and cornfields, I go practising my fantastic fencing all alone, scenting a chance rhyme in every corner, stumbling on words as against cobblestones, sometimes striking on verses I had long dreamt of.

This providing father, enemy of anaemias, wakens verses as well as roses in the fields; he makes our cares vanish into the sky; he fills our brains and all the hives with honey. It is he who gives youth to those who hobble on crutches, and makes them gay and gentle as young girls; he bids the crops to grow and ripen in the immortal heart that ever longs to flower again.

Quand, ainsi qu'un poète, il descend dans les villes,
Il ennoblit le sort des choses les plus viles,
Et s'introduit en roi, sans bruit et sans valets,
Dans tous les hôpitaux et dans tous les palais.

When, like a poet he comes down into cities, he ennobles the lot of
even the vilest things, and, like a monarch, silent and unattended, he
enters all the hospitals and palaces.

[An early work. FM 1857]

LXXXVIII
À UNE MENDIANTE ROUSSE

Blanche fille aux cheveux roux,
Dont la robe par ses trous
Laisse voir la pauvreté
 Et la beauté,

Pour moi, poète chétif,
Ton jeune corps maladif,
Plein de taches de rousseur,
 A sa douceur.

Tu portes plus galamment
Qu'une reine de roman
Ses cothurnes de velours
 Tes sabots lourds.

Au lieu d'un haillon trop court,
Qu'un superbe habit de cour
Traîne à plis bruyants et longs
 Sur tes talons;

To a Redheaded Beggar Girl

Pale ginger-haired streetwalker, whose ragged frock gives glimpses of poverty and beauty,

 for a wretched poet like me your young and seedy freckled frame has its attractions.

 You wear your heavy clogs more stylishly than a novelette queen showing off her velvet buskins.

 Instead of your skimpy tatters, I would like a splendid courtly robe to hang in long swishing folds down to your heels;

En place de bas troués,
Que pour les yeux des roués
Sur ta jambe un poignard d'or
Reluise encor;

Que des nœuds mal attachés
Dévoilent pour nos péchés
Tes deux beaux seins, radieux
Comme des yeux;

Que pour te déshabiller
Tes bras se fassent prier
Et chassent à coups mutins
Les doigts lutins,

Perles de la plus belle eau,
Sonnets de maître Belleau
Par tes galants mis aux fers
Sans cesse offerts,

Valetaille de rimeurs
Te dédiant leurs primeurs
Et contemplant ton soulier
Sous l'escalier,

instead of your undarned stockings, may a golden dagger glint on
your leg to catch the eyes of playboys.

May loose bows of ribbon unveil for our sins your lovely twin
breasts as radiant as eyes;

may your arms coquettishly refuse to undress you, and with arch
taps discourage teasing fingers

and the choicest pearls and sonnets of Master Belleau which your
lovers clapped in irons ceaselessly offer you.

The rabble of rhymers dedicating the first fruits – or rather, vege-
tables – of their Muse to you and studying your shoe from below stairs;

Maint page épris du hasard,
Maint seigneur et maint Ronsard
Épieraient pour le déduit
 Ton frais réduit!

Tu compterais dans tes lits
Plus de baisers que de lis
Et rangerais sous tes lois
 Plus d'un Valois!

– Cependant tu vas gueusant
Quelque vieux débris gisant
Au seuil de quelque Véfour
 De carrefour;

Tu vas lorgnant en dessous
Des bijoux de vingt-neuf sous
Dont je ne puis, oh! pardon!
 Te faire don.

Va donc, sans autre ornement,
Parfum, perles, diamant,
Que ta maigre nudité,
 Ô ma beauté!

 many a young page with an eye to the main chance, many a squire and many a Ronsard would gladly spy on your cool lodging for an erotic thrill.

 You would count more kisses than lilies in your beds, and subject many a Valois to your laws.

 Meanwhile you go cadging for any old scraps at the door of some shabby-chic cornerhouse,

 you goggle from a distance at the cheap beads which – God forgive me – I can't afford to offer you for nothing.

 Go, then, with no adornment – neither scent nor pearls nor diamonds – but your skinny nakedness, my beauty.

 [An early poem, anywhere between 1840–45. FM 1857]

LXXXIX
LE CYGNE

À Victor Hugo.

I

Andromaque, je pense à vous! Ce petit fleuve,
Pauvre et triste miroir où jadis resplendit
L'immense majesté de vos douleurs de veuve,
Ce Simoïs menteur qui par vos pleurs grandit,

A fécondé soudain ma mémoire fertile,
Comme je traversais le nouveau Carrousel.
Le vieux Paris n'est plus (la forme d'une ville
Change plus vite, hélas! que le cœur d'un mortel);

Je ne vois qu'en esprit tout ce camp de baraques,
Ces tas de chapiteaux ébauchés et de fûts,
Les herbes, les gros blocs verdis par l'eau des flaques,
Et, brillant aux carreaux, le bric-à-brac confus.

The Swan

for Victor Hugo

I

Andromache – my thoughts are turned to you. That narrow stream, that unworthy, sad mirror that long ago resplended with the awesome majesty of your widow's grief, that false Simoïs swelled by your tears,

has suddenly enriched my fertile memory, as I was crossing the new Carrousel. The Paris of old is there no more – a city's pattern changes, alas, more swiftly than a human heart –

only in my mind's eye can I see those makeshift booths, those piles of rough-hewn capitals and pillars, the weeds, the massive blocks of stone stained by the puddles' green, the jumble of cheap bric-à-brac glittering in shopfronts.

Là s'étalait jadis une ménagerie;
Là je vis, un matin, à l'heure où sous les cieux
Froids et clairs le Travail s'éveille, où la voirie
Pousse un sombre ouragan dans l'air silencieux,

Un cygne qui s'était évadé de sa cage,
Et, de ses pieds palmés frottant le pavé sec,
Sur le sol raboteux traînait son blanc plumage.
Près d'un ruisseau sans eau la bête ouvrant le bec

Baignait nerveusement ses ailes dans la poudre,
Et disait, le cœur plein de son beau lac natal:
«Eau, quand donc pleuvras-tu? quand tonneras-tu, foudre?»
Je vois ce malheureux, mythe étrange et fatal,

Vers le ciel quelquefois, comme l'homme d'Ovide,
Vers le ciel ironique et cruellement bleu,
Sur son cou convulsif tendant sa tête avide,
Comme s'il adressait des reproches à Dieu!

A menagerie used to sprawl just here, where one morning, at the hour when beneath the chill clear sky Toil stirs from sleep, when the roadmenders drive a dark dust-storm into the silent air, I saw
a swan who had escaped out of his cage. Rubbing the parched road-way with his webbed feet, he went trailing his white wings on the rough ground. Beside a dried-up gutter the poor creature, with gaping beak,
was frantically bathing his wings in the dust, and with his heart full of longing for his beautiful native lake, cried out 'O water, when will you ever rain down? When will you resound, thunderbolt?' I can see that unhappy bird, that strange symbol of doom,
sometimes like Ovid's man lifting his hungry head on his twisted neck towards the ironic, cruelly blue sky, as if to reproach God.

II

Paris change! mais rien dans ma mélancolie
N'a bougé! palais neufs, échafaudages, blocs,
Vieux faubourgs, tout pour moi devient allégorie,
Et mes chers souvenirs sont plus lourds que des rocs.

Aussi devant ce Louvre une image m'opprime:
Je pense à mon grand cygne, avec ses gestes fous,
Comme les exilés, ridicule et sublime,
Et rongé d'un désir sans trêve! et puis à vous,

Andromaque, des bras d'un grand époux tombée,
Vil bétail, sous la main du superbe Pyrrhus,
Auprès d'un tombeau vide en extase courbée;
Veuve d'Hector, hélas! et femme d'Hélénus!

Je pense à la négresse, amaigrie et phtisique,
Piétinant dans la boue, et cherchant, l'œil hagard,
Les cocotiers absents de la superbe Afrique
Derrière la muraille immense du brouillard;

II

Paris is changing, but naught in my melancholy has moved. These new palaces and scaffoldings, blocks of stone, old suburbs – everything for me is turned to allegory, and my memories are heavier than rocks.

And so beside the Louvre I am oppressed by a vision: I think of my great swan with his frenzied gestures, like all exiles ridiculous and sublime, gnawed by an unremitting nostalgia: and then of you,

O Andromache, fallen from the arms of an heroic spouse to be a vile chattel in the hands of proud Pyrrhus, bent in ecstasy before an empty tomb; widow of Hector, alas, then wife of Helenus.

I think of the lean consumptive negress trudging through the mud, with her haggard eyes peering in vain through the huge wall of fog for the absent palm-trees of her noble Africa;

À quiconque a perdu ce qui ne se retrouve
Jamais, jamais! à ceux qui s'abreuvent de pleurs
Et tètent la Douleur comme une bonne louve!
Aux maigres orphelins séchant comme des fleurs!

Ainsi dans la forêt où mon esprit s'exile
Un vieux Souvenir sonne à plein souffle du cor!
Je pense aux matelots oubliés dans une île,
Aux captifs, aux vaincus!... à bien d'autres encor!

I think of all those who have lost what they can never, never hope
to find again; of those who quench their thirst with their own tears and
suck the breast of Sorrow like a good mother-wolf's. I think of the
starved orphans withering away like flowers.

Thus, in the forest where my mind is exiled, an old memory winds
its horn: I think of sailors abandoned on a desert isle, of those who are
captive, those who are defeated – and of many another.

[1859. FM 1861]

XC
LES SEPT VIEILLARDS

À Victor Hugo.

Fourmillante cité, cité pleine de rêves,
Où le spectre en plein jour raccroche le passant!
Les mystères partout coulent comme des sèves
Dans les canaux étroits du colosse puissant.

Un matin, cependant que dans la triste rue
Les maisons, dont la brume allongeait la hauteur,
Simulaient les deux quais d'une rivière accrue,
Et que, décor semblable à l'âme de l'acteur,

Un brouillard sale et jaune inondait tout l'espace,
Je suivais, roidissant mes nerfs comme un héros
Et discutant avec mon âme déjà lasse,
Le faubourg secoué par les lourds tombereaux.

Tout à coup, un vieillard dont les guenilles jaunes
Imitaient la couleur de ce ciel pluvieux,
Et dont l'aspect aurait fait pleuvoir les aumônes,
Sans la méchanceté qui luisait dans ses yeux,

The Seven Old Men

for Victor Hugo

O swarming city, city full of dreams, where ghosts accost the passers-by in broad daylight! Mysteries flow everywhere like sap in the narrow veins of this mighty giant.

One morning, when in the dingy street the houses seemed to be stretched upwards by the mist and looked like the two quays of some swollen river, and when − a background not unlike the actor's soul −

a dirty yellow fog flooded the whole of space, I was making my way, heroically steeling my nerves and arguing with my already weary soul, through the suburbs which were shaken by ponderous tumbrils.

Then suddenly an old man whose yellow rags were the same colour as the rainy sky, and whose appearance was enough to invite showers of alms were it not for the wicked glint in his eyes,

M'apparut. On eût dit sa prunelle trempée
Dans le fiel; son regard aiguisait les frimas,
Et sa barbe à longs poils, roide comme une épée,
Se projetait, pareille à celle de Judas.

Il n'était pas voûté, mais cassé, son échine
Faisant avec sa jambe un parfait angle droit,
Si bien que son bâton, parachevant sa mine,
Lui donnait la tournure et le pas maladroit

D'un quadrupède infirme ou d'un juif à trois pattes.
Dans la neige et la boue il allait s'empêtrant,
Comme s'il écrasait des morts sous ses savates,
Hostile à l'univers plutôt qu'indifférent.

Son pareil le suivait: barbe, œil, dos, bâton, loques,
Nul trait ne distinguait, du même enfer venu,
Ce jumeau centenaire, et ces spectres baroques
Marchaient du même pas vers un but inconnu.

hove in sight. You would have thought his eyes were steeped in gall; his sharp glance made the winter frost still more acute, and his long beard, as stiff as any sword, jutted out like the beard of Judas himself.

He was not so much bent, as broken, his backbone making a perfect right-angle with his legs, so that his walking-stick, adding the finishing touch to his appearance, gave him the ungainly shape and gait of a sick quadruped or a three-legged Jew. He scuffled along, sinking into the mud and snow as if crushing the dead under his old beetle-crushers, not just indifferent to the world but hating it.

This old man was followed by his double – beard, eye, back, stick, rags, not a single feature distinguished this centenarian twin out of the same hell, and these two outlandish ghosts went plodding at the same speed towards some unknown destination.

À quel complot infâme étais-je donc en butte,
Ou quel méchant hasard ainsi m'humiliait?
Car je comptai sept fois, de minute en minute,
Ce sinistre vieillard qui se multipliait!

Que celui-là qui rit de mon inquiétude,
Et qui n'est pas saisi d'un frisson fraternel,
Songe bien que malgré tant de décrépitude
Ces sept monstres hideux avaient l'air éternel!

Aurais-je, sans mourir, contemplé le huitième,
Sosie inexorable, ironique et fatal,
Dégoûtant Phénix, fils et père de lui-même?
— Mais je tournai le dos au cortège infernal.

Exaspéré comme un ivrogne qui voit double,
Je rentrai, je fermai ma porte, épouvanté,
Malade et morfondu, l'esprit fiévreux et trouble,
Blessé par le mystère et par l'absurdité!

What infamous conspiracy was I the victim of? What evil chance was now humiliating me? For, *seven times*, minute by minute, I counted the same sinister, multiple old man!

Whoever laughs at my uneasiness and does not feel a brotherly chill run down his spine, let him not forget that in spite of their senility these seven hideous freaks had a look of eternity about them!

Could I, without being stricken dead, have looked on yet an eighth, a pitiless, ironical, deadly twin, a loathsome phoenix who was his own son and his own father? But I turned my back on that satanical procession,

irritated beyond endurance like some drunkard seeing double. I went home and locked my door, terrified and nauseated and depressed, my mind feverish and disturbed, hurt by this enigma, this absurdity.

Vainement ma raison voulait prendre la barre;
La tempête en jouant déroutait ses efforts,
Et mon âme dansait, dansait, vieille gabarre
Sans mâts, sur une mer monstrueuse et sans bords!

My reason tried to take over, but in vain: its efforts were all thwarted by the storm, and my soul danced and danced like some old mastless barge heaved on a monstrous shoreless sea.

[Written and published 1859; one of a series of *Parisian Ghosts*]

XCI

LES PETITES VIEILLES

À Victor Hugo.

I

Dans les plis sinueux des vieilles capitales,
Où tout, même l'horreur, tourne aux enchantements,
Je guette, obéissant à mes humeurs fatales,
Des êtres singuliers, décrépits et charmants.

Ces monstres disloqués furent jadis des femmes,
Éponine ou Laïs! Monstres brisés, bossus
Ou tordus, aimons-les! ce sont encor des âmes.
Sous des jupons troués et sous de froids tissus

Ils rampent, flagellés par les bises iniques,
Frémissant au fracas roulant des omnibus,
Et serrant sur leur flanc, ainsi que des reliques,
Un petit sac brodé de fleurs ou de rébus;

The Little Old Women

for Victor Hugo

I

In the twisting folds of old capital cities, where everything, even
horror, turns to magic, obeying my irresistible impulses I spy on odd,
decrepit, charming creatures.

Let us love these disjointed freaks who once were women – hero-
ines, courtesans – broken-down monsters, humped or distorted, for
they are still human souls. Under their tattered skirts and flimsy
garments

they crawl along whipped by the malignant winds, trembling at the
din of buses thundering past, clutching against their ribs, like holy
relics, their tiny handbags embroidered with flowers or puzzling
patterns.

Ils trottent, tout pareils à des marionnettes;
Se traînent, comme font les animaux blessés,
Ou dansent, sans vouloir danser, pauvres sonnettes
Où se pend un Démon sans pitié! Tout cassés

Qu'ils sont, ils ont des yeux perçants comme une vrille,
Luisants comme ces trous où l'eau dort dans la nuit;
Ils ont les yeux divins de la petite fille
Qui s'étonne et qui rit à tout ce qui reluit.

– Avez-vous observé que maints cercueils de vieilles
Sont presque aussi petits que celui d'un enfant?
La Mort savante met dans ces bières pareilles
Un symbole d'un goût bizarre et captivant,

Et lorsque j'entrevois un fantôme débile
Traversant de Paris le fourmillant tableau,
Il me semble toujours que cet être fragile
S'en va tout doucement vers un nouveau berceau;

They trot along like puppets or limp like lame animals, or, though they don't intend to, they do a kind of jig, like puny bells swung by a merciless demon. Although they are falling to pieces,
their eyes are as piercing as drills, they glint like holes where water sleeps at night; or they have the divine eyes of little girls, full of wonder and laughing at whatever shines.
Have you ever noticed that many old women's coffins are almost as small as little children's? Cunning old Death gives these similar coffins a strange and entrancing symbolism:
when I catch a glimpse of a sickly ghost passing through the swarming Parisian landscape, I always have the feeling that the frail creature is gently progressing towards a second cradle;

À moins que, méditant sur la géométrie,
Je ne cherche, à l'aspect de ces membres discords,
Combien de fois il faut que l'ouvrier varie
La forme de la boîte où l'on met tous ces corps.

– Ces yeux sont des puits faits d'un million de larmes,
Des creusets qu'un métal refroidi pailleta . . .
Ces yeux mystérieux ont d'invincibles charmes
Pour celui que l'austère Infortune allaita !

II

De Frascati défunt Vestale enamourée;
Prêtresse de Thalie, hélas! dont le souffleur
Enterré sait le nom; célèbre évaporée
Que Tivoli jadis ombragea dans sa fleur,

Toutes m'enivrent! mais parmi ces êtres frêles
Il en est qui, faisant de la douleur un miel,
Ont dit au Dévouement qui leur prêtait ses ailes:
Hippogriffe puissant, mène-moi jusqu'au ciel!

unless, my thoughts turning to geometry as I see those incongruent limbs, I reflect on how often the undertaker has to modify the shape of the one box into which all those bodies are laid . . .

Those eyes are the wells of a million tears, crucibles spangled with cool metal. Those enigmatic eyes have compelling charms for whoever was suckled on the milk of austere Misfortune!

II

Vestal enamoured of some dead Frascati; priestess of Thalia, alas, whose name is known only to the buried prompter; illustrious beauty whom Tivoli long ago sheltered in her bloom –

they all intoxicate me! But among those fragile beings there are those who, turning their grief into honey, have implored the Devotion which lent them wings, saying, 'O mighty hippogriff, lead me to Heaven!'

L'une, par sa patrie au malheur exercée,
L'autre, que son époux surchargea de douleurs,
L'autre, par son enfant Madone transpercée,
Toutes auraient pu faire un fleuve avec leurs pleurs!

III

Ah! que j'en ai suivi de ces petites vieilles!
Une, entre autres, à l'heure où le soleil tombant
Ensanglante le ciel de blessures vermeilles,
Pensive, s'asseyait à l'écart sur un banc,

Pour entendre un de ces concerts, riches de cuivre,
Dont les soldats parfois inondent nos jardins,
Et qui, dans ces soirs d'or où l'on se sent revivre,
Versent quelque héroïsme au cœur des citadins.

Celle-là, droite encor, fière et sentant la règle,
Humait avidement ce chant vif et guerrier;
Son œil parfois s'ouvrait comme l'œil d'un vieil aigle;
Son front de marbre avait l'air fait pour le laurier!

One, whose homeland schooled her in misfortune; another, whom her husband overwhelmed with sufferings; or she who through her child became a Madonna pierced to the heart – all could have made a river with their tears!

III

Ah, how many of those little old ladies have I followed! One of them, at the hour when the setting sun bloodens the sky with scarlet wounds, used to sit deep in thought, alone on a bench,

listening to one of those brass-band concerts with which the military sometimes flood our parks, and which, on those golden evenings when you feel yourself coming to life again, inject a certain heroism into the hearts of city folk.

This woman, still upright and full of pride and radiating a sense of discipline, eagerly drank in that lively warlike song: sometimes her eye would open like an old eagle's, and then her marble brow seemed shaped for a laurel crown.

IV

Telles vous cheminez, stoïques et sans plaintes,
À travers le chaos des vivantes cités,
Mères au cœur saignant, courtisanes ou saintes,
Dont autrefois les noms par tous étaient cités.

Vous qui fûtes la grâce ou qui fûtes la gloire,
Nul ne vous reconnaît! un ivrogne incivil
Vous insulte en passant d'un amour dérisoire;
Sur vos talons gambade un enfant lâche et vil.

Honteuses d'exister, ombres ratatinées,
Peureuses, le dos bas, vous côtoyez les murs;
Et nul ne vous salue, étranges destinées!
Débris d'humanité pour l'éternité mûrs!

Mais moi, moi qui de loin tendrement vous surveille,
L'œil inquiet, fixé sur vos pas incertains,
Tout comme si j'étais votre père, ô merveille!
Je goûte à votre insu des plaisirs clandestins:

IV

Thus you pass on, stoical and uncomplaining, through the chaos of living cities: mothers whose hearts are bleeding, courtesans or saints whose names were once on everybody's lips.

You who were once the embodiment of grace or glory, nobody recognizes you now: a foul-mouthed drunkard insults you as he goes by with his mock advances; or some cowardly despicable urchin dances at your heels.

Ashamed to be still alive, shrivelled shadows, timorous and bent-backed, you hug the walls and nobody raises his hat to you, O strangely-fated women! O human wreckage, ripe for eternity!

But I who watch you tenderly from afar, with my uneasy eye fixed on your tottering steps, as though by some miracle I were your father – unknown to you I enjoy secret pleasures:

Je vois s'épanouir vos passions novices;
Sombres ou lumineux, je vis vos jours perdus;
Mon cœur multiplié jouit de tous vos vices!
Mon âme resplendit de toutes vos vertus!

Ruines! ma famille! ô cerveaux congénères!
Je vous fais chaque soir un solennel adieu!
Où serez-vous demain, Èves octogénaires,
Sur qui pèse la griffe effroyable de Dieu?

I watch your untutored passions flower and, dark or bright, I relive your vanished days; my manifold heart delights in all your vices, and my soul resplends with all your virtues.

O ruins, O you my flesh and blood, O you, minds of the same stamp, I bid you every evening grave farewells! Where will you be tomorrow, octogenarian Eves, on whom God's terrible claw is already poised?

[One of the projected series of *Parisian Ghosts*. Written and published 1859 and FM 1861. See the prose-poems 'Le Désespoir de la vieille' and 'Les Veuves']

XCII

LES AVEUGLES

Contemple-les, mon âme; ils sont vraiment affreux!
Pareils aux mannequins; vaguement ridicules;
Terribles, singuliers comme les somnambules;
Dardant on ne sait où leurs globes ténébreux.

Leurs yeux, d'où la divine étincelle est partie,
Comme s'ils regardaient au loin, restent levés
Au ciel; on ne les voit jamais vers les pavés
Pencher rêveusement leur tête appesantie.

Ils traversent ainsi le noir illimité,
Ce frère du silence éternel. Ô cité!
Pendant qu'autour de nous tu chantes, ris et beugles,

Éprise du plaisir jusqu'à l'atrocité,
Vois! je me traîne aussi! mais, plus qu'eux hébété,
Je dis: Que cherchent-ils au Ciel, tous ces aveugles?

The Blind Men

Observe them, O my soul – they are truly frightful, like tailors'
dummies, faintly ridiculous, terrifying and strange as sleep-walkers,
darting this way and that their lightless orbs.

Their eyes, from which the divine spark has departed, as though
they were staring into the distance, remain lifted towards the sky: you
never see them dreamily bow their weighed-down heads to the
cobbled road.

Thus they pass on their way through boundless dark, that brother of
eternal silence. O city, while you sing and laugh and bellow all around
us,

abominably bent on pleasure, behold, I also drag myself along; but
even more stupefied than they, I ask myself – what are they seeking in
the heavens, all these blind men?

[Written and published 1860. FM 1861]

XCIII

À UNE PASSANTE

La rue assourdissante autour de moi hurlait.
Longue, mince, en grand deuil, douleur majestueuse,
Une femme passa, d'une main fastueuse
Soulevant, balançant le feston et l'ourlet;

Agile et noble, avec sa jambe de statue.
Moi, je buvais, crispé comme un extravagant,
Dans son œil, ciel livide où germe l'ouragan,
La douceur qui fascine et le plaisir qui tue.

Un éclair... puis la nuit! – Fugitive beauté
Dont le regard m'a fait soudainement renaître,
Ne te verrai-je plus que dans l'éternité?

Ailleurs, bien loin d'ici! trop tard! *jamais* peut-être!
Car j'ignore où tu fuis, tu ne sais où je vais,
Ô toi que j'eusse aimée, ô toi qui le savais!

To a Woman Passing By

The deafening street was howling round me when a woman passed on
her way, so tall and slender, all in black mourning, majestical in her
grief, with her stately hand lifting and swaying the scallop and hem,
 light-footed and noble and with a statue's leg. And I tense as a man
out of his wits, drank from her eye – a pallid sky in which a tempest
brews – that gentleness which bewitches, that pleasure which destroys.
 A flash of lightning – then darkness. O vanishing beauty whose
glance brought me suddenly to life again, shall I never see you once
more except in eternity?
 Elsewhere, far from here, too late or perhaps never? For whither
you flee I know not, nor do you know whither I am bound – O you
whom I could have loved, O you who knew it!

[1860. FM 1861]

XCIV
LE SQUELETTE LABOUREUR

I

Dans les planches d'anatomie
Qui traînent sur ces quais poudreux
Où maint livre cadavéreux
Dort comme une antique momie,

Dessins auxquels la gravité
Et le savoir d'un vieil artiste,
Bien que le sujet en soit triste,
Ont communiqué la Beauté,

On voit, ce qui rend plus complètes
Ces mystérieuses horreurs,
Bêchant comme des laboureurs,
Des Écorchés et des Squelettes.

The Digging Skeleton

I

In those anatomical plates which languish [in book-boxes] on the dusty quays [along the Seine], where many a shrivelled volume sleeps like an ancient mummy –

in drawings to which the gravity and learning of some forgotten artist gave some beauty, however depressing the theme,

you can see (to make these mysterious horrors more complete) flayed men and skeletons digging the soil like farm-hands.

II

You poor gloomy devils who seem resigned to your fate, tell me – what strange horror do you dig up from the soil you hack with all that straining of your backbones and skinned muscles,

II

De ce terrain que vous fouillez,
Manants résignés et funèbres,
De tout l'effort de vos vertèbres,
Ou de vos muscles dépouillés,

Dites, quelle moisson étrange,
Forçats arrachés au charnier,
Tirez-vous, et de quel fermier
Avez-vous à remplir la grange?

Voulez-vous (d'un destin trop dur
Épouvantable et clair emblème!)
Montrer que dans la fosse même
Le sommeil promis n'est pas sûr;

Qu'envers nous le Néant est traître;
Que tout, même la Mort, nous ment,
Et que sempiternellement,
Hélas! il nous faudra peut-être

Dans quelque pays inconnu
Écorcher la terre revêche
Et pousser une lourde bêche
Sous notre pied sanglant et nu?

you hard-labourers dragged out of the boneyard, tell me what
farmer's barns are you condemned to fill?
 Do you want to show us – O shocking and unmistakable emblem
of too harsh a fate – that even in the grave the sleep we are promised
may be denied us;
 that the Void can cheat us; that all things lie to us, including Death;
and that for ever and ever, alas, perhaps
 in some land unknown to us we will have to scrape the sullen earth,
and shove a heavy spade beneath our bleeding naked feet?

[1859. FM 1861]

XCV
LE CRÉPUSCULE DU SOIR

Voici le soir charmant, ami du criminel;
Il vient comme un complice, à pas de loup; le ciel
Se ferme lentement comme une grande alcôve,
Et l'homme impatient se change en bête fauve.

Ô soir, aimable soir, désiré par celui
Dont les bras, sans mentir, peuvent dire: Aujourd'hui
Nous avons travaillé! – C'est le soir qui soulage
Les esprits que dévore une douleur sauvage,
Le savant obstiné dont le front s'alourdit,
Et l'ouvrier courbé qui regagne son lit.
Cependant des démons malsains dans l'atmosphère
S'éveillent lourdement, comme des gens d'affaire,
Et cognent en volant les volets et l'auvent.
À travers les lueurs que tourmente le vent
La Prostitution s'allume dans les rues;
Comme une fourmilière elle ouvre ses issues;
Partout elle se fraye un occulte chemin,
Ainsi que l'ennemi qui tente un coup de main;

Evening Twilight

Here is the delightful evening, the criminal's friend. It comes like an
accomplice, with slinking wolf-like strides. The sky is slowly closing
like an immense alcove, and restless man turns into a wild beast.

O evening, pleasant evening, desired by those whose arms can say
without lying, 'We have worked today!' It is evening that refreshes
minds devoured by savage grief, or the poring scholar whose head
begins to nod, or the back-bent workman returning home to bed. But
now mischievous demons rouse lumpishly in the air like businessmen,
and flounder in their flight against shutters and sheds.

Through glimmering gas-jets wincing in the wind, Prostitution
lights up in the streets, like an ant-heap opening all its entrances and
exits; it weaves its furtive passage everywhere, like an enemy planning a
surprise attack; it burrows through the city's filth like a worm filching

Elle remue au sein de la cité de fange
Comme un ver qui dérobe à l'Homme ce qu'il mange.
On entend çà et là les cuisines siffler,
Les théâtres glapir, les orchestres ronfler;
Les tables d'hôte, dont le jeu fait les délices,
S'emplissent de catins et d'escrocs, leurs complices,
Et les voleurs, qui n'ont ni trêve ni merci,
Vont bientôt commencer leur travail, eux aussi,
Et forcer doucement les portes et les caisses
Pour vivre quelques jours et vêtir leurs maîtresses.

Recueille-toi, mon âme, en ce grave moment,
Et ferme ton oreille à ce rugissement.
C'est l'heure où les douleurs des malades s'aigrissent!
La sombre Nuit les prend à la gorge; ils finissent
Leur destinée et vont vers le gouffre commun;
L'hôpital se remplit de leurs soupirs. – Plus d'un
Ne viendra plus chercher la soupe parfumée,
Au coin du feu, le soir, auprès d'une âme aimée.

Encore la plupart n'ont-ils jamais connu
La douceur du foyer et n'ont jamais vécu!

away men's food. Here and there you can hear the whistling from kitchens, the yapping of theatres, the droning of orchestras: the cheap joints whose main attraction is gambling are filling with whores and their crony crooks, and the burglars, who have neither rest nor mercy, will soon be setting to work, tenderly cracking doors and safes, so as to keep themselves for a few days and buy togs for their molls.

O my soul, withdraw into yourself at this grave hour, and stop your ears against this roaring din. It is the hour when the pangs of the sick increase in pain. Cheerless Night grips them by the throat, they are reaching their destiny's end and approach the universal common grave, the hospitals are overflowing with their sighs. More than one will never again return to sup the fragrant soup by the fireside, of an evening, beside the one he loves;

and in any case, most of them have never known the solace of a home, and have never lived.

[1851; published 1852. FM 1857]

XCVI

LE JEU

Dans des fauteuils fanés des courtisanes vieilles,
Pâles, le sourcil peint, l'œil câlin et fatal,
Minaudant, et faisant de leurs maigres oreilles
Tomber un cliquetis de pierre et de métal;

Autour des verts tapis des visages sans lèvre,
Des lèvres sans couleur, des mâchoires sans dent,
Et des doigts convulsés d'une infernale fièvre,
Fouillant la poche vide ou le sein palpitant;

Sous de sales plafonds un rang de pâles lustres
Et d'énormes quinquets projetant leurs lueurs
Sur des fronts ténébreux de poètes illustres
Qui viennent gaspiller leurs sanglantes sueurs;

Voilà le noir tableau qu'en un rêve nocturne
Je vis se dérouler sous mon œil clairvoyant.
Moi-même, dans un coin de l'antre taciturne,
Je me vis accoudé, froid, muet, enviant,

The Gambling-Den

In faded armchairs agèd courtesans, sallow, with eyebrows painted on,
with their come-hither compelling eyes, simpering and making their
skinny ears rattle with rings of metal and stones;

round the green baize, lipless faces, bloodless lips, toothless jaws,
fingers convulsed by a satanic fever, rummaging in an empty pocket or
a heaving bosom,

hanging from the dirty ceilings a row of dim glass chandeliers and
massive lamps casting their dingy gleams on the glowering brows of
poets of renown who have come here to squander their sweat and
blood –

– Such is the sombre picture that in a dream, one night, I saw unfold
beneath my seer's gaze. I saw myself in a corner of that silent den, my-
self there leaning on my elbows, cold and speechless, actually envying,

Enviant de ces gens la passion tenace,
De ces vieilles putains la funèbre gaieté,
Et tous gaillardement trafiquant à ma face,
L'un de son vieil honneur, l'autre de sa beauté!

Et mon cœur s'effraya d'envier maint pauvre homme
Courant avec ferveur à l'abîme béant,
Et qui, soûl de son sang, préférerait en somme
La douleur à la mort et l'enfer au néant!

yes, *envying* the intensity of those people's passion, the old whores'
dismal sprightliness, all of them as they cheerfully sold, under my very
nose, one, his long-established honour, the other, her beauty.

And my heart swelled with fear that I should envy many a poor soul
hastening so eagerly towards the gaping pit, who, drunk with his own
blood, would really prefer agony to death, and Hell to nothingness.

[FM 1857]

XCVII
DANSE MACABRE

À Ernest Christophe.

Fière, autant qu'un vivant, de sa noble stature,
Avec son gros bouquet, son mouchoir et ses gants,
Elle a la nonchalance et la désinvolture
D'une coquette maigre aux airs extravagants.

Vit-on jamais au bal une taille plus mince?
Sa robe exagérée, en sa royale ampleur,
S'écroule abondamment sur un pied sec que pince
Un soulier pomponné, joli comme une fleur.

La ruche qui se joue au bord des clavicules,
Comme un ruisseau lascif qui se frotte au rocher,
Défend pudiquement des lazzi ridicules
Les funèbres appas qu'elle tient à cacher.

The Dance of Death

to Ernest Christophe

As proud of her noble figure as anyone alive, with her outsize bouquet, handkerchief and gloves, she has the ease and casualness of a skinny flirt with her affected poses.

Did you ever see such a narrow waist at any ball? Her flashy gown, ample enough for a queen, sweeps generously down to her neat foot which is pinched into a pomponned slipper as pretty as a flower.

The frills on her dress hug her collarbones like a randy stream rubbing against a rock, demurely protecting the lifeless charms which she does her best to hide from hilarious jeers.

Ses yeux profonds sont faits de vide et de ténèbres,
Et son crâne, de fleurs artistement coiffé,
Oscille mollement sur ses frêles vertèbres.
Ô charme d'un néant follement attifé!

Aucuns t'appelleront une caricature,
Qui ne comprennent pas, amants ivres de chair,
L'élégance sans nom de l'humaine armature.
Tu réponds, grand squelette, à mon goût le plus cher!

Viens-tu troubler, avec ta puissante grimace,
La fête de la Vie? ou quelque vieux désir,
Éperonnant encor ta vivante carcasse,
Te pousse-t-il, crédule, au sabbat du Plaisir?

Au chant des violons, aux flammes des bougies,
Espères-tu chasser ton cauchemar moqueur,
Et viens-tu demander au torrent des orgies
De rafraîchir l'enfer allumé dans ton cœur?

Her fathomless eyes are pits of emptiness and dark. Her hairless skull is crowned with an arty garland and gently tilts from side to side, poised on her vertebrae's delicate bones. What charm there is in Nothingness dressed to kill!

But some will dismiss you as a mere caricature, such as those flesh-obsessed lovers who fail to appreciate the nameless elegance of the human frame. But for me, grand skeleton, you are the answer to my fondest tastes.

Have you come here to disturb the feast of life with your compelling grin, or does some lingering lust spur your living carcass on and trick you into joining our saturnalia?

To the strains of violins, the flaming candle-lights, are you still hoping to drive the nightmare of derision away? Have you come to ask the flood of orgies to cool the inferno blazing in your breast?

Inépuisable puits de sottise et de fautes!
De l'antique douleur éternel alambic!
À travers le treillis recourbé de tes côtes
Je vois, errant encor, l'insatiable aspic.

Pour dire vrai, je crains que ta coquetterie
Ne trouve pas un prix digne de ses efforts;
Qui, de ces cœurs mortels, entend la raillerie?
Les charmes de l'horreur n'enivrent que les forts!

Le gouffre de tes yeux, plein d'horribles pensées,
Exhale le vertige, et les danseurs prudents
Ne contempleront pas sans d'amères nausées
Le sourire éternel de tes trente-deux dents.

Pourtant, qui n'a serré dans ses bras un squelette,
Et qui ne s'est nourri des choses du tombeau?
Qu'importe le parfum, l'habit ou la toilette?
Qui fait le dégoûté montre qu il se croit beau.

Inexhaustible pit of stupidity and errors, grisly vessel of age-old griefs, I can see the hungry aspic still at work in the rounded vessel of your ribs.

To tell the truth, I fear that your coquetry will never win the prize your efforts deserve, for which of these mortal hearts will ever grasp the meaning of your mockery? The charms of horror can seduce none but the strong.

The abyss of your eyes, full of unspeakable thoughts, casts an hypnotic vertigo all around you. No prudent partner in the dance will ever glimpse the permanent smile of your perfect set of thirty-two teeth without wanting to vomit bile.

Yet who has never held a skeleton in his arms, who has never fed on the carrion of the grave, of what avail are scents and clothes and jewels? Anyone who turns aside in disgust is only proving that he thinks himself beautiful.

Bayadère sans nez, irrésistible gouge,
Dis donc à ces danseurs qui font les offusqués:
«Fiers mignons, malgré l'art des poudres et du rouge
Vous sentez tous la mort! Ô squelettes musqués,

«Antinoüs flétris, dandys à face glabre,
Cadavres vernissés, lovelaces chenus,
Le branle universel de la danse macabre
Vous entraîne en des lieux qui ne sont pas connus!

«Des quais froids de la Seine aux bords brûlants du Gange,
Le troupeau mortel saute et se pâme, sans voir
Dans un trou du plafond la trompette de l'Ange
Sinistrement béante ainsi qu'un tromblon noir.

«En tout climat, sous tout soleil, la Mort t'admire
En tes contorsions, risible Humanité,
Et souvent, comme toi, se parfumant de myrrhe,
Mêle son ironie à ton insanité!»

Noseless ballerina, magnetic whore, you should tell those dancers whom you fill with nausea, 'You stiff-necked squeamish fools, in spite of all your perfumes and cosmetics you all stink of death. Skeletons tarted with musk,
'shabby wizened old fops, smooth-faced senile dandies, glorified cadavers, doddering Don Juans – the universal maelstrom of the Dance of Death will whirl you all into realms unknown to the living.
'From the Seine's cold quays to Ganges' sultry shores the herds of mortals jig and swoon, without ever noticing that gaping hole in the ceiling, through which the archangel's final trump yawns sinisterly like the jaws of a black cannon.
'In every clime and wherever the sun shines down, Death has her eye on you and marvels at your antics, O ridiculous human race; and often, like you, she scents herself with myrrh, matching your madness with her irony.'

[Ms. 1859; FM 1861]

XCVIII
L'AMOUR DU MENSONGE

Quand je te vois passer, ô ma chère indolente,
Au chant des instruments qui se brise au plafond
Suspendant ton allure harmonieuse et lente,
Et promenant l'ennui de ton regard profond;

Quand je contemple, aux feux du gaz qui le colore,
Ton front pâle, embelli par un morbide attrait,
Où les torches du soir allument une aurore,
Et tes yeux attirants comme ceux d'un portrait,

Je me dis: Qu'elle est belle! et bizarrement fraîche!
Le souvenir massif, royale et lourde tour,
La couronne, et son cœur, meurtri comme une pêche,
Est mûr, comme son corps, pour le savant amour.

Es-tu le fruit d'automne aux saveurs souveraines?
Es-tu vase funèbre attendant quelques pleurs,
Parfum qui fait rêver aux oasis lointaines,
Oreiller caressant, ou corbeille de fleurs?

The Love of Falsehood

When I watch you passing by, my dear indolent one, to the band's tune refracted on the ceiling, pausing in your harmonious unhurried progress and casting the boredom of your deep gaze all around you;

when I observe your pallid forehead tinted by the gas-jets, the lovelier for its morbid charm, in which evening's torches light a dawn, and your eyes that are as magnetic as those in a painted portrait,

then I say to myself – 'How beautiful she is, how curiously unspoiled! Memory, as massive as a regal, cumbrous tower, crowns her head, while her heart, bruised like a peach, is ripe like her body for the lore of love.'

Are you the fruit of autumn with its peerless savours? Are you a funeral urn awaiting tears? a perfume that sets one dreaming of far oases? a pampering pillow, a basket of flowers?

Je sais qu'il est des yeux, des plus mélancoliques,
Qui ne recèlent point de secrets précieux;
Beaux écrins sans joyaux, médaillons sans reliques,
Plus vides, plus profonds que vous-mêmes, ô Cieux!

Mais ne suffit-il pas que tu sois l'apparence,
Pour réjouir un cœur qui fuit la vérité?
Qu'importe ta bêtise ou ton indifférence?
Masque ou décor, salut! J'adore ta beauté.

I know there are eyes of deepest melancholy but which contain no hidden secrets, fine caskets empty of jewels, lockets with no relics in them, emptier and deeper than you heavens are –
but is it not enough for you to be no more than a semblance, in order to rejoice a heart that flees from truth? What matter your stupidity and indifference? I hail you, whether a mask or a sham display, and worship your beauty.

[Perhaps wrongly attributed to the Marie Daubrun cycle by some critics: in any case oddly situated in this group of poems. Published 1860, FM 1861]

XCIX

Je n'ai pas oublié, voisine de la ville,
Notre blanche maison, petite mais tranquille;
Sa Pomone de plâtre et sa vieille Vénus
Dans un bosquet chétif cachant leurs membres nus,
Et le soleil, le soir, ruisselant et superbe,
Qui, derrière la vitre où se brisait sa gerbe,
Semblait, grand œil ouvert dans le ciel curieux,
Contempler nos dîners longs et silencieux,
Répandant largement ses beaux reflets de cierge
Sur la nappe frugale et les rideaux de serge.

I have not forgotten . . .

I have not forgotten our white house near the city, small but quiet, with its plaster Pomona and old statue of Venus hiding their naked limbs in the meagre grove; while the evening sun, sumptuously streaming down through the pane on which its sheaf of light broke, like a huge open eye in the curious sky, seemed to be keeping watch over our long, silent dinners, generously spreading its lovely candle-beams on the frugal table-cloth and the serge curtains.

[Early poem. FM 1857]

C

La servante au grand cœur dont vous étiez jalouse,
Et qui dort son sommeil sous une humble pelouse,
Nous devrions pourtant lui porter quelques fleurs.
Les morts, les pauvres morts, ont de grandes douleurs,
Et quand Octobre souffle, émondeur des vieux arbres,
Son vent mélancolique à l'entour de leurs marbres,
Certe, ils doivent trouver les vivants bien ingrats,
À dormir, comme ils font, chaudement dans leurs draps,
Tandis que, dévorés de noires songeries,
Sans compagnon de lit, sans bonnes causeries,
Vieux squelettes gelés travaillés par le ver,
Ils sentent s'égoutter les neiges de l'hiver
Et le siècle couler, sans qu'amis ni famille
Remplacent les lambeaux qui pendent à leur grille.

Lorsque la bûche siffle et chante, si le soir,
Calme, dans le fauteuil je la voyais s'asseoir,

The great-hearted servant . . .

The great-hearted servant of whom you were so jealous, and who is sleeping her last sleep under a humble grassy mound – we really ought to be taking her some flowers. The dead, the poor dead, have their great griefs, and when October, which comes to prune old trees, blows its doleful wind around their marble graves, they must surely think the living are most ungrateful, who sleep so snugly in their sheets; whereas, devoured by gloomy reflections, with no bedfellow and never a cosy chat, those frozen old skeletons riddled with worms feel the winter snows drip down, and the century flowing on, without friends or relations replacing the scraps of wreaths that hang on their tombs' railings.

When the log whistles and sings, if some evening calm in the armchair where I used to watch her sit – if on some December night,

Si, par une nuit bleue et froide de décembre,
Je la trouvais tapie en un coin de ma chambre,
Grave, et venant du fond de son lit éternel
Couver l'enfant grandi de son œil maternel,
Que pourrais-je répondre à cette âme pieuse,
Voyant tomber des pleurs de sa paupière creuse?

cold and blue, I could find her huddling in a corner of my room,
solemn-faced and risen from her eternal bed in order to watch with
her motherly eye over the grown child – what could I answer that
pious soul, seeing the tears fall from her hollow lids?

[An early poem. The servant was Mariette,
to whom C.B. prayed in later life. FM 1857]

CI
BRUMES ET PLUIES

Ô fins d'automne, hivers, printemps trempés de boue,
Endormeuses saisons! je vous aime et vous loue
D'envelopper ainsi mon cœur et mon cerveau
D'un linceul vaporeux et d'un vague tombeau.

Dans cette grande plaine où l'autan froid se joue,
Où par les longues nuits la girouette s'enroue,
Mon âme mieux qu'au temps du tiède renouveau
Ouvrira largement ses ailes de corbeau.

Rien n'est plus doux au cœur plein de choses funèbres,
Et sur qui dès longtemps descendent les frimas,
Ô blafardes saisons, reines de nos climats,

Que l'aspect permanent de vos pâles ténèbres,
– Si ce n'est, par un soir sans lune, deux à deux,
D'endormir la douleur sur un lit hasardeux.

Mists and Rains

O ends of autumn, winters, springs soaked in mud, O drowsy seasons, I love and praise you for wrapping both my heart and mind in a misty shroud, a shadowy tomb.

In this great plain through which the cold south wind plays, where through the long nights the weather-cock shrieks himself hoarse, my soul, far better than in the days of warm renewal, will stretch its raven wings out wide.

Nothing is dearer to the heart, so full of gloomy things, and on which the hoar-frosts long ago began to fall, O sallow seasons, queens of our climes,

than the look of permanence in your colourless shadows – unless it be, on a moonless night, two by two, to lay our suffering to sleep on an uncertain bed.

[This totally irregular 'sonnet' was first published in FM 1857. Related to the 'Spleen' poems.]

CII
RÊVE PARISIEN

À Constantin Guys.

I

De ce terrible paysage,
Tel que jamais mortel n'en vit,
Ce matin encore l'image,
Vague et lointaine, me ravit.

Le sommeil est plein de miracles!
Par un caprice singulier,
J'avais banni de ces spectacles
Le végétal irrégulier,

Et, peintre fier de mon génie,
Je savourais dans mon tableau
L'enivrante monotonie
Du métal, du marbre et de l'eau.

Babel d'escaliers et d'arcades,
C'était un palais infini,
Plein de bassins et de cascades
Tombant dans l'or mat ou bruni;

A Parisian Dream

for Constantin Guys

I

The blurred, remote vista of this terrifying landscape, the like of which no mortal ever saw, entranced me once again this morning.

Sleep is rich in miracles. By some strange caprice I had banished shapeless organic forms from those scenes,

and like some painter proud of his own genius, I enjoyed in my picture the entrancing monotony of metal, marble and water.

A Babel of staircases and arcades, there was an infinite palace full of fountains and waterfalls falling into basins of dulled or burnished gold,

Et des cataractes pesantes,
Comme des rideaux de cristal,
Se suspendaient, éblouissantes,
À des murailles de métal.

Non d'arbres, mais de colonnades
Les étangs dormants s'entouraient,
Où de gigantesques naïades,
Comme des femmes, se miraient.

Des nappes d'eau s'épanchaient, bleues,
Entre des quais roses et verts,
Pendant des millions de lieues,
Vers les confins de l'univers;

C'étaient des pierres inouïes
Et des flots magiques; c'étaient
D'immenses glaces éblouies
Par tout ce qu'elles reflétaient!

Insouciants et taciturnes,
Des Ganges, dans le firmament,
Versaient le trésor de leurs urnes
Dans des gouffres de diamant.

and massy cataracts hung dazzling as crystal curtains from the metallic walls.

Not trees, but colonnades encircled the sleeping pools, in which colossal naiads admired their own reflections like living women.

Vast expanses of water stretched blue between the rosy and green embankments for millions of leagues, towards the ends of the universe.

There were fabulous stones and magic waves, and enormous mirrors dazzled by all that was reflected in them.

Impassive and silent Ganges rivers in the sky poured down the treasure of their urns into diamond abysses.

Architecte de mes féeries,
Je faisais, à ma volonté,
Sous un tunnel de pierreries
Passer un océan dompté;

Et tout, même la couleur noire,
Semblait fourbi, clair, irisé;
Le liquide enchâssait sa gloire
Dans le rayon cristallisé.

Nul astre d'ailleurs, nuls vestiges
De soleil, même au bas du ciel,
Pour illuminer ces prodiges,
Qui brillaient d'un feu personnel!

Et sur ces mouvantes merveilles
Planait (terrible nouveauté!
Tout pour l'œil, rien pour les oreilles!)
Un silence d'éternité.

The architect of my own wonderland, at will I tamed an ocean and sent it through a tunnel of precious jewels,

and everything, even the colour black, seemed polished and pellucid and iridescent, the liquid enshrining its glory like a gem in the crystalline light.

Nor was there a single star, no trace of the sun even at the lowest levels of the sky, nothing to illuminate these marvels which shone with their own intrinsic fire.

And, most terrible novelty of all, with everything for the eye and nothing for the ear, a silence of eternity hovered over all those moving wonders.

II

En rouvrant mes yeux pleins de flamme
J'ai vu l'horreur de mon taudis,
Et senti, rentrant dans mon âme,
La pointe des soucis maudits;

La pendule aux accents funèbres
Sonnait brutalement midi,
Et le ciel versait des ténèbres
Sur le triste monde engourdi.

II

Opening my flame-filled eyes, I saw the horror of my wretched lodging and felt the barb of infernal cares re-entering my soul.

The clock with mournful chimes was striking noon brutally, and the sky poured its dark shadows down on the sad, sluggish world.

[1860; FM 1861. See the prose-poem 'La Chambre double']

CIII
LE CRÉPUSCULE DU MATIN

La diane chantait dans les cours des casernes,
Et le vent du matin soufflait sur les lanternes.

C'était l'heure où l'essaim des rêves malfaisants
Tord sur leurs oreillers les bruns adolescents;
Où, comme un œil sanglant qui palpite et qui bouge,
La lampe sur le jour fait une tache rouge;
Où l'âme, sous le poids du corps revêche et lourd,
Imite les combats de la lampe et du jour.
Comme un visage en pleurs que les brises essuient,
L'air est plein du frisson des choses qui s'enfuient,
Et l'homme est las d'écrire et la femme d'aimer.

Les maisons çà et là commençaient à fumer.
Les femmes de plaisir, la paupière livide,
Bouche ouverte, dormaient de leur sommeil stupide;
Les pauvresses, traînant leurs seins maigres et froids,
Soufflaient sur leurs tisons et soufflaient sur leurs doigts.

Morning Twilight

The bugles were sounding the reveille in the barrack-squares, and the morning wind was blowing at the streetlamps.

It was the hour when a swarm of evil dreams makes swarthy adolescents writhe on their pillows; when like a bloodshot eye that throbs and jerks, the lamp makes a red stain on the daylight; when the soul, crushed by the body's sullen, leaden weight, enacts the struggle between lamp and day. Like a face in tears which the wind wipes dry, the air is full of the tremble of fleeting things, when men grow weary of writing and women weary of love.

The houses here and there began to puff smoke out. The women of 'pleasure', with bleary eyelids and gaping mouths, were sleeping their stupid sleep; while poor old women, dragging their scraggy frozen breasts, blew now upon the embers and then on their own fingers. It

C'était l'heure où parmi le froid et la lésine
S'aggravent les douleurs des femmes en gésine;
Comme un sanglot coupé par un sang écumeux
Le chant du coq au loin déchirait l'air brumeux;
Une mer de brouillards baignait les édifices,
Et les agonisants dans le fond des hospices
Poussaient leur dernier râle en hoquets inégaux.
Les débauchés rentraient, brisés par leurs travaux.

L'aurore grelottante en robe rose et verte
S'avançait lentement sur la Seine déserte,
Et le sombre Paris, en se frottant les yeux,
Empoignait ses outils, vieillard laborieux.

was the hour when amid the cold and poverty the pangs of mothers in childbirth grew more sharp; and like a sob cut off by frothing blood the cock-crow from afar tore through the hazy air; a sea of fog was swirling round the buildings, and dying men in hospitals and workhouses groaned their last death-rattle in heaving gasps. The debauched made their way homewards, racked by their labours.

The shuddering dawn in her pink green dress wended her way slowly alongside the deserted Seine, and gloomy Paris, rubbing his eyes, laid hold of his tools, an old man doomed to toil.

[Pre-1843. Published 1852, 1855; FM 1857]

Le Vin

L'ÂME DU VIN

Un soir, l'âme du vin chantait dans les bouteilles:
«Homme, vers toi je pousse, ô cher déshérité,
Sous ma prison de verre et mes cires vermeilles,
Un chant plein de lumière et de fraternité!

«Je sais combien il faut, sur la colline en flamme,
De peine, de sueur et de soleil cuisant
Pour engendrer ma vie et pour me donner l'âme;
Mais je ne serai point ingrat ni malfaisant,

«Car j'éprouve une joie immense quand je tombe
Dans le gosier d'un homme usé par ses travaux,
Et sa chaude poitrine est une douce tombe
Où je me plais bien mieux que dans mes froids caveaux.

WINE

The Soul of Wine

One evening the wine's soul sang in the bottles, 'Man, dear disinherited Man, from my glass prison with its scarlet seals of wax I send you a song which is full of light and brotherhood.

'I know what labour, sweat and scorching sun the flaming hillside needs, to engender my life and provide me with a soul; but I shall never be ungrateful or malign,

'as I feel tremendous joy when I flow down the throat of a man worn out with his toil, and his hot breast is a snug grave where I am happier than in my chilly cellars.

«Entends-tu retentir les refrains des dimanches
Et l'espoir qui gazouille en mon sein palpitant?
Les coudes sur la table et retroussant tes manches,
Tu me glorifieras et tu seras content;

«J'allumerai les yeux de ta femme ravie;
À ton fils je rendrai sa force et ses couleurs
Et serai pour ce frêle athlète de la vie
L'huile qui raffermit les muscles des lutteurs.

«En toi je tomberai, végétale ambroisie,
Grain précieux jeté par l'éternel Semeur,
Pour que de notre amour naisse la poésie
Qui jaillira vers Dieu comme une rare fleur!»

'Can you hear the sabbath choruses echoing, and the hope that babbles in my throbbing breast? With your elbows on the table, sleeves rolled up, you will glorify me and find happiness;

'I shall set a light in the eyes of your delighted wife, and restore his strength and colour to your son, and for that frail athlete of existence I shall be as the oil that fortifies the muscles of wrestlers.

'Into you I shall fall as vegetal ambrosia, a precious seed cast by the eternal Sower, so that poetry may be born from our love and spring towards God like a rare flower.'

[An early poem, 1843. Published in the
Magasin des Familles 1850, etc. FM 1857]

CV
LE VIN DES CHIFFONNIERS

Souvent, à la clarté rouge d'un réverbère
Dont le vent bat la flamme et tourmente le verre,
Au cœur d'un vieux faubourg, labyrinthe fangeux
Où l'humanité grouille en ferments orageux,

On voit un chiffonnier qui vient, hochant la tête,
Butant, et se cognant aux murs comme un poète,
Et, sans prendre souci des mouchards, ses sujets,
Épanche tout son cœur en glorieux projets.

Il prête des serments, dicte des lois sublimes,
Terrasse les méchants, relève les victimes,
Et sous le firmament comme un dais suspendu
S'enivre des splendeurs de sa propre vertu.

Oui, ces gens harcelés de chagrins de ménage,
Moulus par le travail et tourmentés par l'âge,
Éreintés et pliant sous un tas de débris,
Vomissement confus de l'énorme Paris,

The Rag-and-Bone-Men's Wine

Often, in the red glare of a streetlamp, with the wind flailing its gas-jet and racking the glass panes, in the heart of some old suburb, a slimy labyrinth where mankind seethes in a stormy fermentation,

you will see a rag-and-bone-man heave in sight, wagging his head from side to side, stumbling along and banging himself against the walls like a poet, and, ignoring his thralls the stool-pigeons, unburdening his heart of his world-shaking ambitions.

He takes oaths and decrees sublime laws, lays low the wicked and exalts the down-trodden, and beneath the firmament spread like a canopy he waxes drunk on the splendours of his own virtue.

Yes, these people, harassed by domestic sorrows, ground down by toil and racked by encroaching age, fagged and bending under a load of scrap, the confused vomit of gigantic Paris –

Reviennent, parfumés d'une odeur de futailles,
Suivis de compagnons, blanchis dans les batailles,
Dont la moustache pend comme les vieux drapeaux.
Les bannières, les fleurs et les arcs triomphaux

Se dressent devant eux, solennelle magie!
Et dans l'étourdissante et lumineuse orgie
Des clairons, du soleil, des cris et du tambour,
Ils apportent la gloire au peuple ivre d'amour!

C'est ainsi qu'à travers l'Humanité frivole
Le vin roule de l'or, éblouissant Pactole;
Par le gosier de l'homme il chante ses exploits
Et règne par ses dons ainsi que les vrais rois.

Pour noyer la rancœur et bercer l'indolence
De tous ces vieux maudits qui meurent en silence,
Dieu, touché de remords, avait fait le sommeil;
L'Homme ajouta le Vin, fils sacré du Soleil!

they reel home scented with the reek of wine-casks, followed by their comrades, white-haired from their battles, whose moustaches droop down like old flags. Banners and garlands and triumphal arches
loom by solemn magic before their eyes. And in the ear-splitting and dazzling orgy of trumpet-calls, sunshine, bawling and beaten drums, they bring glory to the masses, drunk with love.

Thus among frivolous mankind wine flows, full of gold, a blinding Eldorado; through the throat of man it sings its exploits and reigns by virtue of its bounty, as true monarchs do.

To drown the rancour and comfort the idle hours of all those old vagrants who die in silence, God, touched with remorse, created Sleep; Man added Wine, the sacred son of the Sun.

[Pre-1843. Published in a wine-growers'
journal, *Jean Raisin*, 1854; FM 1857]

CVI
LE VIN DE L'ASSASSIN

Ma femme est morte, je suis libre!
Je puis donc boire tout mon soûl.
Lorsque je rentrais sans un sou,
Ses cris me déchiraient la fibre.

Autant qu'un roi je suis heureux;
L'air est pur, le ciel admirable...
Nous avions un été semblable
Lorsque j'en devins amoureux!

L'horrible soif qui me déchire
Aurait besoin pour s'assouvir
D'autant de vin qu'en peut tenir
Son tombeau; – ce n'est pas peu dire:

Je l'ai jetée au fond d'un puits,
Et j'ai même poussé sur elle
Tous les pavés de la margelle.
– Je l'oublierai si je le puis!

The Murderer's Wine

My wife is dead, and I am free. So now I can get tight as much as I like.
Whenever I came home without a cent in my pocket her screeching
used to tear me apart.

Now I'm as happy as a king: how clean the air is, what a marvellous
sky! – a summer like when I first fell in love with her.

The cruel thirst that's always racking my innards would take all the
wine her grave can hold, to drown it, and that's saying something,

as I flung her down a well and shoved all the well-head stones on
top of her. Now I'll forget her, if I can.

Au nom des serments de tendresse,
Dont rien ne peut nous délier,
Et pour nous réconcilier
Comme au beau temps de notre ivresse,

J'implorai d'elle un rendez-vous,
Le soir, sur une route obscure.
Elle y vint! – folle créature!
Nous sommes tous plus ou moins fous!

Elle était encore jolie,
Quoique bien fatiguée! et moi,
Je l'aimais trop! voilà pourquoi
Je lui dis: Sors de cette vie!

Nul ne peut me comprendre. Un seul
Parmi ces ivrognes stupides
Songea-t-il dans ses nuits morbides
À faire du vin un linceul?

Cette crapule invulnérable
Comme les machines de fer
Jamais, ni l'été ni l'hiver,
N'a connu l'amour véritable,

In the name of all the vows of tenderness from which nothing can ever release us, and to make things up again like in the good old days when we were both drunk with love,

I begged her to meet me at night on a dark road, and she was mad enough to come. But we are all a bit mad, aren't we.

She was still pretty enough, though a bit worn. I was too fond of her, and that's why I said 'You can say goodbye to this existence.'

Nobody will ever understand me – for what drunk, even in his most miserable nights, would ever dream of making a burial-sheet of wine?

That invulnerable hag who was no more capable of feeling than an iron machine, never once in winter or summer did she have the least idea of what true love is,

Avec ses noirs enchantements,
Son cortège infernal d'alarmes,
Ses fioles de poison, ses larmes,
Ses bruits de chaîne et d'ossements!

– Me voilà libre et solitaire!
Je serai ce soir ivre mort;
Alors, sans peur et sans remords,
Je me coucherai sur la terre,

Et je dormirai comme un chien!
Le chariot aux lourdes roues
Chargé de pierres et de boues,
Le wagon enragé peut bien

Écraser ma tête coupable
Ou me couper par le milieu,
Je m'en moque comme de Dieu,
Du Diable ou de la Sainte Table!

what with her black magic and diabolic tricks and little bottles of
poison, her crocodile tears and all her rattling of chains and bones.
　　Now I am free and all alone. Tonight I'll get drunk as a lord.
Without fear and without remorse, I'll throw myself on the ground
　　and sleep like a dog. The night-cart with its lumbering wheels and
load of stones and filth, the furious railway car can easily
　　shatter my guilty skull or slice me in two, but I'll not care a damn,
just as I don't give a damn for God or the Devil or the blessed altar
itself.

[1843 (Prarond). Published 1848]

CVII
LE VIN DU SOLITAIRE

Le regard singulier d'une femme galante
Qui se glisse vers nous comme le rayon blanc
Que la lune onduleuse envoie au lac tremblant,
Quand elle y veut baigner sa beauté nonchalante;

Le dernier sac d'écus dans les doigts d'un joueur;
Un baiser libertin de la maigre Adeline;
Les sons d'une musique énervante et câline,
Semblable au cri lointain de l'humaine douleur,

Tout cela ne vaut pas, ô bouteille profonde,
Les baumes pénétrants que ta panse féconde
Garde au cœur altéré du poète pieux;

Tu lui verses l'espoir, la jeunesse et la vie,
– Et l'orgueil, ce trésor de toute gueuserie,
Qui nous rend triomphants et semblables aux Dieux!

The Lonely Man's Wine

The significant gleam in a loose woman's eyes sliding towards us, like the white beam the snaking Moon casts on the rippling lake where she would bathe her nonchalant beauty;

the last bag of dollars in the gambler's hand; a licentious kiss from skinny Adeline; the notes of an annoying and caressing melody like some distant cry of human suffering –

none of those things, O profound bottle, can ever equal the pungent balms which your fertile belly reserves for the pious poet's thirsting heart.

For him you pour out Hope and Youth and Life itself, and Pride, the treasure of the most deprived, which makes us triumphant and similar to the Gods.

[An early work. FM 1857]

CVIII
LE VIN DES AMANTS

Aujourd'hui l'espace est splendide!
Sans mors, sans éperons, sans bride,
Partons à cheval sur le vin
Pour un ciel féerique et divin!

Comme deux anges que torture
Une implacable calenture,
Dans le bleu cristal du matin
Suivons le mirage lointain!

Mollement balancés sur l'aile
Du tourbillon intelligent,
Dans un délire parallèle,

Ma sœur, côte à côte nageant,
Nous fuirons sans repos ni trêves
Vers le paradis de mes rêves!

·

Lovers' Wine

How splendid Space is, today! Without bit or spurs or bridle, let us
mount wine like a horse, and ride away to a divine, faery heaven!

Like two Angels goaded by a merciless sea-fever, let us pursue that
far-off mirage into the blue crystal of the morning.

Gently swaying on the wing of the wise whirlwind, in parallel
transcendence,

my sister, swimming side by side we'll speed away without repose or
pause, to the paradise of my dreams.

[FM 1857]

Fleurs du mal

CIX

LA DESTRUCTION

Sans cesse à mes côtés s'agite le Démon;
Il nage autour de moi comme un air impalpable;
Je l'avale et le sens qui brûle mon poumon
Et l'emplit d'un désir éternel et coupable.

Parfois il prend, sachant mon grand amour de l'Art,
La forme de la plus séduisante des femmes,
Et, sous de spécieux prétextes de cafard,
Accoutume ma lèvre à des philtres infâmes.

Il me conduit ainsi, loin du regard de Dieu,
Haletant et brisé de fatigue, au milieu
Des plaines de l'Ennui, profondes et désertes,

Et jette dans mes yeux pleins de confusion
Des vêtements souillés, des blessures ouvertes,
Et l'appareil sanglant de la Destruction!

FLOWERS OF EVIL

Destruction

The Demon is always nagging at my side, swirling round me like
untouchable vapour. As I gulp this down it sears my lungs and fills my
breast with never-ending, guilty lust.

Knowing my great love of Art, sometimes he assumes the most
entrancing female forms, and with specious, hypocritical pretexts
accustoms my lips to degrading potions.

Thus he lures me far from God's sight, and when I pant and faint
with exhaustion, sets me in the centre of enormous deserts of ennui:

and into my eyes full of confusion he hurls filthy rags and festering
sores, and every blood-soaked weapon of destruction.

[Prarond dates this 1846. Published 1855]

CX
UNE MARTYRE

DESSIN D'UN MAÎTRE INCONNU

Au milieu des flacons, des étoffes lamées
 Et des meubles voluptueux,
Des marbres, des tableaux, des robes parfumées
 Qui traînent à plis somptueux,

Dans une chambre tiède où, comme en une serre,
 L'air est dangereux et fatal,
Où des bouquets mourants dans leurs cercueils de verre
 Exhalent leur soupir final,

Un cadavre sans tête épanche, comme un fleuve,
 Sur l'oreiller désaltéré
Un sang rouge et vivant, dont la toile s'abreuve
 Avec l'avidité d'un pré.

Semblable aux visions pâles qu'enfante l'ombre
 Et qui nous enchaînent les yeux,
La tête, avec l'amas de sa crinière sombre
 Et de ses bijoux précieux,

A Martyred Woman

FROM A DRAWING BY AN UNKNOWN MASTER

Surrounded with scent-bottles, lamé draperies, luxurious furniture, marble sculptures, oil-paintings, perfumed dresses scattered around in sumptuous folds;

in a close bedchamber like a hothouse with its threatening morbid atmosphere in which drooping bouquets sigh their last in their crystal tombs –

on the sodden pillow a headless body pours a stream of scarlet living blood which the linen soaks up greedily like a parched field.

Like one of those hazy visions born of darkness which hypnotize our eyes, the severed head with its mass of pitch-black hair and precious jewels

Sur la table de nuit, comme une renoncule,
Repose; et, vide de pensers,
Un regard vague et blanc comme le crépuscule
S'échappe des yeux révulsés.

Sur le lit, le tronc nu sans scrupules étale
Dans le plus complet abandon
La secrète splendeur et la beauté fatale
Dont la nature lui fit don;

Un bas rosâtre, orné de coins d'or, à la jambe,
Comme un souvenir est resté;
La jarretière, ainsi qu'un œil secret qui flambe,
Darde un regard diamanté.

Le singulier aspect de cette solitude
Et d'un grand portrait langoureux,
Aux yeux provocateurs comme son attitude,
Révèle un amour ténébreux,

reposes on the night-table – a grotesque dandelion! – a head empty
of thoughts, whose reversed eyeballs gaze with a stare as vague and
colourless as twilight.

The naked torso, on the bed, wantonly exhibits the intimate splen-
dours and foredoomed beauty which were nature's gifts.

A flesh-coloured stocking, prettified with clocks of gold, clings like
a reminiscence to her leg, on which a garter, like a secret blazing eye,
glints with a gemlike glare.

This singular aspect of this solitude, completed by her large volup-
tuous portrait in which the eyes are as provocative as her pose, points to
some shady love-affair,

Une coupable joie et des fêtes étranges
 Pleines de baisers infernaux,
Dont se réjouissait l'essaim des mauvais anges
 Nageant dans les plis des rideaux;

Et cependant, à voir la maigreur élégante
 De l'épaule au contour heurté,
La hanche un peu pointue et la taille fringante
 Ainsi qu'un reptile irrité,

Elle est bien jeune encor! – Son âme exaspérée
 Et ses sens par l'ennui mordus
S'étaient-ils entr'ouverts à la meute altérée
 Des désirs errants et perdus?

L'homme vindicatif que tu n'as pu, vivante,
 Malgré tant d'amour, assouvir,
Combla-t-il sur ta chair inerte et complaisante
 L'immensité de son désir?

Réponds, cadavre impur! et par tes tresses roides
 Te soulevant d'un bras fiévreux,
Dis-moi, tête effrayante, a-t-il sur tes dents froides
 Collé les suprêmes adieux?

 guilty joys, perverted rituals full of diabolical embraces, gloated on by hordes of evil angels floating among the curtains' folds –
 and yet to judge from the elegant slimness of the shoulder's clean outlines, the slightly pointed hip, the waist as lithe as a writhing snake's,
 she must be still quite young. Did her exasperated soul, her senses suffering from the bite of boredom, half open themselves to a thirsty pack of wandering, lost desires?
 Did the avenger whom your vast love could never satisfy while you lived, assuage his immense longing on your inert and unresisting flesh?
 Answer me, impure carcass – as his feverish arms lifted you up by your stiff hair, tell me, terrifying head, did he print his last farewell on your ice-cold teeth?

– Loin du monde railleur, loin de la foule impure,
 Loin des magistrats curieux,
Dors en paix, dors en paix, étrange créature,
 Dans ton tombeau mystérieux;

Ton époux court le monde, et ta forme immortelle
 Veille près de lui quand il dort;
Autant que toi sans doute il te sera fidèle,
 Et constant jusques à la mort.

Far from the mockery of the world, far from the foul multitude, far from inquiring magistrates sleep now in peace, strange being, in your mysterious tomb.

Now your husband roams the earth, and your immortal shade keeps watch over him while he sleeps; and no doubt as steadfastly as you, he will be faithful and constant to the death.

[FM 1857. Perhaps an early work, based on
The Death of Sardanapalus by Delacroix]

CXI
FEMMES DAMNÉES

Comme un bétail pensif sur le sable couchées,
Elles tournent leurs yeux vers l'horizon des mers,
Et leurs pieds se cherchant et leurs mains rapprochées
Ont de douces langueurs et des frissons amers.

Les unes, cœurs épris des longues confidences,
Dans le fond des bosquets où jasent les ruisseaux,
Vont épelant l'amour des craintives enfances
Et creusent le bois vert des jeunes arbrisseaux;

D'autres, comme des sœurs, marchent lentes et graves
À travers les rochers pleins d'apparitions,
Où saint Antoine a vu surgir comme des laves
Les seins nus et pourprés de ses tentations;

Il en est, aux lueurs des résines croulantes,
Qui dans le creux muet des vieux antres païens
T'appellent au secours de leurs fièvres hurlantes,
Ô Bacchus, endormeur des remords anciens!

Doomed Women

Lying like ruminating cattle on the sand, they turn their eyes towards the seas' horizons, and their feet seeking each other's, their hands drawing more close, they feel sweet languors, bitter thrills.

Some of them, hearts given to long intimate talks, deep in the groves where streams are purling, go spelling out their shy virgin loves and carving their names on the green bark of saplings.

Others, like nuns, tread slow and grave among the vision-haunted rocks where St Anthony saw the bare ruby breasts of his temptations surge like lava.

There are others who, in the melting resin's glimmer in the silent hollows of pagan caves, implore you to assuage their shrieking fevers, O Bacchus, soother of many a past remorse.

Et d'autres, dont la gorge aime les scapulaires,
Qui, recélant un fouet sous leurs longs vêtements,
Mêlent, dans le bois sombre et les nuits solitaires,
L'écume du plaisir aux larmes des tourments.

Ô vierges, ô démons, ô monstres, ô martyres,
De la réalité grands esprits contempteurs,
Chercheuses d'infini, dévotes et satyres,
Tantôt pleines de cris, tantôt pleines de pleurs,

Vous que dans votre enfer mon âme a poursuivies,
Pauvres sœurs, je vous aime autant que je vous plains,
Pour vos mornes douleurs, vos soifs inassouvies,
Et les urnes d'amour dont vos grands cœurs sont pleins!

And others whose throats love wearing scapularies, and who, hiding a whip under their trailing robes, unite the froth of pleasure and the tears of pain in the lightless wood on lonely nights.

O virgins, demons, monsters, martyrs, great minds who despise reality, seekers of the Infinite; whether pious or lustful ones, now crying out aloud, now bathed in tears,

you whom my soul has followed into your inferno, my poor sisters – I have as much love as compassion for your melancholy griefs and unquenchable thirsts, and the urns of love which overflow in your great hearts.

[1846? FM 1857]

CXII
LES DEUX BONNES SŒURS

La Débauche et la Mort sont deux aimables filles,
Prodigues de baisers et riches de santé,
Dont le flanc toujours vierge et drapé de guenilles
Sous l'éternel labeur n'a jamais enfanté.

Au poète sinistre, ennemi des familles,
Favori de l'enfer, courtisan mal renté,
Tombeaux et lupanars montrent sous leurs charmilles
Un lit que le remords n'a jamais fréquenté.

Et la bière et l'alcôve en blasphèmes fécondes
Nous offrent tour à tour, comme deux bonnes sœurs,
De terribles plaisirs et d'affreuses douceurs.

Quand veux-tu m'enterrer, Débauche aux bras immondes?
Ô Mort, quand viendras-tu, sa rivale en attraits,
Sur ses myrtes infects enter tes noirs cyprès?

The Two Kind Sisters

Debauch and Death are two amiable girls, generous kissers, hearty with health, whose ever-virginal sides, decked in rags and tatters, have never borne a child despite their endless labours.

To the sinister poet, that foe of families, the blue-eyed-boy of hell, that underpaid hanger-on, graves and midnight revels show the way to a bed in their bowers on which Remorse has never lain.

Coffin and bed, fertile in blasphemies, like two indulgent sisters offer us in turn terrible pleasures, horrible delights.

When will you bury me, Debauch with her loathsome embrace? And when, O Death, her rival in charms, will you come and graft your black cypresses on her leprous myrtles?

[1844? (Le Vavasseur). FM 1857]

CXIII
LA FONTAINE DE SANG

Il me semble parfois que mon sang coule à flots,
Ainsi qu'une fontaine aux rythmiques sanglots.
Je l'entends bien qui coule avec un long murmure,
Mais je me tâte en vain pour trouver la blessure.

À travers la cité, comme dans un champ clos,
Il s'en va, transformant les pavés en îlots,
Désaltérant la soif de chaque créature,
Et partout colorant en rouge la nature.

J'ai demandé souvent à des vins captieux
D'endormir pour un jour la terreur qui me mine;
Le vin rend l'œil plus clair et l'oreille plus fine!

J'ai cherché dans l'amour un sommeil oublieux;
Mais l'amour n'est pour moi qu'un matelas d'aiguilles
Fait pour donner à boire à ces cruelles filles!

The Fountain of Blood

Sometimes my blood seems to be flowing out in waves like a rhythmically sobbing fountain. I can hear it running with a steady murmur, yet I feel my body in vain to find the wound.

Across the city, as in a tourney field, my blood goes; it makes islands of the streets, it slakes the thirst of all living things, it dyes all nature red.

I have often begged the most intoxicating wines to bring a day's respite to the terror which is sapping my strength; but wine undims the eye and makes the ear more sharp.

I have sought the sleep of oblivion in love; but for me love is no more than a bed of spikes, designed to draw our blood for these cruel whores to drink.

[1851–2. FM 1857]

CXIV

ALLÉGORIE

C'est une femme belle et de riche encolure,
Qui laisse dans son vin traîner sa chevelure.
Les griffes de l'amour, les poisons du tripot,
Tout glisse et tout s'émousse au granit de sa peau.
Elle rit à la Mort et nargue la Débauche,
Ces monstres dont la main, qui toujours gratte et fauche,
Dans ses jeux destructeurs a pourtant respecté
De ce corps ferme et droit la rude majesté.
Elle marche en déesse et repose en sultane;
Elle a dans le plaisir la foi mahométane,
Et dans ses bras ouverts, que remplissent ses seins,
Elle appelle des yeux la race des humains.
Elle croit, elle sait, cette vierge inféconde
Et pourtant nécessaire à la marche du monde,
Que la beauté du corps est un sublime don
Qui de toute infamie arrache le pardon.
Elle ignore l'Enfer comme le Purgatoire,
Et quand l'heure viendra d'entrer dans la Nuit noire,
Elle regardera la face de la Mort,
Ainsi qu'un nouveau-né, – sans haine et sans remords.

Allegory

She is a handsome strong-necked woman, who lets her hair trail in her wine. The talons of love and the poisons of the dens glance off her granite hide which blunts their power. She laughs at death and taunts debauchery; but those monsters whose paws are forever scratching and scything, in their destructive games have never failed to respect the primitive majesty of her firm and upright body. She moves like a goddess, and like an empress she reclines. She has a moorish faith in pleasure, her eyes invite the human race to the welcome of her breast-filled arms.

This infertile vestal, so essential to the working of the world, believes and knows that physical beauty is a sublime gift which exacts forgiveness for all infamies. Careless of hell and purgatory alike, when her hour comes to step into the black night, she will look upon death's face without hatred or remorse, like a newborn child.

[1843, Prarond. FM 1857]

CXV
LA BÉATRICE

Dans des terrains cendreux, calcinés, sans verdure,
Comme je me plaignais un jour à la nature,
Et que de ma pensée, en vaguant au hasard,
J'aiguisais lentement sur mon cœur le poignard,
Je vis en plein midi descendre sur ma tête
Un nuage funèbre et gros d'une tempête,
Qui portait un troupeau de démons vicieux,
Semblables à des nains cruels et curieux.
À me considérer froidement ils se mirent,
Et, comme des passants sur un fou qu'ils admirent,
Je les entendis rire et chuchoter entre eux,
En échangeant maint signe et maint clignement d'yeux:

– «Contemplons à loisir cette caricature
Et cette ombre d'Hamlet imitant sa posture,
Le regard indécis et les cheveux au vent.
N'est-ce pas grand-pitié de voir ce bon vivant,
Ce gueux, cet histrion en vacances, ce drôle,
Parce qu'il sait jouer artistement son rôle,

The Poet's Beatrice

Across the ashen vacant lots, burnt to a cinder, where no green grew,
while one day I was complaining to Nature and, aimlessly wandering,
went sharpening the dagger of my thoughts on my own heart,
although it was high noon I saw a sinister, storm-heavy cloud descend
upon my head, bearing with it a horde of vicious demons like cruel
inquisitive dwarfs. They began to examine me coldly and, like street-
idlers gaping at a halfwit, I heard them chuckle and whisper to one
another, exchanging many a nudge and many a wink.

 'Let us gaze our fill on this human caricature, this shade of Hamlet
imitating his poses, with his distraught gaze and unkempt hair. Isn't it an
awful shame to see this epicure, this pauper, this unemployed actor, this
oddfellow, just because he knows how to play his part like a professional,

Vouloir intéresser au chant de ses douleurs
Les aigles, les grillons, les ruisseaux et les fleurs,
Et même à nous, auteurs de ces vieilles rubriques,
Réciter en hurlant ses tirades publiques?»

J'aurais pu (mon orgueil aussi haut que les monts
Domine la nuée et le cri des démons)
Détourner simplement ma tête souveraine,
Si je n'eusse pas vu parmi leur troupe obscène,
Crime qui n'a pas fait chanceler le soleil!
La reine de mon cœur au regard nonpareil,
Qui riait avec eux de ma sombre détresse
Et leur versait parfois quelque sale caresse.

trying to interest eagles and crickets, streams and flowers in his tale of
woe, and even bellowing his public speeches at us, of all people, who
invented all that mumbo-jumbo ourselves!'

As my mountain-high pride stands far above the clouds and cries of
demons, I could simply have turned my princely head the other way –
had I not seen among that obscene mob – O crime which failed to
rock the Sun! – the queen of my heart, whose eyes arc beyond
compare, laughing with them at my dire affliction, and giving them
here and there a lewd caress.

[An early poem which ought to be situated in the Jeanne Duval
cycle, as both 'De profundis clamavi' and 'Le Vampire'
were originally entitled 'La Béatrix'. FM 1857]

CXVI
UN VOYAGE À CYTHÈRE

Mon cœur, comme un oiseau, voltigeait tout joyeux
Et planait librement à l'entour des cordages;
Le navire roulait sous un ciel sans nuages,
Comme un ange enivré d'un soleil radieux.

Quelle est cette île triste et noire? – C'est Cythère,
Nous dit-on, un pays fameux dans les chansons,
Eldorado banal de tous les vieux garçons.
Regardez, après tout, c'est une pauvre terre.

– Île des doux secrets et des fêtes du cœur!
De l'antique Vénus le superbe fantôme
Au-dessus de tes mers plane comme un arome,
Et charge les esprits d'amour et de langueur.

Belle île aux myrtes verts, pleine de fleurs écloses,
Vénérée à jamais par toute nation,
Où les soupirs des cœurs en adoration
Roulent comme l'encens sur un jardin de roses

A Voyage to the Isle of Venus

My heart was hovering gaily as a bird, gliding with ease around the rigging; the ship sailed on beneath a cloudless sky like an angel drunk with blinding sun.

'But what can that sad, black island be?' – 'It's Cythera,' they said, 'a place much famed in song, the boring Eldorado of all old bachelors: as you can see, it's not much of a place, when all is said and done.'

– The isle of the sweet secrets and festivities of the heart! The majestic Shade of the Venus of ancient days wafts like a perfume over the seas around you, filling our minds with love and soft repose.

Fair Isle of green myrtle glades, filled with flowers in full bloom, revered throughout the ages by all nations, where the sighs of adoring hearts roll like incense through a garden of roses,

Ou le roucoulement éternel d'un ramier!
– Cythère n'était plus qu'un terrain des plus maigres,
Un désert rocailleux troublé par des cris aigres.
J'entrevoyais pourtant un objet singulier!

Ce n'était pas un temple aux ombres bocagères,
Où la jeune prêtresse, amoureuse des fleurs,
Allait, le corps brûlé de secrètes chaleurs,
Entrebâillant sa robe aux brises passagères;

Mais voilà qu'en rasant la côte d'assez près
Pour troubler les oiseaux avec nos voiles blanches,
Nous vîmes que c'était un gibet à trois branches,
Du ciel se détachant en noir, comme un cyprès.

De féroces oiseaux perchés sur leur pâture
Détruisaient avec rage un pendu déjà mûr,
Chacun plantant, comme un outil, son bec impur
Dans tous les coins saignants de cette pourriture;

or like the endless cooing of the dove! – But Cythera had now become the most barren of all lands, a desert of rocks haunted by shrill cries. However, I glimpsed a strange thing there.

It was no temple with shady groves in which some flower-loving young priestess walked, her body aflame with obscure desires, half-opening her robe to catch the passing breeze.

Oh no: as we passed close enough to the shore for our white sails to alarm the birds, we saw it was a three-branched gibbet, looming black against the sky like a cypress tree.

Ferocious birds perched on their prey were savagely tearing the ripened corpse of a hanged man, all driving their filthy beaks like a tool into every bleeding corner of that putridness.

Les yeux étaient deux trous, et du ventre effondré
Les intestins pesants lui coulaient sur les cuisses,
Et ses bourreaux, gorgés de hideuses délices,
L'avaient à coups de bec absolument châtré.

Sous les pieds, un troupeau de jaloux quadrupèdes,
Le museau relevé, tournoyait et rôdait;
Une plus grande bête au milieu s'agitait
Comme un exécuteur entouré de ses aides.

Habitant de Cythère, enfant d'un ciel si beau,
Silencieusement tu souffrais ces insultes
En expiation de tes infâmes cultes
Et des péchés qui t'ont interdit le tombeau.

Ridicule pendu, tes douleurs sont les miennes!
Je sentis, à l'aspect de tes membres flottants,
Comme un vomissement, remonter vers mes dents
Le long fleuve de fiel des douleurs anciennes;

His eyes were already two empty sockets, and from his caved-in belly the heavy intestines were rolling down his thighs, and his tormentors, gorged on hideous titbits, had thoroughly castrated him with their beaks.

At his feet a pack of jealous beasts were circling and prowling to and fro with uplifted maws, while one bigger than the rest was leaping higher in their midst, like an executioner surrounded by his henchmen.

Oh son of Cythera, child of such a lovely sky, silently you suffered those insults in expiation of your infamous practices and for sins which denied you a grave.

O grotesque gallow-bird, your sufferings are my own! As I looked on your swinging limbs, I felt the long stream of gall of past sufferings rise like a vomit to my teeth.

Devant toi, pauvre diable au souvenir si cher,
J'ai senti tous les becs et toutes les mâchoires
Des corbeaux lancinants et des panthères noires
Qui jadis aimaient tant à triturer ma chair.

– Le ciel était charmant, la mer était unie;
Pour moi tout était noir et sanglant désormais,
Hélas! et j'avais, comme en un suaire épais,
Le cœur enseveli dans cette allégorie.

Dans ton île, ô Vénus! je n'ai trouvé debout
Qu'un gibet symbolique où pendait mon image . . .
– Ah! Seigneur! donnez-moi la force et le courage
De contempler mon cœur et mon corps sans dégoût!

At the sight of you, poor devil whose memory I hold dear, I felt all
the beaks and jaws of swooping ravens and black panthers which once
delighted in reducing my flesh to pulp.

– The sky was entrancing, the sea a sheet of calm; but for me all was
now darkness and blood. Alas, my heart lay buried in that allegory as in
the thick shrouds of death.

O Venus, in your Isle I found nothing standing but a symbolic
gallows with my own image hanged upon it. – O heavenly Father, give
me the strength and courage to contemplate my heart and body with-
out disgust!

[One of the twelve poems sent to Gautier, 1852. Published
1855 and in FM 1857. The poem was probably prompted
by Nerval's description of Cerigo in 1844. I suggest that
Baudelaire probably knew Gentil-Bernard's *La Ménagerie
de Cythère*, a burlesque description of Cythera which
would explain the 'Eldorado banal' etc.]

CXVII
L'AMOUR ET LE CRÂNE

VIEUX CUL-DE-LAMPE

L'Amour est assis sur le crâne
De l'Humanité,
Et sur ce trône le profane,
Au rire effronté,

Souffle gaiement des bulles rondes
Qui montent dans l'air,
Comme pour rejoindre les mondes
Au fond de l'éther.

Le globe lumineux et frêle
Prend un grand essor,
Crève et crache son âme grêle
Comme un songe d'or.

J'entends le crâne à chaque bulle
Prier et gémir:
– «Ce jeu féroce et ridicule,
Quand doit-il finir?

Love and the Skull

AN OLD TAIL-PIECE

Profanely perched on mankind's skull as on a throne, with insolent laughter

Cupid is cheerfully blowing bubbles, which float into the air as though to join other worlds in the ethereal heights,

The luminous frail globe soars heavenwards then bursts, spitting its feeble soul out like a golden dream.

I can hear the skull praying and groaning at each one 'When will this crazy heartless game come to an end?

«Car ce que ta bouche cruelle
Éparpille en l'air,
Monstre assassin, c'est ma cervelle,
Mon sang et ma chair!»

'Murderous monster, what your cruel mouth is scattering in the air
is my brain, my flesh, my blood.'

[Published 1855. The theme has been traced
to an etching by Hendrick Goltzius]

Révolte

CXVIII
LE RENIEMENT DE SAINT PIERRE

Qu'est-ce que Dieu fait donc de ce flot d'anathèmes
Qui monte tous les jours vers ses chers Séraphins?
Comme un tyran gorgé de viande et de vins,
Il s'endort au doux bruit de nos affreux blasphèmes.

Les sanglots des martyrs et des suppliciés
Sont une symphonie enivrante sans doute,
Puisque, malgré le sang que leur volupté coûte,
Les cieux ne s'en sont point encor rassasiés!

– Ah! Jésus, souviens-toi du Jardin des Olives!
Dans ta simplicité tu priais à genoux
Celui qui dans son ciel riait au bruit des clous
Que d'ignobles bourreaux plantaient dans tes chairs vives,

REVOLT

Saint Peter's Denial

What does God do with the stream of curses which rise day after day
to the ears of his beloved Seraphim? Like some tyrant glutted with
flesh and wine he falls asleep to the soothing clamour of our outra-
geous blasphemies.

The sobs of martyrs and tortured victims must be an intoxicating
symphony, as in spite of all the bloodshed which is the price of their
entertainment, those in heaven have not yet had their fill.

Ah, Jesus, never forget the Mount of Olives. In your simplicity you
fell on your knees and prayed to your Father above, but he laughed
aloud in his heaven as he heard the hammering of the nails being
driven by the hangmen into your living flesh.

Lorsque tu vis cracher sur ta divinité
La crapule du corps de garde et des cuisines,
Et lorsque tu sentis s'enfoncer les épines
Dans ton crâne où vivait l'immense Humanité;

Quand de ton corps brisé la pesanteur horrible
Allongeait tes deux bras distendus, que ton sang
Et ta sueur coulaient de ton front pâlissant,
Quand tu fus devant tous posé comme une cible,

Rêvais-tu de ces jours si brillants et si beaux
Où tu vins pour remplir l'éternelle promesse,
Où tu foulais, monté sur une douce ânesse,
Des chemins tout jonchés de fleurs et de rameaux,

Où, le cœur tout gonflé d'espoir et de vaillance,
Tu fouettais tous ces vils marchands à tour de bras,
Où tu fus maître enfin? Le remords n'a-t-il pas
Pénétré dans ton flanc plus avant que la lance?

When you saw the scum of guards and scullions spit on your divinity;
when you felt the crown of thorns thrust into your head, that home of
immense Humanity;

when the unbearable weight of your broken body stretched your
distended arms; when your blood and sweat oozed from your paling
brow, when you were placed before everyone like a target –

did you not dream of those radiant beautiful days when you came
to fulfil the eternal promise; when you mounted on a humble ass and
trod the paths all strewn with flowers and sprays of palm,

when with a heart swollen with hope and courage you whipped the
money-lenders from the temple – when at last you were the Master,
did not remorse penetrate your side more deeply than the lance?

– Certes, je sortirai, quant à moi, satisfait
D'un monde où l'action n'est pas la sœur du rêve;
Puissé-je user du glaive et périr par le glaive!
Saint Pierre a renié Jésus . . . il a bien fait!

For my part I shall certainly be glad to leave a world where action is not the sister of dream: if only I could wield the sword and perish by the sword! Saint Peter denied Jesus: he was right.

[1851–2. FM 1857]

CXIX

ABEL ET CAÏN

I

Race d'Abel, dors, bois et mange;
Dieu te sourit complaisamment.

Race de Caïn, dans la fange
Rampe et meurs misérablement.

Race d'Abel, ton sacrifice
Flatte le nez du Séraphin!

Race de Caïn, ton supplice
Aura-t-il jamais une fin?

Race d'Abel, vois tes semailles
Et ton bétail venir à bien;

Race de Caïn, tes entrailles
Hurlent la faim comme un vieux chien.

Abel and Cain

I

Tribe of Abel, sleep, drink and eat, for God gives you his indulgent smile.

Tribe of Cain, crawl in the shit, die like a dog.

Tribe of Abel, how sweet your offerings smell in the nostrils of the Seraphim.

Tribe of Cain, will your agony never end?

Tribe of Abel, see how your seed prospers, how your cattle thrive.

Tribe of Cain, your guts howl with hunger like an old cur.

Race d'Abel, chauffe ton ventre
À ton foyer patriarcal;

Race de Caïn, dans ton antre
Tremble de froid, pauvre chacal!

Race d'Abel, aime et pullule!
Ton or fait aussi des petits.

Race de Caïn, cœur qui brûle,
Prends garde à ces grands appétits.

Race d'Abel, tu croîs et broutes
Comme les punaises des bois!

Race de Caïn, sur les routes
Traîne ta famille aux abois.

Tribe of Abel, warm your belly before your patriarchal hearth.

Tribe of Cain, tremble with cold in your hole in the ground, you miserable jackal.

Tribe of Abel, be amorous and increase: your gold also will multiply.

Tribe of Cain, however much your heart might burn with love, beware these great desires.

Tribe of Abel, bloat and guzzle like woodlice.

Tribe of Cain, drag your hounded wife and children with you down the roads.

II

Ah! race d'Abel, ta charogne
Engraissera le sol fumant!

Race de Caïn, ta besogne
N'est pas faite suffisamment;

Race d'Abel, voici ta honte:
Le fer est vaincu par l'épieu!

Race de Caïn, au ciel monte,
Et sur la terre jette Dieu!

II

Tribe of Abel, one day your carcass will manure the fetid soil.
　　Tribe of Cain, your task is not yet done.
　　Tribe of Abel, your shame will come when the sword is shattered by the peasants' stake.
　　Tribe of Cain, ascend to heaven, and throw God down to earth.

[1847–8. FM 1857]

CXX
LES LITANIES DE SATAN

Ô toi, le plus savant et le plus beau des Anges,
Dieu trahi par le sort et privé de louanges,

Ô Satan, prends pitié de ma longue misère !

Ô Prince de l'exil, à qui l'on a fait tort,
Et qui, vaincu, toujours te redresses plus fort,

Ô Satan, prends pitié de ma longue misère !

Toi qui sais tout, grand roi des choses souterraines,
Guérisseur familier des angoisses humaines,

Ô Satan, prends pitié de ma longue misère !

Toi qui, même aux lépreux, aux parias maudits,
Enseignes par l'amour le goût du Paradis,

Ô Satan, prends pitié de ma longue misère !

The Litanies of Satan

O you, the most omniscient and most beautiful of all Angels, a god betrayed by Fate and bereft of praises; O Satan, have compassion on my endless misery!

O Prince of exile, to whom injustice has been done, and who in your defeat arise more firm; O Satan, have compassion on my endless misery!

You who know all, great King of all things in the underworld, familiar healer of all human anguishes; O Satan, have compassion on my endless misery!

You who, even to lepers and to outcasts under ban, teach through love the taste of Paradise; O Satan, have compassion on my endless misery!

Ô toi qui de la Mort, ta vieille et forte amante,
Engendras l'Espérance, – une folle charmante!

Ô Satan, prends pitié de ma longue misère!

Toi qui fais au proscrit ce regard calme et haut
Qui damne tout un peuple autour d'un échafaud,

Ô Satan, prends pitié de ma longue misère!

Toi qui sais en quels coins des terres envieuses
Le Dieu jaloux cacha les pierres précieuses,

Ô Satan, prends pitié de ma longue misère!

Toi dont l'œil clair connaît les profonds arsenaux
Où dort enseveli le peuple des métaux,

Ô Satan, prends pitié de ma longue misère!

Toi dont la large main cache les précipices
Au somnambule errant au bord des édifices,

Ô Satan, prends pitié de ma longue misère!

O you who through your old and mighty consort, Death, begot that charming maniac, Hope; O Satan, have compassion on my endless misery!

You who give the outlaw that serene and haughty look which damns an entire nation thronging round the scaffold; O Satan, have compassion on my endless misery!

You who know in what recesses of covetous lands the jealous God hid the precious stones; O Satan, have compassion on my endless misery!

You whose bright eye knows the deep arsenals where the buried race of metals slumbers; O Satan, have compassion on my endless misery!

You whose vast hand conceals the precipice from the somnambulist as he strays on the brink of buildings; O Satan, have compassion on my endless misery!

Toi qui, magiquement, assouplis les vieux os
De l'ivrogne attardé foulé par les chevaux,

Ô Satan, prends pitié de ma longue misère!

Toi qui, pour consoler l'homme frêle qui souffre,
Nous appris à mêler le salpêtre et le soufre,

Ô Satan, prends pitié de ma longue misère!

Toi qui poses ta marque, ô complice subtil,
Sur le front du Crésus impitoyable et vil,

Ô Satan, prends pitié de ma longue misère!

Toi qui mets dans les yeux et dans le cœur des filles
Le culte de la plaie et l'amour des guenilles,

Ô Satan, prends pitié de ma longue misère!

Bâton des exilés, lampe des inventeurs,
Confesseur des pendus et des conspirateurs,

Ô Satan, prends pitié de ma longue misère!

You whose magic makes supple the old bones of the belated drunk-ard, trampled by hooves of horses; O Satan, have compassion on my endless misery!

You who, to console frail Man in his suffering, taught us to mingle saltpetre and sulphur; O Satan, have compassion on my endless misery!

You who set your mark, O subtle accomplice, on the brow of the pitiless vile millionaire; O Satan, have compassion on my endless misery!

You who implant in women's eyes and hearts the cult of wounds and love of rags; O Satan, have compassion on my endless misery!

Staff of the exiled, lamp of inventors, confessor of the hanged and of the terrorist; O Satan, have compassion on my endless misery!

Père adoptif de ceux qu'en sa noire colère
Du paradis terrestre a chassés Dieu le Père,

Ô Satan, prends pitié de ma longue misère !

PRIÈRE

Gloire et louange à toi, Satan, dans les hauteurs
Du Ciel, où tu régnas, et dans les profondeurs
De l'Enfer, où, vaincu, tu rêves en silence !
Fais que mon âme un jour, sous l'Arbre de Science,
Près de toi se repose, à l'heure où sur ton front
Comme un Temple nouveau ses rameaux s'épandront !

Foster-father of those who in his black anger God drove out of the earthly Paradise; O Satan, have compassion on my endless misery!

PRAYER

Glory and praise to you, Satan, in the heights of Heaven where once you reigned, and in the depths of Hell where, vanquished, you dream in silence. Grant that my soul, some day, may rest beside you under the Tree of Knowledge, at the hour when on your brow, like a new Temple, its branches will all spread.

[An early poem, perhaps 1846 (F. Caussy). FM 1857]

La Mort

LA MORT DES AMANTS

Nous aurons des lits pleins d'odeurs légères,
Des divans profonds comme des tombeaux,
Et d'étranges fleurs sur des étagères,
Écloses pour nous sous des cieux plus beaux.

Usant à l'envi leurs chaleurs dernières,
Nos deux cœurs seront deux vastes flambeaux,
Qui réfléchiront leurs doubles lumières
Dans nos deux esprits, ces miroirs jumeaux.

Un soir fait de rose et de bleu mystique,
Nous échangerons un éclair unique,
Comme un long sanglot, tout chargé d'adieux;

Et plus tard un Ange, entrouvrant les portes,
Viendra ranimer, fidèle et joyeux,
Les miroirs ternis et les flammes mortes.

DEATH

The Death of Lovers

We shall have beds scented with delicate perfumes; divans with the deepness of the tomb, and mysterious flowers decking our shelves, that bloom for us beneath more lovely skies.

Vying with one another to exhaust their final fires our two hearts will be two vast torches, reflecting their twin lights in our two minds, which are twin mirrors.

On an evening all rosiness and mystic blue, we shall exchange a single flash of light, like a long sob heavy with our farewells;

and afterwards an Angel, discreetly opening the doors, faithful and full of joy, will come in to revive the lustreless mirrors and lifeless flames.

[Published 1851 and FM 1857: set to music by Debussy and others]

CXXII
LA MORT DES PAUVRES

C'est la Mort qui console, hélas! et qui fait vivre;
C'est le but de la vie, et c'est le seul espoir
Qui, comme un élixir, nous monte et nous enivre,
Et nous donne le cœur de marcher jusqu'au soir;

À travers la tempête, et la neige, et le givre,
C'est la clarté vibrante à notre horizon noir;
C'est l'auberge fameuse inscrite sur le livre,
Où l'on pourra manger, et dormir, et s'asseoir;

C'est un Ange qui tient dans ses doigts magnétiques
Le sommeil et le don des rêves extatiques,
Et qui refait le lit des gens pauvres et nus;

C'est la gloire des dieux, c'est le grenier mystique,
C'est la bourse du pauvre et sa patrie antique,
C'est le portique ouvert sur les Cieux inconnus!

The Death of the Poor

It is Death, alas, which brings us consolation and makes us keep on living. Death is the aim and end of life, and is the only hope which, like some elixir, rouses and intoxicates us and gives us courage to fare on till evening.

Through tempest, snow and frost, it is the lamp that glimmers on our black horizon, the marvellous inn the Book tells of, where a man may eat and sleep and sit himself down.

It is an Angel whose magnetic fingers impart sleep and the gift of dreams of ecstasy, that Angel who makes the bed of poor and naked folk.

It is the glory of the gods, the mystic granary, the poor man's purse, his historic motherland: it is the gate which opens onto unknown skies.

[Sent to Gautier in 1852. FM 1857. The book is taken
by critics to mean the Gospel (Luke, x.30–35),
but it could be an allusion to the Koran]

CXXIII
LA MORT DES ARTISTES

Combien faut-il de fois secouer mes grelots
Et baiser ton front bas, morne caricature?
Pour piquer dans le but, de mystique nature,
Combien, ô mon carquois, perdre de javelots?

Nous userons notre âme en de subtils complots,
Et nous démolirons mainte lourde armature,
Avant de contempler la grande Créature
Dont l'infernal désir nous remplit de sanglots!

Il en est qui jamais n'ont connu leur Idole,
Et ces sculpteurs damnés et marqués d'un affront,
Qui vont se martelant la poitrine et le front,

N'ont qu'un espoir, étrange et sombre Capitole!
C'est que la Mort, planant comme un soleil nouveau,
Fera s'épanouir les fleurs de leur cerveau!

The Death of Artists

How often must I rattle my bells and kiss your beetling brow, you gloomy caricature? To score a bull's-eye on that metaphysical target, how many javelins must my quiver waste?

We shall wear our souls out in sly stratagems and destroy many a [sculptor's] framework, before coming face to face with that gigantic Creature, whose infernal desire fills us with lamentations.

There are some who have never known their Idol; and these sculptors damned and branded with humiliation, who turn the hammer against their own breast and brow

have one hope only, one strange, dark Capitol: the hope that Death, soaring aloft like a new sun, will enable the flowers of their mind to bloom at last.

[Published 1851. FM 1857]

CXXIV
LA FIN DE LA JOURNÉE

Sous une lumière blafarde
Court, danse et se tord sans raison
La Vie, impudente et criarde.
Aussi, sitôt qu'à l'horizon

La nuit voluptueuse monte,
Apaisant tout, même la faim,
Effaçant tout, même la honte,
Le Poète se dit: «Enfin!

«Mon esprit, comme mes vertèbres,
Invoque ardemment le repos;
Le cœur plein de songes funèbres,

«Je vais me coucher sur le dos
Et me rouler dans vos rideaux,
Ô rafraîchissantes ténèbres!»

The Day's End

In bloodless daylight, Life rushes along and jigs and writhes, shameless and shrill; so as soon as
 voluptuous Night looms in the sky, appeasing all things and even hunger, effacing all things, even shame, the Poet says to himself, 'At last!
 'My mind, like my spine, craves ardently for rest. With my heart full of morbid visions,
 'I shall now lie on my back and roll myself in your curtains, refreshing shadows.'

[1860. FM 1861]

CXXV
LE RÊVE D'UN CURIEUX

À F. N.

Connais-tu, comme moi, la douleur savoureuse,
Et de toi fais-tu dire: «Oh! l'homme singulier!»
– J'allais mourir. C'était dans mon âme amoureuse,
Désir mêlé d'horreur, un mal particulier;

Angoisse et vif espoir, sans humeur factieuse.
Plus allait se vidant le fatal sablier,
Plus ma torture était âpre et délicieuse;
Tout mon cœur s'arrachait au monde familier.

J'étais comme l'enfant avide du spectacle,
Haïssant le rideau comme on hait un obstacle . . .
Enfin la vérité froide se révéla:

J'étais mort sans surprise, et la terrible aurore
M'enveloppait. – Eh quoi! n'est-ce donc que cela?
La toile était levée et j'attendais encore.

A Curious Fellow's Dream

for Félix Nadar

Do you know delicious pain, the way I do? And do you get others to say, 'What an odd man?' – I was about to die. There was a peculiar queasiness in my soul, desire and horror,
 anguish and keen hope, and no fault-finding bile. The more doom's hour-glass emptied, the more harsh and exquisite my torment became as my heart was cutting loose from the familiar world.
 I was like a child agog for the show to start, loathing the lowered curtain as we hate any obstacle. Then at last the naked truth became plain to me –
 I had died unsurprised and was wrapped in a terrible dawn. What, can that be all? The curtain had gone up, but I was still waiting for the show.

[Written and published 1860. FM 1861]

CXXVI

LE VOYAGE

À Maxime Du Camp.

I

Pour l'enfant, amoureux de cartes et d'estampes,
L'univers est égal à son vaste appétit.
Ah! que le monde est grand à la clarté des lampes!
Aux yeux du souvenir que le monde est petit!

Un matin nous partons, le cerveau plein de flamme,
Le cœur gros de rancune et de désirs amers,
Et nous allons, suivant le rythme de la lame,
Berçant notre infini sur le fini des mers:

Les uns, joyeux de fuir une patrie infâme;
D'autres, l'horreur de leurs berceaux, et quelques-uns,
Astrologues noyés dans les yeux d'une femme,
La Circé tyrannique aux dangereux parfums.

The Voyage

for Maxime Du Camp

I

For the child who adores maps and prints, the universe matches his vast appetite. Ah, how big the world is in the lamplight, but how small when viewed through the eyes of memory!

One morning we set out, our minds aflame, our heart swelling with resentment and frustrated longings, and we fare onwards in rhythm with the waves, soothing our infinity on the finite of the seas.

Some are overjoyed to quit an infamous homeland; others, to leave the horror of their cradles behind; some are astrologers drowned in a woman's eyes, the tyrannical Circe with her destructive perfumes.

Pour n'être pas changés en bêtes, ils s'enivrent
D'espace et de lumière et de cieux embrasés;
La glace qui les mord, les soleils qui les cuivrent,
Effacent lentement la marque des baisers.

Mais les vrais voyageurs sont ceux-là seuls qui partent
Pour partir; cœurs légers, semblables aux ballons,
De leur fatalité jamais ils ne s'écartent,
Et, sans savoir pourquoi, disent toujours: Allons!

Ceux-là dont les désirs ont la forme des nues,
Et qui rêvent, ainsi qu'un conscrit le canon,
De vastes voluptés, changeantes, inconnues,
Et dont l'esprit humain n'a jamais su le nom!

II

Nous imitons, horreur! la toupie et la boule
Dans leur valse et leurs bonds; même dans nos sommeils
La Curiosité nous tourmente et nous roule,
Comme un Ange cruel qui fouette des soleils.

To avoid being changed into beasts they drug themselves with space
and light and blazing skies, and the ice that bites them, the suns that
burn them bronze, gradually efface the stigmata of kisses.

But the true travellers are those, and those alone, who set out only
for the journey's sake, and with light balloon-like hearts they never
swerve from their destiny, and, without knowing why, keep saying 'Let
us fare forward!'

– those whose desires are shaped like clouds, and who, like the
conscript dreaming of his cannon, have visions of boundless, ever-
changing, unexplored ecstasies which the human mind has never been
able to name.

II

Horribly, we imitate the spinning-top's waltz and the bouncing ball.
Even as we sleep, curiosity torments us and drives us along, like a cruel
Angel whipping suns.

Singulière fortune où le but se déplace,
Et, n'étant nulle part, peut être n'importe où!
Où l'Homme, dont jamais l'espérance n'est lasse,
Pour trouver le repos court toujours comme un fou!

Notre âme est un trois-mâts cherchant son Icarie;
Une voix retentit sur le pont: «Ouvre l'œil!»
Une voix de la hune, ardente et folle, crie:
«Amour... gloire... bonheur!» Enfer! c'est un écueil!

Chaque îlot signalé par l'homme de vigie
Est un Eldorado promis par le Destin;
L'Imagination qui dresse son orgie
Ne trouve qu'un récif aux clartés du matin.

Ô le pauvre amoureux des pays chimériques!
Faut-il le mettre aux fers, le jeter à la mer,
Ce matelot ivrogne, inventeur d'Amériques
Dont le mirage rend le gouffre plus amer?

A strange destiny, this, in which the target is ever shifting and which, being nowhere, can be anywhere; in which mankind, with untiring hope, is forever rushing like a madman in search of rest.

Our soul is a galleon in search of its Icaria: a voice from the bridge booms 'Watch out!' but another from aloft, eager and demented, cries 'Love is in sight, and Glory, and Happiness!' – but no, it's hell let loose, we have struck a rock!

Every island sighted by the look-out in the crow's-nest is an Eldorado promised by Destiny – our imagination conjures up an orgy in advance, but in the morning light it proves to be a reef.

Poor lover of non-existent Utopias! – Should he be cast into irons and hurled into the sea, this drunken sailor who invents Americas, whose mirage only adds more acid to the deep?

Tel le vieux vagabond, piétinant dans la boue,
Rêve, le nez en l'air, de brillants paradis;
Son œil ensorcelé découvre une Capoue
Partout où la chandelle illumine un taudis.

III

Étonnants voyageurs! quelles nobles histoires
Nous lisons dans vos yeux profonds comme les mers!
Montrez-nous les écrins de vos riches mémoires,
Ces bijoux merveilleux, faits d'astres et d'éthers.

Nous voulons voyager sans vapeur et sans voile!
Faites, pour égayer l'ennui de nos prisons,
Passer sur nos esprits, tendus comme une toile,
Vos souvenirs avec leurs cadres d'horizons.

Dites, qu'avez-vous vu?

Like some old tramp trudging in the mud and dreaming with his nose in the air of dazzling paradises, his bewitched eyes find a Capua in every candle-lit hovel.

III

Astounding travellers! What noble tales we can read in your sea-deep eyes! Show us the caskets crammed with your rich memories, those wondrous gems fashioned from stars and ethers!

We long to travel without steam or sail. To enliven the tedium of our prisons, project onto our minds, stretched tight like sails, your horizon-framed remembrances!

Tell us, what have you seen?

IV

«Nous avons vu des astres
Et des flots; nous avons vu des sables aussi;
Et, malgré bien des chocs et d'imprévus désastres,
Nous nous sommes souvent ennuyés, comme ici.

«La gloire du soleil sur la mer violette,
La gloire des cités dans le soleil couchant,
Allumaient dans nos cœurs une ardeur inquiète
De plonger dans un ciel au reflet alléchant.

«Les plus riches cités, les plus grands paysages,
Jamais ne contenaient l'attrait mystérieux
De ceux que le hasard fait avec les nuages.
Et toujours le désir nous rendait soucieux!

«– La jouissance ajoute au désir de la force.
Désir, vieil arbre à qui le plaisir sert d'engrais,
Cependant que grossit et durcit ton écorce,
Tes branches veulent voir le soleil de plus près!

IV

'We have seen stars and waves, and deserts also, and despite many an alarm and many an unforeseen disaster, we were often bored, just as you are here.

'The glory of the sunlight on the violet sea, the glory of cities in the declining sun, kindled an unquiet longing in our hearts, to plunge into a sky's alluring reflection.

'The richest of cities, the most magnificent of landscapes, never contained the mysterious magnetism of those which Chance wrought with the clouds. Besides, we were always fretful with desire.

'– Enjoyment adds more strength to all desires. O Desire, you ancient tree whose manure is pleasure, while your bark thickens and hardens, your branches yearn to view the sun more near!

«Grandiras-tu toujours, grand arbre plus vivace
Que le cyprès? – Pourtant nous avons, avec soin,
Cueilli quelques croquis pour votre album vorace,
Frères qui trouvez beau tout ce qui vient de loin!

«Nous avons salué des idoles à trompe;
Des trônes constellés de joyaux lumineux;
Des palais ouvragés dont la féerique pompe
Serait pour vos banquiers un rêve ruineux;

«Des costumes qui sont pour les yeux une ivresse;
Des femmes dont les dents et les ongles sont teints,
Et des jongleurs savants que le serpent caresse.»

v

Et puis, et puis encore?

'Will you grow for ever, mighty tree, hardier than any cypress is? –
However, we carefully collected a few sketches for your greedy album,
O brothers who find beauty in whatever comes from afar.

'We have hailed idols trunked like elephants; thrones that were
bestarred with luminous gems; sculptured palaces whose faery splen-
dour would be a ruinous dream for all your bankers;

costumes which would make you see double; women with painted
teeth and painted nails, and jugglers full of lore, caressed by snakes.'

v

And then – what else?

VI

«Ô cerveaux enfantins!

«Pour ne pas oublier la chose capitale,
Nous avons vu partout, et sans l'avoir cherché,
Du haut jusques en bas de l'échelle fatale,
Le spectacle ennuyeux de l'immortel péché:

«La femme, esclave vile, orgueilleuse et stupide,
Sans rire s'adorant et s'aimant sans dégoût;
L'homme, tyran goulu, paillard, dur et cupide,
Esclave de l'esclave et ruisseau dans l'égout;

«Le bourreau qui jouit, le martyr qui sanglote;
La fête qu'assaisonne et parfume le sang;
Le poison du pouvoir énervant le despote,
Et le peuple amoureux du fouet abrutissant;

«Plusieurs religions semblables à la nôtre,
Toutes escaladant le ciel; la Sainteté,
Comme en un lit de plume un délicat se vautre,
Dans les clous et le crin cherchant la volupté;

VI

'Infantile minds!

'Lest we forget the most important thing of all – everywhere, without even looking for it, from top to bottom of the deadly scale we saw the tedious sight of immortal Sin:

'woman, that vile slave, arrogant and stupid, in all seriousness adoring and loving herself without disgust; and man, that gutsy tyrant, lewd and merciless and grasping, the slave of a slave, the tributary of the sewer;

'the torturer delighting in his task; the sobbing martyr; the banquet seasoned and perfumed with blood; the poison of power exasperating the despot; the masses enamoured of the stupefying lash;

'several religions like our own, so many ladders up to heaven; saintliness seeking a thrill in nails and hair-shirts, enjoying their pain like a weakling snug in his feather bed;

«L'Humanité bavarde, ivre de son génie,
Et, folle maintenant comme elle était jadis,
Criant à Dieu, dans sa furibonde agonie:
"Ô mon semblable, ô mon maître, je te maudis!"

«Et les moins sots, hardis amants de la Démence,
Fuyant le grand troupeau parqué par le Destin,
Et se réfugiant dans l'opium immense!
– Tel est du globe entier l'éternel bulletin.»

VII

Amer savoir, celui qu'on tire du voyage!
Le monde, monotone et petit, aujourd'hui,
Hier, demain, toujours, nous fait voir notre image:
Une oasis d'horreur dans un désert d'ennui!

Faut-il partir? rester? Si tu peux rester, reste;
Pars, s'il le faut. L'un court, et l'autre se tapit
Pour tromper l'ennemi vigilant et funeste,
Le Temps! Il est, hélas! des coureurs sans répit,

'tongue-wagging mankind drunk with their own wit, as crazy today as in the past, shrieking to God in insane agony, "O Thou, my likeness, my master, I curse thee!"

'– and least stupid of all, the dauntless lovers of insanity fleeing the fate-guarded herd and taking refuge in the infinity of opium – such is the eternal balance-sheet of the entire globe.'

VII

Bitter is the knowledge we learn from voyaging! Monotonous and mean, today, yesterday, tomorrow, always, the world presents us our own image – an oasis of horror in a desert of tedium.

Ought we to go, or stay? Stay, if you can stay; go, if you must go. One man will up and go, another crouches at home in order to outwit Time, the watchful, hateful enemy. Alas, there are runners who never find a respite,

Comme le Juif errant et comme les apôtres,
À qui rien ne suffit, ni wagon ni vaisseau,
Pour fuir ce rétiaire infâme; il en est d'autres
Qui savent le tuer sans quitter leur berceau.

Lorsque enfin il mettra le pied sur notre échine,
Nous pourrons espérer et crier: En avant!
De même qu'autrefois nous partions pour la Chine,
Les yeux fixés au large et les cheveux au vent,

Nous nous embarquerons sur la mer des Ténèbres
Avec le cœur joyeux d'un jeune passager.
Entendez-vous ces voix, charmantes et funèbres,
Qui chantent: «Par ici! vous qui voulez manger

«Le Lotus parfumé! c'est ici qu'on vendange
Les fruits miraculeux dont votre cœur a faim;
Venez vous enivrer de la douceur étrange
De cette après-midi qui n'a jamais de fin?»

like the Wandering Jew or the Apostles, those for whom nothing is ever enough, neither railway car nor ship, to outdistance the infamous slave-driver: but there are others who can kill him without ever stirring from the cradle.

When at last he sets his foot on our spine, we can still hope and cry out 'Fare forward!' – just as when we once set out for China, with our eyes fixed on the open sea, our hair streaming in the wind,

we shall set sail across the sea of Shadows with a young passenger's joyful heart. Can you hear those seductive, mournful voices chanting, 'Come this way, all you who would eat

of the scented Lotus: here we harvest the miraculous fruits for which your heart is longing! Come and drink the marvellous bliss of this unending afternoon!'

À l'accent familier nous devinons le spectre;
Nos Pylades là-bas tendent leurs bras vers nous.
«Pour rafraîchir ton cœur nage vers ton Électre!»
Dit celle dont jadis nous baisions les genoux.

VIII

Ô Mort, vieux capitaine, il est temps! levons l'ancre!
Ce pays nous ennuie, ô Mort! Appareillons!
Si le ciel et la mer sont noirs comme de l'encre,
Nos cœurs que tu connais sont remplis de rayons!

Verse-nous ton poison pour qu'il nous réconforte!
Nous voulons, tant ce feu nous brûle le cerveau,
Plonger au fond du gouffre, Enfer ou Ciel, qu'importe?
Au fond de l'Inconnu pour trouver du *nouveau!*

But we scent the ghost behind those familiar tones. Yonder our Pylades are stretching their arms towards us: 'To refresh your heart, now swim to your Electra!' calls she whose knees we once embraced.

VIII

O Death, you ancient mariner, the hour has come. Let us weigh anchor! O Death, we are weary of this land, let us spread sail! Though sea and sky be black as ink, our hearts which you know so well are full of shafts of light.

Pour us your hemlock, for our comfort: its fire so burns our brains that we long to dive into the gulf's depths, and – what matters if it is heaven, or hell? – into the depths of the Unknown, in quest of *something new.*

[Written and published 1859. FM 1861]

Projets d'épilogues

I
ÉPILOGUE

Le cœur content, je suis monté sur la montagne
D'où l'on peut contempler la ville en son ampleur,
Hôpital, lupanar, purgatoire, enfer, bagne,

Où toute énormité fleurit comme une fleur.
Tu sais bien, ô Satan, patron de ma détresse,
Que je n'allais pas là pour répandre un vain pleur;

Mais, comme un vieux paillard d'une vieille maîtresse,
Je voulais m'enivrer de l'énorme catin,
Dont le charme infernal me rajeunit sans cesse.

DRAFT EPILOGUES
for the second edition, 1861

I
Epilogue

It was with a contented heart that I climbed the hill [up to Montmartre] from which one can survey the city in her totality – with her hospitals and brothels, purgatory, inferno, prison-houses,

where every outrage blooms like a flower. You know full well, Satan, patron of my anguish, that I did not go to shed a futile tear;

but like an old rake with his old mistress I wanted to intoxicate myself with the sight of that enormous bawd, whose diabolical charms never fail to restore my youth.

Que tu dormes encor dans les draps du matin,
Lourde, obscure, enrhumée, ou que tu te pavanes
Dans les voiles du soir passementés d'or fin,

Je t'aime, ô capitale infâme! Courtisanes
Et bandits, tels souvent vous offrez des plaisirs
Que ne comprennent pas les vulgaires profanes.

Whether you drowse abed in your morning sheets [of cloud and smoke], leaden and opaque and rheumy, or whether you strut in your evening gauze braided with fine threads of gold,

I love you, foul metropolis, who with your harlots and apaches have delights to offer which godless, commonplace minds can never understand.

[This poem, incorrectly thought to be an epilogue to the *Petits Poèmes en prose*, was published posthumously in 1869. However, when Baudelaire wrote his draft epilogue below in 1860, intended for the second edition of *Les Fleurs du mal* (1861), the poet told his editor that it would be developed in *terza rima*. As the above Epilogue is written in that form, though unfinished, it is reasonable to assume that it is a versified amplification of the next epilogue's opening lines.]

II

Tranquille comme un sage et doux comme un maudit,
 J'ai dit:
Je t'aime, ô ma très belle, ô ma charmante . . .
Que de fois . . .
Tes débauches sans soif et tes amours sans âme,
 Ton goût de l'infini,
Qui partout, dans le mal lui-même, se proclame . . .

Tes bombes, tes poignards, tes victoires, tes fêtes,
Tes faubourgs mélancoliques,
Tes hôtels garnis,
Tes jardins pleins de soupirs et d'intrigues,
Tes temples vomissant la prière en musique,
Tes désespoirs d'enfant, tes jeux de vieille folle,
 Tes découragements;

Et tes feux d'artifice, éruptions de joie,
Qui font rire le Ciel, muet et ténébreux.

Ton vice vénérable étalé dans la soie,
Et ta vertu risible, au regard malheureux,
Douce, s'extasiant au luxe qu'il déploie.

II

Calm as a sage and docile as one on whom the curse is laid, I said: 'I love you, my very beautiful one, my charmer. Many a time . . . your debauches though you did not thirst, your soulless love affairs; your longing for the Infinite, which everywhere is manifest, and even in Evil;

'your bombs, your daggers, your triumphs, your public festivals, your dismal suburbs, your hired furnished rooms, your parks alive with sighs and conspiracies, your chapels vomiting musical prayers, your infantile despairs, your old madwife's tricks, and your discouragements;

'and your firework displays, eruptions of joy, which cheer the dumb gloomy Heaven.

'Your venerable vice displayed in silk, and your laughable virtue with its sad gaze, gentle, delighting in the luxury it exhibits.

Tes principes sauvés et tes lois conspuées,
Tes monuments hautains où s'accrochent les brumes,
Tes dômes de métal qu'enflamme le soleil,
 Tes reines de Théâtre aux voix enchanteresses,
Tes tocsins, tes canons, orchestre assourdissant,
Tes magiques pavés dressés en forteresses,
Tes petits orateurs, aux enflures baroques
Prêchant l'amour, et puis tes égouts pleins de sang,
S'engouffrant dans l'Enfer comme des Orénoques,
Tes sages, tes bouffons neufs aux vieilles défroques.
Anges revêtus d'or, de pourpre et d'hyacinthe,
Ô vous! soyez témoins que j'ai fait mon devoir
Comme un parfait chimiste et comme une âme sainte.
 Car j'ai de chaque chose extrait la quintessence,
Tu m'as donné ta boue et j'en ai fait de l'or.

'Your rescued "principles", your flouted laws, your haughty monuments on which the mists are caught, your metal domes fired by the sun, your theatre-queens with their seductive voices, your tocsins, your cannons, a deafening orchestra, your magic cobbles piled for barricades, your cheap orators' baroque rhetoric, preaching of love while your sewers run with blood, swirling to Hell like mighty rivers, your sages, your latterday clowns dressed in old rags. Angels in gold and purple and hyacinth, O you, bear witness that I fulfilled my task like a perfect alchemist, a saintly soul;
 'for from all these things I extracted the quintessence. The mud you gave me I have turned to gold.'

[See note to 'Epilogue' on p .249. The second half of
this draft is often spaced to indicate the latent tercets.
'Tes sages. . .', six lines from the end, is the 1976
Pléiade's silent emendation for 'Tes anges. . .'.]

II
Other Poems

Nouvelles Fleurs du mal
1868

NEW FLOWERS OF EVIL

Les Épaves
1866

FLOTSAM

and other poems

Nouvelles *Fleurs du mal*

(POÈMES APPORTÉS PAR L'ÉDITION DE 1868)

ÉPIGRAPHE
POUR UN LIVRE CONDAMNÉ

Lecteur paisible et bucolique,
Sobre et naïf homme de bien,
Jette ce livre saturnien,
Orgiaque et mélancolique.

Si tu n'as fait ta rhétorique
Chez Satan, le rusé doyen,
Jette! tu n'y comprendrais rien,
Ou tu me croirais hystérique.

Mais si, sans se laisser charmer,
Ton œil sait plonger dans les gouffres,
Lis-moi, pour apprendre à m'aimer;

Âme curieuse qui souffres
Et vas cherchant ton paradis,
Plains-moi!... Sinon, je te maudis!

NEW FLOWERS OF EVIL
(poems brought into the 1868 edition)

Epigraph for a Condemned Book

Harmless nature-loving Reader, sober and simple well-meaning fellow – throw away this saturnine, lustful and melancholy book.

Unless you learnt your Rhetoric from that cunning old Dean of Studies, Satan, throw it away! You would never understand a word of it, or would think me hysterical.

But if your eye refuses to be mesmerized and is capable of plumbing the depths, then read me, so as to learn how to love me.

Inquiring, suffering soul in search of your paradise, give me your sympathy – or else I'll curse you!

[Written and published 1861]

MADRIGAL TRISTE

I

Que m'importe que tu sois sage?
Sois belle! et sois triste! Les pleurs
Ajoutent un charme au visage,
Comme le fleuve au paysage;
L'orage rajeunit les fleurs.

Je t'aime surtout quand la joie
S'enfuit de ton front terrassé;
Quand ton cœur dans l'horreur se noie;
Quand sur ton présent se déploie
Le nuage affreux du passé.

Je t'aime quand ton grand œil verse
Une eau chaude comme le sang;
Quand, malgré ma main qui te berce,
Ton angoisse, trop lourde, perce
Comme un râle d'agonisant.

J'aspire, volupté divine!
Hymne profond, délicieux!

Sad Madrigal

I

What should I care if you're as good as gold? Be beautiful, and be sad.
Tears add a charm to the face, as a river to a landscape; the storm rejuvenates the flowers.

I love you especially when happiness quits your anguished brow; when your heart drowns in horror; when your Present is smothered by the dreadful cloud of the Past.

I love you when your wide eye sheds tears as hot as blood; when despite my lulling hand your anguish grows too heavy for you to bear, and blurts out like the death-rattle of a man in his last throes.

I breathe in with divine voluptuousness – O profound delicious

Tous les sanglots de ta poitrine,
Et crois que ton cœur s'illumine
Des perles que versent tes yeux!

II

Je sais que ton cœur, qui regorge
De vieux amours déracinés,
Flamboie encor comme une forge,
Et que tu couves sous ta gorge
Un peu de l'orgueil des damnés;

Mais tant, ma chère, que tes rêves
N'auront pas reflété l'Enfer,
Et qu'en un cauchemar sans trêves,
Songeant de poisons et de glaives,
Éprise de poudre et de fer,

N'ouvrant à chacun qu'avec crainte,
Déchiffrant le malheur partout,
Te convulsant quand l'heure tinte,
Tu n'auras pas senti l'étreinte
De l'irrésistible Dégoût,

hymn – every sob escaping from your breast, and believe your heart
grows brighter from those pearls that drip from your eyes.

II

I know that your heart, which is choked with old uprooted loves, still
flames like a forge, and that you still nourish in your breast something
like the pride of the damned.

But so long, my dear, as your dreams have not mirrored Hell itself,
so long as in a relentless nightmare – dreaming of poisons and daggers,
obsessed with gunpowder and steel blades,

full of dread whenever you open your door to anyone, reading
disaster into everything, falling into a fit when the clock strikes the hour
– so long as you have never felt the embrace of irresistible Disgust –

Tu ne pourras, esclave reine
Qui ne m'aimes qu'avec effroi,
Dans l'horreur de la nuit malsaine
Me dire, l'âme de cris pleine:
«Je suis ton égale, ô mon Roi!»

then, my enslaved queen who love me out of fear alone, you will
never be able to say, in the horror of the queasy night, your soul shriek-
ing within you, 'I am your equal, O my King!'

[1861. Dedicated to 'L. L.']

LA PRIÈRE D'UN PAÏEN

Ah! ne ralentis pas tes flammes;
Réchauffe mon cœur engourdi,
Volupté, torture des âmes!
Diva! supplicem exaudî!

Déesse dans l'air répandue,
Flamme dans notre souterrain!
Exauce une âme morfondue,
Qui te consacre un chant d'airain.

Volupté, sois toujours ma reine!
Prends le masque d'une sirène
Faite de chair et de velours,

Ou verse-moi tes sommeils lourds
Dans le vin informe et mystique,
Volupté, fantôme élastique!

A Pagan's Prayer

Ah, slow not thy flames; warm my numb heart again, voluptuousness,
torturer of souls: O goddess, grant my prayer!

Goddess, who are one with the air itself, our torch flaming in the
darkness of our cellar, grant the prayer of a defeated soul who offers
thee a hymn of bronze.

Voluptuousness, be ever my queen: assume the Siren's mask of flesh
and velvet

or pour me thy heavy slumbers in incorporeal, mystic wine, O
Voluptuousness, elastic shade!

[1861]

LE REBELLE

Un Ange furieux fond du ciel comme un aigle,
Du mécréant saisit à plein poing les cheveux,
Et dit, le secouant: «Tu connaîtras la règle!
(Car je suis ton bon Ange, entends-tu?) Je le veux!

«Sache qu'il faut aimer, sans faire la grimace,
Le pauvre, le méchant, le tortu, l'hébété,
Pour que tu puisses faire à Jésus, quand il passe,
Un tapis triomphal avec ta charité.

«Tel est l'Amour! Avant que ton cœur ne se blase,
À la gloire de Dieu rallume ton extase;
C'est la Volupté vraie aux durables appas!»

Et l'Ange, châtiant autant, ma foi! qu'il aime,
De ses poings de géant torture l'anathème;
Mais le damné répond toujours: «Je ne veux pas!»

The Rebel

A furious Angel swoops down from Heaven like an eagle and grips the wrongdoer's hair in his fist, saying as he shakes him, 'Now you will learn the rule! For I am your good Angel, do you hear? Such is my will.

'Know that you must love, without wincing, the poor and the wicked, the twisted and the stupid, so that you will make for Jesus, when he comes, a carpet of triumph with your charity.

'Such is Love! Before your heart becomes indifferent, rekindle your ecstasy for the glory of God; that is the true voluptuousness, whose charms endure.'

And the Angel, chastising as much – heaven knows – as he loves, tortures the blasphemer with his gigantic fists. But the damned man keeps on answering, 'No, I will not!'

[Perhaps an early poem, rehandled. Published 1861]

L'AVERTISSEUR

Tout homme digne de ce nom
A dans le cœur un Serpent jaune,
Installé comme sur un trône,
Qui, s'il dit: «Je veux!» répond: «Non!»

Plonge tes yeux dans les yeux fixes
Des Satyresses ou des Nixes,
La Dent dit: «Pense à ton devoir!»

Fais des enfants, plante des arbres,
Polis des vers, sculpte des marbres,
La Dent dit: «Vivras-tu ce soir?»

Quoi qu'il ébauche ou qu'il espère,
L'homme ne vit pas un moment
Sans subir l'avertissement
De l'insupportable Vipère.

The Warner

Every man worthy of the name has a yellow Serpent in his heart, squatting there as on a throne, and whenever he says 'I will!' it answers, 'No, you will not!'

If your eyes plunge into the staring eyes of female satyrs or nixies, the Tooth says, 'Think of your duty!'

Whether you are making children, planting trees, polishing verses or sculpting marbles, the Tooth says, 'Do you think you will still be alive tonight?'

Whatever he undertakes or hopes for, no man ever lives a second without having to endure the insufferable Viper's warning.

[Published 1861]

RECUEILLEMENT

Sois sage, ô ma Douleur, et tiens-toi plus tranquille.
Tu réclamais le Soir; il descend; le voici:
Une atmosphère obscure enveloppe la ville,
Aux uns portant la paix, aux autres le souci.

Pendant que des mortels la multitude vile,
Sous le fouet du Plaisir, ce bourreau sans merci,
Va cueillir des remords dans la fête servile,
Ma Douleur, donne-moi la main; viens par ici,

Loin d'eux. Vois se pencher les défuntes Années,
Sur les balcons du ciel, en robes surannées;
Surgir du fond des eaux le Regret souriant;

Le Soleil moribond s'endormir sous une arche,
Et, comme un long linceul traînant à l'Orient,
Entends, ma chère, entends la douce Nuit qui marche.

Composure

Have patience, O my sorrow, fret no more. You longed for evening: look, it is falling now. An opaque atmosphere enfolds the city, to some men bringing peace, to others, care.

While the base herd of mortals, driven by the lash of pleasure, that pitiless torturer, sets out to reap remorse in the sports of slaves, my Sorrow, give me your hand, come this way,

far from them. See where the lost years are leaning from the balconies of heaven, in their faded bygone robes; where Regret, with a smile on her lips, is rising from the waters' depths;

where the dying Sun seeks sleep beneath an arch; and, like a long, long shroud trailed from the East, listen, my dear, O listen to the gentle Night's approach.

[1861]

LE COUVERCLE

En quelque lieu qu'il aille, ou sur mer ou sur terre,
Sous un climat de flamme ou sous un soleil blanc,
Serviteur de Jésus, courtisan de Cythère,
Mendiant ténébreux ou Crésus rutilant,

Citadin, campagnard, vagabond, sédentaire,
Que son petit cerveau soit actif ou soit lent,
Partout l'homme subit la terreur du mystère,
Et ne regarde en haut qu'avec un œil tremblant.

En haut, le Ciel! ce mur de caveau qui l'étouffe,
Plafond illuminé pour un opéra bouffe
Où chaque histrion foule un sol ensanglanté;

Terreur du libertin, espoir du fol ermite;
Le Ciel! couvercle noir de la grande marmite
Où bout l'imperceptible et vaste Humanité.

The Lid

Wherever he goes, on land or sea, in torrid zones or polar sunlight; whether he serves Jesus or courts Venus, a gloomy beggar or a glittering millionaire;

be he townsman or countryman, rolling-stone or stay-at-home; whether his puny brain be quick or slow – Man endures the fear of Mystery wherever he is, and only looks heavenwards with trembling eye.

Above stretches the sky, like the wall of a burial vault that stifles him, or a ceiling lit by a comic opera in which every actor treads a blood-drenched stage;

the freethinker's terror, the crazed hermit's hope – the sky, the black lid of the huge cauldron in which, countless but insignificant, mankind boils.

[1861. Perhaps suggested by Breughel and/or Goya]

LA LUNE OFFENSÉE

Ô Lune qu'adoraient discrètement nos pères,
Du haut des pays bleus où, radieux sérail,
Les astres vont te suivre en pimpant attirail,
Ma vieille Cynthia, lampe de nos repaires,

Vois-tu les amoureux sur leurs grabats prospères,
De leur bouche en dormant montrer le frais émail?
Le poète buter du front sur son travail?
Ou sous les gazons secs s'accoupler les vipères?

Sous ton domino jaune, et d'un pied clandestin,
Vas-tu, comme jadis, du soir jusqu'au matin,
Baiser d'Endymion les grâces surannées?

«— Je vois ta mère, enfant de ce siècle appauvri,
Qui vers son miroir penche un lourd amas d'années,
Et plâtre artistement le sein qui t'a nourri!»

The Offended Moon

O Moon, whom our fathers worshipped secretly: from the heights of the blue realms where the radiant harem of stars attend you in their bright attire, my old Cynthia, the lanthorn of our dens –

can you see the lovers on their carefree beds, when as they sleep they show the cool enamel of their teeth; and the poet, bruising his brow over his task; or the snakes coupling in the dry grasses?

Under your yellow mantle, with furtive step, do you still, as in the past, from eve till morn, come down to kiss Endymion's faded charms?

'O child of this degenerate century, I can see your mother bending her heavy load of years over her looking-glass, and artistically improving the breast that suckled you.'

[Perhaps an early poem. Published 1861]

LE GOUFFRE

Pascal avait son gouffre, avec lui se mouvant.
– Hélas! tout est abîme, – action, désir, rêve,
Parole! et sur mon poil qui tout droit se relève
Mainte fois de la Peur je sens passer le vent.

En haut, en bas, partout, la profondeur, la grève,
Le silence, l'espace affreux et captivant . . .
Sur le fond de mes nuits Dieu de son doigt savant
Dessine un cauchemar multiforme et sans trêve.

J'ai peur du sommeil comme on a peur d'un grand trou,
Tout plein de vague horreur, menant on ne sait où;
Je ne vois qu'infini par toutes les fenêtres,

Et mon esprit, toujours du vertige hanté,
Jalouse du néant l'insensibilité.
– Ah! ne jamais sortir des Nombres et des Êtres!

The Pit

Pascal had a fathomless pit which followed him wherever he went. Alas,
all things are a gaping void – actions, desires, and dreams and words! –
and many a time I feel the gust of Fear sweep through my hair, making
it stand on end.

High and low and all around I find nothing but depth, shore,
silence, a terrifying and hypnotic emptiness of space. Upon the back-
cloth of my nights God's expert finger draws a multitudinous and
unrelenting nightmare.

I am afraid of sleep, as of some yawning pit full of nameless horror,
leading who knows where? I can see nothing but Infinity through
every window,

and my mind, obsessed by the dread of falling through space, envies
the insensibility of Nothingness. Ah, is there no escape from Numbers
and Beings?

[Published 1862, the year in which Baudelaire felt himself 'touched
by the wind of imbecility's wing'. Critics agree on the ambiguity of
the last line, which could also be translated in the opposite sense.]

LES PLAINTES D'UN ICARE

Les amants des prostituées
Sont heureux, dispos et repus;
Quant à moi, mes bras sont rompus
Pour avoir étreint des nuées.

C'est grâce aux astres nonpareils,
Qui tout au fond du ciel flamboient,
Que mes yeux consumés ne voient
Que des souvenirs de soleils.

En vain j'ai voulu de l'espace
Trouver la fin et le milieu;
Sous je ne sais quel œil de feu
Je sens mon aile qui se casse;

Et brûlé par l'amour du beau,
Je n'aurai pas l'honneur sublime
De donner mon nom à l'abîme
Qui me servira de tombeau.

Laments of an Icarus

Lovers of harlots are happy, content and satiated: but as for me, my arms are racked because I embraced clouds.

It is thanks to the incomparable stars which blaze in the sky's remotest depths, that my burnt-out eyes see nothing but memories of suns.

In vain I have sought to discover the end and centre of space: beneath I know not what eye of fire I feel my wings [melt and] break

and, scorched by the love of beauty, I shall not have the sublime honour of giving my name to the pit which will be my grave.

[Published and probably written in 1862]

L'EXAMEN DE MINUIT

La pendule, sonnant minuit,
Ironiquement nous engage
À nous rappeler quel usage
Nous fîmes du jour qui s'enfuit:
– Aujourd'hui, date fatidique,
Vendredi, treize, nous avons,
Malgré tout ce que nous savons,
Mené le train d'un hérétique.

Nous avons blasphémé Jésus,
Des Dieux le plus incontestable!
Comme un parasite à la table
De quelque monstrueux Crésus,
Nous avons, pour plaire à la brute,
Digne vassale des Démons,
Insulté ce que nous aimons
Et flatté ce qui nous rebute;

Contristé, servile bourreau,
Le faible qu'à tort on méprise;
Salué l'énorme Bêtise,
La Bêtise au front de taureau;

The Poet Examines His Conscience at Midnight

As it strikes midnight the clock ironically summons us to take stock of
what use we made of this now vanishing day. Today – an unpropitious
date, Friday the Thirteenth – although we know better we played the
heretic.

We blasphemed against Jesus, the least questionable of Gods. Like a
parasite at some monstrous millionaire's table, we have – in toadying to
the brute, a worthy servant of the Demons – insulted what we love and
praised all that we loathe;

humiliated, like a servile torturer, a weak man whom others unjustly
look down on; we paid our respects to enormous bull-browed Stupidity;

Baisé la stupide Matière
Avec grande dévotion,
Et de la putréfaction
Béni la blafarde lumière.

Enfin, nous avons, pour noyer
Le vertige dans le délire,
Nous, prêtre orgueilleux de la Lyre,
Dont la gloire est de déployer
L'ivresse des choses funèbres,
Bu sans soif et mangé sans faim!...
– Vite soufflons la lampe, afin
De nous cacher dans les ténèbres!

we kissed mindless Matter with enormous devotion; we blessed the
sickly radiance of decay.

Finally, as if we could drown the mind's vortex in delirium, we,
proud priest of the Lyre, whose glory should lie in portraying the
rapture of sad things, we drank without thirst and gorged without
hunger. Quick, blow out that lamp, so as to hide our face in the dark!

[Published 1863, 1866. See the prose-poem 'À une heure du matin']

BIEN LOIN D'ICI

C'est ici la case sacrée
Où cette fille très parée,
Tranquille et toujours préparée,

D'une main éventant ses seins,
Et son coude dans les coussins,
Écoute pleurer les bassins:

C'est la chambre de Dorothée.
– La brise et l'eau chantent au loin
Leur chanson de sanglots heurtée
Pour bercer cette enfant gâtée.

Du haut en bas, avec grand soin,
Sa peau délicate est frottée
D'huile odorante et de benjoin.
– Des fleurs se pâment dans un coin.

Far Away

This hut is the sanctuary where that young lady in all her finery, composed and always ready,

is fanning her breasts with one hand and reclining on her elbow among the cushions, and listening to the fountains weep.

It is Dorothy's boudoir. The wind and water are singing their sobbing song in the distance, the spoiled child's lullaby.

From tip to toe, with great care, her delicate skin is anointed with aromatic oil and benjamin. A few wild flowers are swooning in a corner.

[Published 1864. See the prose-poem 'La Belle Dorothée']

Les Épaves

I
LE COUCHER DU SOLEIL ROMANTIQUE

Que le Soleil est beau quand tout frais il se lève,
Comme une explosion nous lançant son bonjour!
– Bienheureux celui-là qui peut avec amour
Saluer son coucher plus glorieux qu'un rêve!

Je me souviens!... J'ai vu tout, fleur, source, sillon,
Se pâmer sous son œil comme un cœur qui palpite...
– Courons vers l'horizon, il est tard, courons vite,
Pour attraper au moins un oblique rayon!

Mais je poursuis en vain le Dieu qui se retire;
L'irrésistible Nuit établit son empire,
Noire, humide, funeste et pleine de frissons;

FLOTSAM

The Sunset of Romanticism

How beautiful the Sun is when he rises up all fresh, bidding us good morning like an explosion. Happy is the man who can, with love, salute the sundown more glorious than any dream.

I remember seeing everything – flower, spring, the ploughed furrow – faint like a throbbing heart beneath the Sun's gaze. Let us speed towards the horizon, it is late now, we must run fast to catch at least one slanting ray!

But vainly I pursue the retiring God. Irresistible Night is establishing its empire, black and damp, dismal, making all things shudder.

Une odeur de tombeau dans les ténèbres nage,
Et mon pied peureux froisse, au bord du marécage,
Des crapauds imprévus et de froids limaçons.

The smell of the grave is floating in the shadows, and my faltering
foot on the borders of the bog, stumbles on unexpected toads, cold
slugs.

> [1862. A note on the proof reads 'It is obvious that by "irresistible
> Night" M. Charles Baudelaire was seeking to characterize the
> present state of literature, and that the unexpected toads and
> cold slugs are writers who are not of his school.']

BANNED POEMS
withdrawn from *The Flowers of Evil*

Lesbos

Lesbos, mother of the Latin games and the voluptuous rites of Greece,
where kisses of languor or rapture, sun-scorching or melon-cool, make
lovelier the glorious nights and days; mother of the Latin games and the
voluptuous rites of Greece:

Pièces condamnées

TIRÉES DES *FLEURS DU MAL*

II
LESBOS

Mère des jeux latins et des voluptés grecques,
Lesbos, où les baisers, languissants ou joyeux,
Chauds comme les soleils, frais comme les pastèques,
Font l'ornement des nuits et des jours glorieux;
Mère des jeux latins et des voluptés grecques,

Lesbos, où les baisers sont comme les cascades
Qui se jettent sans peur dans les gouffres sans fonds,
Et courent, sanglotant et gloussant par saccades,
Orageux et secrets, fourmillants et profonds;
Lesbos, où les baisers sont comme les cascades!

Lesbos, où les Phrynés l'une l'autre s'attirent,
Où jamais un soupir ne resta sans écho,
À l'égal de Paphos les étoiles t'admirent,
Et Vénus à bon droit peut jalouser Sapho!
Lesbos, où les Phrynés l'une l'autre s'attirent,

Lesbos, where kisses are like waterfalls hurling themselves fearlessly
into fathomless depths, sobbing or chuckling, stormy or secretive,
seething or profound; Lesbos where kisses are like waterfalls:

Lesbos, whose Phrynian vestals are magnets each to each, where
every sigh is echoed by a sigh, the galaxies of stars admire you no less
than Paphos, and gave Venus good cause for envying Sappho; Lesbos
whose vestals are magnets each to each:

Lesbos, terre des nuits chaudes et langoureuses,
Qui font qu'à leurs miroirs, stérile volupté!
Les filles aux yeux creux, de leurs corps amoureuses,
Caressent les fruits mûrs de leur nubilité;
Lesbos, terre des nuits chaudes et langoureuses,

Laisse du vieux Platon se froncer l'œil austère;
Tu tires ton pardon de l'excès des baisers,
Reine du doux empire, aimable et noble terre,
Et des raffinements toujours inépuisés.
Laisse du vieux Platon se froncer l'œil austère.

Tu tires ton pardon de l'éternel martyre,
Infligé sans relâche aux cœurs ambitieux,
Qu'attire loin de nous le radieux sourire
Entrevu vaguement au bord des autres cieux!
Tu tires ton pardon de l'éternel martyre!

Lesbos, isle of sultry swooning nights which drive the deep-eyed virgins, enamoured of their own bodies, to fondle the ripe fruits of their adolescence in their glasses, in sterile ecstasy; Lesbos the isle of sultry swooning nights:

let greybeard Plato frown with his reproving eye; you are redeemed by the very excess of your embraces, Lesbos, queen of the realms of gentleness, lovable and noble motherland, queen of the inexhaustible subtleties of loving; let greybeard Plato frown with his reproving eye.

You earn forgiveness through the eternal martyrdom relentlessly endured by aspiring hearts, our hearts compelled by the radiant smile glimpsed on the distant shores of other skies; you earn forgiveness through eternal martyrdom.

Qui des Dieux osera, Lesbos, être ton juge
Et condamner ton front pâli dans les travaux,
Si ses balances d'or n'ont pesé le déluge
De larmes qu'à la mer ont versé tes ruisseaux?
Qui des Dieux osera, Lesbos, être ton juge?

Que nous veulent les lois du juste et de l'injuste?
Vierges au cœur sublime, honneur de l'archipel,
Votre religion comme une autre est auguste,
Et l'amour se rira de l'Enfer et du Ciel!
Que nous veulent les lois du juste et de l'injuste?

Car Lesbos entre tous m'a choisi sur la terre
Pour chanter le secret de ses vierges en fleurs,
Et je fus dès l'enfance admis au noir mystère
Des rires effrénés mêlés aux sombres pleurs;
Car Lesbos entre tous m'a choisi sur la terre.

Lesbos, which of the gods shall presume to be your judge and condemn your brow grown pale with toil, if the golden scales fail to weigh the deluge of tears your streams have poured into the sea? Lesbos, which of the gods shall presume to be your judge?

What do the laws of the just and unjust want of us? Sublime-hearted vestals, pride of the archipelago, your religion is as noble as any other, and love will laugh off both Hell and Heaven: what do the laws of the just and unjust want of us?

For Lesbos ordained me above all others on earth to sing the secret of her nubile vestals: from childhood I was initiate to the dark mystery of unbridled laughter mingled with tears of sorrow, for Lesbos ordained me above all others on earth.

Et depuis lors je veille au sommet de Leucate,
Comme une sentinelle à l'œil perçant et sûr,
Qui guette nuit et jour brick, tartane ou frégate,
Dont les formes au loin frissonnent dans l'azur;
Et depuis lors je veille au sommet de Leucate

Pour savoir si la mer est indulgente et bonne,
Et parmi les sanglots dont le roc retentit
Un soir ramènera vers Lesbos, qui pardonne,
Le cadavre adoré de Sapho, qui partit
Pour savoir si la mer est indulgente et bonne!

De la mâle Sapho, l'amante et le poète,
Plus belle que Vénus par ses mornes pâleurs!
– L'œil d'azur est vaincu par l'œil noir que tachette
Le cercle ténébreux tracé par les douleurs
De la mâle Sapho, l'amante et le poète!

And since that time I keep watch on Leucate's peak, a sentinel whose sharp eyes never fail, who night and day look out for brig or tartane or frigate whose outline shimmers afar on the azure sea, and since that time I keep watch on Leucate's peak,

to learn whether the sea is favourable and kind, for where the sobbing voices echo on the cliff, some evening will restore to a forgiving Lesbos the worshipped body of Sappho, who long ago left these shores to learn whether the sea is favourable and kind;

the body of the male Sappho, lover and poet, more lovely than Venus even in her deathly paleness, the azure eye outshone by her eye's darkness ringed by the shadowy circle traced by grief, the body of the male Sappho, lover and poet;

— Plus belle que Vénus se dressant sur le monde
Et versant les trésors de sa sérénité
Et le rayonnement de sa jeunesse blonde
Sur le vieil Océan de sa fille enchanté;
Plus belle que Vénus se dressant sur le monde!

— De Sapho qui mourut le jour de son blasphème,
Quand, insultant le rite et le culte inventé,
Elle fit son beau corps la pâture suprême
D'un brutal dont l'orgueil punit l'impiété
De celle qui mourut le jour de son blasphème.

Et c'est depuis ce temps que Lesbos se lamente,
Et, malgré les honneurs que lui rend l'univers,
S'enivre chaque nuit du cri de la tourmente
Que poussent vers les cieux ses rivages déserts!
Et c'est depuis ce temps que Lesbos se lamente!

lovelier than Venus standing erect above the world and pouring out the treasures of her serenity, radiating her golden youth on old Ocean enchanted with his daughter, more beautiful than Venus standing erect above the world;

of Sappho who died on her day of blasphemy, when she transgressed the rites of the cult she had created, when she allowed her perfect form to be the supreme conquest of a brute, whose pride punished the impiousness of her who died on her day of blasphemy.

And it is ever since that day that Lesbos mourns, and notwithstanding all the honours paid to her by the world, she is drunk each night with the cry of torment which her deserted shores lift to the skies, and it is ever since that day that Lesbos mourns.

[Published 1850]

III
FEMMES DAMNÉES

DELPHINE ET HIPPOLYTE

À la pâle clarté des lampes languissantes,
Sur de profonds coussins tout imprégnés d'odeur,
Hippolyte rêvait aux caresses puissantes
Qui levaient le rideau de sa jeune candeur.

Elle cherchait, d'un œil troublé par la tempête,
De sa naïveté le ciel déjà lointain,
Ainsi qu'un voyageur qui retourne la tête
Vers les horizons bleus dépassés le matin.

De ses yeux amortis les paresseuses larmes,
L'air brisé, la stupeur, la morne volupté,
Ses bras vaincus, jetés comme de vaines armes,
Tout servait, tout parait sa fragile beauté.

Doomed Women

DELPHINE AND HIPPOLYTA

In the wan glimmer of the dwindling lamps, on some deep and heavily scented cushions Hippolyta lay dreaming of those irresistible caresses which had initiated her girlish candour.

With an eye distraught after the tempest she was seeking for the already distant sky of her lost innocence, just as some traveller turns his head towards the blue horizons he crossed that morning.

The languid tears in her dulling eyes, her air of weariness, her stupor and sad feeling of voluptuousness, her defeated arms flung down like futile weapons – everything served and enhanced her fragile loveliness.

Étendue à ses pieds, calme et pleine de joie,
Delphine la couvait avec des yeux ardents,
Comme un animal fort qui surveille une proie,
Après l'avoir d'abord marquée avec les dents.

Beauté forte à genoux devant la beauté frêle,
Superbe, elle humait voluptueusement
Le vin de son triomphe, et s'allongeait vers elle,
Comme pour recueillir un doux remercîment.

Elle cherchait dans l'œil de sa pâle victime
Le cantique muet que chante le plaisir,
Et cette gratitude infinie et sublime
Qui sort de la paupière ainsi qu'un long soupir.

— «Hippolyte, cher cœur, que dis-tu de ces choses?
Comprends-tu maintenant qu'il ne faut pas offrir
L'holocauste sacré de tes premières roses
Aux souffles violents qui pourraient les flétrir?

Stretched at her feet, full of calm and joy, Delphine watched over
her with glowing eyes, like a powerful animal watching his prey after
setting the mark of his fangs on it.

Strong beauty on her knees beside frail beauty, proudly and sensu-
ally she breathed the wine of her victory, and leaned towards Hippolyta
as if to win some tender sign of gratitude.

In her pale victim's eyes she was seeking the silent hymn which
pleasure intones, and that infinite and sublime thanksgiving which
eyelids yield after a lingering sigh.

— 'Hippolyta, sweetheart, what do you think of these things? Do
you understand now that you must never offer the sacred sacrifice of
your first roses to violent blasts which would make them fade and die?

«Mes baisers sont légers comme ces éphémères
Qui caressent le soir les grands lacs transparents,
Et ceux de ton amant creuseront leurs ornières
Comme des chariots ou des socs déchirants;

«Ils passeront sur toi comme un lourd attelage
De chevaux et de bœufs aux sabots sans pitié . . .
Hippolyte, ô ma sœur! tourne donc ton visage,
Toi, mon âme et mon cœur, mon tout et ma moitié,

«Tourne vers moi tes yeux pleins d'azur et d'étoiles!
Pour un de ces regards charmants, baume divin,
Des plaisirs plus obscurs je lèverai les voiles
Et je t'endormirai dans un rêve sans fin!»

Mais Hippolyte alors, levant sa jeune tête:
— «Je ne suis point ingrate et ne me repens pas,
Ma Delphine, je souffre et je suis inquiète,
Comme après un nocturne et terrible repas.

'My kisses are light as those ephemerids which skim and caress great glassy lakes at sundown, while those of your lover would carve furrows in you, like chariot wheels or cutting ploughshares;

'they pass over you like a heavy team of horses and oxen with their pitiless hooves. Hippolyta, O my sister, now turn your face my way, my soul, my heart, my all, my second self,

'turn your eyes towards me brimming with azure and stars: in return for one of those charming glances, O divine balm, I shall lift the veils of even more uncharted delights, and lull you to sleep in a dream that has no ending.'

But, raising up her youthful head, Hippolyta replied: 'I am not ungrateful and have no regrets, my Delphine; but I am pained and uneasy as though after some terrible nocturnal feast.

«Je sens fondre sur moi de lourdes épouvantes
Et de noirs bataillons de fantômes épars,
Qui veulent me conduire en des routes mouvantes
Qu'un horizon sanglant ferme de toutes parts.

«Avons-nous donc commis une action étrange?
Explique, si tu peux, mon trouble et mon effroi:
Je frissonne de peur quand tu me dis: "Mon ange!"
Et cependant je sens ma bouche aller vers toi.

«Ne me regarde pas ainsi, toi, ma pensée!
Toi que j'aime à jamais, ma sœur d'élection,
Quand même tu serais une embûche dressée
Et le commencement de ma perdition!»

Delphine secouant sa crinière tragique,
Et comme trépignant sur le trépied de fer,
L'œil fatal, répondit d'une voix despotique:
– «Qui donc devant l'amour ose parler d'enfer?

'I feel crushing terrors and black battalions of phantoms, trying to drive me down shifting paths, blocked on all sides by a bloody horizon, closing in upon me.

'Can we have committed some forbidden deed? If you can, then explain this distress and alarm of mine. I tremble with fear when you call me "my angel" and yet I feel my lips seeking for yours.

'Do not look at me like that, you who are my very thought and whom I love for ever, my sister, my heart's choice, even though you might be an ambush laid against me, and the first step to my damnation.'

Delphine, shaking her tragic mane of hair, and as though stamping on the [Oracle's] iron tripod, her eye fateful, replied in tyrannic tones, 'Who dares to speak of hell, when faced with love?

«Maudit soit à jamais le rêveur inutile
Qui voulut le premier, dans sa stupidité,
S'éprenant d'un problème insoluble et stérile,
Aux choses de l'amour mêler l'honnêteté!

«Celui qui veut unir dans un accord mystique
L'ombre avec la chaleur, la nuit avec le jour,
Ne chauffera jamais son corps paralytique
À ce rouge soleil que l'on nomme l'amour!

«Va, si tu veux, chercher un fiancé stupide;
Cours offrir un cœur vierge à ses cruels baisers;
Et, pleine de remords et d'horreur, et livide,
Tu me rapporteras tes seins stigmatisés . . .

«On ne peut ici-bas contenter qu'un seul maître!»
Mais l'enfant, épanchant une immense douleur,
Cria soudain: «– Je sens s'élargir dans mon être
Un abîme béant; cet abîme est mon cœur!

'May the futile dreamer be damned who first, in his stupidity, when facing an insoluble and sterile problem, thought he could confuse honesty with love's ways.

'Whoever seeks to contrive some mysterious union between shade and light and night and day, will never be able to warm his paralytic flesh with the scarlet sun which we call Love.

'Go then, if you will, in pursuit of some stupid oaf's betrothal, run and submit a virgin heart to his bloodthirsty kisses – then full of remorse and horror, pale as death, you will run back to me with your disfigured breasts.

'Here on earth we can only satisfy one master.' But the child, unable to contain her immense suffering, suddenly cried out, 'I feel a gaping void opening in my being, and that abyss is my own heart.

«Brûlant comme un volcan, profond comme le vide!
Rien ne rassasiera ce monstre gémissant
Et ne rafraîchira la soif de l'Euménide
Qui, la torche à la main, le brûle jusqu'au sang.

«Que nos rideaux fermés nous séparent du monde,
Et que la lassitude amène le repos!
Je veux m'anéantir dans ta gorge profonde
Et trouver sur ton sein la fraîcheur des tombeaux!»

– Descendez, descendez, lamentables victimes,
Descendez le chemin de l'enfer éternel!
Plongez au plus profond du gouffre, où tous les crimes,
Flagellés par un vent qui ne vient pas du ciel,

Bouillonnent pêle-mêle avec un bruit d'orage.
Ombres folles, courez au but de vos désirs;
Jamais vous ne pourrez assouvir votre rage,
Et votre châtiment naîtra de vos plaisirs.

'Burning like a volcano, as deep as the void itself, nothing will ever satisfy that groaning monster's hunger, nothing will ever refresh the thirst of the Fury brandishing her torch to burn my blood away.

'May our closed curtains preserve us from the world, and lassitude bring us repose. I long to extinguish myself in the depths of your bosom, and feel the coldness of the tomb upon your breast.'

Descend, go down, you lamentable victims, go down the road of the everlasting inferno. Dive down into the fathomless depths of the gulf, where all human crimes are whipped by a blast not blown from heaven,

and boil in a chaotic mass with all the uproar of a tempest. Demented shades, run to the very limits of your desiring: you will never be able to calm your rage, your rabies, and your chastisement will be the fruit of your own pleasures.

Jamais un rayon frais n'éclaira vos cavernes;
Par les fentes des murs des miasmes fiévreux
Filtrent en s'enflammant ainsi que des lanternes
Et pénètrent vos corps de leurs parfums affreux.

L'âpre stérilité de votre jouissance
Altère votre soif et roidit votre peau,
Et le vent furibond de la concupiscence
Fait claquer votre chair ainsi qu'un vieux drapeau.

Loin des peuples vivants, errantes, condamnées,
À travers les déserts courez comme les loups;
Faites votre destin, âmes désordonnées,
Et fuyez l'infini que vous portez en vous!

Never will a cool beam come to light your cavern's gloom, but from cracks in the walls feverish miasmas will come filtering through, flaming like lanterns, to pierce your bodies with death-dealing perfumes.

The cruel sterility of your raptures only doubles your thirst and stiffens your skin, and the furious wind of concupiscence makes your flesh flap like an old flag.

Far from all living things, wandering and damned, run like wolves through the deserts; achieve your destiny, disordered souls, and flee from the infinite which you bear within you.

[One of the works in *Les Lesbiennes* projected in 1845–7]

IV

LE LÉTHÉ

Viens sur mon cœur, âme cruelle et sourde,
Tigre adoré, monstre aux airs indolents;
Je veux longtemps plonger mes doigts tremblants
Dans l'épaisseur de ta crinière lourde;

Dans tes jupons remplis de ton parfum
Ensevelir ma tête endolorie,
Et respirer, comme une fleur flétrie,
Le doux relent de mon amour défunt.

Je veux dormir! dormir plutôt que vivre!
Dans un sommeil aussi doux que la mort,
J'étalerai mes baisers sans remords
Sur ton beau corps poli comme le cuivre.

Pour engloutir mes sanglots apaisés
Rien ne me vaut l'abîme de ta couche;
L'oubli puissant habite sur ta bouche,
Et le Léthé coule dans tes baisers.

Lethe

Come, stretch upon my heart, cruel and unhearing soul, beloved
tigress, you indolently posing monster; for I am yearning to plunge my
trembling fingers long and long into the thickness of your massive
mane,

to bury my aching head in your skirts filled with your perfume, to
breathe as a withered flower the honeyed odour of my dead love.

For I would sleep now, sleep rather than live, and in a death-sweet
slumber lavish my kisses without remorse on the glossy bronze of your
exquisite form.

Nothing can rival the abyss of your bed to soothe my sobs; your
mouth is a goblet of oblivion, all Lethe in your kisses flows.

À mon destin, désormais mon délice,
J'obéirai comme un prédestiné;
Martyr docile, innocent condamné,
Dont la ferveur attise le supplice,

Je sucerai, pour noyer ma rancœur,
Le népenthès et la bonne ciguë
Aux bouts charmants de cette gorge aiguë,
Qui n'a jamais emprisonné de cœur.

As a man predestined, henceforth I shall bow to my fate and make it my delight, and be the willing accomplice of my martyrdom, one whose ardour connives to aggravate his anguish.

To drown my thirst for revenge I shall suck the nectar of forgetfulness and the good hemlock from the bewitching tips of that pointed breast, which never held a captive heart.

[Regarded as part of the Jeanne Duval cycle]

V
À CELLE QUI EST TROP GAIE

Ta tête, ton geste, ton air
Sont beaux comme un beau paysage;
Le rire joue en ton visage
Comme un vent frais dans un ciel clair.

Le passant chagrin que tu frôles
Est ébloui par la santé
Qui jaillit comme une clarté
De tes bras et de tes épaules.

Les retentissantes couleurs
Dont tu parsèmes tes toilettes
Jettent dans l'esprit des poètes
L'image d'un ballet de fleurs.

Ces robes folles sont l'emblème
De ton esprit bariolé;
Folle dont je suis affolé,
Je te hais autant que je t'aime!

To Her Who is Too Gay

Your head, your gestures and bearing are as lovely as a beautiful land-
scape: laughter plays over your face like a cool wind in a clear sky.

The glum passer-by you brush against is dazzled by the healthy glow
which flashes from your arms and shoulders like light.

The vivid colours dappling your clothes evoke in poets' minds a
ballet of flowers.

Those motley dresses are the emblem of your mind's variety, you
scatterbrain I'm mad about – I hate you every bit as much as I love you!

Quelquefois dans un beau jardin
Où je traînais mon atonie,
J'ai senti, comme une ironie,
Le soleil déchirer mon sein;

Et le printemps et la verdure
Ont tant humilié mon cœur,
Que j'ai puni sur une fleur
L'insolence de la Nature.

Ainsi je voudrais, une nuit,
Quand l'heure des voluptés sonne,
Vers les trésors de ta personne,
Comme un lâche, ramper sans bruit,

Pour châtier ta chair joyeuse,
Pour meurtrir ton sein pardonné,
Et faire à ton flanc étonné
Une blessure large et creuse,

Et, vertigineuse douceur!
À travers ces lèvres nouvelles,
Plus éclatantes et plus belles,
T'infuser mon venin, ma sœur!

Sometimes in a beautiful garden, weighed down by my listless atony,
I felt the sunshine like an irony wound my breast,
 and the springtime and all its green so humiliated my heart that I
punished the insolence of Nature on a single flower.
 In the same way, some night when the clock strikes the hour of
sensualities, I would like to slink silently like a coward towards your
body's treasures,
 so as to chastise your happy flesh, to bruise your pardoned breast and
cleave into your astounded side a wide deep wound –
 and, giddy sweetness! – through those new lips, more beautiful and
vivid, infuse my poison into you, my sister.

[Sent to Mme Sabatier 1852]

VI

LES BIJOUX

La très chère était nue, et, connaissant mon cœur,
Elle n'avait gardé que ses bijoux sonores,
Dont le riche attirail lui donnait l'air vainqueur
Qu'ont dans leurs jours heureux les esclaves des Mores.

Quand il jette en dansant son bruit vif et moqueur,
Ce monde rayonnant de métal et de pierre
Me ravit en extase, et j'aime à la fureur
Les choses où le son se mêle à la lumière.

Elle était donc couchée et se laissait aimer,
Et du haut du divan elle souriait d'aise
À mon amour profond et doux comme la mer,
Qui vers elle montait comme vers sa falaise.

Les yeux fixés sur moi, comme un tigre dompté,
D'un air vague et rêveur elle essayait des poses,
Et la candeur unie à la lubricité
Donnait un charme neuf à ses métamorphoses;

Beads

My beloved was naked and, knowing my heart's desire, had kept only
her sonorous jewels on, whose rich splendour gave her the triumphant
air that Moorish slave-women have on their happy days.

When it dances and gives out its sharp mocking music, this glitter-
ing world of metal and stone thrills me to ecstasy, and I madly love
those things in which sound and light combine.

So she lay back and let herself be loved, and high on the divan she
smiled for joy upon my love as deep and gentle as the sea, which rose
up to her as towards a cliff.

With her eyes fixed upon me, like a tamed tigress, with a vague
dreamy look she tried this pose and that, and candidness and wanton-
ness together gave a novel charm to her variations.

Et son bras et sa jambe, et sa cuisse et ses reins,
Polis comme de l'huile, onduleux comme un cygne,
Passaient devant mes yeux clairvoyants et sereins;
Et son ventre et ses seins, ces grappes de ma vigne,

S'avançaient, plus câlins que les Anges du mal,
Pour troubler le repos où mon âme était mise,
Et pour la déranger du rocher de cristal
Où, calme et solitaire, elle s'était assise.

Je croyais voir unis par un nouveau dessin
Les hanches de l'Antiope au buste d'un imberbe,
Tant sa taille faisait ressortir son bassin.
Sur ce teint fauve et brun le fard était superbe!

— Et la lampe s'étant résignée à mourir,
Comme le foyer seul illuminait la chambre,
Chaque fois qu'il poussait un flamboyant soupir,
Il inondait de sang cette peau couleur d'ambre!

Her arms and legs, her thighs and loins, glistening like oil, rippling swanlike, passed before my clairvoyant and serene eyes; and her belly and her breasts, those clusters of my vine,

thrust forward, more alluring than the angels of evilness, to trouble the rest my soul had found and dislodge it from the crystal rock it had settled on, calm and solitary.

I thought I saw before me, united in a new structure, the hips of Antiope and a stripling's bust, so strongly her narrow waist accentuated her pelvis. The rouge on her wild tawny complexion looked superb.

And as the lamp had resigned itself to die, and the hearth alone lit up the room, each time it gave a fiery sigh it flowed over that amber skin like blood.

VII
LES MÉTAMORPHOSES DU VAMPIRE

La femme cependant, de sa bouche de fraise,
En se tordant ainsi qu'un serpent sur la braise,
Et pétrissant ses seins sur le fer de son busc,
Laissait couler ces mots tout imprégnés de musc:
– «Moi, j'ai la lèvre humide, et je sais la science
De perdre au fond d'un lit l'antique conscience.
Je sèche tous les pleurs sur mes seins triomphants,
Et fais rire les vieux du rire des enfants.
Je remplace, pour qui me voit nue et sans voiles,
La lune, le soleil, le ciel et les étoiles!
Je suis, mon cher savant, si docte aux voluptés,
Lorsque j'étouffe un homme en mes bras redoutés,
Ou lorsque j'abandonne aux morsures mon buste,
Timide et libertine, et fragile et robuste,
Que sur ces matelas qui se pâment d'émoi,
Les anges impuissants se damneraient pour moi!»

The Vampire's Variations

Meanwhile the woman writhing like a snake on a brazier, chafing her
breasts on the iron ribs of her corset, uttered these musk-scented words
from her strawberry mouth: 'With my wet lips I know the science of
stifling age-old conscience in my bed. I can dry every tear on my
victorious bosom, and can make old men laugh with the laughter of
children. For every man who looks on my unveiled nakedness I will
replace the sun and moon, the sky and all its stars. Dear learned scholar,
know that I am so versed in the lore of voluptuousness that when I
stifle a man in my dreaded embrace or yield my bosom to his teeth,
I can be so shy and so lewd, so fragile and so strong, that on my couch
which swoons with ecstasy the sexless angels would damn themselves
for me.'

Quand elle eut de mes os sucé toute la moelle,
Et que languissamment je me tournai vers elle
Pour lui rendre un baiser d'amour, je ne vis plus
Qu'une outre aux flancs gluants, toute pleine de pus !
Je fermai les deux yeux, dans ma froide épouvante,
Et quand je les rouvris à la clarté vivante,
À mes côtés, au lieu du mannequin puissant
Qui semblait avoir fait provision de sang,
Tremblaient confusément des débris de squelette,
Qui d'eux-mêmes rendaient le cri d'une girouette
Ou d'une enseigne, au bout d'une tringle de fer,
Que balance le vent pendant les nuits d'hiver.

When she had sucked the marrow out of my bones, and languidly I turned to give her a kiss of love, I found nothing there but a leathery gourd all clammy and full of pus. I closed my eyes in a chill of horror, then when I opened them to the light of life I found beside me no longer that powerful machine which seemed to have bloated itself with my blood, but only the rattling bones of a skeleton, which rasped with the grating cry of an iron weathercock or some tavern sign-board dangling from its iron frame, which the wind swings to and fro on a winter's night.

[1851. Also entitled 'L'Outre de la Volupté']

Galanteries

VIII
LE JET D'EAU

Tes beaux yeux sont las, pauvre amante !
Reste longtemps, sans les rouvrir,
Dans cette pose nonchalante
Où t'a surprise le plaisir.
Dans la cour le jet d'eau qui jase
Et ne se tait ni nuit ni jour,
Entretient doucement l'extase
Où ce soir m'a plongé l'amour.

La gerbe épanouie
En mille fleurs,
Où Phœbé réjouie
Met ses couleurs,
Tombe comme une pluie
De larges pleurs.

Ainsi ton âme qu'incendie
L'éclair brûlant des voluptés
S'élance, rapide et hardie,
Vers les vastes cieux enchantés.

GALLANTRIES

The Fountain

Your lovely eyes are weary, my poor darling. Bide a while, without opening them, in that listless pose in which pleasure surprised you. The babbling fountain in the courtyard, never silent night or day, softly accompanies the ecstasy into which love plunged me this evening.

The sheaf of water unfolds into a thousand flowers, to which joyful Diana adds her [moonlight] hues; it falls like a shower of large tears.

Thus your soul, fired by the searing flash of sensual pleasures, springs swift and bold towards the vast enchanted skies. Then it brims over,

Puis, elle s'épanche, mourante,
En un flot de triste langueur,
Qui par une invisible pente
Descend jusqu'au fond de mon cœur.

La gerbe épanouie
En mille fleurs,
Où Phœbé réjouie
Met ses couleurs,
Tombe comme une pluie
De larges pleurs.

Ô toi, que la nuit rend si belle,
Qu'il m'est doux, penché vers tes seins,
D'écouter la plainte éternelle
Qui sanglote dans les bassins !
Lune, eau sonore, nuit bénie,
Arbres qui frissonnez autour,
Votre pure mélancolie
Est le miroir de mon amour.

La gerbe épanouie
En mille fleurs,
Où Phœbé réjouie
Met ses couleurs,
Tombe comme une pluie
De larges pleurs.

dying in a wave of sad languor which falls down some unseen slope into the depths of my heart.

The sheaf of water unfolds into a thousand flowers, to which joyful Diana adds her [moonlight] hues; it falls like a shower of large tears.

O you whom night so beautifies, how I love, as I bend over your breasts, to listen to the eternal lament sobbing in the fountain's basin. O Moon, mellifluous waters, the blessed Night and trees that tremble all around, your pure melancholy is the mirror of my love.

The sheaf of water unfolds into a thousand flowers, to which joyful Diana adds her [moonlight] hues; it falls like a shower of large tears.

[Pre-1853. Published 1865]

IX
LES YEUX DE BERTHE

Vous pouvez mépriser les yeux les plus célèbres,
Beaux yeux de mon enfant, par où filtre et s'enfuit
Je ne sais quoi de bon, de doux comme la Nuit!
Beaux yeux, versez sur moi vos charmantes ténèbres!

Grands yeux de mon enfant, arcanes adorés,
Vous ressemblez beaucoup à ces grottes magiques
Où, derrière l'amas des ombres léthargiques,
Scintillent vaguement des trésors ignorés!

Mon enfant a des yeux obscurs, profonds et vastes,
Comme toi, Nuit immense, éclairés comme toi!
Leurs feux sont ces pensers d'Amour, mêlés de Foi,
Qui pétillent au fond, voluptueux ou chastes.

Bertha's Eyes

You may scorn the most famous eyes, beautiful eyes of my child,
through which distils and vanishes something as good and gentle as the
Night. Beautiful eyes, pour down on me your enchanting darknesses!

Great eyes of my child, adorable enigmas, you strongly resemble
those magic grottoes in which, behind a mass of drowsy shadows,
undiscovered treasures gleam.

My child has dusky eyes, profound and vast as thine, immense
Night, and luminous like thine. Their lights are those thoughts of Love,
combined with Faith, that sparkle in their depths, voluptuous or chaste.

[1843? Jeanne Duval acted under the name *Berthe* in 1838–9: but
the poem was offered to another Berthe at a much later date]

X

HYMNE

À la très chère, à la très belle
Qui remplit mon cœur de clarté,
À l'ange, à l'idole immortelle,
Salut en l'immortalité!

Elle se répand dans ma vie
Comme un air imprégné de sel,
Et dans mon âme inassouvie
Verse le goût de l'éternel.

Sachet toujours frais qui parfume
L'atmosphère d'un cher réduit,
Encensoir oublié qui fume
En secret à travers la nuit,

Comment, amour incorruptible,
T'exprimer avec vérité?
Grain de musc qui gis, invisible,
Au fond de mon éternité!

Hymn

To the very dear and very beautiful one who fills my heart with light,
to the angel and immortal idol, hail in immortality!

She spreads into my life like briny ozone, and into my hungry soul
she pours the taste of the eternal.

Ever-fresh sachet, perfuming the atmosphere of some beloved
retreat, forgotten censer smoking in secret through the night –

O how, my incorruptible love, can I ever express you truthfully, you
grain of musc lying unseen in the depths of my eternity?

À la très bonne, à la très belle,
Qui fait ma joie et ma santé,
À l'ange, à l'idole immortelle,
Salut en l'immortalité!

To the very good and very beautiful one, who are my happiness and
health, to the angel and immortal idol, all hail in immortality!

[Sent to Mme Sabatier 1854. Published 1855]

XI
LES PROMESSES D'UN VISAGE

J'aime, ô pâle beauté, tes sourcils surbaissés,
 D'où semblent couler des ténèbres;
Tes yeux, quoique très noirs, m'inspirent des pensers
 Qui ne sont pas du tout funèbres.

Tes yeux, qui sont d'accord avec tes noirs cheveux,
 Avec ta crinière élastique,
Tes yeux, languissamment, me disent: «Si tu veux,
 Amant de la muse plastique,

«Suivre l'espoir qu'en toi nous avons excité,
 Et tous les goûts que tu professes,
Tu pourras constater notre véracité
 Depuis le nombril jusqu'aux fesses;

«Tu trouveras au bout de deux beaux seins bien lourds,
 Deux larges médailles de bronze,
Et sous un ventre uni, doux comme du velours,
 Bistré comme la peau d'un bonze,

A Face's Promises

I love, my pale beauty, your drooping eyelids which seem to pour out shadows, and though so deeply dark your eyes inspire within me thoughts which are not at all sad.

Your eyes that match your midnight hair, your elastic mane, languorously say, 'If you who love the plastic arts

want to pursue the hope these eyes have stirred within you, and other tastes which you profess to have, then you may verify the truth of us from hip to navel.

On the tips of two heavy shapely breasts you will find two wide medallions of bronze; and under a sleek belly as soft as velvet and olive as the skin of a youthful bonze [Buddhist priest],

«Une riche toison qui, vraiment, est la sœur
De cette énorme chevelure,
Souple et frisée, et qui t'égale en épaisseur,
Nuit sans étoiles, Nuit obscure!»

a downy fleece there, the obvious sister of this flourishing head of
hair, elastic and curly, thick as the starless night, the sombre night.'

[1865–6]

XII

LE MONSTRE

I

Tu n'es certes pas, ma très chère,
Ce que Veuillot nomme un tendron.
Le jeu, l'amour, la bonne chère,
Bouillonnent en toi, vieux chaudron!
Tu n'es plus fraîche, ma très chère,

Ma vieille infante! Et cependant
Tes caravanes insensées
T'ont donné ce lustre abondant
Des choses qui sont très usées,
Mais qui séduisent cependant.

Je ne trouve pas monotone
La verdeur de tes quarante ans;
Je préfère tes fruits, Automne,
Aux fleurs banales du Printemps!
Non! tu n'es jamais monotone!

The Monster

OR THE PARANYMPH OF A MACABRE NYMPH

I

You are certainly not, my dear old girl, what [bigot] Veuillot calls a
chicken: gambling and fornicating and guzzling all bubble in your inside,
you old stewpot; you are no fresh egg,

 my dear old girl. Superannuated Infanta, none the less your knock-
about career has given you that rich patina of old bygones, which can
still seduce us in spite of everything.

 I don't find your sexy middle-age as dull as all that, as I prefer your
ripe Autumnal fruits to the banal flowers that bloom in the Spring – oh
no, you are never a bit dull.

Ta carcasse a des agréments
Et des grâces particulières;
Je trouve d'étranges piments
Dans le creux de tes deux salières;
Ta carcasse a des agréments!

Nargue des amants ridicules
Du melon et du giraumont!
Je préfère tes clavicules
À celles du roi Salomon,
Et je plains ces gens ridicules!

Tes cheveux, comme un casque bleu,
Ombragent ton front de guerrière,
Qui ne pense et rougit que peu,
Et puis se sauvent par derrière
Comme les crins d'un casque bleu.

Tes yeux qui semblent de la boue,
Où scintille quelque fanal,
Ravivés au fard de ta joue,
Lancent un éclair infernal!
Tes yeux sont noirs comme la boue!

Your carcass has charms and graces all its own. I find exotic peppers in the two salt-cellars [of your collar-bones]: your carcass has its beauty-spots!

To hell with the foolish lovers of melons and pumpkins, for I prize your clavicles above King Solomon's, and pity all those foolish people.

Like a blue helmet your hair beetles over your amazonian brow which is rarely the scene of thoughts or blushes, it sweeps behind like a blue helmet's bristles.

Your eyes are pools of mud from which a lantern gleams, heightened by your painted cheeks they flash out hellish rays, yes your eyes are black as mud.

[*Les Clavicules de Salomon* (*clavicule* meaning 'small key') was a magic book wrongly attributed to Solomon. – Ed.]

Par sa luxure et son dédain
Ta lèvre amère nous provoque;
Cette lèvre, c'est un Éden
Qui nous attire et qui nous choque.
Quelle luxure! et quel dédain!

Ta jambe musculeuse et sèche
Sait gravir au haut des volcans,
Et malgré la neige et la dèche
Danser les plus fougueux cancans.
Ta jambe est musculeuse et sèche;

Ta peau brûlante et sans douceur,
Comme celle des vieux gendarmes,
Ne connaît pas plus la sueur
Que ton œil ne connaît les larmes.
(Et pourtant elle a sa douceur!)

II

Sotte, tu t'en vas droit au Diable!
Volontiers j'irais avec toi,
Si cette vitesse effroyable
Ne me causait pas quelque émoi.
Va-t'en donc, toute seule, au Diable!

Your caustic lips taunt us with lewdness and disdain, lips like an Eden
which attracts and shocks with such lechery, such disdain.
 Your scrawny muscled leg can climb volcanoes and dance mad
cancans, come snow or low water, your scrawny muscled leg.
 Your hide is hot and rasping like an old policeman's, a stranger to
sweat as your eyes are strangers to tears, and yet that hide of yours is not
without its comforts.

II

Go to the devil, you silly woman. I would gladly go along with you, if
only your haste did not distress me – so you can go to the devil all by
yourself.

Mon rein, mon poumon, mon jarret
Ne me laissent plus rendre hommage
À ce Seigneur, comme il faudrait.
«Hélas! c'est vraiment bien dommage!»
Disent mon rein et mon jarret.

Oh! très sincèrement je souffre
De ne pas aller aux sabbats,
Pour voir, quand il pète du soufre,
Comment tu lui baises son cas!
Oh! très sincèrement je souffre!

Je suis diablement affligé
De ne pas être ta torchère,
Et de te demander congé,
Flambeau d'enfer! Juge, ma chère,
Combien je dois être affligé,

Puisque depuis longtemps je t'aime,
Étant très logique! En effet,
Voulant du Mal chercher la crème
Et n'aimer qu'un monstre parfait,
Vraiment oui! vieux monstre, je t'aime!

My loins, my lungs, my calves will no longer allow me to pay my respects to His Lowness as I should have to do, and oh what a pity, say my loins and calves.

It grieves me sincerely to be unable to attend your witches' sabbath and watch him farting sulphur while you kiss his parts, oh most sincerely it grieves me.

I am devilishly upset to think I cannot be your torchbearer, and beg to leave you, torch of Hell. You can judge, old girl, how upset I must be,

as I kept on loving you so long, being very logical. Indeed, in my quest for the very cream of Evil and wishing to love nothing but a perfect monster, truly, my old monster, I love you.

[1865–6]

XIII
FRANCISCÆ MEÆ LAUDES

[Voir p. 157]

In Praise of my Francisca: see p. 157

Épigraphes

XIV
VERS POUR LE PORTRAIT
DE M. HONORÉ DAUMIER

Celui dont nous t'offrons l'image,
Et dont l'art, subtil entre tous,
Nous enseigne à rire de nous,
Celui-là, lecteur, est un sage.

C'est un satirique, un moqueur;
Mais l'énergie avec laquelle
Il peint le Mal et sa séquelle,
Prouve la beauté de son cœur.

Son rire n'est pas la grimace
De Melmoth ou de Méphisto
Sous la torche de l'Alecto
Qui les brûle, mais qui nous glace.

INSCRIPTIONS

Lines for the Portrait of Honoré Daumier

He whose image we now offer you and whose supremely subtle art teaches us how to laugh at ourselves, is a wise man, dear reader.

He is a satirist and a mocker, no doubt; but his energy in portraying Evil and its consequences demonstrates the beauty of his heart.

Daumier's laughter is quite unlike the grimace of a Melmoth or Mephistopheles at the Fury's brand, which burns them to ashes but chills us to the bone.

Leur rire, hélas! de la gaîté
N'est que la douloureuse charge;
Le sien rayonne, franc et large,
Comme un signe de sa bonté!

XV

LOLA DE VALENCE

Entre tant de beautés que partout on peut voir,
Je comprends bien, amis, que le désir balance;
Mais on voit scintiller en Lola de Valence
Le charme inattendu d'un bijou rose et noir.

Their laughter is only a painful caricature of gaiety, but Daumier's smile radiates light, frank and generous, a visible sign of his benevolence.

[1865]

Lola de Valence

I quite understand, my friends, how desire may hesitate between the numerous beauties that are everywhere to be seen: but Lola de Valence glitters with the novel charm of a jewel, pink and black.

[1863]

XVI
SUR *LE TASSE EN PRISON*
D'EUGÈNE DELACROIX

Le poète au cachot, débraillé, maladif,
Roulant un manuscrit sous son pied convulsif,
Mesure d'un regard que la terreur enflamme
L'escalier de vertige où s'abîme son âme.

Les rires enivrants dont s'emplit la prison
Vers l'étrange et l'absurde invitent sa raison;
Le Doute l'environne, et la Peur ridicule,
Hideuse et multiforme, autour de lui circule.

Ce génie enfermé dans un taudis malsain,
Ces grimaces, ces cris, ces spectres dont l'essaim
Tourbillonne, ameuté derrière son oreille,

Ce rêveur que l'horreur de son logis réveille,
Voilà bien ton emblème, Âme aux songes obscurs,
Que le Réel étouffe entre ses quatre murs!

On Delacroix's 'Tasso in Prison'

The poet in his cell, unkempt and sick, as he tramples a manuscript under his fevered foot, measures with terror-inflamed eyes the vast stair of madness down which his soul is drawn.

The drunken hilarity which fills the entire gaol is luring his reason into oddness and absurdity. He is surrounded by Doubt, and foolish Fear, hideous and multiform, is prowling round him.

This man of genius caged in a filthy hovel, these grimaces and cries, these visions that whirl in frenzied swarms about his ears,

this dreamer woken by his lodging's horror – such is your emblem, my Soul, you with your darkling dreams, smothered between Reality's four walls.

[Ms dated 1844. Published 1864]

Pièces diverses

XVII
LA VOIX

Mon berceau s'adossait à la bibliothèque,
Babel sombre, où roman, science, fabliau,
Tout, la cendre latine et la poussière grecque,
Se mêlaient. J'étais haut comme un in-folio.
Deux voix me parlaient. L'une, insidieuse et ferme,
Disait: «La Terre est un gâteau plein de douceur;
Je puis (et ton plaisir serait alors sans terme!)
Te faire un appétit d'une égale grosseur.»
Et l'autre: «Viens! oh! viens voyager dans les rêves,
Au-delà du possible, au-delà du connu!»
Et celle-là chantait comme le vent des grèves,
Fantôme vagissant, on ne sait d'où venu,
Qui caresse l'oreille et cependant l'effraie.
Je te répondis: «Oui! douce voix!» C'est d'alors
Que date ce qu'on peut, hélas! nommer ma plaie
Et ma fatalité. Derrière les décors

MISCELLANEOUS PIECES

The Voice

My cradle had its back against the book-case, a dark Babel in which
fiction and science and mediaeval tales, everything including Latin ash
and Greek dust, rubbed shoulders together. I was no bigger than a folio.
 Two voices used to talk to me. The first one, sly and firm, used to
say, 'The Earth is a nice sweet cake: I can give you – and then endless
pleasure will be yours – an appetite just as big as that cake.' And the
second said, 'Come with me and travel in dreamland, beyond the possi-
ble and the known!' And the voice sang like the wind on the sea-shore,
a phantom wailing like a child, from who knows where, both caressing
and frightening the ear.
 I answered you, 'Yes, gentle Voice.' From then dates what, alas, may
be called my wound, my life's misfortune. For behind the scenes of vast

De l'existence immense, au plus noir de l'abîme,
Je vois distinctement des mondes singuliers,
Et, de ma clairvoyance extatique victime,
Je traîne des serpents qui mordent mes souliers.
Et c'est depuis ce temps que, pareil aux prophètes,
J'aime si tendrement le désert et la mer;
Que je ris dans les deuils et pleure dans les fêtes,
Et trouve un goût suave au vin le plus amer;
Que je prends très souvent les faits pour des mensonges,
Et que, les yeux au ciel, je tombe dans des trous.
Mais la Voix me console et dit: «Garde tes songes;
Les sages n'en ont pas d'aussi beaux que les fous!»

existence, in the pit's deepest dark, I distinctly see strange worlds, and, the ecstatic victim of my own insight, I am attended by snakes which snap at my shoes.

And it is since then that, like the prophets of old, I so tenderly love the desert and the sea; that I laugh when others are grieving, and weep when they make merry; that I find a smooth flavour in the tartest wine; that I often mistake facts for lies; and that, with my eyes fixed on the sky, I'm always falling into holes. But the Voice consoles me, saying: 'Keep your dreams – for the wise have not such beautiful dreams as madmen have!'

[Published 1861. Cf. 'Alchimie de la douleur' (p. 182), and Pascal: 'Imagination . . . has its wise men and its madmen. . . . It cannot make madmen wise, but it makes them happy.']

XVIII
L'IMPRÉVU

Harpagon, qui veillait son père agonisant,
Se dit, rêveur, devant ces lèvres déjà blanches:
«Nous avons au grenier un nombre suffisant,
Ce me semble, de vieilles planches?»

Célimène roucoule et dit: «Mon cœur est bon,
Et naturellement, Dieu m'a faite très belle.»
– Son cœur! cœur racorni, fumé comme un jambon,
Recuit à la flamme éternelle!

Un gazetier fumeux, qui se croit un flambeau,
Dit au pauvre, qu'il a noyé dans les ténèbres:
«Où donc l'aperçois-tu, ce créateur du Beau,
Ce Redresseur que tu célèbres?»

Mieux que tous, je connais certain voluptueux
Qui bâille nuit et jour, et se lamente et pleure,
Répétant, l'impuissant et le fat: «Oui, je veux
Être vertueux, dans une heure!»

The Unforeseen

Harpagon, as he watched over his dying father, said to himself as he mused over those already blanched lips, 'I think we have enough old planks in the loft?'

Célimène coos and says, 'I'm a kind-hearted woman, and of course God made me very beautiful.' – Her heart! a shrivelled heart, smoked like a ham, cooks over again in the everlasting fire.

A dimwitted journalist, who thinks he is a torch of light, says to the poor devil whom he has drowned in obscurity, 'Where, then, can you see him, this creator of beauty and righter of wrongs whom you make so much of?'

Better than all that, I know a certain sensualist who yawns all night and day, lamenting and weeping and constantly repeating – 'Yes, I do want to be good – but only in an hour's time!'

L'horloge, à son tour, dit à voix basse: «Il est mûr,
Le damné! J'avertis en vain la chair infecte.
L'homme est aveugle, sourd, fragile, comme un mur
 Qu'habite et que ronge un insecte!»

Et puis, Quelqu'un paraît, que tous avaient nié,
Et qui leur dit, railleur et fier: «Dans mon ciboire,
Vous avez, que je crois, assez communié,
 À la joyeuse Messe noire?

«Chacun de vous m'a fait un temple dans son cœur;
Vous avez, en secret, baisé ma fesse immonde!
Reconnaissez Satan à son rire vainqueur,
 Énorme et laid comme le monde!

«Avez-vous donc pu croire, hypocrites surpris,
Qu'on se moque du maître, et qu'avec lui l'on triche,
Et qu'il soit naturel de recevoir deux prix,
 D'aller au Ciel et d'être riche?

«Il faut que le gibier paye le vieux chasseur
Qui se morfond longtemps à l'affût de la proie.
Je vais vous emporter à travers l'épaisseur,
 Compagnons de ma triste joie,

 In its turn the Clock says in an undertone, 'That doomed man is now ripe. In vain I warn vile bodies that Man is blind and deaf, and as weak as a wall infested and devoured by a beetle.'
 And then Someone appears, one whom they all denied, and says to them, jeering and proud, 'I think you have taken communion often enough from my pyx, at the jolly Black Mass!
 'Each of you has made me a temple in his heart and furtively kissed my loathsome rump. Now, recognize Satan himself by his triumphant laughter, as huge and ugly as the world!
 'Unmasked hypocrites, can you really believe that you can bamboozle the Master and play him false, and that it's quite natural to be given two prizes – to go to heaven, and be rich as well?
 'The game must be worthwhile for the old poacher, who has to cool his heels while he stalks his quarry. I am going to carry you off into the thickness, you partners in my dismal joy –

«À travers l'épaisseur de la terre et du roc,
À travers les amas confus de votre cendre,
Dans un palais aussi grand que moi, d'un seul bloc,
Et qui n'est pas de pierre tendre;

«Car il est fait avec l'universel Péché,
Et contient mon orgueil, ma douleur et ma gloire!»
– Cependant, tout en haut de l'univers juché,
Un Ange sonne la victoire

De ceux dont le cœur dit: «Que béni soit ton fouet,
Seigneur! que la douleur, ô Père, soit bénie!
Mon âme dans tes mains n'est pas un vain jouet,
Et ta prudence est infinie.»

Le son de la trompette est si délicieux,
Dans ces soirs solennels de célestes vendanges,
Qu'il s'infiltre comme une extase dans tous ceux
Dont elle chante les louanges.

'through the thickness of earth and rock, through the chaotic mass of your own ashes, into a palace as spacious as myself, all of a piece and made of no soft stone,
'for it is made of Universal Sin and contains my pride, my sorrow and my glory!' And yet, enthroned on the pinnacle of the universe, an Angel proclaims the victory
of those whose heart says, 'Blessed be thy lash, O Lord, blessed be suffering, O Father! My soul is no idle plaything in thy hands, and thy care is infinite.'
The sound of the trump is so delightful in these solemn evenings of the harvesting of heaven, that it filters like an ecstasy into all those whose praise it sings.

[1863. Baudelaire's note on the poem says 'Here the author of *Les Fleurs du mal* is turning towards the eternal life. It had to end that way. Let us observe that like all the newly-converted he is very strict and very fanatical.']

XIX
LA RANÇON

L'homme a, pour payer sa rançon,
Deux champs au tuf profond et riche,
Qu'il faut qu'il remue et défriche
Avec le fer de la raison;

Pour obtenir la moindre rose,
Pour extorquer quelques épis,
Des pleurs salés de son front gris
Sans cesse il faut qu'il les arrose.

L'un est l'Art, et l'autre l'Amour.
– Pour rendre le juge propice,
Lorsque de la stricte justice
Paraîtra le terrible jour,

Il faudra lui montrer des granges
Pleines de moissons, et des fleurs
Dont les formes et les couleurs
Gagnent le suffrage des Anges.

The Ransom

To pay his ransom with, Man has two fields of deep rich soil, which he
must cultivate with the blade of Reason.

To nurse the smallest rose, to wring a few ears of corn from the earth,
he must water them ceaselessly with the salt tears of his ashen brow.

One is Art, and the other is Love. In order to propitiate the Judge
when the terrible day of strict Justice dawns,

he will have to show him barns full of harvested crops, and flowers
whose forms and colours win the approval of the Angels.

[1851–2]

XX
À UNE MALABARAISE

Tes pieds sont aussi fins que tes mains, et ta hanche
Est large à faire envie à la plus belle blanche;
À l'artiste pensif ton corps est doux et cher;
Tes grands yeux de velours sont plus noirs que ta chair.
Aux pays chauds et bleus où ton Dieu t'a fait naître,
Ta tâche est d'allumer la pipe de ton maître,
De pourvoir les flacons d'eaux fraîches et d'odeurs,
De chasser loin du lit les moustiques rôdeurs,
Et, dès que le matin fait chanter les platanes,
D'acheter au bazar ananas et bananes.
Tout le jour, où tu veux, tu mènes tes pieds nus,
Et fredonnes tout bas de vieux airs inconnus;
Et quand descend le soir au manteau d'écarlate,
Tu poses doucement ton corps sur une natte,
Où tes rêves flottants sont pleins de colibris,
Et toujours, comme toi, gracieux et fleuris.

Pourquoi, l'heureuse enfant, veux-tu voir notre France,
Ce pays trop peuplé que fauche la souffrance,

To a Malabar Woman

Your feet are as slender as your hands, and your hips are broad enough to fill the loveliest white woman with envy. To the thoughtful artist your body is suave and endearing; your great velvet eyes are blacker than your skin. In the torrid blue climes where your God caused you to be born, your task is to light your master's pipe, to fill the vessels with cool water and perfumes, to drive marauding mosquitoes far from his couch, and as soon as morning sets the plane trees singing, to buy pineapples and bananas at the bazaar.

All day long you may take your naked feet wherever you wish, humming forgotten old tunes beneath your breath; and when evening descends in its scarlet cloak, you can lay your body gently down on a straw mat, where your floating dreams are full of hummingbirds and always, like yourself, full of grace and flowers.

Why, happy girl, do you long to see our France, an over-peopled land

Et, confiant ta vie aux bras forts des marins,
Faire de grands adieux à tes chers tamarins?
Toi, vêtue à moitié de mousselines frêles,
Frissonnante là-bas sous la neige et les grêles,
Comme tu pleurerais tes loisirs doux et francs,
Si, le corset brutal emprisonnant tes flancs,
Il te fallait glaner ton souper dans nos fanges
Et vendre le parfum de tes charmes étranges,
L'œil pensif, et suivant, dans nos sales brouillards,
Des cocotiers absents les fantômes épars!

ridden with suffering, and, entrusting your life to the care of sailors' arms, bid your last farewells to your beloved tamarinds?

Under-clad in flimsy muslins, shivering in the snow and hail, how you would pine for your sweet innocent leisure, if with a cruel corset imprisoning your flanks you had to beg for your supper in our mire, and sell the perfume of your exotic charms, with your pensive eyes seeking beyond our grimy fogs the vanished phantoms of your absent coconut trees!

[1840? Published 1846]

Bouffonneries

XXI
SUR LES DÉBUTS D'AMINA BOSCHETTI

AU THÉÂTRE DE LA MONNAIE, À BRUXELLES

Amina bondit, – fuit, – puis voltige et sourit;
Le Welche dit: «Tout ça, pour moi, c'est du prâcrit;
Je ne connais, en fait de nymphes bocagères,
Que celles de *Montagne-aux-Herbes-Potagères.*»

Du bout de son pied fin et de son œil qui rit,
Amina verse à flots le délire et l'esprit;
Le Welche dit: «Fuyez, délices mensongères!
Mon épouse n'a pas ces allures légères.»

Vous ignorez, sylphide au jarret triomphant,
Qui voulez enseigner la valse à l'éléphant,
Au hibou la gaîté, le rire à la cigogne,

BUFFOONERIES

The First Appearance of Amina Boschetti

AT THE THÉÂTRE DE LA MONNAIE, BRUSSELS

Amina leaps, then glides away, then hovers in the air and smiles. The Flem
remarks, 'All that stuff is double-dutch to me: the only woodland nymphs
I've ever seen were in Kitchen Herb Mountain street in Brussels.'

From the tip of her delicate foot and from her laughing eye, Amina
sends out ripples of exuberance and wit: but the Flem says, 'You can stuff
such fancy tricks – my wife don't need any of them lewd poses.

You do not seem to understand, – you sylph with unrivalled legs, who
imagine you can teach an elephant to dance, an owl to smile or a stork
to laugh –

Que sur la grâce en feu le Welche dit: «Haro!»
Et que le doux Bacchus lui versant du bourgogne,
Le monstre répondrait: «J'aime mieux le faro!»

that the Flem just hoots at incandescent grace, or that if kind Bacchus
offered him some Burgundy, this Belgian Caliban would reply, 'I'd rather
a pot of Brussels stingo, any day.'

[1864, in *La Vie parisienne*]

XXII

À M. EUGÈNE FROMENTIN

À PROPOS D'UN IMPORTUN

QUI SE DISAIT SON AMI

Il me dit qu'il était très riche,
Mais qu'il craignait le choléra;
– Que de son or il était chiche,
Mais qu'il goûtait fort l'Opéra;

– Qu'il raffolait de la nature,
Ayant connu monsieur Corot;
– Qu'il n'avait pas encor voiture,
Mais que cela viendrait bientôt;

– Qu'il aimait le marbre et la brique,
Les bois noirs et les bois dorés;
– Qu'il possédait dans sa fabrique
Trois contremaîtres décorés;

– Qu'il avait, sans compter le reste,
Vingt mille actions sur le *Nord*;
– Qu'il avait trouvé, pour un zeste,
Des encadrements d'Oppenord;

TO EUGÈNE FROMENTIN

Concerning a Nuisance

WHO CLAIMED TO BE HIS FRIEND

He tells me that he was very well off but afraid of catching the cholera;
that he was close with his money but was an Opera buff;
that he was crazy about Nature and had once known Mister Corot;
that he hadn't his own carriage yet but soon would have;
that he was fond of marble, brick, dark panelling and gilded wood;
that three of his foremen had won awards;
that apart from the rest he held 20,000 shares in the *Nord* newspaper;
that he had picked up some Oppenord frames for a song;

– Qu'il donnerait (fût-ce à Luzarches!)
Dans le bric-à-brac jusqu'au cou,
Et qu'au Marché des Patriarches
Il avait fait plus d'un bon coup;

– Qu'il n'aimait pas beaucoup sa femme,
Ni sa mère; – mais qu'il croyait
À l'immortalité de l'âme,
Et qu'il avait lu Niboyet!

– Qu'il penchait pour l'amour physique,
Et qu'à Rome, séjour d'ennui,
Une femme, d'ailleurs phtisique,
Était morte d'amour pour lui.

Pendant trois heures et demie,
Ce bavard, venu de Tournai,
M'a dégoisé toute sa vie;
J'en ai le cerveau consterné.

S'il fallait décrire ma peine,
Ce serait à n'en plus finir;
Je me disais, domptant ma haine:
«Au moins, si je pouvais dormir!»

that (even at Luzarches) he could always make a splash in the way of antiques and had found many a bargain in the Patriarch's Market;
that he wasn't all that keen on his wife or his mother, but believed in the Immortality of the Soul and had read Niboyet;
that he was keen on sex and that in Rome – such a boring city – a woman who happened to be tubercular – had died of love for him.
For three and a half hours this boor, whelped at Tournai, unloaded all his life onto me so that I still don't feel quite normal.
If I had to describe all my sufferings there would be no end to it, but I managed to keep my hatred in check, saying to myself 'If only I could get some sleep.'

Comme un qui n'est pas à son aise,
Et qui n'ose pas s'en aller,
Je frottais de mon cul ma chaise,
Rêvant de le faire empaler.

Ce monstre se nomme Bastogne;
Il fuyait devant le fléau.
Moi, je fuirai jusqu'en Gascogne,
Ou j'irai me jeter à l'eau,

Si dans ce Paris, qu'il redoute,
Quand chacun sera retourné,
Je trouve encore sur ma route
Ce fléau, natif de Tournai.

Like any uneasy victim who doesn't dare to steal away, I just rubbed my arse on my chair while I imagined ways of impaling him.

This monster was called Bastogne. He was trying to escape from the cholera – but I'll gladly run off to Gascony or go and throw myself in the water,

if in the Paris of which he is so afraid, when everyone has come back, I ever find this pest anywhere near me, that gent from Tournai.

[Brussels, 1865]

XXIII
UN CABARET FOLÂTRE

Vous qui raffolez des squelettes
Et des emblèmes détestés,
Pour épicer les voluptés,
(Fût-ce de simples omelettes!)

Vieux Pharaon, ô Monselet!
Devant cette enseigne imprévue,
J'ai rêvé de vous: *À la vue*
Du Cimetière, Estaminet!

A Jolly Pub

SEEN AT UCCLE. NEAR BRUSSELS

You who delight in skeletons and gruesome emblems which add spice
to enjoyment – even of a plain omelette –
Monselet, you old Pharaoh [*pun, King of Faro*], I thought of you
when I came across this unusual signboard, *Cemetery View Inn.*

[1865]

Bribes

Anges habillés d'or, de pourpre et d'hyacinthe.

Le génie et l'amour sont des Devoirs faciles.

★

J'ai pétri de la boue et j'en ai fait de l'or.

★

Il portait dans ses yeux la force de son cœur.
 Dans Paris son désert vivant sans feu ni lieu,
 Aussi fort qu'une bête, aussi libre qu'un Dieu.

LE GOINFRE

En ruminant, je ris des passants faméliques.

 Je crèverais comme un obus
 Si je n'absorbais comme un chancre.

SCRAPS

Pride

Angels clad in gold and crimson and purple.
 Genius and love: two Duties lightly borne.

★

I kneaded muck till I made gold of it.

★

All his heart's strength showed in his eyes.
 In Paris, his wilderness, without hearth or home,
 as strong as a wild beast, as free as a God.

The glutton

While I chew the cud I laugh at the starved folk who pass by.
 I would burst like a bomb, if I didn't absorb like an ulcer.

Son regard n'était pas nonchalant, ni timide,
Mais exhalait plutôt quelque chose d'avide,
Et, comme sa narine, exprimait les émois
Des artistes devant les œuvres de leurs doigts.

Ta jeunesse sera plus féconde en orages
Que cette canicule aux yeux pleins de lueurs
Qui sur nos fronts pâlis tord ses bras en sueurs,
Et soufflant dans la nuit ses haleines fiévreuses,
Rend de leurs frêles Corps les filles amoureuses,
Et les fait au miroir, stérile volupté,
Contempler les fruits mûrs de leur virginité.

Mais je vois à cet œil tout chargé de Tempêtes
Que ton Cœur n'est pas fait pour les paisibles fêtes,
Et que cette beauté, sombre comme le fer,
Est de celles que forge et que polit l'Enfer
Pour accomplir un jour d'effroyables luxures
Et contrister le Cœur des humbles créatures.

The look in his eyes was neither indifferent nor shy, but gleamed with a sort of greed and, like his nostrils, expressed emotions such as artists feel when gazing at their own handiwork.

Your youth will be richer in storms than the dog-day heat with glinting eyes and which twists its sweating arms round our pallid brows and, gasping with fevered breath in the night, inspires young girls with longing for their own frail bodies and drives them to gloat in their mirrors, with sterile voluptuousness, over the ripe fruits of their virginity.

But I see in that eye of yours, full of storms, that your heart was never designed for peaceful festivities, and that your iron-dark beauty is of the kind which Hell forges and brightens to perform, some day, in terrible orgies of licentiousness, and to fill the hearts of humble creatures with sorrow.

Affaissant sous son poids un énorme oreiller,
Un beau corps était là, doux à voir sommeiller,
Et son sommeil orné d'un sourire superbe
.
L'ornière de son dos par le désir hanté.

L'air était imprégné d'une amoureuse rage;
Les insectes volaient à la lampe et nul vent
Ne faisait tressaillir le rideau ni l'auvent.
C'était une nuit chaude, un vrai bain de jouvence.

<div align="center">★</div>

Grand ange qui portez sur votre fier visage
La noirceur de l'Enfer d'où vous êtes monté;
Dompteur féroce et doux qui m'avez mis en cage
Pour servir de spectacle à votre cruauté,

Cauchemar de mes Nuits, Sirène sans corsage,
Qui me tirez, toujours debout à mon côté,
Par ma robe de saint ou ma barbe de sage
Pour m'offrir le poison d'un amour effronté;
.

DAMNATION

Crushing an enormous pillow under its weight, a beautiful body lay there, sweet to look upon in sleep, a sleep the lovelier for its sublime smile . . . The furrow in her back haunted by desire.

The air was full of the rage of love. The insects were flying to the lamp. No wind trembled the curtain or the mantel. It was a sultry night, truly a bath of youthfulness.

<div align="center">★</div>

Great Angel whose proud face bears the blackness of the Hell from which you rose, fierce and gentle tamer of men who have caged me to serve as a side-show of your cruelty;

horror of my Nights, bare-breasted Siren who stand ever at my side to drag me by my saint's robe or sage's beard to offer me the poison of a shameless love . . .

Damnation

Le banc inextricable et dur,
La passe au col étroit, le maëlstrom vorace,
Agitent moins de sable et de varech impur

Que nos cœurs où pourtant tant de ciel se reflète;
Ils sont une jetée à l'air noble et massif,
Où le phare reluit, bienfaisante vedette,
Mais que mine en dessous le taret corrosif;

On peut les comparer encore à cette auberge,
Espoir des affamés, où cognent sur le tard,
Blessés, brisés, jurants, priant qu'on les héberge,
L'écolier, le prélat, la gouge et le soudard.

Ils ne reviendront pas dans les chambres infectes;
Guerre, science, amour, rien ne veut plus de nous.
L'âtre était froid, les lits et le vin pleins d'insectes;
Ces visiteurs, il faut les servir à genoux!

SPLEEN

The inextricable unyielding shoal, the narrow-necked pass, the insatiable
maelstrom, all vomit less sand and wrack
 than our hearts which yet reflect so much of the sky; our hearts are
as a pier which looks so noble and solidly built, on which a beacon shines
in merciful warning, but which is undermined and rotten with worms
and barnacles.
 They might be compared with that Inn, the hope of starving travel-
lers, where late at night the wounded and broken, schoolboy, priest,
whore and soldier, beg with oaths and prayers to be given refuge.
 But they will never come again to those foul rooms – neither war
nor learning nor love, there is nothing that wants us any more. The
hearth was cold, the beds and the wine crawled with bugs, whereas such
visitors ought to be served on bended knees.

Spleen
[These fragments appear to have been written at different
dates and recopied, the subtitles added in pencil]

Poésies de jeunesse

I
INCOMPATIBILITÉ

Tout là-haut, tout là-haut, loin de la route sûre,
Des fermes, des vallons, par-delà les coteaux,
Par-delà les forêts, les tapis de verdure,
Loin des derniers gazons foulés par les troupeaux,

On rencontre un lac sombre encaissé dans l'abîme
Que forment quelques pics désolés et neigeux;
L'eau, nuit et jour, y dort dans un repos sublime,
Et n'interrompt jamais son silence orageux.

Dans ce morne désert, à l'oreille incertaine
Arrivent par moments des bruits faibles et longs,
Et des échos plus morts que la cloche lointaine
D'une vache qui paît aux penchants des vallons.

JUVENILIA

Incompatibility

High, high up above, far from the beaten track and the farms and valleys,
beyond the hilly slopes and forests and carpets of green, far from the last
meadows trodden by flocks,
 you come upon a dark lake sunk in the hollow between a few empty
snowy peaks; night and day the water slumbers there in sublime repose
and never breaks its louring silence.
 In this gloomy desert, from time to time there come faint steady
sounds, and echoes more muffled than the far-off bell of a cow browsing
on the dellside.

Sur ces monts où le vent efface tout vestige,
Ces glaciers pailletés qu'allume le soleil,
Sur ces rochers altiers où guette le vertige,
Dans ce lac où le soir mire son teint vermeil,

Sous mes pieds, sur ma tête et partout, le silence,
Le silence qui fait qu'on voudrait se sauver,
Le silence éternel et la montagne immense,
Car l'air est immobile et tout semble rêver.

On dirait que le ciel, en cette solitude,
Se contemple dans l'onde, et que ces monts, là-bas,
Écoutent, recueillis, dans leur grave attitude,
Un mystère divin que l'homme n'entend pas.

Et lorsque par hasard une nuée errante
Assombrit dans son vol le lac silencieux,
On croirait voir la robe ou l'ombre transparente
D'un esprit qui voyage et passe dans les cieux.

On these mountains where the wind sweeps every trace away, on
these spangled glaciers fired by the sun, on these lofty rocks where
giddiness threatens you, in this lake where evening reflects its rosy hues,

below my feet, above my head and all around, there is nothing but
silence, a silentness that makes you long to escape from here, the eternal
silence and the vast mountain, where the air is still and everything seems
lost in a dream.

It is as though the sky, in this solitude, were contemplating itself in
the lake, and yonder mountains listening, in their solemn attitude, to
some divine mystery unheard by man.

And when perchance a wandering cloud in its flight overcasts the
silent lake, you might think you saw the robe or transparent shadow of
some spirit, travelling and vanishing across the heavens.

[1838–9. Published 1872]

II

N'est-ce pas qu'il est doux, maintenant que nous sommes
Fatigués et flétris comme les autres hommes,
De chercher quelquefois à l'Orient lointain
Si nous voyons encor les rougeurs du matin,
Et, quand nous avançons dans la rude carrière,
D'écouter les échos qui chantent en arrière
Et les chuchotements de ces jeunes amours
Que le Seigneur a mis au début de nos jours? . . .

III

Il aimait à la voir, avec ses jupes blanches,
Courir tout au travers du feuillage et des branches,
Gauche et pleine de grâce, alors qu'elle cachait
Sa jambe, si la robe aux buissons s'accrochait . . .

Is it not pleasant . . .

Is it not pleasant, now that we are weary and wilted like other men,
sometimes to try and see in the distant East, whether we can still see the
glow of morning, and as we press onwards in life's rough arena, to listen
to the echoes singing behind us, and the whispering of those young loves
which the Lord allowed us in our early days?

[1837. Published 1864]

He loved to watch her . . .

He loved to watch her in her white skirts, running through the leafage
and branches, awkward and full of grace, while she hid her leg when her
dress caught on the bushes . . .

IV

[À Henri Hignard.]

Tout à l'heure je viens d'entendre
Dehors résonner doucement
Un air monotone et si tendre
Qu'il bruit en moi vaguement,

Une de ces vielles plaintives,
Muses des pauvres Auvergnats,
Qui jadis aux heures oisives
Nous charmaient si souvent, hélas!

Et, son espérance détruite,
Le pauvre s'en fut tristement;
Et moi je pensai tout de suite
À mon ami que j'aime tant,

Qui me disait en promenade
Que pour lui c'était un plaisir
Qu'une semblable sérénade
Dans un long et morne loisir.

To Henri Hignard

I have just been listening to the sweet strains of a monotonous tune outside, so touching that it is still vaguely echoing within me.

It came from one of those doleful barrel-organs which are the muses of the poor wandering minstrels of Auvergne and which so often charmed us, alas, in the old days in our hours of idleness.

With his hopes unrewarded the poor fellow went sadly on his way, before I remembered my old friend whom I care for so much

and who once said, during one of our walks together, how he enjoyed such serenades in his long sad hours of leisure.

Nous aimions cette humble musique
Si douce à nos esprits lassés
Quand elle vient, mélancolique,
Répondre à de tristes pensers.

– Et j'ai laissé les vitres closes,
Ingrat, pour qui m'a fait ainsi
Rêver de si charmantes choses,
Et penser à mon cher Henri!

We used to love that music of the poor, so sweet to our weary minds
when its melancholy tallied with our sad thoughts.
 – But I left the window closed, ungrateful to that man who had made
me daydream of such charming things and to think of my dear Henri.

[Published 1892]

V

Hélas! qui n'a gémi sur autrui, sur soi-même?
Et qui n'a dit à Dieu: «Pardonnez-moi, Seigneur,
Si personne ne m'aime et si nul n'a mon cœur?
Ils m'ont tous corrompu; personne ne vous aime!»

Alors lassé du monde et de ses vains discours,
Il faut lever les yeux aux voûtes sans nuages,
Et ne plus s'adresser qu'aux muettes images,
De ceux qui n'aiment rien, consolantes amours.

Alors, alors il faut s'entourer de mystère,
Se fermer aux regards, et sans morgue et sans fiel,
Sans dire à vos voisins: «Je n'aime que le ciel»,
Dire à Dieu: «Consolez mon âme de la terre!»

Tel, fermé par son prêtre, un pieux monument,
Quand sur nos sombres toits la nuit est descendue,
Quand la foule a laissé le pavé de la rue,
Se remplit de silence et de recueillement.

Alas, who has never grieved . . .

Alas, who has never grieved for others or himself? Who has never said
to God, 'Forgive me, Lord, if no one cares for me and no one has my
heart. They have all corrupted me and no one loves you.'

Then, weary of the world and its idle talk, a man must raise his eyes
towards the cloudless vaults, and address himself only to the mute images
of those who care for nothing – consoling loves.

Then one must wrap oneself in mystery, make oneself inscrutable, and
without pride or bitterness, without saying to one's fellows 'I care for
nothing but heaven', say to God 'Comfort my soul for earthly things.'

Just as a holy building, when the priest has closed its doors, when
night has fallen on our dark rooftops, when the crowd has vanished from
the cobbles of the streets, is filled with silence and composure.

[Sent to Henri Hignard 1839]

VI

SONNET

Vous avez, chère sœur dont le cœur est poète,
Passé par quelque bourg tout paré, tout vermeil,
Quand le ciel et la terre ont un bel air de fête,
Un dimanche éclairé par un joyeux soleil.

Quand le clocher s'agite, et qu'il chante à tue-tête,
Et tient dès le matin le village en éveil,
Quand tous, pour écouter l'office qui s'apprête,
S'en vont, jeunes et vieux en pimpant appareil,

Lors s'élevant au fond de votre âme mondaine,
Des sons d'orgue mouvants et de cloche lointaine
Vous ont-ils pas tiré malgré vous un soupir?

Cette dévotion des champs, joyeuse et franche,
Ne vous a-t-elle pas – triste et doux souvenir –
Rappelé qu'autrefois vous aimiez le dimanche?

Sonnet

Dear sister, who have a poet's heart, you must have wandered through
some little country place when it looked all trim and gilded, when earth
and sky seemed to be on holiday, on a Sunday morning bright with gay
sunshine,

the belfry trembling with the boom of bells and rousing the whole
village, when young and old step out in their Sunday best to attend the
mass now being made ready.

Then, as they rise from the depths of your townswoman's soul, don't
the touching tones of the organ and the distant bell draw a sigh from
you in spite of yourself?

Has this rustic worship, so carefree and candid, never reminded you,
as a sad and gentle memory, how fond you were of Sundays, long ago?

[1840? Offered by C.B. to his sister-in-law Félicité Baudelaire
and also, with some modification, to Antony Bruno]

VII

Il est de chastes mots que nous profanons tous;
Les amoureux d'encens font un abus étrange.
Je n'en connais pas un qui n'*adore* quelque *ange*
Dont ceux du Paradis sont, je crois, peu jaloux.

On ne doit accorder ce nom sublime et doux
Qu'à de beaux cœurs bien purs, vierges et sans mélange.
Regardez! il lui pend à l'aile quelque fange
Quand votre *ange* en riant s'assied sur vos genoux.

J'eus, quand j'étais enfant, ma naïve folie
– Certaine fille aussi mauvaise que jolie –
Je l'appelais *mon ange.* Elle avait cinq galants.

Pauvres fous! nous avons tant soif qu'on nous caresse
Que je voudrais encor tenir quelque drôlesse
À qui dire: *mon ange* – entre deux draps bien blancs.

Chaste Words

There are some chaste words that we all tend to profane. Those who go in for incense abuse them in odd ways. I've never met one who doesn't *adore* some *angel* whom no angel in Paradise, I think, can envy.

We should reserve such a sublime sweet name for the pure in heart, the virginal and unadulterated. See! – surely some smut soils those wings of hers when your *angel* smirks and sits on your knee.

When I was a child I was simple and foolish enough to call a tart *my angel*, though she was as naughty as she was pretty and had five hangers-on.

Poor fools that we are, we are all so keen to be petted that even now I'd be glad to hug some hussy to whom I could whisper *my angel* – between two clean white sheets.

[Sent by C. B. to his half-brother, 1840]

VIII

Je n'ai pas pour maîtresse une lionne illustre;
La Gueuse de mon âme emprunte tout son lustre.
Invisible aux regards de l'univers moqueur,
Sa beauté ne fleurit que dans mon triste cœur –

Pour avoir des souliers elle a vendu son âme;
Mais le bon Dieu rirait si près de cette infâme
Je tranchais du Tartufe, et singeais la hauteur,
Moi qui vends ma pensée, et qui veux être auteur.

Vice beaucoup plus grave, elle porte perruque.
Tous ses beaux cheveux noirs ont fui sa blanche nuque;
Ce qui n'empêche pas les baisers amoureux
De pleuvoir sur son front plus pelé qu'un lépreux.

Elle louche, et l'effet de ce regard étrange,
Qu'ombragent des cils noirs plus longs que ceux d'un ange,
Est tel que tous les yeux pour qui l'on s'est damné
Ne valent pas pour moi son œil juif et cerné.

My mistress . . .

My mistress is no pin-up lioness. My beggar-girl's glory all comes from my soul. Unmoved by the world's mocking stares, her beauty blooms in my sad heart alone.

She sold her soul to buy herself a pair of shoes, but the dear Lord would laugh if alongside this infamous creature I were to play the hypocrite and pretend to be her superior, as I sell my thoughts and hope to be a writer.

An even more serious crime is that she wears a wig: all her silky black hair has long since left her lilywhite neck; but that doesn't stop my amorous kisses from raining down on her brow although it's as peeled as any leper's.

She has a squint, and the effect of this peculiar gaze, dimmed by black eyelashes longer than any angel's, is such that all the orbs for which a fellow gets himself damned cannot compete with her jewish dark-ringed eyeballs.

Elle n'a que vingt ans; sa gorge – déjà basse
Pend de chaque côté comme une calebasse,
Et pourtant me traînant chaque nuit sur son corps,
Ainsi qu'un nouveau-né, je la tète et la mords –

Et bien qu'elle n'ait pas souvent même une obole
Pour se frotter la chair et pour s'oindre l'épaule –
Je la lèche en silence avec plus de ferveur,
Que Madeleine en feu les deux pieds du Sauveur –

La pauvre Créature au plaisir essoufflée
A de rauques hoquets la poitrine gonflée,
Et je devine au bruit de son souffle brutal
Qu'elle a souvent mordu le pain de l'Hôpital.

Ses grands yeux inquiets durant la nuit cruelle
Croient voir deux autres yeux au fond de la ruelle –
Car ayant trop ouvert son cœur à tous venants,
Elle a peur sans lumière et croit aux revenants. –

Although she is only twenty her breasts stick out like calabashes at
each side; yet when I stretch on her body every night I suck and nibble
them like a newborn.

And although she often hasn't a scent for soaping her body and
creaming her shoulders, I lick her in silence with more fervour than love-
sick Magdalene kissing her Saviour's feet.

The poor soul, as she pants with pleasure, feels her chest shattered
with spasms of coughing, and to judge by the wheeze of her agonized
breathing I dare say she has often chewed hospital bread.

In the cruel night her dilated feverish eyes imagine she can see two
eyes at the end of her bed, for as she has unburdened her heart to
allcomers she is scared without a light on and thinks there are ghosts,

Ce qui fait que de suif elle use plus de livres
Qu'un vieux savant couché jour et nuit sur ses livres
Et redoute bien moins la faim et ses tourments
Que l'apparition de ses défunts amants.

Si vous la rencontrez, bizarrement parée,
Se faufilant au coin d'une rue égarée,
Et la tête et l'œil bas – comme un pigeon blessé –
Traînant dans les ruisseaux un talon déchaussé,

Messieurs, ne crachez pas de jurons ni d'ordure,
Au visage fardé de cette pauvre impure
Que déesse Famine a par un soir d'hiver
Contrainte à relever ses jupons en plein air.

Cette bohème-là, c'est mon tout, ma richesse,
Ma perle, mon bijou, ma reine, ma duchesse,
Celle qui m'a bercé sur son giron vainqueur,
Et qui dans ses deux mains a réchauffé mon cœur.

and she wastes more money on tallow candles than any old scholar poring night and day over his books: she is less afraid of hunger and all its torments than of the reappearance of her dead loves.

If you ever happen to meet her, weirdly dressed up and slinking at the corner of some back street, with her head and eyes cast down like a wounded pigeon, dragging a broken shoeheel in the gutter,

Gentlemen, please don't spit out any of your oaths and insults on this poor fallen waif with a painted face, whom the goddess Hunger has forced to lift her skirts on a winter's night –

for this gipsy-girl is my treasure, my pearl, my gem, my queen, my duchess, who has rocked me in the cradle of her lap and warmed my heart in her hands.

[Published 1875: said to have been written in a M. Bouchon's album]

IX

Ci-gît qui, pour avoir par trop aimé les gaupes,
Descendit jeune encore au royaume des taupes.

A Poet's Epitaph

Here lies a man who was too fond of molls,
a youthful migrant to the realm of moles.

X

Tous imberbes alors, sur les vieux bancs de chêne,
Plus polis et luisants que des anneaux de chaîne,
Que jour à jour la peau des hommes a fourbis,
– Nous traînions tristement nos ennuis, accroupis
Et voûtés sous le ciel carré des solitudes,
Où l'enfant boit, dix ans, l'âpre lait des études.

– C'était dans ce vieux temps mémorable et marquant,
Où forcés d'élargir le classique carcan,
Les professeurs encor rebelles à vos rimes,
Succombaient sous l'effort de nos folles escrimes,
Et laissaient l'écolier, triomphant et mutin,
Faire à l'aise hurler Triboulet en latin.

– Qui de nous, en ces temps d'adolescences pâles,
N'a connu la torpeur des fatigues claustrales,
– L'œil perdu dans l'azur morne d'un ciel d'été,
Ou l'éblouissement de la neige, – guetté,
L'oreille avide et droite, – et bu, comme une meute,
L'écho lointain d'un livre, ou le cri d'une émeute?

The Epistle to Sainte-Beuve

There we all sat, still beardless, on the old oaken benches, more polished
and glossy than the links of chains furbished day after day by the skins
of galley-slaves; we sat and endured our cares, huddled and round-
shouldered under the square skylight of solitudes beneath which, for ten
years, a boy must drink the bitter milk of lessons.

It was in those far-off memorable days which leave their mark on one
that, forced at last to relax the classical yoke, our schoolmasters, though
still hostile to your rhymes, yielded to the onslaught of our wild skir-
mishes and allowed us triumphant and mischievous schoolboys to make
Triboulet [Hugo's buffoon] bellow in Latin to his heart's content. Which
of us, in those days of our wan adolescence, never suffered the tedium
of those cloistered lassitudes, his eye lost in the depressing azure of a
summer sky or a dazzlement of snow, watching, with his hungry ears
pricked, then drinking like a pack of hounds the distant echo of some
book, or the clamour of a riot in the streets?

C'était surtout l'été, quand les plombs se fondaient,
Que ces grands murs noircis en tristesse abondaient,
Lorsque la canicule ou le fumeux automne
Irradiait les cieux de son feu monotone,
Et faisait sommeiller dans les sveltes donjons,
Les tiercelets criards, effroi des blancs pigeons;
Saison de rêverie, où la Muse s'accroche
Pendant un jour entier au battant d'une cloche;
Où la Mélancolie, à midi, quand tout dort,
Le menton dans la main, au fond du corridor, –
L'œil plus noir et plus bleu que la Religieuse
Dont chacun sait l'histoire obscène et douloureuse,
– Traîne un pied alourdi de précoces ennuis,
Et son front moite encor des langueurs de ses nuits.

– Et puis venaient les soirs malsains, les nuits fiévreuses,
Qui rendent de leur corps les filles amoureuses,
Et les font aux miroirs – stérile volupté –
Contempler les fruits mûrs de leur nubilité –
Les soirs italiens, de molle insouciance,
– Qui des plaisirs menteurs révèlent la science,

It was particularly in summer that when the leads melted on the roof,
the blackened walls were full of sadness, when a heat-wave or the hazy
autumn made the skies radiant with a monotonous blaze, and made the
shrill falcons, the white pigeons' terror, drowse in the narrow turrets of
our school; the season of daydreams when the Muse waits all day long
for the school-bell to ring; when Melancholy, at noon when all is sleep-
ing, chin in hand, at the end of the corridor, and with an eye darker and
bluer than Diderot's Nun's (whose lewd and painful story is known to
all) drags a foot heavy with precocious cares, its brow still moist with the
labours of its nights.

And then the troubled evenings at last came, the feverish nights
which make girls love their own flesh and – sterile pleasure – make them
inspect the ripened fruits of their nubility in the mirror; Italian evenings
of indolent nonchalance, which reveal the secrets of deceitful pleasures,

– Quand la sombre Vénus, du haut des balcons noirs,
Verse des flots de musc de ses frais encensoirs.

. .

Ce fut dans ce conflit de molles circonstances,
Mûri par vos sonnets, préparé par vos stances,
Qu'un soir, ayant flairé le livre et son esprit,
J'emportai sur mon cœur l'histoire d'Amaury.
Tout abîme mystique est à deux pas du Doute.

– Le breuvage infiltré, lentement, goutte à goutte,
En moi qui dès quinze ans vers le gouffre entraîné,
Déchiffrais couramment les soupirs de René,
Et que de l'inconnu la soif bizarre altère,
– A travaillé le fond de la plus mince artère.

J'en ai tout absorbé, les miasmes, les parfums,
Le doux chuchotement des souvenirs défunts,
Les longs enlacements des phrases symboliques,
– Chapelets murmurants de madrigaux mystiques;
– Livre voluptueux, si jamais il en fut.

Et depuis, soit au fond d'un asile touffu,
Soit que, sous les soleils des zones différentes,
L'éternel bercement des houles enivrantes,
Et l'aspect renaissant des horizons sans fin,

when the dark Venus pours waves of musk from her cool censers from
high black balconies.

It was in this struggle between dispiriting circumstances that, matured
by your sonnets and prepared by your stanzas, one evening when I had
sensed the inner meaning and spirit of your book, I took the story of
Amaury to my heart. Every abyss of mysticism is only two steps away
from doubt. The drug slowly filtered drop by drop into my mind, and
from the age of fifteen I was swept away towards the bottomless pit as I
swiftly interpreted René's sighs – I who am so athirst for the unknown
– and it worked upon even the slightest springs of my being. I absorbed
it whole – the miasmas, perfumes, the gentle whispers of dead memories,
long intertwining of symbolic phrases, murmurous rosaries of mystic
madrigals – a voluptuous book if ever there was one!

And since that time, whether in some leafy sanctuary or beneath the
suns of other hemispheres, the eternal swaying of the hypnotic swell of
seas and often reborn vistas of endless horizons bring my heart back to

Ramenassent ce cœur vers le songe divin, –
Soit dans les lourds loisirs d'un jour caniculaire,
Ou dans l'oisiveté frileuse de frimaire –
Sous les flots du tabac qui masque le plafond,
– J'ai partout feuilleté le mystère profond
De ce livre si cher aux âmes engourdies
Que leur destin marqua des mêmes maladies,
Et devant le miroir j'ai perfectionné
L'art cruel qu'un Démon en naissant m'a donné,
– De la Douleur pour faire une volupté vraie, –
D'ensanglanter son mal et de gratter sa plaie.

Poète, est-ce une injure ou bien un compliment?
Car je suis vis-à-vis de vous comme un amant
En face du fantôme, au geste plein d'amorces,
Dont la main et dont l'œil ont pour pomper les forces
Des charmes inconnus. – Tous les êtres aimés
Sont des vases de fiel qu'on boit les yeux fermés,
Et le cœur transpercé que la douleur allèche
Expire chaque jour en bénissant sa flèche.

a divine dreaming; whether in the heavy leisure hours of a midsummer day or in the chill idleness of early winter, under waves of tobacco smoke obscuring the ceiling, I have everywhere perused the profound mystery of this book, so dear to those numbed souls whose fate has stamped them with the same disorders [as Amaury's]; and before the mirror I have practised the cruel art which a demon bestowed on me at birth – the need for pain to create true voluptuousness – the need to draw blood from one's suffering, then scratch the wound.

Poet, is it an insult or a compliment? For beside you I am as a lover towards a ghost, whose gestures are full of caresses, whose hand and eye have hidden charms which can drain strength away. All the beings we love are vessels of gall which we drink with our eyes closed, and the heart, pierced and lured on by pain, dies every day, blessing its arrow.

[Sent to Sainte-Beuve in 1844. The references are to
Diderot's *La Réligieuse*, Sainte-Beuve's novel *Volupté*
and its hero Amaury, and Chateaubriand's *René*]

XI

À THÉODORE DE BANVILLE

Vous avez empoigné les crins de la Déesse
Avec un tel poignet, qu'on vous eût pris, à voir
Et cet air de maîtrise et ce beau nonchaloir,
Pour un jeune ruffian terrassant sa maîtresse.

L'œil clair et plein du feu de la précocité,
Vous avez prélassé votre orgueil d'architecte
Dans des constructions dont l'audace correcte
Fait voir quelle sera votre maturité.

– Poète, notre sang nous fuit par chaque pore –
Est-ce que par hasard la robe du Centaure
Qui changeait toute veine en funèbre ruisseau

Était teinte trois fois dans les baves subtiles
De ces vindicatifs et monstrueux reptiles
Que le petit Hercule étranglait au berceau?

To Théodore de Banville

So tightly you have gripped the Goddess's hair that with your air of authority and marvellous cool, you might have been taken for a young ruffian knocking his mistress down.

With your bright eye full of the fire of precocious youth you have thrown all your architect's pride into bold and exact structures which foretell what the art of your maturity will be.

Poet, our blood [of poets] ebbs from every pore; is it by chance that the shirt of Nessus, which transformed every vein into a stream of death, was thrice dipped in the subtle venom of those vindictive monstrous snakes which infant Hercules once strangled in his cot?

[1842]

XII

Noble femme au bras fort, qui durant les longs jours
Sans penser bien ni mal dors ou rêves toujours
 Fièrement troussée à l'antique,
Toi que depuis dix ans qui pour moi se font lents
Ma bouche bien apprise aux baisers succulents
 Choya d'un amour monastique –

————

Prêtresse de débauche et ma sœur de plaisir
Qui toujours dédaignas de porter et nourrir
 Un homme en tes cavités saintes,
Tant tu crains et tu fuis le stigmate alarmant
Que la vertu creusa de son soc infamant
 Au flanc des matrones enceintes.

Fragment

Noble strong-armed woman, who sleep or dream always throughout
long days with no thought of good or evil, wearing robes proudly slung
in Grecian style; you whom for ten years (which seem slow to me now)
my lips, well-versed in luscious kisses, cherished with all the devotion of
a monk:

 priestess of debauch, my sister in lust, who disdained to carry and
nourish a male child in your hallowed urn, you so much fear and flee
the appalling stigmata which virtue carved with its degrading blade in
pregnant matrons' flanks . . .

[Ms 1844. Published 1902. Pichois implies
that these lines refer to Jeanne Duval]

XIII
[SUR L'ALBUM DE MME ÉMILE CHEVALET]

Au milieu de la foule, errantes, confondues,
Gardant le souvenir précieux d'autrefois,
Elles cherchent l'écho de leurs voix éperdues,
Tristes, comme le soir, deux colombes perdues
Et qui s'appellent dans les bois.

XIV

Je vis, et ton bouquet est de l'architecture;
C'est donc lui la beauté, car c'est moi la nature.
Si toujours la nature embellit la beauté,
Je fais valoir tes fleurs . . . me voilà trop flatté!

Lines for Mme Émile Chevalet's Album

Wandering here and there confusedly in the crowd, holding to the precious memory of bygone days, they try to find the echo of their distraught voices; sad as evening, two lost doves calling each other through the woods.

[Published 1908]

Thanks for a Bouquet

I am alive, whereas your bouquet is a work of architecture; therefore it is Beauty, while I am Nature. If Nature always embellishes Beauty, then I add lustre to your flowers: I am only too flattered . . .

XV

[À Charles Asselineau.]

D'un esprit biscornu le séduisant projet
– Qui de tant de héros va choisir Bruandet!!

XVI

MONSELET PAILLARD

VERS DESTINÉS À SON PORTRAIT

On me nomme *le petit chat*;
Modernes petites-maîtresses,
J'unis à vos délicatesses
La force d'un jeune pacha.

La douceur de la voûte bleue
Est concentrée en mon regard;
Si vous voulez me voir hagard,
Lectrices, mordez-moi la queue.

To Charles Asselineau

A stroke of genius for an addle-pate –
To count a *Bruandet* among the great!

[Asselineau had written an article on *Lazare Bruandet, peintre de l'école française, 1753–1803*, published in 1855 but previously a source of amusement for Baudelaire]

Another Epigram on Randy Monselet

ON HIS PORTRAIT

They call me *the wee kitten*: so, you latter-day minxes, to your refined ways I add the prowess of a young pasha.

A sky-blue gentleness is concentrated in my eyes, so to make me look haggard you have only to bite my tail.

[Published 1881]

Vers de circonstance

[VERS LAISSÉS CHEZ UN AMI ABSENT]

5 heures, à l'Hermitage.

Mon cher, je suis venu chez vous
Pour entendre une langue humaine;
Comme un, qui, parmi les Papous,
Chercherait son ancienne Athêne.

Puisque chez les Topinambous
Dieu me fait faire quarantaine,
Aux sots je préfère les fous
– Dont je suis, chose, hélas! certaine.

Offrez à Mam'selle Fanny
(Qui ne répondra pas: Nenny,
Le salut n'étant pas d'un âne),

L'hommage d'un bon écrivain,
– Ainsi qu'à l'ami Lécrivain
Et qu'à Mam'selle Jeanne.

OCCASIONAL VERSE

Lines Left for an Absent Friend

Dear old man, I came round to your place in order to hear a human language, just as a man stranded among a lot of Papuans might look for his lost Athena.

As God has quarantined me among a tribe of savages, I prefer lunatics (of whom I am unfortunately one) to fools.

Please give Miss Fanny (who won't have to reply *nay* as this is no asinine greeting) the compliments of a good writer, and ditto to my friend Lécrivain and Miss Jenny.

[To Poulet-Malassis. 1865]

389

SONNET POUR S'EXCUSER DE NE PAS ACCOMPAGNER UN AMI À NAMUR

Puisque vous allez vers la ville
Qui, bien qu'un fort mur l'encastrât,
Défraya la verve servile
Du fameux poète castrat;

Puisque vous allez en vacances
Goûter un plaisir recherché,
Usez toutes vos éloquences,
Mon bien cher Coco-Malperché,

(Comme je le ferais moi-même)
À dire là-bas combien j'aime
Ce tant folâtre monsieur Rops,

Qui n'est pas un grand prix de Rome,
Mais dont le talent est haut comme
La pyramide de Chéops!

Sonnet

APOLOGIES FOR NOT ACCOMPANYING
A FRIEND TO NAMUR

As you are off to the town which (though it had a strong wall round it) put paid to the servile verve of the famous castrato poet, Boileau, and as you are going on holiday to enjoy a highly desirable pleasure, please use all your eloquence (as I would do myself) dear Poulet-Malassis, to say how fond I am of jolly old Félicien Rops, who is no Prix de Rome laureate but whose talent tops the Pyramid of Cheops.

[To Poulet-Malassis. Published 1865]

[SUSCRIPTION RIMÉE]

Monsieur Auguste Malassis
 Rue de *Mercélis*
Numéro *trente-cinq* bis
Dans le faubourg d'*Ixelles*,
 Bruxelles.
(Recommandée à l'Arioste
 De la poste,
C'est-à-dire à quelque facteur
 Versificateur.)

A Postal Address

Mr Augustus Malassis
Rue de Mercélis
35A if you please
in the district of Ixelles
a dingy suburb of Brussels
care of some Ariosto
of the Po-
stal Service who
in the art of verse excels.

[1866]

Amœnitates Belgicæ

VENUS BELGA

(MONTAGNE DE LA COUR)

Ces mollets sur ces pieds montés,
Qui vont sous des cottes peu blanches,
Ressemblent à des troncs plantés
Dans des planches.

Les seins des moindres femmelettes,
Ici, pèsent plusieurs quintaux,
Et leurs membres sont des poteaux
Qui donnent le goût des squelettes.

Il ne me suffit pas qu'un sein soit gros et doux;
Il le faut un peu ferme, ou je tourne casaque.
Car, sacré nom de Dieu! je ne suis pas Cosaque
Pour me soûler avec du suif et du saindoux.

THE DELIGHTS OF BELGIUM

The Belgian Venus

IN THE MONTAGNE DE LA COUR

Such calves planted on such feet, walking in once-white petticoats, look more like tree-trunks planted into floorboards.

Here the puniest female's tits weigh a few bushels, and their limbs are hefty poles which inspire a taste for skeletons.

For me it is not enough for tits to be fat and spongy: if they are not a bit firm I turn tail, not being – thank God – a Cossack who can get high on tallow and lard.

LA PROPRETÉ DES DEMOISELLES BELGES

Elle puait comme une fleur moisie.
Moi, je lui dis (mais avec courtoisie):
«Vous devriez prendre un bain régulier
Pour dissiper ce parfum de bélier.»

Que me répond cette jeune hébétée?
«Je ne suis pas, moi, de vous dégoûtée!»
– Ici pourtant on lave le trottoir
Et le parquet avec du savon noir!

The Cleanliness of Belgian Girls

She stank like a decaying flower. I said politely, 'Maybe you should take a regular bath, to get rid of that smell of ram.' What do you think the astonished girl replied? 'But you don't turn me off at all.' Yet in this place they wash pavements and floors with black soap.

LA PROPRETÉ BELGE

«*Bains*». – J'entre et je demande un bain. Alors le maître
Me regarde avec l'œil d'un bœuf qui vient de paître,
Et me dit: «Ça n'est pas possible, ça, sais-tu,
Monsieur!» – Et puis, d'un air plus abattu:
«Nous avons au grenier porté nos trois baignoires.»

J'ai lu, je m'en souviens, dans les vieilles histoires
Que le Romain mettait son vin au grenier; mais,
Si barbare qu'il fût, ses baignoires, jamais!
Aussi, je m'écriai: «Quelle idée, ô mon Dieu!»

Mais l'ingénu: «Monsieur, c'est qu'on venait si peu!»

Belgian Hygiene

Baths. I go in and ask for a bath. The attendant eyes me with the orbs of a browsing ox, and says 'Sorry, nothing doing, Sir.' Then he looks a bit more down in the mouth and adds, 'We've stored all our three baths in the loft.'

I remember reading in ancient-history books that the Romans used to store their wine in the loft; but, however barbarian, they would never store their baths there. So I shouted 'Good God, what a daft idea!'

The gormless fellow replied 'You see, Sir, there were hardly any takers.'

L'AMATEUR DES BEAUX-ARTS EN BELGIQUE

Un ministre, qu'on dit le Mecenas flamand,
Me promenait un jour dans son appartement,
Interrogeant mes yeux devant chaque peinture,
Parlant un peu de *l'art*, beaucoup de la *nature*,
Vantant le *paysage*, expliquant le *sujet*,
Et surtout me marquant *le prix* de chaque objet.
– Mais voilà qu'arrivé devant un portrait d'Ingres,
(Pédant dont j'aime peu les facultés malingres)
Je fus pris tout à coup d'une sainte fureur
De célébrer David, le grand peintre empereur!
– Lui, se tourne vers son fournisseur ordinaire,
Qui se tenait debout comme un factionnaire,
Ou comme un chambellan qui savoure avec foi
Les sottises tombant des lèvres de son roi,
Et lui dit, avec l'œil d'un marchand de la Beauce:
«Je crois, mon cher, je crois que David est en hausse!»

A Belgian Art-Lover

A Minister, who was known as a great Belgian patron of the arts, showed me round his collection one day, questioning my eyes in front of every painting, chatting a bit about *art*, a lot about *nature*, praising the *landscape*, explaining the *subject*,

but above all informing me of the *price* of everything. But when we came to a portrait by Ingres (a dullard whose feeble faculties have little appeal for me) I was suddenly seized by an unholy urge to sing the praises of the great emperor of painting, David.

My host turns to his pet agent, who was hovering round like an auctioneer or one of those chamberlains who slavishly go into raptures at all his monarch's nonsensical remarks, and says, with a glint like a provincial shopkeeper's in his eyes, 'Yes, I do believe, dear fellow, that Davids are going up.'

UNE EAU SALUTAIRE

Joseph Delorme a découvert
Un ruisseau si clair et si vert
Qu'il donne aux malheureux l'envie
D'y terminer leur triste vie.
– Je sais un moyen de guérir
De cette passion malsaine
Ceux qui veulent ainsi périr:
Menez-les au bords de la Senne.

«Voyez – dit ce Belge badin
Qui n'est certes pas un ondin –
La *contrefaçon* de la Seine.»
– «Oui – lui dis-je – une Seine obscène!»

Car cette Senne, à proprement
Parler, où de tout mur et de tout fondement
L'indescriptible tombe en foule,
Ce n'est guère qu'un excrément
Qui coule.

[W]holesome Water

Sainte-Beuve's Joseph Delorme found a stream so clear and green that it made unhappy young men want to end their miserable existence in it.

But I know a way of curing fellows who have the unhealthy urge to peg out that way – just take them to the banks of the Senne in Brussels.

This Belgian wag, who is certainly no water-sprite, exclaimed 'Behold, our replica of the Seine!' 'Yes,' I replied, 'an obscene Seine!'

For to tell the truth their river Senne, with its loads of the unmentionable dripping and dropping from every wall and (so to speak) fundament of every building, is little better than running excrement.

LES BELGES ET LA LUNE

On n'a jamais connu de race si baroque
Que ces Belges. Devant le joli, le charmant,
Ils roulent de gros yeux et grognent sourdement.
Tout ce qui réjouit nos cœurs mortels les choque.

Dites un mot plaisant, et leur œil devient gris
Et terne comme l'œil d'un poisson qu'on fait frire;
Une histoire touchante; ils éclatent de rire,
Pour faire voir qu'ils ont parfaitement compris.

Comme l'esprit, ils ont en horreur les lumières;
Parfois sous la clarté calme du firmament,
J'en ai vu, qui rongés d'un bizarre tourment,

Dans l'horreur de la fange et du vomissement,
Et gorgés jusqu'aux dents de genièvre et de bières,
Aboyaient à la Lune, assis sur leurs derrières.

The Belgians and the Moon

You never saw such a fantastic race as these Belgians. When they see anything pretty or charming they just roll their huge eyes and grunt dully. They are shocked by whatever delights our mortal hearts.

If you make a joke, their eyes turn as glazed and dull as a fish's in a frying-pan. Or if you tell them some touching tale they split their sides laughing, just to show that they have completely understood.

Just as they are terrified of wit, they have a horror of lights, and many a time, under a calm and sunny sky, I've seen them, bitten by some queer torment of their own,

among disgusting filth and vomit and full to the teeth with gin and beer, sit down on their backsides in the street and start barking like dogs at the moon.

ÉPIGRAPHE

POUR L'ATELIER DE M. ROPS,
FABRICANT DE CERCUEILS, À BRUXELLES

Je rêvais, contemplant ces bières,
De palissandre ou d'acajou,
Qu'un habile ébéniste orne de cent manières:
«Quel écrin! et pour quel bijou!
Les morts, ici, sont sans vergognes!
Un jour, des cadavres flamands
Souilleront ces cercueils charmants.
Faire de tels étuis pour de telles charognes!»

An Epigraph

FOR THE WORKSHOP OF MR ROPS, COFFIN-MAKER IN BRUSSELS

I thought to myself as I examined those coffins in teak and mahogany which a skilled craftsman can carve into a hundred patterns, 'What an admirable casket – but to hold what sort of gem? The dead here have no shame, for sooner or later Flemish corpses will desecrate these exquisite coffins. Fancy making such shrines as these, for such offal.'

LA NYMPHE DE LA SENNE

«Je voudrais bien – me dit un ami singulier,
Dont souvent la pensée alterne avec la mienne, –
Voir la Naïade de la Senne;
Elle doit ressembler à quelque charbonnier
Dont la face est toute souillée.»

– «Mon ami, vous êtes bien bon.
Non, non! Ce n'est pas de charbon
Que cette nymphe est barbouillée!»

OPINION DE M. HETZEL SUR LE FARO

«Buvez-vous du faro?» – dis-je à monsieur Hetzel;
Je vis un peu d'horreur sur sa mine barbue.
– «Non, jamais! le faro (je dis cela sans fiel!)
C'est de la bière deux fois bue.»

The Nymph of the Senne

A rather odd friend of mine, whose thoughts often run on the same lines as my own, remarked 'I wouldn't mind having a glimpse of the Naiad of the river Senne – she must have a face like a coalman's, smudged all over.'

'You're much too kind, old man. Far from it – her face is smeared with something dirtier than coal-dust.'

Mr Hetzel's Views on Faro

I asked Mr Hetzel, 'Do you even drink Belgian beer?' I saw a look of dismay cross his bearded face. 'No, never on your life. Faro – and I say this without malice – Faro is a beer which has been drunk twice over.'

Hetzel parlait ainsi, dans un Café flamand,
Par prudence sans doute, énigmatiquement;
Je compris que c'était une manière fine
De me dire: «Faro, synonyme d'urine!»

«Observez bien que le faro
Se fait avec de l'eau de Senne.»
– «Je comprends d'où lui vient sa saveur citoyenne.
Après tout, c'est selon ce qu'on entend par eau!»

UN NOM DE BON AUGURE

Sur la porte je lus: «*Lise Van Swieten*».
(C'était dans un quartier qui n'est pas un Éden)
– Heureux l'époux, heureux l'amant qui la possède,
Cette Ève qui contient en elle son remède!
Cet homme enviable a trouvé,
Ce que nul n'a jamais rêvé,
Depuis le pôle nord jusqu'au pôle antarctique:
Une épouse prophylactique!

Hetzel said this in a Flemish café and – no doubt for the sake of prudence – somewhat enigmatically. I understand it was a polite way of telling me that Faro is a synonym for P. . .

'Note that faro is brewed from the waters of the river Senne.' – 'Now I understand where it gets that plebeian flavour from – after all, it all depends on what you people mean by water.'

A Promising Surname

On the door I read the name *Lise van Swieten*. That was in a part of Brussels which was far from being a Garden of Eden. Happy the husband or lover who possesses this Eve, who contains her own cure. This enviable fellow has found what nobody between the Poles ever dreamt of – a prophylactic mate.

LE RÊVE BELGE

La Belgique se croit toute pleine d'appas;
Elle dort. Voyageur, ne la réveillez pas.

L'INVIOLABILITÉ DE LA BELGIQUE

«Qu'on ne me touche pas! Je suis inviolable!»
Dit la Belgique. – C'est, hélas! incontestable.
Y toucher? Ce serait, en effet, hasardeux,
 Puisqu'elle est un bâton merdeux.

The Belgian Dream

Belgium dreams that she has no end of charms. Now she is fast asleep –
but, tourist, don't wake her up at any price.

Belgian Inviolability

'Don't you touch me – I'm *inviolable*,' Belgium says. Alas, there's not the
slightest doubt about that. It would certainly be a risky thing to do,
touching a stick with shit on.

ÉPITAPHE POUR LÉOPOLD I^er

Ci-gît un roi constitutionnel,
(Ce qui veut dire : Automate en hôtel
 Garni),
Qui se croyait sempiternel.
Heureusement, c'est bien fini !

ÉPITAPHE POUR LA BELGIQUE

On me demande une épitaphe
Pour la Belgique morte. En vain
Je creuse, et je rue et je piaffe ;
Je ne trouve qu'un mot : « Enfin ! »

Epitaph for King Leopold I

Here lies a *constitutional* King (which means a dumb-waiter in a boarding-house) who thought he could go on eternally. Happily, that eternity is over now.

Epitaph for Belgium

They've asked me to write an epitaph for the lately-deceased Belgium. After racking my brains and lashing out and pawing the ground, all I can come up with is 'At last!'

L'ESPRIT CONFORME

[1]

Cet imbécile de Tournai
Me dit: «J'ai l'esprit mieux tourné
Que vous, Monsieur. Ma jouissance
Dérive de l'obéissance;

J'ai mis toute ma volupté
Dans l'esprit de Conformité;
Mon cœur craint toute façon neuve
En fait de plaisir ou d'ennui,
Et veut que le bonheur d'autrui
Toujours au sien serve de preuve.»

Ce que dit l'homme de Tournai,
(Dont vous devinez bien, je pense,
Que j'ai retouché l'éloquence)
N'était pas aussi bien tourné.

The Conformist Mentality

I

That chump from Tournai says to me: 'I have a better *turn of mind* than you, old man. I owe all my enjoyment of life to *obedience*. I've centred my every possible pleasure on the spirit of *conformity*: my heart shrinks from any fresh form of delight or boredom, and it wants the happiness of others to be only a constant proof of its own.

But what the Tournai fellow had to say – you've no doubt guessed that I've touched up his style of eloquence a bit – wasn't so well 'turned' as all that.

L'ESPRIT CONFORME

[II]

Les Belges poussent, ma parole!
L'imitation à l'excès,
Et s'ils attrapent la vérole,
C'est pour ressembler aux Français.

LES PANÉGYRIQUES DU ROI

Tout le monde, ici, parle un français ridicule:
On proclame immortel ce vieux principicule.
Je veux bien qu'immortalité
Soit le synonyme
De longévité,
La différence est si minime!

Bruxelles, ces jours-ci, déclarait (c'est grotesque!)
Léopold immortel. – Au fait, il le fut presque.

The Conformist Mentality
II
I must say the Belgians push their habit of imitation too far – catching the pox just to be like the French.

Royal Panegyrics
Everyone here speaks an absurd sort of French. Now they're proclaiming that their little old Kinglet is *immortal*. Well, I don't really mind if they use *immortality* as a synonym for *longevity*, as there's such a trifling distance between the two.

In the past few days Brussels has, grotesquely enough, announced that Leopold is immortal – as indeed he almost was.

LE MOT DE CUVIER

«En quel genre, en quel coin de l'animalité
Classerons-nous le Belge?» Une Société
Scientifique avait posé ce dur problème.
Alors le grand Cuvier se leva, tremblant, blême,
Et pour toutes raisons criant: «Je jette aux chiens
Ma langue! Car, messieurs les Académiciens,
L'espace est un peu grand depuis les singes jusques
 Jusques aux mollusques!»

AU CONCERT, À BRUXELLES

On venait de jouer de ces airs ravissants
Qui font rêver l'esprit et transporter les sens;
Mais un peu lâchement; hélas! à la flamande.
«Tiens! l'on n'applaudit pas ici?» fis-je. – Un voisin,
Amoureux comme moi de musique allemande,
Me dit: «Vous êtes neuf dans ce pays malsain,
 Monsieur? Sans ça, vous sauriez qu'en musique,
 Comme en peinture et comme en politique,

Cuvier's Little Joke

'In what species, order or whatever should we classify the *Belgian*?'
When a scientific society raised this tough problem, the Great Cuvier
rose to his feet with a shudder, pale with anger, and shouted without
further explanation, 'I really have to give up, gentlemen of the Academy,
as there's a quite considerable gap between the apes and molluscs.'

A Brussels Concert

They'd just finished playing one of those exquisite airs which fill your
mind with dreams and steal all your senses away – only they'd performed
it rather slackly, Flemish-style, alas . . . 'Don't people ever applaud here?'
I exclaimed. A gentleman who was sitting near me, who is fond of
German music as I am, remarked 'You must be a newcomer to this
sick country, Sir? Otherwise you would know that where music is
concerned, as well as painting and politics, every Belgian imagines that

Le Belge croit qu'on le veut attraper,
– Et puis qu'il craint surtout de se tromper. »

UNE BÉOTIE BELGE

La Belgique a sa Béotie!
C'est une légende, une scie,
Un proverbe! – Un comparatif
Dans un état superlatif!
Bruxelles, ô mon Dieu! méprise Poperinghe!
Un vendeur de trois-six blaguant un mannezingue!
Un clysoir, ô terreur! raillant une seringue!
Bruxelles n'a pas droit de railler Poperinghe!
Comprend-on le comparatif
(C'est une épouvantable scie!)
À côté du superlatif?
La Belgique a sa Béotie!

somebody's trying to cheat him, and at the same time he's dead scared of being wrong.'

A Belgian Boeotia

Belgium has its own Brummagem! It's a legend, a gag, a proverb. Fancy a comparative in a superlative –

good heavens, *Brussels* looks down on *Poperinghe*, it's like a hooch-merchant taking the piss out of a poteen-merchant! Or – wait for it – an enema-tube insulting a syringe! Brussels has no right to jeer at Poperinghe.

Don't they realize the difference between a comparative and a superlative? It's a hell of a joke, Belgium having its Brummagem.

[Boeotia was proverbial for stupidity to the ancient Greeks. The local name for the English town Birmingham and its dialect suggests the spurious, counterfeit, or tawdry. – Ed.]

LA CIVILISATION BELGE

Le Belge est très civilisé;
Il est voleur, il est rusé;
Il est parfois syphilisé;
Il est donc très civilisé.

Il ne déchire pas sa proie
Avec ses ongles; met sa joie
À montrer qu'il sait employer
À table fourchette et cuiller;
Il néglige de s'essuyer,
Mais porte paletot, culottes,
Chapeau, chemise même et bottes;
Fait de dégoûtantes ribotes;
Dégueule aussi bien que l'Anglais;
Met sur le trottoir des engrais;
Rit du Ciel et croit au progrès
Tout comme un journaliste d'Outre-
Quiévrain; – de plus, il peut foutre
Debout comme un singe avisé.

Il est donc très civilisé.

Belgian Civilization

The Belgian is highly civilized. He is a thief and a slyboots and he
sometimes catches the pox, so he must be highly civilized. He doesn't
tear at his prey with his fingernails, but he delights in proving at table
that he can handle a fork and spoon together. He never wipes his arse,
but wears a coat and trousers, a hat, even a shirt and boots. He goes on
disgusting binges and he vomits as heartily as the English. He manures
his pavements, he laughs at the idea of Heaven, he believes in Progress
like any Frog journalist across the border. What's more, he can copulate
standing like any sensible monkey.
 So he really is highly civilized.

LA MORT DE LÉOPOLD I^{er}

[I]

Le grand juge de paix d'Europe
A donc dévissé son billard!
(Je vous expliquerai ce trope).
Ce Roi n'était pas un fuyard
Comme notre Louis-Philippe.
Il pensait, l'obstiné vieillard,
Qu'il n'était jamais assez tard
Pour *casser* son ignoble *pipe.*

LA MORT DE LÉOPOLD I^{er}

[II]

Léopold voulait sur la Mort
Gagner sa première victoire.
Il n'a pas été le plus fort;
Mais dans l'impartiale histoire
Sa résistance méritoire
Lui vaudra ce nom fulgurant:
«Le cadavre récalcitrant».

The Death of King Leopold I

I

The *Great Arbiter of European Peace* has at last pegged out, unscrewed his knob. I'll explain that figure of speech for you: this monarch was no flitter like our Louis-Philippe; the obstinate old chap thought it was never too late to kick his dirty bucket.

II

Leopold was hoping to win his first victory – over Death. He wasn't the stronger of the two, but in impartial history-books his heroic resistance will earn him this sublime title, 'the corpse that wouldn't lie down'.

III

Verse Translations

LE CALUMET DE PAIX

IMITÉ DE LONGFELLOW

I

Or Gitche Manito, le Maître de la Vie,
Le Puissant, descendit dans la verte prairie,
Dans l'immense prairie aux coteaux montueux;
Et là, sur les rochers de la Rouge Carrière,
Dominant tout l'espace et baigné de lumière,
Il se tenait debout, vaste et majestueux.

Alors il convoqua les peuples innombrables,
Plus nombreux que ne sont les herbes et les sables.
Avec sa main terrible il rompit un morceau
Du rocher, dont il fit une pipe superbe,
Puis, au bord du ruisseau, dans une énorme gerbe,
Pour s'en faire un tuyau, choisit un long roseau.

from *The Song of Hiawatha*
by Henry Wadsworth Longfellow

I

THE PEACE-PIPE

On the Mountains of the Prairie,
On the great Red Pipe-stone
 Quarry,
Gitche Manito, the mighty,
He the Master of Life, descending,
On the red crags of the quarry
Stood erect, and called the nations,
Called the tribes of men together.

 From his footprints flowed a river,
Leaped into the light of morning,
O'er the precipice plunging down-
 ward
Gleamed like Ishkoodah, the comet.
And the Spirit, stooping earthward,
With his finger on the meadow
Traced a winding pathway for it,
Saying to it, 'Run in this way!'

 From the red stone of the quarry
With his hand he broke a fragment,
Moulded it into a pipe-head,
Shaped and fashioned it with
 figures;
From the margin of the river
Took a long reed for a pipe-stem,
With its dark green leaves upon it;
Filled the pipe with bark of willow,
With the bark of the red willow;

Pour la bourrer il prit au saule son écorce;
Et lui, le Tout-Puissant, Créateur de la Force,
Debout, il alluma, comme un divin fanal,
La Pipe de la Paix. Debout sur la Carrière
Il fumait, droit, superbe et baigné de lumière.
Or pour les nations c'était le grand signal.

Et lentement montait la divine fumée
Dans l'air doux du matin, onduleuse, embaumée.
Et d'abord ce ne fut qu'un sillon ténébreux;
Puis la vapeur se fit plus bleue et plus épaisse,
Puis blanchit; et montant, et grossissant sans cesse,
Elle alla se briser au dur plafond des cieux.

Des plus lointains sommets des Montagnes Rocheuses,
Depuis les lacs du Nord aux ondes tapageuses,
Depuis Tawasentha, le vallon sans pareil,
Jusqu'à Tuscaloosa, la forêt parfumée,
Tous virent le signal et l'immense fumée
Montant paisiblement dans le matin vermeil.

Breathed upon the neighbouring
 forest,
Made its great boughs chafe
 together,
Till in flame they burst and kindled
And erect upon the mountains,
Gitche Manito, the mighty,
Smoked the calumet, the Peace-
 Pipe,
As a signal to the nations.

 And the smoke rose slowly,
 slowly,
Through the tranquil air of
 morning,
First a single line of darkness,
Then a denser, bluer vapour,

Then a snow-white cloud
 unfolding,
Like the tree-tops of the forest,
Ever rising, rising, rising,
Till it touched the top of heaven,
Till it broke against the heaven,
And rolled outward all around it.

 From the Vale of Tawasentha,
From the Valley of Wyoming,
From the groves of Tuscaloosa,
From the far-off Rocky Mountains,
From the Northern lakes and rivers
All the tribes beheld the signal,
Saw the distant smoke ascending,
The Pukwana of the Peace-Pipe.

Les Prophètes disaient: «Voyez-vous cette bande
De vapeur, qui, semblable à la main qui commande,
Oscille et se détache en noir sur le soleil?
C'est Gitche Manito, le Maître de la Vie,
Qui dit aux quatre coins de l'immense prairie:
"Je vous convoque tous, guerriers, à mon conseil!"»

Par le chemin des eaux, par la route des plaines,
Par les quatre côtés d'où soufflent les haleines
Du vent, tous les guerriers de chaque tribu, tous,
Comprenant le signal du nuage qui bouge,
Vinrent docilement à la Carrière Rouge
Où Gitche Manito leur donnait rendez-vous.

Les guerriers se tenaient sur la verte prairie,
Tous équipés en guerre, et la mine aguerrie,
Bariolés ainsi qu'un feuillage automnal;
Et la haine qui fait combattre tous les êtres,
La haine qui brûlait les yeux de leurs ancêtres
Incendiait encor leurs yeux d'un feu fatal.

And the Prophets of the nations
Said: 'Behold it, the Pukwana!
By the signal of the Peace-Pipe,
Bending like a wand of willow,
Waving like a hand that beckons,
Gitche Manito, the mighty,
Calls the tribes of men together,
Calls the warriors to his council!'

Down the rivers, o'er the prairies,
Came the warriors of the nations,
Came the Delawares and Mohawks,
Came the Choctaws and
Camanches,
Came the Shoshonies and Blackfeet,
Came the Pawnees and Omahas,

Came the Mandans and Dacotahs,
Came the Hurons and Ojibways,
All the warriors drawn together
By the signal of the Peace-Pipe,
To the Mountains of the Prairie,
To the great Red Pipe-stone
Quarry,

And they stood there on the
meadow,
With their weapons and their war-
gear,
Painted like the leaves of Autumn,
Painted like the sky of morning,
Wildly glaring at each other;
In their faces stern defiance,
In their hearts the feuds of ages,
The hereditary hatred,

Et leurs yeux étaient pleins de haine héréditaire.
Or Gitche Manito, le Maître de la Terre,
Les considérait tous avec compassion,
Comme un père très bon, ennemi du désordre,
Qui voit ses chers petits batailler et se mordre.
Tel Gitche Manito pour toute nation.

Il étendit sur eux sa puissante main droite
Pour subjuguer leur cœur et leur nature étroite,
Pour rafraîchir leur fièvre à l'ombre de sa main;
Puis il leur dit avec sa voix majestueuse,
Comparable à la voix d'une eau tumultueuse
Qui tombe et rend un son monstrueux, surhumain:

II

«Ô ma postérité, déplorable et chérie!
Ô mes fils! écoutez la divine raison.
C'est Gitche Manito, le Maître de la Vie,
Qui vous parle! celui qui dans votre patrie
A mis l'ours, le castor, le renne et le bison.

The ancestral thirst of vengeance.

 Gitche Manito, the mighty,
The creator of the nations,
Looked upon them with
 compassion,
With paternal love and pity;
Looked upon their wrath and
 wrangling
But as quarrels among children,
But as feuds and fights of children!

 Over them he stretched his right
 hand,
To subdue their stubborn natures,
To allay their thirst and fever,
By the shadow of his right hand;

Spake to them with voice majestic
As the sound of far-off waters,
Falling into deep abysses,
Warning, chiding, spake in this
 wise:

 'O my children! my poor
 children!
Listen to the words of wisdom,
Listen to the words of warning,
From the lips of the Great Spirit,
From the Master of Life, who made
 you!

 'I have given you lands to hunt in,
I have given you streams to fish in,
I have given you bear and bison,

«Je vous ai fait la chasse et la pêche faciles;
Pourquoi donc le chasseur devient-il assassin?
Le marais fut par moi peuplé de volatiles;
Pourquoi n'êtes-vous pas contents, fils indociles?
Pourquoi l'homme fait-il la chasse à son voisin?

«Je suis vraiment bien las de vos horribles guerres.
Vos prières, vos vœux mêmes sont des forfaits!
Le péril est pour vous dans vos humeurs contraires,
Et c'est dans l'union qu'est votre force. En frères
Vivez donc, et sachez vous maintenir en paix.

«Bientôt vous recevrez de ma main un Prophète
Qui viendra vous instruire et souffrir avec vous.
Sa parole fera de la vie une fête;
Mais si vous méprisez sa sagesse parfaite,
Pauvres enfants maudits, vous disparaîtrez tous!

I have given you roe and reindeer,
I have given you brant and beaver,
Filled the marshes full of wild-fowl,
Filled the rivers full of fishes:
Why then are you not contented?
Why then will you hunt each
 other?

 'I am weary of your quarrels,
Weary of your wars and bloodshed,
Weary of your prayers for
 vengeance,
Of your wranglings and dissensions;
All your strength is in your union,

All your danger is in discord;
Therefore be at peace henceforward,
And as brothers live together.

 'I will send a Prophet to you,
A Deliverer of the nations,
Who shall guide you and shall
 teach you,
Who shall toil and suffer with you.
If you listen to his counsels,
You will multiply and prosper;
If his warnings pass unheeded,
You will fade away and perish!

«Effacez dans les flots vos couleurs meurtrières.
Les roseaux sont nombreux et le roc est épais;
Chacun en peut tirer sa pipe. Plus de guerres,
Plus de sang! Désormais vivez comme des frères,
Et tous, unis, fumez le Calumet de Paix!»

III

Et soudain tous, jetant leurs armes sur la terre,
Lavent dans le ruisseau les couleurs de la guerre
Qui luisaient sur leurs fronts cruels et triomphants.
Chacun creuse une pipe et cueille sur la rive
Un long roseau qu'avec adresse il enjolive.
Et l'Esprit souriait à ses pauvres enfants!

'Bathe now in the stream before you,
Wash the war-paint from your faces,
Wash the blood-stains from your fingers,
Bury your war-clubs and your weapons,
Break the red stone from this quarry,
Mould and make it into Peace-Pipes,
Take the reeds that grow beside you,
Deck them with your brightest feathers,
Smoke the calumet together,
And as brothers live henceforward!'

Then upon the ground the warriors
Threw their cloaks and shirts of deer-skin,
Threw their weapons and their war-gear,
Leaped into the rushing river,
Washed the war-paint from their faces.
Clear above them flowed the water,
Clear and limpid from the foot-prints
Of the Master of Life descending;
Dark below them flowed the water,
Soiled and stained with streaks of crimson,
As if blood were mingled with it!

From the river came the warriors,
Clean and washed from all their war-paint;
On the banks their clubs they buried,
Buried all their warlike weapons.
Gitche Manito, the mighty,
The Great Spirit, the creator,
Smiled upon his helpless children!

Chacun s'en retourna, l'âme calme et ravie,
Et Gitche Manito, le Maître de la Vie,
Remonta par la porte entrouverte des cieux.
– À travers la vapeur splendide du nuage
Le Tout-Puissant montait, content de son ouvrage,
Immense, parfumé, sublime, radieux!

L'ENFANCE D'HIAWATHA

La belle Wénonah, la douce et tendre mère
D'Hiawatha, mourut dans une angoisse amère;
Car Vent-d'Ouest, guerrier parjure, abandonna
Ta fille, ô Nokomis! la tendre Wénonah.

And in silence all the warriors
Broke the red stone of the quarry,
Smoothed and formed it into
 Peace-Pipes,
Broke the long reeds by the river,
Decked them with their brightest
 feathers,
And departed each one homeward,
While the Master of Life, ascending,
Through the opening of cloud-
 curtains,
Through the doorways of the
 heaven,
Vanished from before their faces,
In the smoke that rolled around
 him,
The Pukwana of the Peace-Pipe!

from III
HIAWATHA'S CHILDHOOD

. . . Thus was born my Hiawatha,
Thus was born the child of wonder;
But the daughter of Nokomis,
Hiawatha's gentle mother,
In her anguish died deserted
By the West-Wind, false and
 faithless,
By the heartless Mudjekeewis. . . .

Sur les bords de Gitche Gumee, nappe vermeille,
S'élevait le wigwam de Nokomis la vieille;
La forêt de pins noirs par-derrière ondulait,
Et la Grosse-Eau-de-Mer par-devant déferlait.

La vieille Nokomis, malgré tant de détresses,
A trouvé dans son cœur de nouvelles tendresses;
C'est elle qui, berçant le pauvre Hiawatha,
Dans son sein amaigri longtemps le dorlota.

La patiente aïeule, aux tempes racornies,
De l'enfant gémissant calmait les agonies,
Disant, s'il criait trop: «Chut! l'Ours-Nu t'entendra!
Sois bien sage! Sinon l'Ours-Nu te mangera!»

Dans son petit berceau fait de joncs et de mousses
Elle amusait son âme avec des chansons douces;
Et l'enfant aux grands yeux ébahis l'écoutait.
La vieille, deux fois mère, ainsi parfois chantait:

> morceau de chant

By the shores of Gitchee Gumee
By the shining Big-Sea-Water,
Stood the wigwam of Nokomis,
Daughter of the Moon, Nokomis.
Dark behind it rose the forest,
Rose the black and gloomy pine-
 trees,
Rose the firs with cones upon
 them;
Bright before it beat the water,
Beat the clear and sunny water,
Beat the shining Big-Sea-Water.

There the wrinkled, old Nokomis
Nursed the little Hiawatha,

Rocked him in his linden cradle,
Bedded soft in moss and rushes,
Safely bound with reindeer sinews;
Stilled his fretful wail by saying,
'Hush! the Naked Bear will hear
 thee!'
Lulled him into slumber, singing,
'Ewa-yea! my little owlet!
Who is this, that lights the wigwam?
With his great eyes lights the
 wigwam?
Ewa-yea! my little owlet!'

LE PONT DES SOUPIRS

TRADUIT DE THOMAS HOOD

En voici une encore plus infortunée
Qui fatiguée de respirer
Et follement impatiente
Est allée à sa mort.

Prends-la tendrement;
Soulève-la avec soin,
Elle est faite si délicatement
Et si jeune et si belle!

Regarde ses vêtements
Qui collent comme un suaire,
Pendant que le flot constamment
Coule de sa robe.
Soulève-la immédiatement
Avec amour et non avec dégoût.

Touche-la sans mépris,
Pense à elle avec tristesse,
Avec douceur, avec humanité.

The Bridge of Sighs

'Drown'd! drown'd!' – HAMLET

One more Unfortunate,
 Weary of breath,
Rashly importunate,
 Gone to her death!

Take her up tenderly,
 Lift her with care;
Fashioned so slenderly
 Young, and so fair!

Look at her garments
 Clinging like cerements;
Whilst the wave constantly
 Drips from her clothing;
Take her up instantly,
 Loving, not loathing.

Touch her not scornfully;
Think of her mournfully,
 Gently and humanly;

Ne pense pas à ses souillures.
Tout ce qui reste d'elle
Maintenant est pur fémininement.

Ne fais pas un trop profond examen
De sa révolte
Téméraire et coupable.
Tout déshonneur est effacé.
La mort n'a laissé sur elle
Que la beauté.

Cependant à cause de toutes ses erreurs,
Car elle était de la famille d'Ève,
Essuie ses pauvres lèvres
Suintant si visqueusement.

Ramasse ses tresses
Échappées au peigne,
Ses belles tresses châtaines,
Cependant qu'on cherche avec étonnement
Où était son logis.

Qui était son père?
Qui était sa mère?
Avait-elle une sœur?

Not of the stains of her,
All that remains of her
 Now is pure womanly.

Make no deep scrutiny
Into her mutiny
 Rash and undutiful:
Past all dishonour,
Death has left on her
 Only the beautiful.

Still, for all slips of hers,
 One of Eve's family –

Wipe those poor lips of hers
 Oozing so clammily.

Loop up her tresses
 Escaped from the comb,
Her fair auburn tresses;
Whilst wonderment guesses
 Where was her home?

Who was her father?
 Who was her mother?
Had she a sister?

Avait-elle un frère ?
Ou existait-il pour elle quelqu'un plus cher
Encore, quelqu'un plus précieux
Encore que tout autre.

Hélas ! ô rareté
De la chrétienne charité
Sous le soleil !
Oh ! c'était à faire pitié !
Près d'une grande cité toute pleine
Elle n'avait pas un logis.

Du côté de la sœur, du frère,
Du père, de la mère
Les sentiments avaient changé.
L'amour par une cruelle révélation
Avait été précipité de sa hauteur,
Et même la Divine Providence
Semblait lui être devenue étrangère.

Là où les réverbères tremblaient
Au loin sur la rivière,
Avec mille lumières
De la fenêtre et de la lucarne,

Had she a brother?
Or was there a dearer one
Still, and a nearer one
 Yet, than all other?

Alas! for the rarity
Of Christian charity
 Under the sun!
O, it was pitiful!
Near a whole city full,
 Home she had none.

Sisterly, brotherly,
Fatherly, motherly
 Feelings had changed:
Love, by harsh evidence,
Thrown from its eminence;
Even God's providence
 Seeming estranged.

Where the lamps quiver
So far in the river,
 With many a light
From window and casement,

Depuis la mansarde jusqu'à la base,
Elle se tenait avec stupéfaction
Seule, sans logis dans la nuit.

Le vent glacial de mars
La faisait trembler et frissonner
Mais non pas l'arche sombre
Ou la rivière coulant noire.
Folle du roman de la vie,
Souriant au mystère de la Mort,
Impatiente d'être engloutie . . .
N'importe où, n'importe où
Hors de ce monde!

Elle a plongé bravement
Sans s'inquiéter si glacialement
L'âpre rivière coulait.
Sur le bord de cette eau
Figure-toi cela, pense à cela,
Homme dissolu!
Lave-toi dans cette eau, bois de cette eau
Maintenant, si tu peux!

From garret to basement,
She stood, with amazement,
　　Houseless by night.

The bleak wind of March
　　Made her tremble and shiver;
But not the dark arch,
Or the black flowing river:
Mad from life's history,
Glad to death's mystery,
　　Swift to be hurled —

Anywhere, anywhere
　　Out of the world!

In she plunged boldly —
No matter how coldly
　　The rough river ran —
Over the brink of it,
Picture it — think of it,
　　Dissolute Man!
Lave in it, drink of it,
　　Then, if you can!

Prends-la tendrement!
Soulève-la avec soin,
Elle est faite si délicatement!
Et si jeune et si belle!

Avant que ses membres glacés
Ne se raidissent trop rigidement,
Avec décence, avec bonté,
Assouplis-les et arrange-les;
Et ses yeux, ferme-les,
Ses yeux dardés aveuglément!
Ses yeux terriblement dardés
À travers la vase impure,
Et comme gardant l'audacieux
Dernier regard du désespoir
Fixés sur le futur.

Elle a péri lugubrement,
Aiguillonnée par l'outrage,
Par la froide inhumanité,
Par la brûlante insanité,
Vers son repos FINAL . . .

Take her up tenderly,
 Lift her with care;
Fashioned so slenderly,
 Young, and so fair!

Ere her limbs frigidly
Stiffen too rigidly,
 Decently, kindly,
Smooth and compose them;
And her eyes, close them,
 Staring so blindly!

Dreadfully staring
 Thro' muddy impurity,
As when with the daring
Last look of despairing
 Fixed on futurity.

Perishing gloomily,
Spurred by contumely,
Cold inhumanity,
Burning insanity,
 Into her rest. –

Croise ses mains humblement,
Comme si elle priait silencieusement,
Sur sa poitrine!
Comme si elle avouait sa faiblesse,
Sa coupable conduite,
Et confiait avec humilité
Ses péchés à son Sauveur!

Cross her hands humbly
As if praying dumbly,
Over her breast!

Owning her weakness,
Her evil behaviour,
And leaving, with meekness,
Her sins to her Saviour!

[1865. Translation dictated by Baudelaire]

IV

Poems Attributed
to Baudelaire

LE RACCOMMODEUR DE FONTAINES

À l'heure où le cœur se délabre,
Où l'estomac est mal rempli,
Le gaz meurt dans le candélabre;
Paris d'ombre est enseveli.

Sur le pavé sec et poli
Passe un long cheval qui se cabre,
Portant sur son dos assoupi
Un spectre grimaçant et glabre.

Dans un vieux clairon tout cassé,
Sous son suaire de futaine,
Il pousse une note incertaine.

C'est le squelette encore glacé
Du raccommodeur de fontaine
Qui mourut de froid l'an passé.

The Fountain-Mender

At the hour when the heart breaks and the stomach fills with hunger,
the gas-jet sinks in its socket and Paris is buried in gloom.

Then over the smooth dry cobbles a long horse plods along and shies,
carrying a grinning moon-faced ghost on its sagging back.

The wraith blows a quavering note on his battered old bugle, from
under his shoddy shroud.

It's the frozen skeleton of the old fountain-mender, who died of cold
last year.

[Published 1926]

429

«QUANT À MOI...»

Quant à moi, si j'avais un beau parc planté d'ifs,
Si, pour mettre à l'abri mon bonheur dans l'orage,
J'avais, comme ce riche, un parc au vaste ombrage,
Dédale s'égarant sous de sombres massifs;

Si j'avais vos bosquets, ô rossignols craintifs,
Ô cygnes, vos bassins; votre sentier sauvage,
Vers luisants qui, le soir, étoilez le feuillage;
Vos prés au grand soleil, petits grillons plaintifs;

Je sais qui je voudrais cacher sous mes feuillées,
Avec qui secouer dans les herbes mouillées
Les perles que la nuit y verse de ses doigts,

Avec qui respirer les odeurs des rivières,
Ou dormir à midi dans les chaudes clairières,
Et tu le sais aussi, belle aux yeux trop adroits.

As for me . . .

As for me, if only I had a fine park planted with yews; if to shelter my
happiness in a storm I had, like that rich fellow, a park with a vast spread
of shade and a maze carved in thick hedges;

 if your groves, shy nightingales, were mine, or mine your ornamental
pools, O swans, or the rustic paths where glow-worms star the foliage at
evening, or sunny meadows alive with the crickets' melancholy song –

 then I know whom I should love to hide beneath my leafy walks;
with whom to scatter on the wet grass the pearls which night's fingers
sprinkle there;

 with whom to breathe the fragrance of the rills, or to sleep at noon
with in the cosy clearings – and you know all that also, my beauty, whose
eyes are only too shrewd.

[1839? Published 1871 by Antony Bruno, see p. 375]

LE PAUVRE DIABLE

Père	Chaque	Pâle
Las!	Vent	Fou,
Mère	Claque	Pas le
Pas.	Dent.	Sou!
Erre	Rude	Couve
Sur	Jeu . . .	Port
Terre . . .	Plus de	Trouve
Dur! . . .	Feu!	Mort!
Maigre	Rêve	Bière . . .
Flanc,	Pain	Trou . . .
Nègre	Crève	Pierre
Blanc,	Faim . . .	Où
Blême!	Cherche	Sale
Pas	Rôt,	Chien
Même	Perche	Pâle
Gras.	Haut,	Vient,
Songe	Trotte	Sur le
Vain . . .	Loin,	Bord,
Ronge	Botte	Hurle
Frein.	Point.	Fort
Couche	Traîne	Clame
Froid,	Sa	Geint
Mouche	Gêne,	Brame . . .
Doigt;	Va,	Fin!

The Poor Devil

Father? – alas! and motherless; rolling stone, skin and bone; skinny hobo, white crow; whey-faced, run to waste; dreams, idle, chews bridle; sleeps out, fingers snout; winds batter, teeth chatter; tough game, snuffed flame; dreams of bread, starves instead; dreams meat and veg, dosses in hedge; roams the streets on toe-rag feet, hawking his mawk; white as chalk, pauper gawk, go, stay at home and let death come – a bier – a hole – a tombstone where a dirty bitch prowls round your ditch, and howls and growls and groans among the bones: the end, my friend.

[Published in *Le Figaro* by an anonymous donor in 1878 and of highly dubious attribution; no doubt a parody of the monosyllabic sonnet: Fort / Belle / Elle / Dort: // Sort, / Frele – / Quelle / Mort! // Rose / Close: / La // Bise / L'a / Prise.]

ÉLÉGIE REFUSÉE AUX JEUX FLORAUX

Mes bottes, pauvres fleurs, sur leurs tiges fanées,
Dans un coin, tristement, gisaient, abandonnées,
 Veuves des soins du décrotteur.
Les jours étaient passés où mon âme ravie
Les voyait recouvrer leur éclat et leur vie,
 Sous le pinceau réparateur.

Et moi, je contemplais avec sollicitude
Le spectacle émouvant de leur décrépitude;
Puis, un de ces soupirs qu'on ne peut étouffer
S'échappa malgré moi de ma gorge oppressée,
Et mon cœur, encor plein de leur grandeur passée,
 Se mit à les apostropher.

Ô bottes! leur disais-je, ô bottes infidèles,
Vous êtes, vous aussi, comme les hirondelles,
 Des oiseaux légers, inconstants!
Vous aimez le ciel pur et les brises amies;
Aussi, d'un vol léger, vous vous êtes enfuies
 Quand est venu le mauvais temps.

Elegy Rejected by the Poetry Festival

(A parody of amateur verses entered for provincial competitions)

My boots, poor flowers on their faded stalks, lay sadly abandoned in a corner, widowed of the cleaner's care. Gone were the days when my delighted soul saw their vitality and gloss restored by the health-giving brush.

Then with anxious care I gazed on the heart-rending sight of their decrepitude, and an irrepressible sigh escaped in spite of myself from my tightened throat, and my heart recalled their past glories and addressed them in these words:

'Oh boots,' I said, 'O unfaithful boots, like swallows you are light inconstant birds! You love pure skies and friendly breezes, and on your airy wings you flew away once the bad weather came.

Ainsi, durant les jours pluvieux de novembre,
Me voilà donc contraint de rester dans ma chambre,
Appelant, mais en vain, les beaux jours d'autrefois;
Car la dent des pavés en grosses cicatrices
A gravé sur vos fronts vos états de services;
Et vous n'entendez plus ma voix.

Le ciel, dont la bonté s'étend sur la nature,
Refuse ses bienfaits à la littérature.
Peut-être, hélas! l'hiver entier,
Traînant cette existence absurde et malheureuse,
J'attendrai vainement d'une âme généreuse
Un crédit chez quelque bottier.

Oh! si pareil bienfait vient à tomber des nues,
Je jure de marcher au travers de nos rues
Avec un légitime orgueil.
Et vous, dont je n'ai plus qu'une triste mémoire,
Ô mes bottes! rentrez au fond de cette armoire
Qui va vous servir de cercueil.

'And so throughout November's rainy days I must remain imprisoned in my room, calling in vain for the happy times of yore to return again; for the cobbles' teeth have carved great scars upon your brow as a record of your services to me, and you no longer hear my voice.

'The heavens, which scatter their bounty over all Nature, withhold their benefits from Literature. Perhaps all winter long I must drag on this absurd and miserable existence, and wait in vain for some generous soul to give me credit at the shoemaker's.

'Oh, should such a godsend come my way, dropped from the clouds, I swear I'll walk the streets with legitimate pride; and you, of whom no more than a mournful memory remains, O my boots, you may return to the bottom of that wardrobe which will be your Tomb.'

[Dated 1851. Baudelaire thought of writing
for a shoe-trade publication in 1853]

À MADAME DU BARRY

Vous étiez du bon temps des robes à paniers,
Des bichons, des manchons, des abbés, des rocailles,
Des gens spirituels, polis et cancaniers,
Des filles, des marquis, des soupers, des ripailles.

Moutons poudrés à blanc, poètes familiers,
Vieux sèvres et biscuits, charmantes antiquailles,
Amours dodus, pompons de rubans printaniers,
Meubles en bois de rose et caprices d'écailles;

Le peuple a tout brisé, dans sa juste fureur,
Vous seule avez pleuré, vous seule avez eu peur,
Vous seule avez trahi votre fraîche noblesse.

Les autres souriaient sur les noirs tombereaux,
Et, tués sans colère, ils mouraient sans faiblesse,
Car vous seule étiez femme en ce temps de héros.

To Madame du Barry

Yours were the 'good old days' of hooped gowns, velvet pads, muffs, abbots, rockeries, smooth scandal-mongering wits, wenches and marquises, suppers and revelries.

White-powdered sheep, pet salon poets, old Sèvres and porcelains, curious bygones, plump Cupids, knots and tassels of springtime ribbons, rosewood furniture, trinkets of rocaille –

all those were demolished by the masses in their righteous anger – but you alone allowed yourself to weep, you alone were afraid, you alone betrayed your newly-found nobility.

All the rest wore a smile in the black tumbrils; killed without anger, they died without weakness – for you alone were a woman in an age of heroes.

[Published 1844, signed by Privat d'Anglemont]

À IVONNE PEN-MOORE

Te souvient-il, enfant, des jours de ta jeunesse,
Et des grandes forêts où tu courais pieds nus,
Rêveuse et vagabonde, oubliant ta détresse
Et laissant le zéphir baiser tes bras charnus?

Tes cheveux crespelés, ta peau de mulâtresse
Rendaient plus attrayants tes charmes ingénus:
Telle avant ses amours Diane chasseresse
Courait dans la bruyère et sur les monts chenus.

Il ne reste plus rien de ta beauté sauvage;
Le flot ne mordra plus tes pieds sur le rivage,
Et l'herbe a recouvert l'empreinte de tes pas.

Paris t'a faite riche entre les plus hautaines.
Tes frères les chasseurs ne reconnaîtraient pas
Leur sœur qui, dans ses mains, buvait l'eau des fontaines.

To Ivonne Pen-Moore

My child, do you remember the days when you were young, the vast forests through which you ran barefoot or rambled in a daydream, forgetting all your troubles and letting the warm breeze kiss your rounded arms?

Your crinkled hair and mulatto skin gave your innocent attractions all the more appeal; like you, huntress Diana raced before her lovers through the heather and up snowy hills.

Nothing of your untamed beauty now remains. The waves will no longer nip your bare feet on the shore. The grass has grown over the imprint of your steps.

Paris has made you rich among the snobs; your hunting companions would no longer know, in you, their sister who drank with cupped hands from the springs.

[1845, signed Pierre d'Anglemont]

AVRIL

À Mme Joséphine de Fer...

La muse est de retour! La campagne s'allume.
Partez, ma fantaisie; errez parmi les prés;
Voici le soleil d'or et les cieux sidérés,
La nature s'éveille et le bois se parfume.

Le printemps, jeune oiseau, vêt sa première plume.
Avril vient en chantant dans les champs diaprés,
Ouvrir sous un baiser les bourgeons empourprés,
Et la terre en moiteur s'enveloppe de brume.

Le printemps engloutit la neige et les chagrins
Et dispense à chacun des jours purs et sereins.
Vous dont les rigueurs font que sur ma tête il neige,

N'êtes-vous pas d'avis, belle qui dès longtemps
De me faire mourir avez le privilège,
Qu'il serait sage et bon d'imiter le printemps?

April

to Miss Joséphine de Ferrières

The muse is here again. The countryside is coming alight. Go roaming through the meadows, my fantasy, observe the golden sun, star-dappled skies; Nature is waking, fresh odours fill the woods.

The fledgling spring is showing her first feathers. Here comes April singing through pied fields, kissing open the crimson buds, and the moist earth is clothed in mist.

Spring drinks away the snows and all our griefs, gives pure and serene days to everyone. You, whose rigours heap my head with snow,

can you not agree, my lovely one who were privileged so long to make me die, that it would be kind and wise of you to emulate the spring.

[Published in *L'Artiste* 1845 and *L'Écho* 1846 by
Privat d'Anglemont – a poem so full of clichés that it is
more like a caricature than a serious poem by C.B.]

À UNE BELLE DÉVOTE

Que n'avons-nous pu voir ce siècle – même un jour –
Où les abbés galants, sans trouver de cruelles,
Lisaient leur bréviaire à l'oreiller des belles;
Quand Bernis pour Madone adorait Pompadour!

Ils sont passés, ces temps, et passés sans retour,
Où, d'un pied libertin, ils couraient les ruelles,
Et bravaient de l'enfer les flammes éternelles
Dans les boudoirs rocaille enflammés par l'amour!

Oh! que n'existions-nous, – vous, toute à Dieu, madame!
Moi, tout au sentiment que votre vertu blâme;
À notre culte vrai l'un et l'autre attachés.

J'aurais pris la tonsure, – et, qu'en sait-on? peut-être,
Tout en vous confessant, m'auriez-vous permis d'être
De moitié quelque soir dans vos divins péchés.

To a Pious Beauty

If only we could have seen that century, if only for a day, when amorous
abbots found no lady cold and recited their breviary at the ladies' pillow;
when Bernis worshipped Pompadour as his madonna.

Those days are gone and never to return, when clerics sped on
passionate feet to ladies' bedsides, braving the everlasting flames of hell
in rococo boudoirs, afire with love.

Oh why did we not live then, Lady; you who belong to God alone,
and I devoted to the passion which your virtue blames, each of us vowed
to his authentic cult.

For then I would have taken the tonsure and – how can we ever
know? – perhaps while I was hearing your confession you would have
allowed me to be, some evening, your partner in your divine sins.

[Published in *L'Artiste* 1845, signed Henry Vernot]

À UNE JEUNE SALTIMBANQUE

Nous t'aimions bien jadis, quand sur ta triste harpe
Tu raclais la romance, et qu'en un carrefour,
Pour attirer la foule à voir tes sauts de carpe,
Un enfant scrofuleux tapait sur un *tambour*,

Quand tu couvais de l'œil, en tordant ton écharpe,
Quelque athlète en maillot, Alcide fait au tour,
Qu'admire le bourgeois, que la police écharpe,
Qui porte cent kilos et t'appelle *mamour*.

Ta guitare enrouée et ta jupe à paillettes
Étalaient à nos yeux le rêve des poètes,
La danseuse d'Hoffmann, Esmeralda, Mignon.

Mais déchue à présent, te voilà, ma pauvre ange,
Sultane du trottoir, ramassant dans la fange
L'argent qui doit soûler ton rude compagnon.

To a Young Street-Acrobat

How we all adored you in those days, when you scraped a heart-rending
ballad on your pathetic 'harp' while an urchin hammered his toy drum
to fetch a crowd in the square to watch you hop like a fish out of water.

When you twirled your shawl and gazed with adoration at some
acrobat in a leotard, one of those vulgar Hercules whom the crowd gape
at and the police tear apart, weighing fifteen stone and calling you his
Duck,

your whining guitar and star-spangled skirt spread the poet's dream
before our eyes, a Hoffmann ballerina, an Esmeralda, a Mignon.

But now, fallen from your glory, we see you, poor angel, Sultana of
the pavements, scrabbling in the dirt for a few coppers to get your coarse
pimp drunk.

[*La Silhouette* 1845, signed Privat d'Anglemont]

[SUR L'ALBUM D'UNE DAME INCONNUE]

Vos cheveux sont-ils blonds, vos prunelles humides?
Avez-vous de beaux yeux à ravir l'univers?
Sont-ils doux ou cruels? sont-ils fiers ou timides?
Méritez-vous enfin qu'on vous fasse des vers?

Drapez-vous galamment vos châles en chlamydes?
Portez-vous un blason de gueules ou de vairs?
Savez-vous le secret des hautaines Armides?
Ou bien soupirez-vous sous les ombrages verts?

Si votre corps poli se tord comme un jeune arbre,
Et si le lourd damas, sur votre sein de marbre,
Comme un fleuve en courroux déborde en flots mouvants,
Si toutes vos beautés valent qu'on s'inquiète,
Ne laissez plus courir mon rêve à tous les vents,
Belle, venez poser devant votre poète.

Lines written in an unknown lady's album

Is your hair fair, are your pupils moist? Have you lovely eyes to entrance
the whole world with? Are they gentle, cruel; proud, or shy? Do you
really deserve to have verses written for you?

Do you wear your shawls draped round you stylishly? Do you sport
a coat of arms with gold or ermine? Do you know the secret of haughty
heroines like Armida? Or do you simply sigh in woodland shades?

If your body twists like a young sapling's, or if the heavy damask on
your marble breast heaves like an angry river's impetuous waves;

if all your beauties are such as might disturb us, then why do you let
my dreams search everywhere for you? Come, then, fair lady, and pose
now for your poet.

[*L'Artiste* 1846, signed Pierre d'Anglemont]

SONNET CAVALIER

À Mme E.M...., Gentille Femme.

Pourquoi donc m'aimez-vous, ô ma belle maîtresse?
Vous avez pour moi seul des sourires joyeux,
Et bien après le jour, sur le divan soyeux
Vous savez d'un baiser caresser ma paresse.

Suis-je, pour vous aimer, ô blonde enchanteresse,
Un timide écolier qui rêve de vos yeux
Et rougit quand son front sent frémir vos cheveux
Dont la brise lascive éparpille une tresse?...

Suis-je un beau raffiné, vainqueur de l'univers,
Mettant flamberge au vent pour un mot de travers,
Prenant pour vous aimer sa plus farouche pose?...

Non! mais je suis le seul dont le souffle hardi,
Ô froide Galatée, arrive, quand je l'ose,
À réchauffer un peu votre marbre engourdi.

A Saucy Sonnet

to Miss E.M., gentlewoman

Why do you love me, then, my lovely mistress? You keep all your happiest smiles for me, and long after the day dies you know how to woo my apathy with a kiss on the silky divan.

O blonde spell-binder, when I make love to you am I some timid schoolboy dreaming of your eyes, blushing when he feels your hair rustle against his brow when a lock is blown by the lascivious breeze?

Or am I some exquisite dandy, a world-conqueror drawing his sword to avenge some ill-chosen epithet, adopting his fiercest stance to prove his love?

No, but I'm the only one whose dauntless breath, whenever I dare to, can warm the numbness of your marble, O frigid Galatea.

[Published in *Le Corsaire-Satan* 1846 by Privat d'Anglemont]

«COMBIEN DURERONT NOS AMOURS?»

«Combien dureront nos amours?»
Dit la pucelle, au clair de lune.
L'amoureux répond: «Ô ma brune,
Toujours! toujours!»

Quand tout sommeille aux alentours,
Élise, se tortillant d'aise,
Dit qu'elle veut que je la baise
Toujours! toujours!

Moi je dis: «Pour charmer mes jours
Et le souvenir de mes peines,
Bouteilles, que n'êtes-vous pleines
Toujours! toujours!»

Mais le plus chaste des amours,
L'amoureux le plus intrépide,
Comme un flacon s'use et se vide
Toujours! toujours!

A Song

'How long will your love and mine endure?' the virgin asked in the moonlight. And her lover replies, 'For ever and ever, my nut-brown maid.'

When everything around us is fast asleep, Élise writhes with delight and says she wants me to pleasure her for ever and ever.

But I say, 'To charm my days away and the remembrance of my sorrows, dear bottles, why can't you be full for ever and ever?'

For the chastest love and the boldest womanizer are soon worn out and empty like a flask, for ever and for ever.

[1848: Privat d'Anglemont]

«J'AIME SES GRANDS YEUX BLEUS...»

J'aime ses grands yeux bleus, sa chevelure ardente
 Aux étranges senteurs,
Son beau corps blanc et rose, et sa santé puissante
 Digne des vieux jouteurs.

J'aime son air superbe et sa robe indécente
 Laissant voir les rondeurs
De sa gorge charnue à la forme abondante,
 Qu'admirent les sculpteurs.

J'aime son mauvais goût, sa jupe bigarrée,
Son grand châle boiteux, sa parole égarée
 Et son front rétréci.

Je l'aime ainsi! Tant pis... Cette fille des rues
M'enivre et me fascine avec ses beautés crues.
 Tant pis, je l'aime ainsi!

I love her great blue eyes...

I love her great blue eyes, her blazing hair so full of strange aromas, her lovely white rosy body, her strong vitality worthy of the jousters of old.

I love her haughty air, her shameless dress which shows the curves of her abundant breasts which have the ample shape sculptors admire.

I love her vulgar taste, her gaudy skirts, her large and mangled shawl, her mindless babble, her low and narrow brow.

I love her as she is, it can't be helped: this street-girl turns my head and fascinates me with her crude charms. It can't be helped, I love her as she is.

[1843? Published by Privat d'Anglemont 1848]

SONNET

À Mme Anna B...

Quand la brise d'avril a chassé les autans,
 Et doré toutes choses,
Anna, vous revenez avec le doux printemps
 Qui fait les fleurs écloses.

Vous voyant si charmante, on croirait que le temps
 En ses métamorphoses,
A, pour vous embellir, dans les prés éclatants
 Pris la pourpre des roses.

Lorsque nous vous avons, que nous fait le soleil
Aux rayons d'or, les fleurs au calice vermeil?
 Votre joue est plus belle!

Pourquoi donc imiter, à l'hiver pluvieux,
 La sauvage hirondelle,
Et nous priver aussi de l'éclat de vos yeux?

To Madame Anna B...

When the April breeze has driven the south winds away and touched all things with gold, Anna, you return with sweet spring as it is opening the flowers.

When we see you in all your charm, we can imagine that ever-changing Time has robbed the glistening meadows of the rose's crimson to make you lovelier still.

Since you are with us now, what need have we of the sun's golden beams or the vermilion chalices of flowers, when your cheek is more beautiful than theirs?

Then why behave like the wild swallow in the winter's rain, robbing us of the brilliance of your eyes?

[*Le Corsaire-Satan* 1847, Pierre d'Anglemont]

SONNET

À Mme Appoline Frantz.

Un livre n'aurait pas suffi
Pour peindre la mignarde flèche
De ton fin regard qui m'allèche
Avec son éternel défi!

Plus d'une belle à front bouffi,
Plus d'une guêpe à taille sèche,
En désespoir de ta calèche,
De tes attraits veut faire fi.

Bast! un fat meurt aussi d'envie,
Envieux non pas de ta vie,
Mais de tes appas entrouverts.

Mais que t'importent tes conquêtes,
Tes vrais amants sont les poètes:
Dont tu sais par cœur les doux vers.

Sonnet

To Madame Appoline Frantz

A whole book would not be enough to portray the coy shaft of your narrow gaze, whose constant challenge tempts me so.

Many a puffed-up lovely, many a slim-waisted wasp, thwarted in her desire to share your carriage, wants to dismiss your charms.

And so what? A fop could also die of envy, not envious of your way of life, but coveting your imperfectly concealed attractions.

But what do such conquests matter to you, whose true lovers are the poets whose tender verses you know by heart?

[Appoline Frantz was an actress at the Odéon, 1847.
The poem was published twice in that year under
the signature of Privat d'Anglemont.]

UN JOUR DE PLUIE

Le 5 juillet 1841

Midi sonne, le jour est bien sombre aujourd'hui;
À peine ce matin si le soleil a lui;
Les nuages sont noirs, et le vent qui les berce
Les heurte, et de leur choc fait ruisseler l'averse;
Leurs arceaux, se courbant sur les toits ardoisés,
Ressemblent aux piliers de draps noirs pavoisés,
Quand de la nef en deuil qui pleure et qui surplombe,
Le dôme s'arrondit comme une large tombe.
Le ruisseau, lit funèbre où s'en vont les dégoûts,
Charrie en bouillonnant les secrets des égouts,
Il bat chaque maison de son flot délétère,
Court, jaunit de limon la Seine qu'il altère,
Et présente sa vague aux genoux du passant.
Chacun, nous coudoyant sur le trottoir glissant,
Egoïste et brutal, passe et nous éclabousse,
Ou, pour courir plus vite, en s'éloignant nous pousse.
Partout fange, déluge, obscurité du ciel;
Noir tableau qu'eût rêvé le noir Ézéchiel!

A Rainy Day

5 July 1841

Now it is striking noon; this is a gloomy day. The sun has hardly shone this morning, the clouds are all black; the wind rocks them, striking them together, and the shock starts a downpour. Arches of cloud curve over the slate roofs like pillars draped in sable hangings, as when the dome swells like an immense tomb over the brooding nave, overhanging the weeping mourners. The gutter's funereal bed carries disgusts along, flows boiling with the secrets of the sewers, slapping in loathsome waves against the houses, rushing along to yellow with silt and pollute the river Seine, fouling the knees of all those who pass by. Everyone elbows us on the slimy pavements, pushing past us with brutal selfishness, splashing us with dirt, thrusting us aside so as to run more quickly. On every side there is nothing but filth, torrential rain, opaque sky, making a scene of gloom such as dour Ezekiel might have dreamt of.

[Hier pourtant le jour, dans sa profondeur vague,
Pur comme l'Océan où s'assoupit la vague,
Semblait jeter sur nous son regard triomphant;
D'Apollon Délien l'attelage piaffant,
À peine s'entourait de cette écume blanche
Qui du flanc des coursiers sur le sable s'épanche;
Hier tout souriait sur les toits, dans les airs;
Les oiseaux dans leur vol sillonnaient des éclairs;
Hier, tout s'agitait aux fenêtres ouvertes;
Hier, se répandait sur nos places désertes
Tout un peuple au plaisir, au travail empressé.
Regardez aujourd'hui: la nuit seule a passé!]

C'est la règle éternelle: aux voluptés d'une heure
Succèdent les longs soirs où l'innocence pleure;
Aux rapides clartés qui brillent sur le front,
L'obscurité des nuits qu'un éclair interrompt;
Au calme firmament, les chaos de nuages
Dont l'accouplement noir enfante les orages.
Le monde où nous vivons, sous sa voûte d'airain,
Semble épaissir sur nous l'ombre d'un souterrain.

[Yet yesterday the day, in its indistinct depth, pure as the Ocean where the waves drowse, seemed to throw its triumphant look on us; Delian Apollo's team of horses, stamping, was barely surrounded by the white foam pouring onto the sand from the chargers' flanks; yesterday everything was smiling on the roofs, in the air; the birds in their flight crisscrossed like lightning; yesterday, everything stirred at open windows; yesterday, a whole people spread through our deserted squares on their way to pleasure, to busy work. Look at today: the lonely night has passed!]
 Such is the eternal rule of life: an hour's delights are followed by long evenings when innocence weeps; after the brief rays that glitter on our brows come the shades of night which a flash of lightning interrupt; after tranquil skies comes a chaos of clouds whose sinister couplings give birth to storms. The world we live in under its vault of bronze seems only to thicken the dungeon's shadow over us. In a fog heavy with subtle

Dans un brouillard chargé d'exhalaisons subtiles,
Les hommes enfouis comme d'obscurs reptiles,
Orgueilleux de leur force en leur aveuglement,
Pas à pas sur le sol glissent péniblement.
Ils ont, creusant sans fin des mystères occultes,
Embrassé tour à tour et nié tous les cultes;
Aux coins qu'à leur tanière assigna le hasard,
Ils meurent en rêvant des palais de lézard;
Et lorsque sur la fange, à travers les ténèbres,
Tombe un peu de clarté des soupiraux funèbres,
En face du rayon qu'ils ont vu flamboyer,
Blasphémant le soleil, ils doutent du foyer.

vapours, men are buried like sneaking reptiles, proud of their strength
in their blindness, with each step they slip painfully on the ground. As
they endlessly explore occult mysteries, they adopt then deny every
religion in turn; in the corners allotted to their den by Chance, they die
while dreaming of lizard palaces; and when a feeble gleam from dismal
basement windows filters through the dense shadow to reveal the filth,
at the sight of the ray which they have seen blazing, they blaspheme
against the sun and lose faith in hearth and home.

[Published 1841, 1843 under Ernest Prarond's name.
Assigned to Baudelaire by Mouquet, who 'leaves' to
Prarond the dozen lines enclosed in square brackets]

«SUR LE TROU DU CERCUEIL...»

Turpe senex miles... – OVIDE.

Sur le trou du cercueil nouvellement creusé,
Immobile, la nuit, un hibou s'est posé.
Son œil est fixe et froid; du milieu des ténèbres,
Sa voix rauque et cassée éclate en cris funèbres;
Sur la chair des tombeaux qu'il déterre et qu'il mord,
Son hymne de triomphe est un hymne de mort.

Et le vieillard pour qui cette fosse est creusée,
Réchauffe sur un sein sa vieillesse blasée,
Et, près du corps vendu qui cède avec dégoût,
Des saintes voluptés cherche un arrière-goût.
Son souffle est un hoquet, ses soupirs sont des râles;
Sa voix, comme l'écho des caves sépulcrales,
Semble venir de loin; son baiser spongieux
Trahit sa route, ainsi qu'un escargot fangeux.
Près de la jeune proie à sa luxure offerte,
Que fait donc ce fantôme en son étreinte inerte?...
Ce que fait le hibou, profanateur de deuil,
Taciturne, la nuit, sur le trou du cercueil.

Over the pit freshly dug...

Turpe senex miles – OVID

Over the pit freshly dug for the coffin, an owl stands motionless in the night. His eye is fixed and cold. His hoarse, cracked voice hoots mournful cries into the gloom. Now he picks flesh from the graves and chews it; his crow of triumph is a hymn of death.

Meanwhile the old man for whom this grave was dug warms his numb senility on a woman's breast; through her sold body which yields to him with disgust he is seeking some after-taste of blessed ecstasies. His breath is hiccups, his sighs are death-rattles, his voice like an echo from the vaults of the dead seems to come from far away, his spongy kiss betrays his path like a slimy slug's. As he stretches there beside the young prey who endures his obscene caresses, what is the ghost in his lifeless grasp doing? – The same as the owl, profaner of mourning, silent, at night, over the pit for the coffin.

[Signed Ernest Prarond, 1843]

SAPHO

Pour aimer les bergers, faut-il être bergère?
Pour avoir respiré la perfide atmosphère
De tes tristes cités, corruptrice Lesbos,
Faut-il donc renoncer aux faveurs d'Antéros?
Et suis-je désormais une conquête indigne
De ce jeune berger, doux et blanc comme un cygne?

Sappho

Must a girl be a shepherdess, in order to love shepherds? Lesbos, isle of corruption, for having breathed the treacherous air of your sad cities, must we renounce the favours of Anteros? Must I now be deemed an unworthy conquest of this shepherd boy, who is as white and smooth as a swan?

[One of the pieces resulting from a collaboration
in 1845 between four poets including Baudelaire]

«LORSQUE DE VOLUPTÉ...»

Lorsque de volupté s'alanguissent tes yeux,
Tes yeux noirs flamboyants de panthère amoureuse,
Dans ta chair potelée, et chaude, et savoureuse,
J'enfonce à belles dents les baisers furieux.

Je suis saisi du rut sombre et mystérieux
Qui jadis transportait la Grèce langoureuse,
Quand elle contemplait, terre trois fois heureuse,
L'accouplement sacré des Hommes et des Dieux.

Puis, sur mon sein brûlant, je crois tenir serrée
Quelque idole terrible et de sang altérée,
À qui les longs sanglots des moribonds sont doux

Et j'éprouve, au milieu des spasmes frénétiques,
L'atroce enivrement des vieux Fakirs Indous,
Les extases sans fin des Brahmes fanatiques.

When your eyes droop...

When your eyes droop with voluptuousness, your pitch-black eyes that
glint like an amorous panther's, into your plump, hot, savoury flesh I sink
my teeth with furious kisses.

I am carried away by the dark mysterious lust which in olden times
inflamed languorous Greece, when that thrice blessed land was the scene
of sacred couplings of men and gods.

Then I feel I am holding tight on my burning breast some terrifying
idol which thirsts for blood, to whom the protracted sobs of dying men
are a delight

and in frenetic spasms I feel the dreadful exaltation of old Hindu
fakirs and the endless ecstasies of fanatic Brahmins.

[Published 1888]

Draft Dedication
and Prefaces
for *Les Fleurs du mal*

Première version de la dédicace

À MON TRÈS CHER ET TRÈS VÉNÉRÉ
MAÎTRE ET AMI
THÉOPHILE GAUTIER

Bien que je te prie de servir de parrain aux *Fleurs du mal*, ne crois pas que je sois assez perdu, assez indigne du nom de poète pour m'imaginer que ces fleurs maladives méritent ton noble patronage. Je sais que dans les régions éthérées de la véritable Poésie, le Mal n'est pas, non plus que le Bien, et que ce misérable dictionnaire de mélancolie et de crime peut légitimer les réactions de la morale, comme le blasphémateur confirme la Religion. Mais j'ai voulu, autant qu'il était en moi, en espérant mieux peut-être rendre un hommage profond à l'auteur d'*Albertus*, de *La Comédie de la Mort* et d'*España*, au poète impeccable, au magicien ès langue française, dont je me déclare, avec autant d'orgueil que d'humilité, le plus dévoué, le plus respectueux et le plus jaloux des disciples.

<div align="right">CHARLES BAUDELAIRE.</div>

FIRST VERSION OF THE DEDICATION
To my most dear and venerated Master and Friend
THÉOPHILE GAUTIER

Although I am now inviting you to act as godfather to *Les Fleurs du mal*, do not think me so misguided or unworthy of the name of Poet as to imagine that these baneful flowers deserve your distinguished patronage. I am aware that in the ethereal realms of authentic Poetry, Evil is no more to be found than Goodness, and that this miserable dictionary of gloom and crime might serve to justify moral reactions in the same way as the blasphemer confirms religion. But I wanted to the utmost of my powers, while perhaps hoping to do better, to offer my profound homage to the creator of *Albertus*, the *Comédie de la Mort*, and *España*; to the impeccable poet, the magician of the French language, of whom I declare myself with as much pride as humility, the most devoted, respectful, and jealous of disciples.

<div align="right">[25 January 1857]</div>

Projets de préfaces

I
PRÉFACE DES FLEURS

Ce n'est pas pour mes femmes, mes filles ou mes sœurs que ce livre a été écrit; non plus que pour les femmes, les filles ou les sœurs de mon voisin. Je laisse cette fonction à ceux qui ont intérêt à confondre les bonnes actions avec le beau langage.

Je sais que l'amant passionné du beau style s'expose à la haine des multitudes. Mais aucun respect humain, aucune fausse pudeur, aucune coalition, aucun suffrage universel ne me contraindront à parler le patois incomparable de ce siècle, ni à confondre l'encre avec la vertu.

Des poètes illustres s'étaient partagé depuis longtemps les provinces les plus fleuries du domaine poétique. Il m'a paru plaisant, et d'autant plus agréable que la tâche était plus difficile, d'extraire la *beauté* du Mal. Ce livre, essentiellement inutile et absolument innocent, n'a pas été fait dans un autre but que de me divertir et d'exercer mon goût passionné de l'obstacle.

DRAFT PREFACES

Preface for the Flowers

This book was not written for my womenfolk, daughters or sisters, nor for the wives, sisters or daughters of my next-door neighbour. I leave that task to those who confuse fine actions and fine words for their own benefit.

I know that the ardent devotee of pure style exposes himself to the hatred of the mob; but no amount of human respect, no false modesty, no coalition, no universal suffrage will ever bring me to express myself in the present century's inimitable cant, or to confuse ink and virtue.

Poets of renown have long shared the most fertile areas of the domain of poetry between them, so I found it amusing and all the pleasanter the harder the job was, to distil beauty from evil. This essentially useless and totally innocuous book was created with no other aim than to entertain myself and indulge my hearty appetite for obstacles.

Quelques-uns m'ont dit que ces poésies pouvaient faire du mal. Je ne m'en suis pas réjoui. D'autres, de bonnes âmes, qu'elles pouvaient faire du bien; et cela ne m'a pas affligé. La crainte des uns et l'espérance des autres m'ont également étonné, et n'ont servi qu'à me prouver une fois de plus que ce siècle avait désappris toutes les notions classiques relatives à la littérature.

Malgré les secours que quelques cuistres célèbres ont apportés à la sottise naturelle de l'homme, je n'aurais jamais cru que notre patrie pût marcher avec une telle vélocité dans la voie du *progrès*. Ce monde a acquis une épaisseur de vulga-rité qui donne au mépris de l'homme spirituel la violence d'une passion. Mais il est des carapaces heureuses que le poison lui-même n'entamerait pas.

J'avais primitivement l'intention de répondre à de nom-breuses critiques et, en même temps, d'expliquer quelques questions très simples, totalement obscurcies par la lumière moderne: qu'est-ce que la Poésie? quel est son but? de la distinction du Bien d'avec le Beau; de la Beauté dans le Mal;

Some people have told me that these poems could have evil effects. That did not delight me. Others, kind souls, said that they could do some good, and that did not distress me. The fears of the first set and the hopes of the second surprised me in equal measure, and only seemed to prove to me once again that this century of ours had forgotten all the classi-cal wisdom about literature.

Despite the help that certain eminent pedants have given to the natural stupidity of mankind, I never imagined that our country would rush so quickly down the path of 'Progress'. Our society has acquired a thick hide of vulgarity which brings all the violence of a passion to its contempt for spiritual man. But there are some fortunate skins which such poison cannot penetrate.

My original intention was to answer numerous criticisms and at the same time explain a few very elementary questions which have become totally obscured by the light of modernity, such as: what is poetry; what is its objective; the distinction between good and the beautiful; the

que le rythme et la rime répondent dans l'homme aux immortels besoins de monotonie, de symétrie et de surprise; de l'adaptation du style au sujet; de la vanité et du danger de l'inspiration, etc., etc.; mais j'ai eu l'imprudence de lire ce matin quelques feuilles publiques; soudain, une indolence, du poids de vingt atmosphères, s'est abattue sur moi, et je me suis arrêté devant l'épouvantable inutilité d'expliquer quoi que ce soit à qui que ce soit. Ceux qui savent me devinent, et pour ceux qui ne peuvent ou ne veulent pas comprendre, j'amoncellerais sans fruit les explications.

<div style="text-align:right">C. B.</div>

beauty to be found in evil; how rhythm and rhyme respond in man to the immortal requirements of monotony, symmetry and surprise; the adaptation of style to subject; the vanity and danger of inspiration, etc. etc. But I was so imprudent as to read a few newspapers this morning, so that an indolence as heavy as twenty atmospheres suddenly fell upon me and I gave up, abashed by the horrifying futility of trying to explain anything to anybody. Those who know these things can easily guess at my thoughts, while for those who cannot or will not understand me, I would be piling up explanations fruitlessly.

<div style="text-align:right">C. B.</div>

II
PRÉFACE

La France traverse une phase de vulgarité. Paris, centre et rayonnement de bêtise universelle. Malgré Molière et Béranger, on n'aurait jamais cru que la France irait si grand train dans la voie du *Progrès*. – Questions d'art, *terræ incognitæ*. Le grand homme est bête.

Mon livre a pu faire du Bien. Je ne m'en afflige pas. Il a pu faire du Mal. Je ne m'en réjouis pas.

Le but de la Poésie. Ce livre n'est pas fait pour mes femmes, mes filles ou mes sœurs.

On m'a attribué tous les crimes que je racontais. Divertissement de la haine et du mépris. Les Élégiaques sont des canailles. *Et verbum Caro factum est.* – Or le poète n'est d'aucun parti. Autrement, il serait un simple mortel.

Le Diable. Le péché originel. Homme bon. Si vous vouliez, vous seriez le favori du Tyran. Il est plus difficile d'aimer Dieu que de croire en lui. Au contraire, il est plus

Preface

France is passing through a phase of vulgarity. Paris – the centre and focus of universal stupidity. Despite Molière and Béranger one could never have believed that France would go so briskly down the path of 'Progress'. – Questions of Art – *terrae incognitae.* The Great Man – nothing but a fool.

My book has perhaps done some good: that does not distress me. It has perhaps done some evil: that does not delight me.

The aim of Poetry. This book was not written for my womenfolk, daughters or sisters.

I have been accused of all the crimes I've written about. The pleasures of hatred and contempt. Elegiac poets – trash. *Et verbum Caro factum est* – the Word became Flesh. – The poet never takes sides, otherwise he would just be an ordinary fellow.

The Devil. Original Sin. Man is [born] good [?]. If you wanted to you could be the Tyrant's blue-eyed boy. It is harder to love God than to believe in him. On the contrary, it is harder for people in this century

difficile pour les gens de ce siècle de croire au Diable que de l'aimer. Tout le monde le sert et personne n'y croit. Sublime subtilité du Diable.

Une âme de mon choix. Le Décor. Ainsi la nouveauté. L'Épigraphe. D'Aurevilly. La Renaissance. Gérard de Nerval. Nous sommes tous pendus ou pendables.

J'avais mis quelques ordures pour plaire à MM. les journalistes. Ils se sont montrés ingrats.

to believe in Satan than to love him. Everyone is at his beck and call but nobody believes in him. The sublime subtlety of Satan.

A soul of my choice. Décor – scenery. Hence the novelty. The Epigraph. D'Aurevilly. The Renaissance. Gérard de Nerval. We are all hanged or hangable.

I threw in a few scraps of filth to please the journalists. They showed their ingratitude.

III

– Comment, par une série d'efforts déterminée, l'artiste peut s'élever à une originalité proportionnelle;

comment la poésie touche à la musique par une prosodie dont les racines plongent plus avant dans l'âme humaine que ne l'indique aucune théorie classique;

que la poésie française possède une prosodie mystérieuse et méconnue, comme les langues latine et anglaise;

pourquoi tout poète qui ne sait pas au juste combien chaque mot comporte de rimes est incapable d'exprimer une idée quelconque;

que la phrase poétique peut imiter (et par là elle touche à l'art musical et à la science mathématique) la ligne horizontale, la ligne droite ascendante, la ligne droite descendante; qu'elle peut monter à pic vers le ciel, sans essoufflement, ou descendre perpendiculairement vers l'enfer avec la vélocité de toute pesanteur; qu'elle peut suivre la spirale, décrire la parabole, ou le zigzag figurant une série d'angles superposés;

[III]

– The way in which by a predetermined series of efforts the artist may ascend to a proportionate degree of originality.

How poetry approaches music by means of a prosody whose roots plunge deeper into the human soul than any classical theory has demonstrated.

That French poetry has a mysterious and misunderstood prosody of its own, just as the Latin and English languages have.

Why any poet who doesn't know exactly how many rhymes every word commands is incapable of expressing any idea whatever.

That poetic phrasing can imitate (thereby bordering on the art of music and the science of mathematics) the horizontal line, the straight ascending and the straight descending lines; that it can rise directly heavenwards without loss of breath or descend perpendicularly towards hell with the speed of weight; that it can describe a spiral, a parabola, or the zigzag figuring a series of superimposed angles.

que la poésie se rattache aux arts de la peinture, de la cuisine et du cosmétique par la possibilité d'exprimer toute sensation de suavité ou d'amertume, de béatitude ou d'horreur par l'accouplement de tel substantif avec tel adjectif, analogue ou contraire;

comment, appuyé sur mes principes et disposant de la science que je me charge de lui enseigner en vingt leçons, tout homme devient capable de composer une tragédie qui ne sera pas plus sifflée qu'une autre, ou d'aligner un poème de la longueur nécessaire pour être aussi ennuyeux que tout poème épique connu.

Tâche difficile que de s'élever vers cette insensibilité divine! Car moi-même, malgré les plus louables efforts, je n'ai su résister au désir de plaire à mes contemporains, comme l'attestent en quelques endroits, apposées comme un fard, certaines basses flatteries adressées à la démocratie, et même quelques ordures destinées à me faire pardonner la tristesse de mon sujet. Mais MM. les journalistes s'étant montrés ingrats envers les caresses de ce genre, j'en ai supprimé la trace, autant qu'il m'a été possible, dans cette nouvelle édition.

That poetry is linked with the arts of painting and cookery and cosmetics through its ability to express sweetness or bitterness, beatitude or horror, by coupling an adjective with a substantive, analogous or contrary.

How, by basing himself on my principles and using the knowledge which I guarantee to teach him in twenty lessons, any man may become capable of writing a tragedy which will be no more heckled than any other, or to line up a poem of the required length which will be just as boring as any known epic poem.

What a difficult task it is to hoist oneself to this state of divine insensibility! For despite the most praiseworthy efforts I myself have been unable to resist the temptation of pleasing my contemporaries, as may be seen here and there from certain flatteries, like dabs of make-up, addressed to democracy, and even a few filthy patches intended as apologies for the sad nature of my material. But as the journalist tribe proved to be ungrateful for blandishments of this sort, as far as possible I have eliminated all trace of them from this new edition.

Que je me propose, pour vérifier de nouveau l'excellence de ma méthode, de l'appliquer prochainement à la célébration des jouissances de la dévotion et des ivresses de la gloire militaire, bien que je ne les aie jamais connues.

Note sur les plagiats. – Thomas Gray. Edgar Poe (2 passages). Longfellow (2 passages). Stace. Virgile (tout le morceau d'Andromaque). Eschyle. Victor Hugo.

In order again to verify the excellence of my method I propose in the near future to apply it to the Pleasure of Piety and the Thrills of Military History, even though I have never experienced either.

A note on my plagiarisms: Thomas Gray; Edgar Poe (two passages); Longfellow (two passages); Statius; Virgil (the whole piece about Andromache); Aeschylus; Victor Hugo.

IV
PROJET DE PRÉFACE
pour *Les Fleurs du mal*

(à fondre peut-être avec d'anciennes notes)

S'il y a quelque gloire à n'être pas compris, ou à ne l'être que très peu, je peux dire, sans vanterie, que, par ce petit livre, je l'ai acquise et méritée d'un seul coup. Offert plusieurs fois de suite à divers éditeurs qui le repoussaient avec horreur, poursuivi et mutilé, en 1857, par suite d'un malentendu fort bizarre, lentement rajeuni, accru et fortifié pendant quelques années de silence, disparu de nouveau, grâce à mon insouciance, ce produit discordant de la *Muse des Derniers jours*, encore avivé par quelques nouvelles touches violentes, ose affronter aujourd'hui pour la troisième fois le soleil de la sottise.

Ce n'est pas ma faute; c'est celle d'un éditeur insistant qui se croit assez fort pour braver le dégoût public. «Ce livre restera sur toute votre vie comme une tache», me prédisait, dès le commencement, un de mes amis qui est un grand poète. En effet, toutes mes mésaventures lui ont, jusqu'à

Draft Preface
for Les Fleurs du mal
(to be worked perhaps into previous notes)

If there is any glory to be drawn from being understood only slightly or not at all, I can say without boasting that I managed and deserved it at one blow with this little book. Offered repeatedly to a series of publishers who rejected it with horror; pursued and mutilated by the Law in 1857 as a result of an extraordinary misunderstanding; slowly rejuvenated, developed and strengthened during a few years of silence, then lost sight of once more thanks to my own neglect, this discordant product of the Latter-Day Muse, further enlivened by a few violent touches, now has the courage to face the glare of foolishness for the third time.

This is not my fault but an insistent publisher's who thinks he is tough enough to brave the disgust of the public. That 'your book will remain a blot on your whole existence' was predicted from the start by one of my friends who is a great poet. Indeed all my misadventures have so far

présent, donné raison. Mais j'ai un de ces heureux caractères qui tirent une jouissance de la haine et qui se glorifient dans le mépris. Mon goût diaboliquement passionné de la bêtise me fait trouver des plaisirs particuliers dans les travestissements de la calomnie. Chaste comme le papier, sobre comme l'eau, porté à la dévotion comme une communiante, inoffensif comme une victime, il ne me déplairait pas de passer pour un débauché, un ivrogne, un impie et un assassin.

Mon éditeur prétend qu'il y aurait quelque utilité, pour moi comme pour lui, à expliquer pourquoi et comment j'ai fait ce livre, quels ont été mon but et mes moyens, mon dessein et ma méthode. Un tel travail de critique aurait sans doute quelques chances d'amuser les esprits amoureux de le rhétorique profonde. Pour ceux-là, peut-être l'écrirai-je plus tard et le ferai-je tirer à une dizaine d'exemplaires. Mais, à un meilleur examen, ne paraît-il pas évident que ce serait là une besogne tout à fait superflue, pour les uns comme pour les autres, puisque les uns savent ou devinent, et que les autres ne comprendront jamais? Pour insuffler au peuple l'intelligence d'un objet d'art, j'ai une trop grande peur du ridicule, et je

proved him right. But mine is one of those cheerful characters which derive some pleasure from hatred and a certain pride from other people's scorn. My diabolically impassioned taste for stupidity makes me find peculiar pleasures in the misrepresentations of slander. As chaste as a blank sheet of paper, as sober as a glass of water, as pious as a woman at communion, as inoffensive as a victim, it would not displease me to be taken for a debauched and drunken lout, a blasphemer or a murderer.

My publisher maintains that it might be of service to me as well as him, if I explained how and why I concocted this book, what my aims and means were, my intentions and method. Such critical effort would no doubt have some hope of amusing such minds as enjoy deep rhetoric. For those, perhaps I'll write all that later on and have a handful of copies printed. But on closer inspection, doesn't it seem obvious that it would be a waste of labour for everyone concerned, as some already know or can guess all that, while the rest will never understand? I'm too afraid of ridicule to try and inculcate any understanding of a work of art into the mob, and in such an undertaking I'd be afraid of resembling

craindrais, en cette matière, d'égaler ces utopistes qui veulent, par un décret, rendre tous les Français riches et vertueux d'un seul coup.

Et puis, ma meilleure raison, ma suprême, est que cela m'ennuie et me déplaît. Mène-t-on la foule dans les ateliers de l'habilleuse et du décorateur, dans la loge de la comédienne? Montre-t-on au public affolé aujourd'hui, indifférent demain, le mécanisme des trucs? Lui explique-t-on les retouches et les variantes improvisées aux répétitions, et jusqu'à quelle dose l'instinct et la sincérité sont mêlés aux rubriques et au charlatanisme indispensable dans l'amalgame de l'œuvre? Lui révèle-t-on toutes les loques, les fards, les poulies, les chaînes, les repentirs, les épreuves barbouillées, bref toutes les horreurs qui composent le sanctuaire de l'art?

D'ailleurs telle n'est pas, aujourd'hui, mon humeur. Je n'ai désir ni de démontrer, ni d'étonner, ni d'amuser, ni de persuader. J'ai mes nerfs, mes vapeurs. J'aspire à un repos absolu et à une nuit continue. Chantre des voluptés folles du vin et de l'opium, je n'ai soif que d'une liqueur inconnue sur la terre, et que la pharmaceutique céleste elle-même ne pourrait

those utopists who want, by decree, to make all Frenchmen rich and virtuous in one fell swoop.

And then my best and supreme reason for refusing is that all this bores and displeases me. Do we ever admit the mob into dressers' workrooms or decorators' workshops or an actress's dressing-room? Do we show the public, which is all enthusiasm one day and indifferent the next, the theatre's machinery back-stage? Do we explain the improvements and variations which are improvised in rehearsals, and to what dose intuition and sincerity are mixed with the tricks and charlatanism necessary for the compound of the work? Do we show the audience all the gladrags and cosmetics, pulleys and chains, second thoughts, scribbled scripts or proofs, in a word all the chamber of horrors which constitutes the inner sanctuary of art?

In any case I have no such inclination today. I have no desire to demonstrate, or astonish or amuse or convince anybody. I have my nerves, my vapours. All I want now is absolute rest, an undisturbed night. I who have sung the wild delights of wine and opium thirst only for an elixir unknown on earth and which the celestial pharmaceutics

pas m'offrir, – d'une liqueur qui ne contiendrait ni la vie/vitalité ni la mort, ni l'excitation, ni le néant. Ne rien savoir, ne rien enseigner, ne rien vouloir, ne rien sentir, dormir et encore dormir, tel est aujourd'hui mon unique vœu. Vœu infâme et dégoûtant, mais sincère.

Toutefois, comme un goût supérieur nous apprend à ne pas craindre de nous contredire un peu nous-mêmes, j'ai rassemblé, à la fin de ce livre abominable, les témoignages de sympathie de quelques-uns des hommes que je prise le plus, pour qu'un lecteur impartial en puisse inférer que je ne suis pas absolument digne d'excommunication et qu'ayant su me faire aimer de quelques-uns, mon cœur, quoi qu'en ait dit je ne sais plus quel torchon imprimé, n'a peut-être pas «*l'épouvantable laideur de mon visage*».

Enfin, par une générosité peu commune, dont MM. les critiques . . .

Comme l'ignorance va croissant . . .

Je dénonce moi-même les imitations . . .

itself could never provide, a liqueur which would contain neither vitality nor death, neither stimulation or nothingness. To know nothing, teach nothing, want nothing, feel nothing, but only to sleep and sleep again, such is my one desire today, an infamous and disgusting desire but sincere none the less.

However, as the gift of superior taste teaches us never to be afraid of contradicting ourselves a little, I have collected at the end of this abominable book the sympathetic testimonies of some of those men whom I hold in the highest esteem, so that an impartial reader might gather that I am not totally fit for excommunication and that, having been able to make myself loved by those few, my heart, whatever some printed rag might say about it, perhaps does not have 'the appalling ugliness of my face.'

And finally, thanks to an uncommon generosity which *messieurs* the critics . . .

As ignorance is on the increase . . .

I myself denounce all imitations . . .

INDEX OF FRENCH TITLES

First lines of untitled poems are given in italic.
Poems attributed to Baudelaire are asterisked.

À celle qui est trop gaie, 329
À Charles Asselineau, 388
À Henri Hignard, 372
*À Ivonne Pen-Moore, 435
*À Madame du Barry, 434
À propos d'un importun, 361
À Sainte-Beuve, 381
À Théodore de Banville, 385
*À une belle dévote, 437
À une dame créole, 159
*À une jeune saltimbanque, 438
À une Madone, 151
À une Malabaraise, 357
À une mendiante rousse, 195
À une passante, 213
Abel et Caïn, 268
L'Albatros, 64
Alchimie de la douleur, 182
Allégorie, 256
L'Amateur des Beaux-Arts en
 Belgique, 396
L'Âme du vin, 237
L'Amour du mensonge, 224
L'Amour et le crâne, 263
L'Aube spirituelle, 130
Au concert, à Bruxelles, 406
Au Lecteur, 55
Au milieu de la foule, errantes,
 confondues, 387
Avec ses vêtements ondoyants et
 nacrés, 99
L'Avertisseur, 303
Les Aveugles, 212
*Avril, 436

Le Balcon, 112
La Béatrice, 257
Le Beau Navire, 140

La Beauté, 85
Les Belges et la Lune, 398
Bénédiction, 59
Une Béotie belge, 407
Bien loin d'ici, 311
Les Bijoux, 331
Bohémiens en voyage, 79
Bribes, 365
Brumes et pluies, 229

Un cabaret folâtre, 364
Le Cadre, 117
Le Calumet de paix, 413
Causerie, 148
Chanson d'après-midi, 154
Chant d'automne, 149
Une charogne, 102
Le Chat: *Dans ma cervelle se*
 promène, 137
Le Chat: *Viens, mon beau chat, sur*
 mon cœur amoureux, 110
Châtiment de l'orgueil, 83
Les Chats, 165
La Chevelure, 94
Ciel brouillé, 136
Ci-gît qui, pour avoir par trop aimé
 les gaupes, 380
La Civilisation belge, 408
La Cloche fêlée, 173
Combien dureront nos amours?, 441
Confession, 127
Correspondances, 67
Le Coucher du soleil romantique,
 313
Le Couvercle, 305
Le Crépuscule du matin, 234
Le Crépuscule du soir, 216
Le Cygne, 198

Danse macabre, 220
De profundis clamavi, 105
La Destruction, 247
Les Deux Bonnes Sœurs, 254
Don Juan aux enfers, 81
Duellum, 111
D'un esprit biscornu le séduisant
 projet, 388

Une eau salutaire, 397
Ébauche d'un épilogue pour la 2e
 édition, 293
*Élégie refusée aux jeux floraux,
 432
Élévation, 65
L'Enfance d'Hiawatha, 419
L'Ennemi, 76
Épigraphe pour l'atelier de
 M. Rops, 399
Épigraphe pour un livre
 condamné, 297
Epilogue, 291
Épitaphe pour la Belgique, 403
Épitaphe pour Léopold I, 403
L'Esprit conforme, I: Cet imbécile
 de Tournai, 404
L'Esprit conforme, II: Les Belges
 poussent, ma parole, 405
L'Examen de minuit, 309

Un fantôme, 115
Femmes damnées ('Comme un
 bétail pensif'), 252
Femmes damnées (Delphine et
 Hippolyte), 320
La Fin de la journée, 278
Le Flacon, 132
Le Flambeau vivant, 124
La Fontaine de sang, 255
Franciscæ meæ laudes, 157, 346

La Géante, 87
Le Gouffre, 307
Le Goût du néant, 181
Une gravure fantastique, 170
Le Guignon, 77

Harmonie du soir, 131
L'Héautontimorouménos, 184
Hélas! Qui n'a gémi sur autrui, sur
 soi-même?, 374
Les Hiboux, 166
L'Homme et la mer, 80
L'Horloge, 189
Horreur sympathique, 183
Hymne, 338
Hymne à la Beauté, 91

L'Idéal, 86
Il aimait à la voir, avec ses jupes
 blanches, 371
Il est de chastes mots que nous
 profanons tous, 376
L'Imprévu, 353
Incompatibilité, 369
L'Inviolabilité de la Belgique, 402
L'Invitation au voyage, 143
L'Irrémédiable, 186
L'Irréparable, 145

J'aime le souvenir de ces époques nues,
 68
*J'aime ses grands yeux bleus, sa
 chevelure ardente, 442
Je n'ai pas oublié, voisine de la ville,
 226
Je n'ai pas pour maîtresse une lionne
 illustre, 377
Je t'adore à l'égal de la voûte
 nocturne, 96
Je te donne ces vers afin que si mon
 nom, 119
Le Jet d'eau, 335
Le Jeu, 218
Je vis, et ton bouquet est de
 l'architecture, 387
*Un jour de pluie, 445

La servante au grand cœur dont vous
 étiez jalouse, 227
Le cœur content, je suis monté sur la
 montagne, 291
Lesbos, 315

Le Léthé, 327
Les Litanies de Satan, 271
Lola de Valence, 348
★*Lorsque de volupté s'alanguissent tes yeux*, 450
La Lune offensée, 306

Madrigal triste, 298
Une martyre, 248
Le Masque, 88
Le Mauvais Moine, 75
Les Métamorphoses du vampire, 333
Moesta et errabunda, 160
Mon cher, je suis venu chez vous, 389
Monselet Paillard, 388
Monsieur Auguste Malassis, 391
Le Monstre, 342
La Mort de Léopold Iᵉʳ, 409
La Mort des amants, 275
La Mort des artistes, 277
La Mort des pauvres, 276
Le Mort joyeux, 171
Le Mot de Cuvier, 406
La Muse malade, 73
La Muse vénale, 74
La Musique, 168

N'est-ce pas qu'il est doux, maintenant que nous sommes, 371
Noble femme au bras fort, qui durant les longs jours, 386
Un nom de bon augure, 401
La Nymphe de la Senne, 400

Obsession, 180
Opinion de M. Hetzel sur le faro, 400

Les Panégyriques du roi, 405
Le Parfum, 116
Parfum exotique, 93
★Le Pauvre diable, 431
Paysage, 191
Les Petites Vieilles, 206
Les Phares, 70

La Pipe, 167
Les Plaintes d'un Icare, 308
Le Poison, 134
Le Pont des soupirs, 421
Le Portrait, 118
Le Possédé, 114
La Prière d'un païen, 301
Les Promesses d'un visage, 340
La Propreté belge, 395
La Propreté des demoiselles belges, 394

★*Quand la brise d'avril a chassé les autans*, 443
★*Quant à moi, si j'avais un beau parc planté d'ifs*, 430
Que diras-tu ce soir, pauvre âme solitaire, 123

★Le Raccommodeur de fontaines, 429
La Rançon, 356
Le Rebelle, 302
Recueillement, 304
Remords posthume, 109
Le Reniement de saint Pierre, 265
Le Rêve belge, 402
Le Rêve d'un curieux, 279
Rêve parisien, 230
Le Revenant, 162
Réversibilité, 125

★Sapho, 449
Sed non satiata, 98
Semper eadem, 120
Les Sept Vieillards, 202
Sépulture, 169
Le Serpent qui danse, 100
Sisina, 156
Le Soleil, 193
★Sonnet cavalier, 440
Sonnet d'automne, 163
Sonnet pour s'excuser de ne pas accompagner un ami à Namur, 390

★Sonnet: *Quand la brise d'avril a chassé les autans,* 443

★Sonnet: *Un livre n'aurait pas suffi,* 444

Sonnet: *Vous avez, chère sœur dont le cœur est poète,* 375

Spleen: *J'ai plus de souvenirs que si j'avais mille ans,* 175

Spleen: *Je suis comme le roi d'un pays pluvieux,* 177

Spleen: *Pluviôse, irrité contre la ville entière,* 174

Spleen: *Quand le ciel bas et lourd pèse comme un couvercle,* 178

Le Squelette laboureur, 214

Sur l'album de Mme Émile Chevalet, 387

★Sur l'album d'une dame inconnue, 439

Sur *Le Tasse en Prison* d'Eugène Delacroix, 349

Sur les débuts d'Amina Boschetti, 359

★ *Sur le trou du cercueil nouvellement creusé,* 448

Suscription rimée, 391

Les Ténèbres, 115

Le Tonneau de la Haine, 172

Tous imberbes, alors, sur les vieux bancs de chêne, 381

Tout à l'heure je viens d'entendre, 372

Tout entière, 121

Tranquille comme un sage et doux comme un maudit, 293

Tristesses de la lune, 164

Tu mettrais l'univers entier dans ta ruelle, 97

★ *Un livre n'aurait pas suffi,* 444

Une nuit que j'étais près d'une affreuse Juive, 108

Le Vampire, 106

Venus belga, 393

Vers laissés chez un ami absent, 389

Vers pour le portrait de M. Honoré Daumier, 347

La Vie antérieure, 78

Le Vin de l'assassin, 241

Le Vin des amants, 245

Le Vin des chiffonniers, 239

Le Vin du solitaire, 244

La Voix, 351

★ *Vos cheveux sont-ils blonds, vos prunelles humides?,* 439

Vous avez, chère sœur dont le cœur est poète, 375

Le Voyage, 280

Un voyage à Cythère, 259

Les Yeux de Berthe, 337

French Poetry in Bilingual Editions from Anvil

GUILLAUME APOLLINAIRE: Selected Poems
Translated by Oliver Bernard

CHARLES BAUDELAIRE: Paris Blues
(Le Spleen de Paris – Petits Poèmes en prose)
Translated by Francis Scarfe

JEAN FOLLAIN: 130 Poems
Chosen and translated by Christopher Middleton

VICTOR HUGO: The Distance, The Shadows
Selected poems translated by Harry Guest

INTO THE DEEP STREET
Seven Modern French Poets
Edited and translated by Jennie Feldman and Stephen Romer

POEMS OF JULES LAFORGUE
Translated by Peter Dale

GÉRARD DE NERVAL: The Chimeras
Translated by Peter Jay with an essay by Richard Holmes

JACQUES RÉDA: Treading Lightly
Selected Poems 1961–1975
Translated by Jennie Feldman

ARTHUR RIMBAUD: A Season in Hell
and other poems
*Translated by Norman Cameron
with an introduction by Michael Hamburger*

RIMBAUD: The Poems
Translated by Oliver Bernard

PAUL VALÉRY: Charms
Translated by Peter Dale

PAUL VERLAINE: Women/Men
Femmes/Hombres
Translated by Alistair Elliot

POEMS OF FRANÇOIS VILLON
Translated by Peter Dale